The Sabarimala Confusion

MENSTRUATION ACROSS CULTURES

A Historical Perspective

Nithin Sridhar

Vitasta

LET KNOWLEDGE SPREAD

www.vitastapublishing.com

Published by
Renu Kaul Verma
Vitasta Publishing Pvt Ltd
4348/4C, Ansari Road, Daryaganj
New Delhi - 110 002
info@vitastapublishing.com

ISBN 978-93-86473-46-2

First Edition 2019
Fourth Reprint 2024
MRP ₹ 895

Editors: Papri Sri Raman and Sangita Menon Malhan
Cover by Somesh Kumar Mishra
Layout by Ram Kumar
Printed at Chaman Enterprises, New Delhi

Dedicated to

Padma, My Mother

Kali & Sundari, My Divine Mothers

&

Pratyasha, my Better Half

Contents

Publisher's Note

As women ourselves, for the last two decades, we have been following India's menstruation story, all its ups and downs, smiles and cries. We are acutely aware that the Sabarimala discourse does not end with court judgements. When Nithin Sridhar started writing online, we felt it was time for an entire book on the subject, of primal importance to half a billion women of this country. We had a tradition, handed down through ages. Our ancient texts prescribed a litany of Dos and Don'ts. Most of these are corrupted after 5,000 years of misuse.

The Essence of it is: The husband must not leave the company of his wife for fifteen days after the start of menstrual period but is not to seek union with her during the menses period. It was customary for the women, after the child-birth to go to the public tank for bathing. During the period of impurity, 'the women were unapproachable' and must not touch the domestic utensils.

In Sangam period (c. 200 BC to 250 AD) literary sources of the age such at *Tolkappiyam, Pattuppattu, Ettuttokai, Cilappatikaram* and *Manimekalai,* much of it written by women poets of the times and with dynamic female protagonists, did refer to menstruation.

It is again India's modern young women poets who are putting menstruation into perspective:

Just remember,
A man bleeds for death.
for agony and for misery.

Do you know why a woman bleeds?

She bleeds for glee.
for happiness.
and to create a new life.

—**Greshma**
HappyToBleed Campaign
Amrita Institute of Medical Sciences

If my body's made of stardust and
my skin matches land,
If my body's geology can make
continents tremble and mountains move
You aren't allowed to tell me that I should be shy
Because I paint the town red for a week,
every month of my life.

—Haiku by
Aranya Johar

So this book.

Foreword

Menstruation is one of the most natural of all processes in this mortal world and yet one which is hedged in by so many mysteries and obfuscations, such a reluctance to talk of it and discuss it in the clear light of day that many misconceptions have grown around it like the ant hill around Maharshi Chyavan.

This book by Nithin Sridhar, who is making a name for himself as a contemporary explorer and explainer of Sanatana Dharma is a timely and excellent attempt to set the record straight about menstruation in the Indic tradition and compare it with ideas from different cultures past and present to put it in perspective.

In 'common' understanding, menstruation in the Indic, and especially the Hindu, tradition is all about taboos and restrictions all leading to unhealthy results.

This book breaks this myth and painstakingly details the meaning and understanding the Hindu Shastras have of menstruation and how it fits in with the philosophy and schema of human life in general.

It is one of the most frustrating paradoxes of contemporary India that Hindus do not know their own roots or traditions. The Islamic invasion, the colonial imposition and the Eurocentrism of the past few centuries have resulted in vast swathes of people being ignorant about themselves. To add to it is the existence today of an alienated urban culture in India which is drifting in a sea of confusion. All roots with the past, the passing down of best practices from mother to daughter and grandmother to granddaughter have been brutally sidelined in the name of modernity.

The discourse is therefore trapped in alien and imported categories which fit neither the reality nor the practices around menstruation which had been followed for centuries. Rest is equated with banishment, care with taboos, attention to reproductive health with chauvinism and there is a forcible attempt to impose fixed categories on to a plethora of different customs.

To be absolutely clear, the thrust is not about moving into the past but about moving the present into a rooted and practical scheme relying on best Indic practices.

Many Abrahamic ideas of impurity have found their way into the mainstream narrative in India and attached themselves to the modern Hindu way of life. This book clarifies the matter by exhaustively setting down Hindu, Buddhist, Christian, Islamic and other traditions relating to menstruation.

Sridhar has shown that the centrality of the Hindu idea of menstruation *as an agent of purity* and *a form of tapa* is far from being the 'punishment' for original sin it is seen as in Christianity or the strong associations with an impurity in the Islamic tradition. It has been the focus of celebration and worship for centuries although today's generation is very often unaware of traditions different from the regurgitated vaguely western ideas that have a strong hold on them.

The comprehensive and three sixty degree treatment of the subject matter is all very well but what, one may ask, is the utility of doing this? Is it academic? No doubt it is, and one hopes to see this book a focal point of academic references in this area as the author has desired, but the real utility is much more immediate and should relate to actual practices.

Menstrual disorders are assuming epic proportions in India. The food, lifestyle, the pressures of modern living, the incessant demand on girls and women leave them with scant time to focus on their own monthly needs and necessities. The message today is to be up and going, no matter what; menstrual periods are an inconvenience which has to be wrestled into submission. The body, however, reacts; nature cannot be repressed without consequences. These consequences have led to an increasing menstrual malaise amongst Indian women.

To deal with this, can we look at an alternative model which is both in sync with today's needs and also incorporates principles proven over millennia adapted for today? With an eye to the reproductive health of women, which is a major area of concern, perhaps each reader can take away something of practical value from this work. The section on Ayurvedic principles and practices for menstruation can be of great significance for this aspect.

Germaine Greer wrote *The Female Eunuch* in 1970 and assumed the place as a high priestess of the exclusive world of women. Feminists swear by her. Interesting then, that the idea of tasting menstrual blood, which caused such a stir, is nothing new for the Indic tradition and the *Chandamaharoshana tantra* discuss this centuries before Greer as this book tells us.

The point being, read this book with an open mind and a desire to learn. To paraphrase Shakespeare, there are more things in Hindu philosophy, Horatio, than are dreamt of in modern times and you will be the richer for having read this book.

Sumedha Verma Ojha
Author, Speaker and Columnist
on Ancient India and the Epics
Geneva, October 2018

Preface

It was towards the end of 2015. The year was coming to a close and the issue of women's entry into the Sabarimala Temple had yet again erupted everywhere in the media. The Sabarimala temple dedicated to Lord Ayyappa Swami is a very important religious, spiritual and pilgrimage center for the Hindus. According to the traditions followed in the temple, women between menarche and menopause are not allowed inside it.

There was a veritable hue and cry in the media and among the activists who shouted in their hoarse voices – day in and day out – about how this practice was anti-women and misogynistic. The narrative soon turned very toxic and the target was no longer limited to just one temple, but the entire Hindu Dharma; its cultures and traditions being called into question.

There was something wrong with this entire narrative. It was built upon misunderstanding, misinformation and obfuscation. For one, it was wrongly portrayed that there was a blanket ban on the entry of all women into the temple, suppressing the fact that young girls and old women regularly visited the temple. Two, it was portrayed as a discrimination against women, without taking into account how the same State – Kerala – has women specific-temples and practices, where men are not allowed, and that there are other Ayyappan temples in Kerala where women of all ages are also allowed, thus making the charge of discrimination quite shallow and without basis. Three, the entire narrative was more or less built on a one-sided and often distorted account of the issue, and no voice or agency was given to Hindu practitioners and devotees of the Ayyappan temple to express their perspective.

More importantly, there was a clever obfuscation of the fact that the question of a person's entry into the temple is a Dharmic issue which has to take into consideration a number of factors including the Agamic rules, the purpose of the temple and the nature of the deity whose presence the temple holds. Instead, it was projected as an issue of women's rights, and used to portray Hinduism as inherently misogynistic.

To counter this obfuscation, I had immediately written an article in January 2016 titled 'Why Sabarimala controversy is religious issue, not women's rights issue'[1] for *NewsGram*. It was my understanding at that time that many people may have been genuinely unaware about the Sabarimala temple and its deity-specific unique practices. But, it was in the following weeks that I realised that ignorance and misinformation run much deeper.

The focus of the activists and media professionals soon shifted from temple-specific restrictions to how there is a general dehumanisation of women in the form of menstruation taboos. It was argued that though menstruation is merely a natural biological activity, Hindu women are dehumanised by considering them dirty, and by keeping them away from temples, which clearly forms gender discrimination.

I must confess that there was a time when even I believed that all these Hindu life-style practices surrounding menstruation were merely a product of superstition. This was further reinforced by the silence and avoidance of the topic by people in general, family elders in particular. Since no answer to the questions posed about the Hindu treatment of menstruation was coming forth from any quarters, I decided to examine the issue intensively.

The following weeks were spent in research into a large number of Hindu texts and living traditions, which fructified in the form of a six-part series titled 'Hindu view of Menstruation',[2] which was published in *IndiaFacts* in 2016. It was during this time that Renu Kaul Verma of Vitasta Publishing approached me with a proposal for expanding my work on menstruation into a full-fledged book.

Now, two years later, I am finally ready with this book. The whole journey in writing this book has been one of learning and discovery. I had never thought I would explore ancient civilisations of the West like the Greek civilisation and the Egyptian civilisation or the history of Abrahamic religions. This book allowed me to explore this realm and to understand religions and civilisations from across the world. More importantly, it helped me dive even deeper into the Hindu civilisation and unravel its knowledge, beauty and diversity. It is my hope that the readers will enjoy reading the book as much as I did writing it.

Finally, I would like to express my deep regards to my parents who have always encouraged me in all my endeavours. My wife Pratyasha has been a constant source of support and inspiration besides being the first reader of the manuscript. Her inputs have been highly valuable to me. I cannot thank Renu Kaul Verma and the entire team of Vitasta Publishing enough for bringing out this book. I am very thankful to Sumedha Verma Ojha for writing the Foreword to the book. I would also like to thank Nagaraja Gundappa and Dr Sammod Acharya for helping with the research at the initial stage, and Sankrant Sanu for sharing his valuable inputs when the original series of articles were written. My deep regards to my employer and mentor Hari Kiran Vadlamani who has been a great source of support and has acted as a facilitator in my various writing projects.

I would also like to thank some of my friends with whom I have discussed my book or took suggestions about the title: Ashish Dhar, Neha Srivastava, Sahana Singh and

Saiswaroopa Iyer. I would also like to thank Dr Ulrike Steinert for sharing her research and helping me appreciate the knowledge embedded in the Mesopotamian civilisation. I thank Madhu Kishwar for the Last Word she provided as a fitting conclusion to this tome.

And last, but not the least, no endeavour will be successful without the blessings of Ishwara and Guru. I submit this book at the lotus feet of my Guru and Kali, my Ishta.

Introduction

Menstruation is a natural biological process that women undergo during a major period of their lives. In many a sense, menstruation, owing to its relationship with fertility and motherhood, is something that is closely associated with womanhood, and it indicates how women as individuals are different from men on many levels. Hence, menstruation has always played an important role in how various societies and cultures across the world have perceived women; man-woman relationships, and the role of women in society, as a whole.

Yet, in contemporary India, the discourse around menstruation has been much skewed and we can see huge obfuscations on the matter. A good example to illustrate this obfuscation is the currently burning issue of Sabarimala temple entry.

In the famous Sabarimala Ayyappa Swamy temple, there has been a prohibition on the entry of women of reproductive age for hundreds of years. While the prohibition itself is part of the temple tradition brought into practice to cater to the unique nature of the deity who resides in this temple in the form of a Naishtika Brahmachari (the eternal celibate) and has nothing to do with menstruation per se, there is a misguided and perhaps motivated narrative in the media and mainstream discourse that posits Sabarimala as a menstruation issue and the prohibition as being due to Hinduism treating menstruation as impure and dirty.

Thus, the obfuscation in the issue is two-fold: that Sabarimala prohibition is related to menstruation, while it clearly is not; and that Hinduism perceives menstruation in a disparaging manner and uses it to oppress women.

While much has been written on the first aspect, very less has been written about Hindu notions of menstruation. Our contemporary narrative has largely focused on sanitary needs, women's health, and hygiene. Media, academic literature, TV Ads – all of them almost exclusively focus on how girls and women in India suffer from unhygienic menstrual practices owing to lack of access to sanitary pads and menstrual taboos imposed by superstitious patriarchy.

An academic paper, for example, states in its abstract that, 'Menstrual hygiene continues to be amongst the most challenging development issues today. Not only do deep-rooted taboos, myths and misinformation create the illusion that menstruation is inherently shameful, gross and weird, but in countries like India, women and girls often lack access to hygienic sanitary materials and basic facilities such as sanitary pads necessary for good menstrual hygiene management'.[1] Media reports routinely quote a 2010 study done by AC Nielsen to point out that only 12 per cent of India's 355 million menstruating women use sanitary napkins with the rest using 'shocking alternatives like unsanitised cloth, ashes and husk sand'.[2] Media reports also note how girls drop out of school or miss classes during menstruation owing to lack of access to sanitary pads, toilets and cultural taboos about menstruation.[3]

Then, there are a number of TV ads telecasted day-in and day-out on various channels, which portray menstruation as an impediment to women's freedom, participating in schools and sports etc. and posit sanitary napkins as the ultimate solution to this. With the production of the popular Akshay Kumar film, *Padman*, this discourse about menstruation, which portrays cultural taboos and lack of access to sanitary pads as the root of all menstrual problems, and then posits sanitary pads as the ultimate solution to all such menstrual issues, has been reinforced.

Further, there are many documentaries and educational videos which explicitly portray Hindu traditions, cultural beliefs and practices regarding menstruation as being patriarchal and oppressive to women. One such example is a Bollywood show titled '*Sex Ki Adalat* – Menstruation' directed by Feroz Abbas Khan.[4] The documentary portrays a court scene involving a Tamil Hindu couple, in which the husband stands accused of oppressing his wife during her monthly periods. The husband is shown as considering menstruation as an impurity due to which he forces his wife to remain in seclusion and separated from him and their children. The documentary neither explores the meaning of terms such as impurity nor does it explore the probable, rational or cultural knowledge associated with practices such as seclusion. It focusses entirely on framing this cultural knowledge and these practices as superstitious and oppressive.

Thus, India's contemporary discourse around menstruation, sanitation needs and associated women's health has been reduced to positing: 1. India as a country with lack of access to hygienic menstrual products and practices; 2. Indian cultural beliefs and practices, especially those derived from Hindu traditions as regressive and patriarchal.

Regarding the portrayal of Indian women as lacking access to hygienic menstrual products and practices, there are some serious issues with such portrayal. First, the assertion about the abysmal reach of sanitary pads in India relies exclusively upon a single study with a very small sample size,[5] while ignoring many other studies with larger sample sizes, but reporting a higher usage of sanitary pads. For example, a study of 138 papers on Menstrual Hygiene Management in India noted that the usage of Sanitary Napkins among adolescents ranges between 32 per cent in rural areas to 67 per cent in urban areas.[6] Second, the contemporary narrative's use of the reach of commercially available sanitary napkins as an almost exclusive criteria to determine the status of menstrual health and hygiene in India is misleading. It is important to understand that use of other absorbent materials like cotton cloth is equally effective and hygienic when properly washed and sun-dried. Being reusable, they are environment friendly as well. In the rural areas, especially, girls and women prefer to use cloths with which they are more familiar.[7]

Sinu Joseph of Mythri Speaks, who has been working in the field of women's health for several years, notes: It is wrong to assume that introducing Sanitary Napkins in itself solves these issues. I have come across cases where just because they use Sanitary Napkins, girls think that it has some super absorbing capacity and do not change it as frequently as they should, or would if it were the good old cloth. Thereby, the harm caused by Sanitary Napkins not being used properly is not greatly different from that of improper usage of cloth. But the point here is that we should be careful not to mislead young girls and women by promoting that hygiene is all about switching to Sanitary Napkins, simply because we (read the urban women) do not know any better. Instead, we need to tell them how to maintain hygiene, regardless of what they use. Why not leave it to them to decide what to use? And respect that decision.[8]

Third, the contemporary narrative has trivialised the issue of serious menstrual disorders by conflating it with hygiene and sanitary pads. Joseph writes: Strangely, it has occurred to very few that Menstrual Disorders have nothing to do with hygiene or the product used. The most common menstrual disorders such as Dysmennorhea (period pain), Mennorhagia (heavy bleeding), Ammenorhea (no bleeding), Oligomenorhea (Menstrual cycles > 35 days) have no association with what product is used or how hygiene is maintained. The more serious disorders like Endometriosis or PCOS are even more cut-off from hygiene correlations. Some write-ups even associate poor menstrual hygiene with cervical cancer, for which there is even lesser evidence.[9]

Then, there is the issue of school absenteeism which is linked to lack of toilets and sanitary pads in developing countries like India. But, if the absenteeism is really due to lack of toilets or sanitary pads, why is such absenteeism prevalent in developed countries as well which supposedly have access to both toilets and sanitary products? Studies indicate that 17 per cent teenagers in Canada, 21 per cent in Washington DC, 24 per cent in Singapore, 26 per cent in Australia and 38 per cent in Texas miss school owing to menstruation.[10] Joseph notes that the 'reasons for missing school have nothing to do with sanitary pads or toilets; in most cases, it has to do with Dysmenorrhea (pain during menses)'.[11] Then, there are a number of studies conducted at various places like Africa[12] and Nepal,[13] which show that menstruation plays a very small role in school absenteeism. There is no reason to assume it is different in India.

Now, coming to the portrayal of Indian cultural practices related to menstruation, especially those rooted in Hindu traditions, as regressive and patriarchal, it must be pointed out that this narrative is as skewed and problematic as the one we discussed above. The Bollywood documentary mentioned above, for example, frames the entire narrative on menstruation by categorising all the cultural knowledge regarding menstruation into a single category of impurity, without even attempting to define impurity! It then brands this impurity as patriarchal and superstitious without even exploring how Indian cultural knowledge – in which these practices are rooted – perceives these menstrual notions and practices. In other words, it perpetrates an image of oppression and blind belief without examining whether these assumptions portray a ground reality.

Another issue with the current narrative is that it has imported western modernity's framework to understand non-western cultures. As a result, all discussions about menstruation revolve exclusively around biology, and the other aspects of the issue like subjective experiences, cultural knowledge and spirituality are reduced to taboos and superstitions. Writing about modernity discourses' distortion of non-western cultural knowledge traditions, Frederique Apffel-Marglin notes that modernity has not only attempted to delegitimise the feelings and vivid experiences of women regarding menstruation, but that using the same 'scientific lens' through anthropology, it has tried to delegitimise cultural experiences and knowledge about menstruation prevalent in other non-western cultures and traditions, by trying to portray them as primitive knowledge as against western scientific understanding, which is considered progressive.[14]

Then, there is the commercial angle to the entire issue. Sinu Joseph observes: Most movements begin with a need. Either a real need or a manufactured one. In the case of the newly emerging space of menstrual hygiene management, the need is a manufactured one; specifically, for sanitary product manufacturing companies to enter the untapped market of India, especially rural India. It is important to note in this context that Coimbatore-based social entrepreneur Arunachalam Muruganantham's effort to produce sanitary napkins has to be seen from the viewpoint of the product's low cost and indigenisation pitted against the high cost products distributed in India in the 1990s by multinationals. Organisations working on menstruation and even sanitary napkin companies (Whisper's 'Don't touch the pickle' ad) have started talking about cultural practices around menstruation by demeaning them as Menstrual Taboos. These institutions, in their attempt to create a market for sanitary products and infrastructure in India, have chosen the path of dismissing all cultural practices around menstruation as regressive taboos, and emphasising that sanitary napkins are the progressive expression of the modern woman. Happily joining hands with such organisations are the sold-out Indian NGOs, who have made menstruation their means of sustenance.[15]

Therefore, the contemporary narrative about Indian women not having access to hygienic menstrual products or that they largely indulge in unhygienic and superstitious menstrual practices owing to poverty, illiteracy, and imposed cultural practices rooted in patriarchy is misleading, incorrect, and may have been manufactured for ulterior motives.

In any case, there is a large gap between the Indian cultural knowledge and practices regarding menstruation prevalent among the common people and the modern discourse created by media, cinema, and academia. To bridge this gap, the present book seeks to undertake a detailed examination of menstrual notions and practices prevalent in Hinduism and other Indic traditions like Buddhism, Jainism, and Sikhism. It further does a comparative analysis of Hindu menstrual notions with notions prevalent in Abrahamic religions, ancient western polytheistic civilisations and other indigenous cultures from across the globe. Finally, a comparative analysis of cultural knowledge regarding menstruation enunciated in Hindu tradition with notions embedded in modernity is undertaken.

I hope this book will lead to a better understanding and appreciation of the Indian cultural knowledge and practices surrounding menstruation. I also believe that this will pave the way for a better understanding of Hindu practices, especially those related to women, and that it will open up new avenues for reexamining various polytheistic traditions in the light of Hindu philosophy and practice.

Kamakhya

Standing Parvati

Metalwork. From the Chola period dated to the first quarter of the tenth century. Parvati is the consort of Shiva who is often associated with feminine power, strength, fertility and motherhood. This magnificent statue is one of the finest Chola representations of Parvati. The genius and obvious skill of the sculptor produced a timeless image of the goddess as well as a female figure of surpassing beauty and grace. Her lyrical, rhythmic carriage and the soft yet firm lines of her body suggest the ideal of the divine and eternal female.

Source: The Metropolitan Museum of Art, US.

Shiva Embracing His Consort, Uma Parvati

From the Chola period dated to the late eleventh century.

Source: The Metropolitan Museum of Art, US.

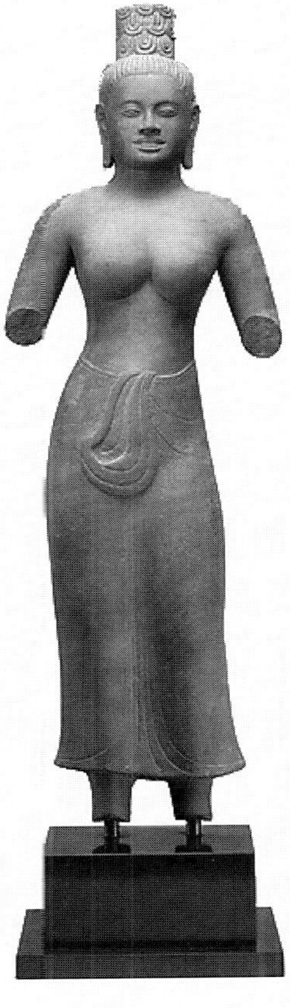

Standing Uma

Stone. From the Angkor period dated to 975 CE.

Source: The Metropolitan Museum of Art, US.

Lajja Gauri

Sandstone Sculpture. From Madhya Pradesh dated to the sixth century. Lajja Gauri is shown in a birthing posture but does not display the swollen belly of one about to give birth, which suggests that the image is of sexual fecundity. The lotus flower in place of her head makes this association with fertility explicit.

Source: The Metropolitan Museum of Art, US.

Artemis

By Arthur B Davies. Oil on canvas, 1909.

Source: The Metropolitan Museum of Art, US.

Bronze Statuette of Artemis

This statuette from the Hellenistic period dated to the third to first century BC shows Artemis, goddess of the hunt and hunters, removing an arrow from a quiver that would have been suspended over her right shoulder.

Source: The Metropolitan Museum of Art, US.

Diana

By Augustus Saint-Gaudens. Bronze Statuette. Date: 1893-94, cast 1894 or after.

Source: The Metropolitan Museum of Art, US.

The Goddess Diana

Jacques Jonghelinck. Date: 1570–80.

Source: The Metropolitan Museum of Art, US.

Hindu View of Menstruation

Introduction

SANATANA DHARMA, which is popularly known as Hinduism or Hindu Dharma is perhaps the most ancient religious tradition of the world, whose roots, recent researches have revealed,[1] go as far back as 6000 BCE or more.[2] It is certainly the oldest civilisation, which has not only survived to this day, but is still flourishing, being true to its name: Sanatana i.e. eternal and perpetual.

Historically, the Hindu civilisation had originated and spread its branches in what is today the Indian-subcontinent or South Asia, and had spread as far as South East Asia. But from the perspective of the practitioners themselves, Dharma is as old as Srishti or the Manifestation of the Universe itself. In fact, unlike the Abrahamic and modern secular worldview, Hinduism does not subscribe to a linear progression of the universe nor does it limit its self-definition or its essential principles to a historical event. Instead, the entire cosmos is perceived as perpetually undergoing a cycle of creation and destruction, and thus, *Sanatana Dharma* or the principles of Dharma, which sustain this perpetual cycle are also perpetual.

Any examination of Hindu beliefs and practices is almost impossible without taking into account its understanding of the cyclical nature of the universe[3] and its rejection of historicism and linear progression. The Hindu framework, instead, suggests an alternate model of Yugas, consisting of four Yugas: Krita, Treta, Dwapara, Kali, through which the universe moves and which together constitute a Maha Yuga. Krita constitutes the age of complete righteousness (Dharma), wherein the bull of Dharma is said to have stood on four legs. In successive ages, righteousness is reduced by one leg and hence, in Kaliyuga, Dharma stands only on one leg, which means the age is full of conflict, violence and unrighteousness. The Hindu tradition locates our current times in this Kaliyuga, which is taken to have started around 5,000 years ago and which is believed to last for another 427,000 years. While such large time-scales cannot be verified using any scientific means, what is important for our consideration is the model of yugas itself and the Hindu tradition's self-location of the present times, as well as much of the attested history in the Kaliyuga.

An analysis of Hindu knowledge and practices, including their perception of menstruation from a purely historical perspective, therefore, would not only be missing crucial perspectives, but also may lead to misleading conclusions. Hence, in the following chapters, we attempt to examine Hindu views of menstruation thematically, exploring different themes and notions that are attached to menstruation in Hindu Dharma.

Moon and Menstruation

Cultures across the world have recognised an intimate relationship between the cycles of menstruation and those of the moon. In fact, the English term menstruation or menses is derived from the Latin word 'mensis', which means 'month' and from the Greek word 'mene', which means 'moon'. Arnold L Lieber in his book, *The Lunar Effect, Biological Tides and Human Emotions*, notes that almost every aspect of human life is affected by the moon, including the menstrual cycle in women.[1]

This observation finds an echo in various Hindu knowledge traditions ranging from texts of medicine (Ayurveda) to texts of Sexology (Kamashastra) and those of Astronomy and Astrology (Jyotisha).

One of the names used for menstruation in Ayurvedic texts is 'Artava', which is derived from the Sanskrit root 'rtu' meaning 'season'.[2] Sandhiya Ramaswamy suggests that 'Rtu also implies ritual suggesting that the rhythm of life comes from the ritual dance of the seasons, and in particular the lunar season'.[3] James G Bailey in his article 'By the Light of the Moon: Ayurveda, Yoga and Menstruation' writes thus about the connection between the menstrual cycle and the lunar cycle as enunciated by the Ayurvedic texts: 'The phases of the moon and the constant transit from one to the other and back again are known as the lunation cycle. It is a symbolic representation of the growth, maturation and death cycle that all things must experience and a principle of life whether it is applied to a living organism, a woman's reproductive physiology, an action, or an emotion. Each phase of the lunation cycle has its own personality, expressed within the human body by an equivalent phase of the physical menstrual cycle.... Associating menstruation with the moon clues us to its cosmic origin (as all seasons are), waxing and waning in sync with the phases of the lunar cycle.'[4] He further adds: Ayurveda suggests that in the ideal cycle, the female human body would be synchronised to the cycles with the moon, ovulating on or near the full moon (a time of fullness) and menstruating on or near the new moon (a time of renewal), a twenty eight day cycle in all. Upon rebuilding the essences of reproduction (shukra), fertility would peak around the time of the full moon, considered the ideal time to conceive as the moon represents the fully awakened mind. At such time, samskaras of both partners are optimal to pass on to a child. Astrologers suggest further that the lunar phase an individual is born under will set a certain tone for the soul's evolution in this lifetime.[5]

In other words, Ayurveda not only recognises a clear connection between the menstrual cycle and the lunar cycle, it also prescribes synchronisation between the two as the best condition for a woman's health and fertility. Similarly, Varahamihira in one of his Jyotisha texts notes: 'Because of the Moon's control on the woman's body, she bleeds regularly once in 28 days.'[6] But it is in the Kamashastric texts such as *Ananga Ranga* and *Ratishastra* that we find a detailed exposition on the connection between women's biology and the moon.

Ananga Ranga, for example, provides details about how sexual passion resides in different parts of a woman's body during different days of the lunar month and how stimulating these parts during sexual intercourse will impart great comfort and pleasure to both the husband and the wife.[7] The text notes that 'passion resides in the woman's right side during the Shuklapaksha, the first or light fortnight of the lunar month, from new moon to full, including the fifteenth day. The reverse is the case on the dark fortnight, including its first day, and lasting from the full to the new moon'.[8] The text then provides a detailed list of the body limbs, arousing which can facilitate sexual passion to reach zenith on that particular day: Starting from the first day of the bright lunar fortnight till the fifteenth day, the following body limbs on the right side of the woman's body act as seats of passion: Big toe, foot, calf of leg, knee, vagina, nates, navel, breasts, side, throat, right cheek, lower lip, right eye and finally head and hair.[9] The order is reversed in the dark lunar fortnight.

A similar description of the different seats of passion in a woman during different lunar days are also given in the text Ratishastra, wherein the narrative is presented as a conversation between Lord Shiva and Goddess Parvati. Ratishastra further dedicates an entire chapter to the description of how the commencement of menstruation in relation to the digits of the moon affects the likely life-path or future of the woman. The chapter opens with a question by Goddess Parvati to her husband, asking thus: 'O Master of the three worlds, the phenomenon of menstruation is a very important phase in the life of a woman. Does this phenomenon influence the life of the woman in any way? I am very anxious to hear your views on this topic.'[10] In response to this query, Lord Shiva begins a detailed exposition of how the lunar day on which menarche commences in a girl affects her future: If menarche commences on the first day of the moon, the girl will be intelligent, but may die prematurely; if menarche occurs on second day of the moon, her mental faculties may be dull; menarche on the third lunar day will imply that the girl will lead a pious and happy life although she may remain without children; menarche on the fourth day may imply repeated pregnancy and abortions; if menarche commences on the fifth day of the moon, the girl's children may be sickly, and her own life short; the sixth day is also not auspicious; menarche on the seventh lunar day is good and may imply that she would have a comfortable rich life with a single child; if menarche commences on the eighth day, the girl is likely to exert great influence on people who come in her contact, but that she will be prone to temper; the ninth day is auspicious and the girl will have a good life; commencement of menarche on the tenth lunar day is considered very auspicious and the woman will be held in high esteem for her good character and noble bearing, she will shine in the midst of other woman just as the moon shines in the midst of the stars; likewise, menarche on the eleventh day of the moon is very auspicious with the woman 'acquiring the beauty of form, etiquette and character'; the twelfth day is also good, although the woman may become prone to temper; if the first menstruation commences on the thirteenth lunar day, the girl will be pious and caring, and she will manage all her responsibilities well and bring prosperity to the family; if a girl has her menarche on the fourteenth day of the moon, the circumstances of her life will be moderate; she will neither have too much fortune and prosperity nor too little; she will, however, be pious and clever. Menarche during full moon is considered most auspicious, and during the new moon most inauspicious.[11]

Contrasting the effects of the first menstruation which commences on a full moon day and a new moon day, Lord Shiva states: If a girl attains her maturity on the full moon, she will shine like a moon in her family and also in her community. She will be very beautiful in appearance, possess a goddess-like grace,and will be pious and wise. Fortune will always smile on her and she is sure to bring luck to her husband; her children, both male and female, will be beautiful, well built, healthy, fortunate and long lived. She herself will live to a pretty old age but will look like a young lady even in her old age. O Gauri, Blessed is the man who gets aswife the girl who first menstruated on the day of the full Moon, for be veritably gets all that the heart of a man craves for. On the other hand, a girl first menstruates on the day of the new Moon, it is an ominous sign. The girl will live a very unlucky and unchaste life. She will be sickly and will continually suffer from diseases peculiar to the female sex, and consequently there is very likelihood of the girls dying prematurely...There will be no redeeming feature whereby she may shine in her family or in society at any time of her life.[12]

It is clear from above passages that much like many native traditions across the globe, even Hindu traditions and knowledge systems, be it Ayurveda, Jyotisha, or Kamashastra, they all associate women's biology in general and menstrual cycle in particular with the motions of the moon. They not only recognise the need for synchronising women's menstrual cycle with the lunar cycle for achieving optimal health and fertility in women, but also have recorded a direct correlation between lunar days and different seats of passion in a woman's body, as well as a correlation between the lunar day on which her menarche commences and her future life events.

The Story of Indra

Indra is the most prominent deity (devata) among the Vedic gods. Known variously as Shakra (powerful one), Vasava (lord of Vasus), Vajrapani (who has thunderbolt in his hands), Vtrahan (slayer of Vrtra), Devaraja (king of Devas) and Svargapati (lord of heaven), he governs and sustains the universe, especially natural phenomenon such as the seasons and the rains. At an individual level, Indra is the lord of the senses and the mind (Indriyas), and he sustains them. It is through the account of this all-powerful deva that the *Vedas*, which are the foremost of all Hindu texts and the source of both Dharma and Moksha, chose to reveal the Hindu views on menstruation.

The account which first appears in the *Yajurveda Taittiriya Samhita* (2.5.1) is also repeated in the *Shatapata Brahmana* among other texts. The narrative revolves around Indra's slaying of Vishvarupa, the three-headed son of Tvastr, who drank Soma from one of the heads, Sura (liquor) from the second head and consumed food from the third head. Here is the full account as it appears in the Yajurveda Taittiriya Samhita, taken from Arthur Berriedale Keith's translation:

Vishvarupa, son of Tvastr, was the domestic priest of the gods, and the sister's son of the Asuras. He had three heads, one which drank Soma, one Sura, and one which ate food. He promised openly the share to the gods, secretly to the Asuras. Men promise openly the share to every one; if they promise any one secretly, his share is indeed promised. Therefore Indra was afraid (thinking), 'Such an one is diverting the sovereignty (from me).' He took his bolt and smote off his heads. (The head) which drank Soma became a hazelcock; (the head) which drank Sura a sparrow; (the head) which ate food a partridge. He seized with his hand the guilt of slaying him, and bore it for a year. Creatures called out upon him, 'Thou art a Brahman slayer.' He appealed to the earth, 'Take a third part of my guilt.' She said, 'Let me choose a boon. I deem that I shall be overcome through digging. Let me not be overcome by that.' He replied, 'Before a year is out it will grow up for thee.' Therefore before the year is out the dug-out portion of earth grows up again, for that was what she chose as a boon. She took a third of his guilt. That became a natural fissure; therefore one who has piled up a fire-altar and whose deity is faith should not choose a natural fissure, for that is the colour of guilt. He appealed to the trees, 'Take a third part of my guilt.' They said, 'Let us choose a boon. We deem that we shall be overcome through pruning. Let us not be overcome by that.' He replied, 'From pruning shall more (shoots) spring up for you.' Therefore from the pruning of trees more (shoots) spring up, for that was what they chose as a boon. They took a third part of his guilt, it became sap; therefore one should not partake of sap, for it is the colour of guilt. Or rather of the sap which is red or which comes from the pruning one should not partake, but of other sap at will. He appealed to a concourse of women, 'Take the third of my guilt.' They said, 'Let us choose a boon; let us obtain offspring from after the menses; let us enjoy intercourse at will up to birth.' Therefore women obtain offspring from after the menses, and enjoy intercourse at will up to birth, for that was what they chose as a boon. They took a third of his

> guilt, it became (a woman) with stained garments; therefore one should not converse with (a woman) stained garments, one should not sit with her, nor eat her food, for she keeps emitting the colour of guilt. Or rather they say, 'Woman's food is unguent, and therefore one should not accept (from her) unguent, but anything else (can be accepted) at will.' The son born of intercourse with (a woman) with stained garments is accursed; (the son born) of intercourse in the forest is a thief; (the son born) of intercourse with a (woman) who turns away is shamefaced and retiring; (the son born) of intercourse with a woman bathing is fated to drown; (the son born) of one who anoints herself has a skin disease; (the son born) of one who combs her hair is bald and feeble; (the son born) of one who anoints (her eyes) is blind; (the son born) of one who cleans her teeth has dirty teeth; (the son born) of one who cuts her nails has bad nails; (the son born) of one who spins is a eunuch; (the son born) of one who weaves ropes is unrestrained; (the son born) of one who drinks from a leaf is drunken; (the son born) of one who drinks from a mutilated (vessel) is mutilated. For three nights he should keep a vow and should drink from his hand or from a perfect vessel, to guard his offspring.[1]

The above account can be divided into two parts: Story Narrative and Menstrual Guidelines. While the story narrative serves the function of etiology, the guidelines constitute the life-style practices and restrictions to be practised by a menstruating woman. The former in fact provides a hermeneutic key for interpreting and understanding the latter.

Let us summarise the story narrative so that we can derive key hermeneutic principles for better understanding of the Hindu views of menstruation. Indra, who was afflicted with the Karmic guilt of Brahmahatya, transferred one-third of his guilt to the earth, one-third to trees, and the remaining one-third to women. In the earth, the guilt manifested as natural fissure; in trees, it manifested as sap; and in women, it manifested as menstrual blood flow once a month, making her a woman with 'stained garment' during that time. In return, all were granted boons. While the earth asked for a boon that she may not be harmed by digging, the trees asked that they may not be harmed by pruning. Women asked that they obtain offsprings after menses and enjoy sexual intimacy at will until the birth of their children. It is because the guilt manifests as stained garment in women that one should not sit with her, not eat her food and not have sexual intercourse with her (since offsprings born of such intercourse will be accursed). Other things to be avoided by menstruating women include bathing, anointing oneself, combing, brushing, cutting nails, spinning and weaving.

The key hermeneutic principles we can derive from this narrative are:

1. Menstruation is a natural phenomenon: The very first thing that strikes a careful reader is that menstruation is portrayed as a natural phenomenon. The account does this by drawing a parallel between the manifestation of menstrual bleeding with the manifestation of sap and natural fissure. Since both the sap and natural fissure are natural phenomena, menstruation should likewise be understood as a natural phenomenon.

2. Menstruation constitutes one-third Brahmahatya: Brahmahatya, i.e. killing of a Brahamna, is considered a great Adharmic action, a Paapam (a sin). By equating the manifestation of menstrual blood with one-third Brahmahatya and then likewise connecting the account with women's ability to give birth in the form of a boon to women, the narrative is making a reference to the biology of women, who are endowed with the monthly menstrual cycle so as to facilitate them to conceive a child. During ovulation, eggs are released to be fertilised by the male sperm. In case fertilisation does not take place, the unfertilised eggs along with blood, endometrium tissue, etc. are thrown out of the body during the monthly periods. It is this unfertilisation of the egg that implies that a potential childbirth did not happen that attracts the guilt of one-third Brahmahatya.

3. Menstruation as Ashaucha: This guilt due to non-fertilisation of egg whose magnitude is one-third of Brahmahatya imparts Ashaucha or impurity on menstruating women. The narrative notes that since natural fissure is associated with one-third guilt, 'one who has piled up a fire-altar and whose deity is faith should not choose a natural fissure', that is, one should not perform any sacred rituals near a fissure. Similarly, one must not consume sap, especially sap which is red. This implies that menstruating women, who are associated with Ashaucha, are not eligible for performance of Vedic rituals.

4. Menstruation as Austerity and Self-purification: The narrative does not end with associating menstruation with Ashaucha. In fact, by limiting the Ashaucha due to the non-fertilisation of the egg to only the three days of menses, the narrative gives clues towards how menstruation is a self-purification process, and notes that the life-style guidelines such as notanointing oneself act as austere measures which facilitate self-purification. Guidelines like no-spinning and no-weaving also indicate that menstruation is a period of rest.

5. Menstruation as Sacred Celebration: By associating menstruation with childbirth, which is considered a very Dharmic act, the narrative portrays menstruation as a sacred celebration.

These hermeneutic principles are very important to understand menstruation practices and restrictions prescribed in important Hindu texts like Vedas, *Smriti*s, *Purana*s, and *Dharmashastra*s. The story of Indra, thus, provides a very important tool for approaching Hindu menstrual beliefs and practices and for arriving at a holistic and wholesome understanding of the Hindu treatment of the issue.

In the subsequent chapters, each of these principles is individually taken up and examined in some depth.

Menstruation as Ashaucha

Menstruation is considered as 'Ashaucha' (which could be roughly translated as 'ritual impurity'). Women who have their periods enter a temporary period (three days to be specific) of ritual impurity.

Angirasa Smriti (Verse 35), for example, tells us that during the fourth day, after menstruation stops, women become Shuddha (pure) through a purification bath.[1] *Vashishta Dharma Sutra* (5.5) goes a step further and explicitly states: 'A woman in her courses will be Ashuchi (impure) during three (days and) nights.' *Baudhayana Dharmasutra* (2.2.4.4) says that the Ashaucha is only 'temporary'.[2] *Parashara Smriti* (7.16-17) informs that even if menstrual blood continues to flow after four days due to some illness (for example: hormonal imbalance), it will cause no further Ashaucha.[3] This is further elaborated in *Stridharmapaddhati* of Tryambakayajvan, wherein the author classifies menstruation into four types based on their causes: due to illness (Rogajam), emotional disturbance (Raagajam), imbalance of humour (Dhatujam), and due to regular monthly cycle; and designates only the last, i.e. menstruation caused due to regular monthly cycle, as being associated with Ashaucha.[4] Stridharmapaddhati further notes that after the three days of Ashaucha, the menstruating women will become pure after cleaning themselves with sixty lumps of earth and then taking a ritual bath with their clothes on.[5] They should then gaze upon the sun, pray to the deity and attend to their duties.[6]

Now, what exactly is Ashaucha? It has been roughly translated to mean uncleanliness/impurity. But the full implication of the term goes beyond the normal notions associated with these terms. To understand this, we must first comprehend the Hindu concept of an Individual and the concepts of Shaucha (purity) and Ashaucha (impurity) associated with such an individual.

Much of the modern scientific view, which is largely rooted in materialism, perceives an Individual as just a physical body. Even the mind and its functions are perceived as being rooted in the physical organ brain. Contrary to this, Hinduism perceives an Individual as a being with five layers of individuality. In other words, each person has five bodies that act as five sheaths that covers his/her innermost Self (Atman). These five sheaths, which are together called as 'Pancha-Koshas'.[7] are: Annamaya Kosha (physical sheath), Pranamaya Kosha (vital sheath), Manomaya Kosha (mental sheath), Vigyanamaya Kosha (sheath of intellect), and Anandamaya Kosha (sheath of bliss). Hence, each Individual is constituted of five bodies – physical, vital, mind, intellect, and bliss. But in day to day life, at the Vyavaharika (transactional) level, a person is mostly active at his physical, vital and mental sheaths. Hence, it is with respect to these three layers of individuality that one must understand the process of menstruation.

One of the names for Menstruation in Sanskrit is 'Rajasraava', which loosely means 'flow of Raja'. Though the term 'Raja' here is often translated as 'blood', it may as well refer to 'Rajas Guna'. Rajas is one among the three Gunas. It denotes flow, movement, passion, energy etc. and imparts a dynamic nature to the Individual, but at the same time it also increases a person's bondage to the worldly cycle.

In the physical body, 'Rajasraava' represents the flow of menstrual blood, which contains blood, cervical mucus, vaginal secretions, and endometrial tissue that are being thrown out of the physical body. In the vital body, Rajasraava represents the flow of excess Rajasic energy, i.e. Prana Shakti (especially the Apana Vayu). Blood is the carrier of Prana Shakti within the physical body. Thus, through the excretion of the blood, excess Prana

Shakti, which is Rajasic in nature, is being thrown out of the body during menstruation. In the mental sheath, Rajas represents thoughts and emotions such as anger, frustration, uneasiness, irritation, mood-swings, etc. to which menstruating women are more prone to. Therefore, menstruation is a complicated physio-psychological process that exposes a woman to the excess Rajasic condition of the physical, vital, and mental levels.

Shaucha or purity is one of the most important tenets of Hinduism.[8] It is considered one of the common duties (Samanya Dharmas) to which each human being is expected to adhere.[9] It is listed as one among the Niyamas (compulsory observances) required to practice Yoga.[10] It is also necessary for the practice of Bhakti[11] and Vedanta.[12] In fact, one of the Smritis goes a step further and states that a person should always try to maintain Shaucha in whatever work he or she engages in, and that without such an adherence to purity, all actions and works becomes fruitless.[13]

From the above, it is clear that the concept of Shaucha or purity is deeply connected with the concept of competency or qualification to perform a particular action. This Shaucha gains even more significance with respect to religious and spiritual actions like performing puja, homam (fire ritual), or visiting temples. Hindu scriptures define Shaucha not only in terms of external purity, but also in terms of internal purity.[14] Thus, purity or impurity is to be understood at the level of physical, vital and mental sheaths.

At the physical level, purity constitutes cleanliness and hygiene of the body and the surroundings. Thus, all body secretions and excretions, be it sweat, urine, feces, blood, or menstrual discharge, are considered as Ashaucha at the physical level. At the vital level, a balance of all the five kinds of vital airs (Pancha-Vayu or Pancha-Prana[15]) within the body is considered as Shaucha. Imbalance in them, for example, due to excess Apana vayu and Rajasic energy during menstruation, is considered as Ashaucha at the vital sheath level. At the level of the mental sheath, a mind that is free from internal passions (Arishadvarga) like lust, anger, jealousy, etc. is considered as Shaucha and a mind afflicted with internal passions is Ashaucha. Hence, menstruation, wherein the internal passions of the mind are at a heightened condition, is considered Ashaucha even at the level of the mental sheath.

For all spiritual and religious activities, the cleanliness of the body, balance in the vital force (Prana) and a calm mind are very important. Without these qualities, at least to some extent, no person will be able to properly perform worship. In other words, purity at the physical, vital and mental levels is among the required competencies for any religious activity, and impurity at these levels makes one incompetent to perform those religious and spiritual activities. Moreover, cleanliness and purity are important, even for the performance of various secular activities. Thus, the Hindu scriptures speak about various kinds of situations wherein a person becomes associated with Ashaucha and becomes incompetent to perform certain religious and secular activities, and certain restrictions are placed on him/her during those situations. One such Ashaucha situation is the death of a close relative, another such situation is the birth of a child, and yet another situation is the monthly menses.

It is important to note that Ashaucha in general is as much about impurity as it is about competency to perform a particular action, especially religious action. *Smritichandrika*, for example, defines Shaucha as the removal of taint (papakshayam) and as the provider of competency to perform Dharma (dharma-yogyatva).[16] Similarly, Rudradhara in *Shuddhiviveka* defines Shuddhi as the 'innate character which gives competence to do all enjoined acts, and Ashuddhi as its opposite, springing from birth or death among kinsfolk'.[17] Govindananda in

Shuddhikaumudhi, explicitly notes that Shaucha provides the competence to do all acts enjoined in the Vedas, and that it springs from fitness in time, place and person.[18] Therefore, while Shaucha is the state of fitness, Ashaucha is the state of incompetence for performing certain Dharmic activities owing to impurity.

Hence, Ashaucha related to menstruation is not only about unhygienic conditions at the physical level, which has been more or less addressed by sanitary pads, tampons etc. in the modern times; Ashaucha is also about the heightened Rajasic state of menstruating women in their physical, vital, and mental sheaths and how this heightened Rajasic state makes:

1. Certain actions unsuitable for menstruating women.
2. Menstruating women unsuitable for certain actions.

Thus, we find Hindu scriptures advising women against performing certain activities. Angirasa Smrithi (verse 37), for example, asks women to not perform any sacred (religious) activities like puja, homam, visiting temple etc. during menstruation. Similarly, *Brihadaranyaka Upanishad* (6.4.13) advices menstruating women to not drink from a metal cup (as metals conduct energy at both physical and subtle levels). Yajurveda Taittiriya Samhita (2.5.1) further advices women to not cook food (because food cooked in a Rajasic condition will be Rajasic in nature) and also asks them to stay away from sexual intercourse, because due to heightened Rajas, if conception happens during menstruation (it is possible,[19] although less likely) or perhaps immediately after menses, the resulting child may suffer from intra-uterine death, early death or some form of deformity. This has been enunciated even in many Ayurvedic texts, which we shall take up in the subsequent sections.

This kind of Ashaucha and the related restrictions are not unique to women. As noted before, both men and women become associated with Ashaucha under different conditions like death of relatives, etc. Thus, calling menstruation Ashaucha neither degrades women nor makes them inferior. Instead, it is a temporary state of impurity that a woman enters, which as we shall see in the next chapter, actually purifies her and makes her remain ever pure.

Nevertheless, it must also be noted that there are Hindu sects, particularly in the tantric traditions, that recognise the menstrual process itself as Shaucha (pure) for certain ritual purposes and have specific rituals for this heightened state as well.

Austerity, Self-purification & Rest

In the previous section, an examination into one facet of Ashaucha (impurity) associated with Menstruation in Hinduism was undertaken, and it was shown how the heightened state of Rajas that a menstruating woman enters makes her unsuitable to perform certain religious and mundane actions during that period.

In this section, let us take up three more principles that inform us of the Hindu views on menstruation: Austerity, Self-Purification and Rest.

Menstruation as a period of austerity

One of the notions that is deeply associated with menstruation in the Hindu scriptures but is often missed in most discussions is the notion of menstruation as a process of austerity (Tapas) and self-purification. This notion is very important because without understanding this one would most likely end up with a distorted view regarding the Hindu conception of menstruation.

First, let us examine the Hindu notion of Tapas. Hindu tradition recognises that some kind of Tapas is necessary to attain any goal – sacred or secular – in life. In the simplest terms, Tapas refers to austerity or hardship. Without facing hardships, without overcoming obstacles, no work is accomplished. Recognising this, the Hindu scriptures have charted out how one can use this Tapas to attain material welfare and spiritual emancipation.

At a deeper level, Tapas is defined as restrainment of the body, mind, and the senses. And all austere practices and self-restrictions have been laid out with an aim to achieve this restrainment. The stress on sense-restrainment has been placed owing to the fact that only through such a restrainment of physical actions and mental thoughts would a person be able to attain detachment and dispassion and free oneself from internal impurities like lust and anger.

Thus, Hindu texts declare that through Tapas, one destroys one's impurities (of the body and mind)[1] and attains self-purification. The importance of austerity in the Hindu tradition can be gauged by the fact that, just like Shaucha, Tapas is also listed among the *Niyama*s of Yoga;[2] among the basic *Samanya Dharma*; and is considered vital for practicing *Vedanta*.[3]

Various Hindu rituals and practices have been designed to act as austerity to help one attain detachment and self-purification. Beginning with Samskaras like Garbadhana (ceremony marking the intention to give birth to a child) and Vivaha (marriage), daily ritual performances like that of Sandhyopasana, and various kinds of vratas (vows of austerity, usually fasting) and pujas along with their different rules and regulations that are performed periodically, are all aimed to act as Tapas or 'Austere practices' that help individuals purify themselves and become free from Adharmic (unrighteous) actions that they may have committed through their body, mind, and speech – intentionally or unintentionally.

In other words, tapas not only aims to help an individual become free of some of the Adharmas committed in the past, it also helps him/her become detached and gain control over the senses, thus helping them prevent committing more Adharma in the future. Hence, Austerity and self-purification play a very vital role in aiding an individual in his journey towards the ultimate Moksha.

It is this notion of austerity and the resulting self-purification that the Hindu scriptures closely associate with the menstruation process experienced by women, making it a very beneficial process, available only to women. This, in fact, honours the process of menstruation as being a form of Sadhana (spiritual effort).

Yajurveda Taittiriya Samhita (Verse 2.5.1) indirectly suggests that menstruating women should not comb their hair, anoint their eyes or cut their nails. Further, they must not have conjugal relations with the husband during that period.[4] Vashishta Dharmasutra (5.6) goes further and explicitly states that during monthly periods, women should not apply collyrium to their eyes, that they should not anoint their body, that they should sleep on the ground, that they must avoid sleeping during the day, that they must not eat meat, mustn't look at the planets, and must not smile.

These regulations and restrictions imply that menstruation must be observed as a period of austerity. For example, take the restriction on the anointment of the eyes and the body. Women are inclined to look beautiful, and they use various means to enhance their physical beauty, which includes anointing the body, adorning ornaments, applying collyrium to the eyes, among other things. Consequently, they develop an attachment to these activities and to their physical body. Adopting these menstruation restrictions make a woman restrain her senses, and as a result, she will develop a better control over thesenses. Similarly, most people sleep on some kind of bed because it is comfortable and many often tend to sleep during the day as well. The former denotes a dependence on material comforts and the latter denotes laziness and an inability to overcome sleep. By restraining oneself, one becomes less attached to material comforts and less addicted to sleep. Similarly, the restriction on meat could make a woman free from her dependency on food. The restriction on intercourse denotes the practice of Brahmacharya, which is one of the most important aspects of any Tapas; it helps overcome lust and the attachment to sexual pleasures.

Thus, according to Hindu tradition, menstruation provides a unique opportunity for women to practice austerity and attain self-purification by developing detachment and better control over the mind and the senses. Moreover, as we shall see next, it is not just the austere practices adopted during menstruation that are beneficial for women. Instead, the menstrual process itself acts as a kind of austerity, which is self-purifying in nature and which frees women from Adharma.

Menstruation as a self-purifying process

Hindu scriptures do not just suggest that the period of menses should be treated as a period of austerity, and that women and girls should observe some austere practices during that phase. They also recognise the process of menstruation itself as being one of austerity and self-purification. One of the reasons behind the segregation of menstruating women is the notion of menstruation being a Tapas by itself, because any Tapas, whether performed by men or women, is best practised in solitude.

Shaucha or Purification as we saw in the chapteron Ashaucha, is not only related to the physical body, but also to the vital body and the mind. And menstruation removes impurity associated with each of the three layers of Individuality. Thus, it purifies the physical body by removing the menstrual fluid that contains blood, cervical mucus, vaginal secretions and endometrial tissue etc.; it purifies the vital body by removing excess Apana Vayu; and it purifies the mind by removing mental impurities.

Thus, menstruation, though associated with Ashaucha, is also a self-purifying process.

Among all its self-purifying functions, the purification with respect to the mind is most significant. The mind is the root of speech and physical action, and is therefore intimately connected with Karma. Hindu scriptures divide Karma into Dharma and Adharma based on whether it is righteous or not, whether it is one's duty or not, and whether it is beneficial to the performer as well as the world or not. All actions that are good, righteous and beneficial, and those that uphold the individual and the world are Dharma, and the opposite – Adharma. Thus, the practice of Dharma is purity and the practice of Adharma is impurity. Purification, therefore, is a process by which one becomes free from the fruits of Adharmic actions through the performance of Tapas or austerity.

To properly understand purification with respect to Adharma, one must first understand Adharma. According to the *Manu Smriti* (12.5-7) Adharma is of three kinds – those committed through the body, through speech, and through the mind. Adharma through the body consists of : taking what has not been given, injuring others without the sanction of the scriptures, and having intercourse with another's spouse. Adharma through speech consists of : abusing others and speaking harshly; speaking the untruth; gossiping and backbiting, and talking idly and without context. Adharma of the mind consists of: desiring the property and belongings of others; thinking in one's heart of what is undesirable (i.e. thinking about committing unrighteous actions that may cause harm to oneself and to others); and adherence to falsehoods and false doctrines. Therefore, a person commits Adharma not only through his body, but also through his mind and speech. Hence, the purification of Adharma will also involve cleansing the Adharma committed through body, mind and speech.

This notion of menstruation as a self-purifying process that frees one from paapam (sin) incurred from Adharmic actions can be traced back to the Vedas. In the section titled 'The Story of Indra', we briefly examined the account from Yajurveda Taittiriya Samhiṭa (2.5.1), which narrates how Indra killed Vishvarupa, the second teacher of the Devas, and incurred the sin (paapa)[5] of Brahmahatya.[6] Indra was able to free himself from this act of Adharma, only when the earth, the trees, and the women agreed to take one-third of the Brahmahatya paapa. As a result of this, women began to menstruate once every 28-30 days. In return, Indra gave women the boon that they will be able to give birth to children after their menses. What is the symbolism of this story?

As we saw before, this story symbolically represents the entire gamut of Hindu notions of menstruation, especially the notion of menstruation as a purification process. On the one hand, it relates menstruation to one-third sin (paapa) of Brahmahatya, and on the other hand, it relates it to the birth of children. Thus, the entire story must be understood with respect to the biological process of menstruation and its relation to child birth.

It is well-known that the menstrual discharge not only contains blood, but also the unfertilised egg. In other words, the monthly discharge represents a failure of conception, a failure to give birth. In the Hindu tradition, giving birth to children is not only considered as an enjoined duty of the householder,[7] it is also considered as a very Dharmic action. It is so because by giving birth, a couple is helping an individual soul (Jivaatma) enter the physical universe and continue its Karmic journey.[8] On the other hand, one commits Adharma, if he/she prevents the birth of a Jivaatma, intentionally or unintentionally. This is so because, in many ways preventing a child from taking a birth is similar to murdering a person: in both cases a Jivaatma is being robbed of its opportunity to experience physical universe.

If it were to be asked, how a person prevents a Jivaatma from taking birth, the answer would be: a) by abortion and b) by unfertilisation of the egg. The former is called 'Bhrunahatya' – killing of the embryo, and as the name denotes, it is counted as murder. The Hindu scriptures count it among the most heinous paapam[9] and equate it to Brahmahatya.[10] Similarly, even the unfertilisation of the egg each month results in the failure of birth, and hence is associated with Adharma. The only difference between abortion and the unfertilisation of the egg is the magnitude of Adharma. The magnitude is severe in the former because it is an embryo which is in the process of developing into a child that is killed, whereas in the latter, only the egg, which was formed for the purpose of mating with the semen, became wasted. It is in this context that Indra's story about women incurring one-third paapa of Brahmahatya must be understood. The one-third of paapa of Brahmahatya is incurred due to the failure of the egg to fertilse and become fit to host a Jivaatma into the physical universe.

The story does not end with women taking upon themselves one-third paapa from Indra. It further says that as a result of women inheriting this one-third paapa of Brahmahatya, they had to menstruate once every month, and after menstruation they would become fertile again. In other words, menstruation acted as a purification process, which helped women get rid of the paapa they had inherited. Thus, there is a clear indication in the Vedas itself about menstruation being a self-purifying process, and among other things, it frees women from the paapam incurred due to the unfertilisation of their egg.

This notion is further elaborated in the Smritis and the Dharmasutras. Angirasa Smriti (Verse 42) explicitly states that women become purified due to menstruation. Manu Smriti (5.108) similarly states that women whose thoughts have become impure, will be purified by menstruation. Vashishta

Dharmasutra (28.2-3) elaborates this further and states: 'A wife, (though) tainted by sin, whether she be quarrelsome, or have left the house, or have suffered criminal force, or have fallen into the hands of thieves, must not be abandoned; to forsake her is not prescribed (by the sacred law). Let him wait for the time of her courses; by her temporary uncleanness she becomes pure.'

Thus, when it is said that menstruation purifies women, it refers to the freeing of women from a large range of Adharmic actions committed through body, mind, and speech. *It also refers to freeing of women from feelings of guilt and dishonour associated with unfortunate incidents like rape, sexual assault etc.* But this does not mean that women have been given a free pass from karmic consequences and that they can freely commit any Adharma. In fact, Vashishta Dharmasutra (28.7) clarifies that Adharmic actions like killing of husband, of Brahmana, and of the embryo will result in a woman losing her Varna. That is, in those cases, menstruation is not enough to free them from those paapas. In short, while menstruation frees women from a large variety of Adharmas committed through body, mind and speech on a day-to-day basis either unintentionally or under unavoidable circumstances, it does not help them in any way in cases where the Adharmas have been performed intentionally or are of a serious magnitude for a selfish purpose without a care for its consequences.

Men do not undergo menstruation and hence they do not have access to this self-purifying process. Instead, the scriptures suggest a variety of rules and ritual practices, based on Varna (inherent quality) and Ashrama (station) in life. Activities like Samskaras, Mantra Japa, Sandhyopasana, etc. have all been prescribed for men to attain purity and become free from Adharmic actions. But, women need not perform any of these spiritual activities to attain purity. They become pure simply by undergoing menstruation. *What comes by special effort to men, comes as part of a natural process to women.* This unique aspect of menstruation and the privilege it provides exclusively for women is repeatedly stressed in the Hindu scriptures.

Baudhayana Dharmasutra (2.2.4.4), for example, says: 'Women (possess) an unrivalled means of purification; they never become (entirely) impure. For month by month their temporary uncleanness removes their sins.' The same is repeated in Vashishta Dharmasutra (28.4), which further elaborates on this and says that women are in the custody of Soma, Gandharva, and Agni who grant them cleanliness, melodious voice and purity of all limbs, respectively, and hence, women are free from stains and cannot be contaminated.[11] It is well known that Soma is one of the names of the Moon, and the moon is intimately connected to the monthly menstrual cycle[12] on the one hand, and to mind, on the other. Similarly, Agni is also associated with the mind. But Agni is also associated with physical actions and is considered as a witness and a purifier of all our actions performed at all levels. Gandharva is clearly associated with the speech in the verses itself. Thus, Agni, Gandharva and Soma are the presiding deities of the actions performed respectively at the physical, verbal, and mental levels. And through these deities, the process of menstruation imparts purity in body, mind, and speech to all women. It is important to note that the verses stress that through these three deities, who are associated with different aspects of the purification process of menstruation, women become 'free from stains, and are not contaminated'.

In a similar verse found in *Yajnavalkya Smriti* (1.71), women are said to be 'all pure'. Vashishta Dharmasutra (28.9) goes a step further and states: *Pure is the mouth of a goat and of a horse, pure is the back of a cow, pure are the feet of a Brâhmana, but women are pure in all (limbs).* Chandamaharoshana-tantra[13] goes even further and declares: *A man should regard every substance discharged from a woman's body as pure and should be willing to touch it and ingest it if requested to do so.* In other words, menstruation, although associating women with temporary Ashaucha, does not make them impure. Instead, it facilitates women to remain ever pure (subject to the condition that they do not perform any intentional Adharma).

It is important to note that as with any Tapas or austerity, even menstruation has certain rules and restrictions that practitioners must follow to the best of their ability and without this, one will not get the complete fruits of the practice.

In other words, though menstruation has a capacity to grant purity and free women from demerits, without a proper realisation of the austere and purifying nature of menstruation and an adherence to menstruation practices suggested by various Hindu texts, the ability of the menstruation process to purify women and make them free from impurities at all levels would be limited, and such women will end up gaining only partial benefits from the whole process.

Menstruation as a period of rest

Menstruation as a period of rest is another notion that is widely prevalent throughout India. Menstruating women often face discomfort, mood swings, and abdominal cramps. Most experience menstrual pain of varying intensity and ten out of hundred women experience such a severe pain that they are unable to carry out their usual daily activities.[14] Though, this is not an India-specific estimate, it does give us a general idea regarding the prevalence of menstrual discomfort across the world. This discomfort forces women to take rest during this period, even making them take one or two days off from their schools and workplaces.[15] Therefore, the notion of rest is widely prevalent among modern urban women. But what is interesting is the fact that this notion of rest is not only well-recognised in the Hindu scriptures, it is also a dominant notion attached to traditional menstrual beliefs and practices among various communities.

Angirasa Smriti (Verse 37), for example, advises women to resume their household work only after their monthly periods stop. Similarly, Vashishta Dharmasutra (5.6) says that menstruating women should not indulge in physical exertion, be it household work, or activities like running. During Ambubachi festival in Kamakhya temple in Assam, the temple is closed for three days to give rest to the Goddess, who is believed to be menstruating during that time. Similarly, during the Tulu festival called Keddasa in Karnataka, mother earth is believed to have begun her earthly menstrual cycle and is given a rest for three days. This is also practised during the Raja Parva (menstruation festival) in Odisha, where farmers don't plough the land and give rest to Goddess earth. The State of Bihar in India, for example, grants government teachers leave every month for this.

Frederique Apffel-Marglin, in her book, *Rhythms of Life: Enacting the World with the Goddesses of Orissa,* quotes a village woman from Odisha saying thus: *During the menses of the earth, women do no work; they play and sing with their friends. The sole reason is for them to rest, just like during their monthly periods, when they do not work and must not be disturbed, they should not be touched*.[16]

Mitoo Das, in her paper 'Menstruation as Pollution: Taboos in Simlitola, Assam', mentions that both the notions of menstruation as impurity and as a period of rest are prevalent among the people of Simlitola, Assam. She writes: *The taboos prescribed are not only present, because women are taken to be 'pollutants' or 'impure' during menstruation but also because women are considered to be physically weak during menses and thus the following of taboos, at least some of it, allow her ample 'rest'. Thus, Similitola society has a second way of explaining the need for the existence of such taboos, i.e. to make women rest.*[17]

In the modern times, Swami Chinmayananda has explained[18] that menstruation restrictions were used as a means for providing rest to women, who otherwise indulged in physically demanding household tasks in the past, and who suffered from pain, stress, and discomfort during the menses. Therefore, the notion of menstruation as a period of rest that the women need, owing to stress and physical discomfort, is clearly recognised by Hinduism and some menstrual practices like preventing women from doing household work are aimed to serve that purpose.

Menstruation as a Sacred Celebration

In the previous two sections an examination into the facets of Ashaucha and the facets of austerity, self-purification and rest associated with Menstruation in the Hindu tradition was undertaken, and it was shown how inspite of menstruating women entering a temporary period of Ashaucha (ritual impurity), the process itself is very beneficial and purificatory in nature. We further saw how Hindu scriptures implore women to consider menstruation as a period of austerity and rest and take full benefit of the purification process, which is available exclusively to them.

In this section let us take up another facet of the Hindu view of menstruation: as a period of sacred celebration.

Celebrating Menarche

The Hindu way of life perceives each element of an Individual's life as sacred and worthy of worship and celebration. Thus, from the moment of birth, intake of the first food, writing the first letters, and until marriage and death, every life event is associated with sacredness, worship, and celebration. Even in death, wherein people always mourn, it is recognised that the journey of the Jivaatma has not ended, and the death rites aim to aid the Jivaatma regain new birth and continue its journey further. Thus, even the Death rites are sacred and have the utmost importance in the Hindu scheme of things.

This attachment of sacredness – of a notion of worship and celebration – to the various elements of life can be observed with respect to menstruation and menstruating women as well. The best example that illustrates this is the celebration of 'Ritu Kala Samskara' which is the coming of age ceremony that celebrates the onset of menstruation among young girls. This is a highly localised ceremony that is celebrated across India, based on local customs and traditions.

In his book, *The Cochin Tribes and Castes* (Vol 1), LK Anantha Krishna Iyer writes thus about the menarche rituals observed in a Kerala community of astrologers and umbrella makers called Kaniyans:

> When a girl reaches puberty, she is bathed and dressed in a cloth dyed yellow with turmeric. She is lodged in a room of the house for the period of her seclusion, which is generally four days, during which only her girl-friends associate with her. On the fourth day, she and her friends have an oil bath in a stream or tank close by. A triangular figure made of the bark of a plantain tree, with lighted candles and pieces of tender leaves of a coconut tree thrust on the three sides, on which is sprinkled the blood of a fowl just killed, is waved round the head of the girl as she plunges into the water. As they return home after the bath, they are escorted by a few Nairs provided with swords and guns, and there is music from the drum and the pipe. The girl is seated in a conspicuous part of the house, when a woman waves round her face, a vessel containing water mixed with turmeric powder and lime, which is believed to free her from the power of the evil-eye or any demoniacal influence. Another woman of the family throws pieces of bread to the four corners of the house to invoke the blessings of the deities presiding over the cardinal points. The women of the caste who are invited are then feasted, after which the men are fed. This

> is followed by a circular dance of the women. A woman of the washerman caste is also engaged to be present to sing at the time. She has also to give a newly washed cloth to the girl to wear after her bath in order to be free from pollution.[1]

Frederique Apffel-Marglin in her essay 'The Sacred Groves' recounts this account of menarche practices among Odisha women as narrated by Sisulata, an Odiya woman in her 40s:

> I was 13 when I saw my first blood. I was afraid. I came and told my father, mother and paternal grandmother who were all sitting together...Then, my mother took me to the back of our house where the manure pile is and made me stand on it for about an hour. Then she took me to the house and gave me a bath, pouring water over me. She and the other women didn't touch me; I was polluted. They called the washerwoman and she took all my clothes and they gave me a new sari. That sari was later given to the washerwoman. Then, for the four days that I lay on the mat inside, I did not bathe, comb and oil my loose hair, or decorate myself at all.
>
> Then my parents brought nine kinds of navasasya (seeds) rice, black gram, mugha (another lentil), horse gram, sesame, mustard, wild rice, wheat and bean. They also brought five pitchers with water in them, covered with mango leaves topped by a coconut (purna khumba). They spread a mat, and on that, a red cloth for me to lie on. At the four corners, they placed four pitchers and the fifth midway between two of the others. Then they spread the seeds all around the mat.
>
> My mother told me, 'come here and sit on the mat'. She taught me how to wear the napkin and said: 'Don't be afraid, it is not bad; you'll bleed [for] four days and it will happen every month. You must not work, not cook, not cut any vegetables. You will rest and eat separately'. I stayed in that room with the windows closed so that no man would see me and the sun would not fall on me. I only went out in the night to relieve myself. My girlfriends came and brought me food: fruits,

> flattened rice, puffed rice; only raw and dry food; no boiled food. I ate no fish, meat, eggs, onions, garlic, and no salt or turmeric. This means I ate no cooked rice or curry because these must always have salt and turmeric. I could chat with my friends. Every day I was given a new sari. All these four saris were later given to the washerwoman. On the fifth day, before dawn, seven married women came to take me to the pond and we all bathed. They poured water over me, rubbed my body with oil and turmeric, blew the conch shell and did hula-huli (women's trill, an auspicious sound). The barber's wife cut my nails and painted auspicious designs with alata (red dye) on my test [sic]. They combed, oiled and braided my hair. They dressed me with all new garments and I wore my mother's gold ornaments. We all came back to the house in a procession and I was so happy to be out and to be able to touch everybody! I was also happy because everyone brought me presents and fussed about me.
>
> My parents had sent the news out to all our relatives and neighbours and they came to our house that day with presents for me. That day I had to feed sweets to seven small children. I stayed decorated the whole day and people kept coming and giving me clothes, oil, turmeric [and] combs, lots of things for me. I got so many saris, blouse pieces, bangles, sindur (red powder for the dot on the forehead)! These were my first saris, before menarche I wore only frocks. At one point in the day my mother prepared offerings for the temple; on a winnowing tray, she placed a lamp, incense, a bit of food [and] some coins, and I carried it to the temple and offered these to Siva. Then, I ate consecrated food. In the evening, my mother had cooked a grand feast for all the guests. I remember that feast so vividly, when everybody kept me happy.[2]

In Karnataka, the young girl, who has started menstruating, is dressed up, and the Sumangali women (married women) from the neighborhood perform her Aarti (showing of lamp, light from a wick as in Puja) and sing songs. The girl is then given Chigali unde (a dish made of sesame seeds and jaggery that is believed to help in proper flow), Tambula (a combination of coconut, betel leaves, and a few other items offered to the deity in puja or given to guests) and gifts. A similar ceremony is observed in Kerala and Andhra Pradesh, as well.

The celebration is carried out with much fanfare for three full days in Tamil Nadu, where it is called 'Manjal Neerattu Vizha' (turmeric bathing ceremony). The highlight of this festival is that the girl undergoes ritual seclusion, ritual bathing, and many other local customs, including the turmeric bathing ceremony. Friends and family are invited and the girl is gifted silk sarees, and she wears a Saree (or a half-saree) for the first time. The elaborate ceremony happens with much pomp, and in many ways, is a mini-marriage.[3]

In North India, the celebration happens quietly. Young girls are taught about menstruation practices and are asked to maintain seclusion. In Assam, the celebration is called 'Xoru Biya', or 'small marriage'.

Historian NN Bhattacharyya notes that menarche rituals have been in vogue among various tribes and castes of Bengal, Madhya Pradesh, Odisha, Tamil Nadu, Karnataka, Andhra, Kerala and other parts of India.[4] Summarising how different communities practice Menarche rituals, he writes:

> The Rarhi Brahmins of Bengal compel a girl at puberty to live alone, and do not allow her to see the face of any male. For three days she remains shut up in a dark room, and [she] has to undergo certain penances. She must not eat fish, flesh, egg or sweetmeat; she must live on rice and ghee. Among the Deshast Brahmins, the first menstruation of a girl is celebrated. The secluded girl sits on a little throne and is attended constantly by a Maratha maid-servant. The neighbours and relatives pay visits, bring presents for her and wash her in oil. The Aradhya Brahmins of Mysore observe the first menstruation with a

ceremonial bath. The Dikshitar Brahmins of South India also perform the first menstrual celebration with pomp and splendour, the rites being essentially similar to those of the Nayars. The Malayalam-speaking Ksatriyas of the same region also seclude their girls at the first menstruation.

The Kadirs who chiefly inhabit the Nelliampathi and Kadasseri mountains in Cochin and the Annamalai hills in the Coimbatore district strictly observe the first menstruation of the girls. During the menstruation, seclusion in a hut is compulsory for them. Among the Pulayans or Cherumans, a girl's first menstruation is celebrated with a certain amount of pomp and splendour. The girl has to remain secluded in a hut for seven days. The bleeding girl with a company of seven friends has to [take a] dip in a river and then paint her face in yellow. In the period of her seclusion no one else may enter the hut, not even her mother. Women stand a little way off and lay down food for her. At the end of the time she is brought home clad in a new or clean cloth, and friends are honoured with betel-nut, toddy and arack. Among the Tiyans of Madura, a girl is thought to be polluted for four days from the beginning of her first menstruation. She has to reside in the northern side of the house and sleep on a grass mat. Another girl keeps her company and sleeps with her, and the girl concerned must not touch any person, tree or plant and see the sky. Her diet must be strictly vegetarian, without salt and tamarind. She has also to keep a knife with her. More or less similar puberty rites are found among the Kappilions of Madura and Tinnevelly as well as among the Parivarams of Madura. The menstrual rites of the Parayans or Malas are more or less similar to the Pulayans described above. The girl has to remain in seclusion for a considerable period of time, and this is to be followed by a ceremonial bath. At the final ceremony, the girl in question takes her seat in an open place, very often in the middle of her parent's courtyard. Flowers and betel-leaves are kept in front of her, and she has to accept the gifts offered by the festival guests.

The puberty rites of the Nayars are called Thirandukuli. The girl concerned has to remain secluded in a room. In the room, there must be a lamp, a brass pot, a bundle of coconut blossoms and other things. The girl holds a handled mirror made of a round brass plate. The event is properly announced among the relatives. The neighbouring women visit the girl and dress her [up]in new garments. On the third day, the relatives and friends are invited. The Manans and Velans arrive on the fourth day. The menstruating girl along with her other girl-friends undergoes a ceremonial bath. The whole party then returns in procession. The ceremony is followed by a great feast. The Velans sing before the assembly. Sometimes, the girl is led to a neighbouring house. On her return, drums are beaten, and shouts of joy are given. Sometimes the feast is postponed to a more suitable day before the completion of which the girl is not allowed to enter the kitchen or go to the temple for worship.

Puberty rites of the girls are also celebrated among the Haddis, Jalaris, Jogis, Kapus, Karna Sales, Kurubas, Muka Doras, Mutrachas, Maravans, Malas, Toreyas and Tsakalas of South India. Menstrual rites at puberty are also performed by the Bili Maggas, Budubudukis, Darizis, Dasaris, Dombs, Gangadikara Okkalus, Ganigas, Gollas, Halepaiks, Halikar Okkaligas, Hasalars, Helavas, Holeyas, Idigas, Jains, Jangalas, Jettis, Kacha-Gauligas. Kare-Okkalus, Killekyatas, Komatis, Korachas, Kumbaras, Kunchitigas, Ladars, Medigas, Mcdas, Mondarus, Nagarthas, Nattuvans, Nayindas, Patvegaras, Reddis, Sadarus, Salahuva-Vakkalus, Padmasales, Saniyasis, Satanis, Tigalas, Togatas, Upparas and Woddas of the same region. Similar menstrual rites are also current among the Bavuris of Ganjam, the Malapantaram, Malapulayam and Malankudi peasants of Kerala as well as among many other castes and tribes of Southern India.

The first menstruation is regarded as an occasion of ceremonial importance among some tribes and castes of Central India....[5]

Thus, across India, one observes various localised customs and ceremonies that celebrate the onset of menstruation. What is common in all these ceremonies is the fact that the ceremonies are aimed at:

1. Imparting a positive notion about menstruation to young women. They are treated as special and given gifts. The girl is perceived to be a manifestation of the Supreme Goddess and is worshipped with Aarti. She is welcomed with open hands into womanhood, and the ritual allows her to accept the changes that come along with puberty positively. She is made to feel confident and happy with her feminine identity.
2. Imparting knowledge that equips the young girl to adjust well to her on-coming physical and emotional changes during puberty; imparting knowledge regarding various menstruation practices that the girl must follow, including practices related to Ashaucha, austerity and diet, and the reasons and benefits of those practices.

In a private communication to this author, Prof Nagaraja Gundappa observed thus: There is one practice among Hindus that sheds more light on the positive attitude of the Rishis towards Menstruation, and it may be fast disappearing, but traces of that practice can still be found. This is about the celebration that parents carry out when a girl enters the menstrual cycle for the first time. She is then called 'Pushpavathi', and is decorated beautifully in a 'Moggina Jede' – a flower-bedecked plait. There will be a small celebration in the family and certain rituals are followed. In Karnataka, there are also some specifications to the decoration in this ceremony including the way the plait should be woven. The girl is called Pushpavathi as Pushpa (flower) is the first stage of bearing fruit, and it is this transition into the menstrual cycles that leads to conception and bearing children subsequently. In a tree, the fruit sprouts as a flower first and then transforms and ripens into a fruit. The future motherhood of a woman is thus a cause for celebration and also a way of educating her, assuring her and making her feel comfortable about that process. Secondly, the rituals are also aimed to awaken certain spiritual centres or petals of the shatchakras (from Muladhara to Sahasrara). To signify this spiritual awakening, the plait is modelled around the places of inner awakening.The plait is called Triveni in Kannada, meaning confluence of three. Inside the spinal cord, three nadis or paths of flow of Prana Shakthi are supposed to run through in an intertwined manner. These are Ida, Pingala and Sushumna. Ida and Pingala run around the Sushumna and Sushumna stays inside. The Triveni plait is woven in such a way that it resembles the Trinadis. And in the case of a 'Moggina Jede', the flowers are supposed to be decked in such a way that the bedecking of the flowers happen at the places coinciding with the Shatchakras (Muladhara to Ajna) and the Sahasrara with the number of petals in each flower-deck corresponding to the petals in the spiritual chakra located in the Trinadis.[6]

Bhattacharyya notes interesting parallels between Menarche rituals and Upanayana. He writes that Upanayana is nothing but puberty rites for boys[7] and in places like Bengal, a boy must remain secluded for three days during Upanayana, very much like Ritu Samskara.[8] Similarly, they should not see the sun or touch the earth, practices which are also observed by menarche girls in some Hindu communities.[9] Then, there are the practices of hair-shaving and ear-piercing, which are observed by both boys and girls during Upanayana and menarche rituals, respectively.[10] These parallels show that Ritu Samskara served as the girl counterpart of boy's undergoing Upanayana. It is no surprise then that many Hindu texts note that women, especially in Kaliyuga, have no Upanayana for them. But Upanayana serves two purposes in men: First, it imparts competency to men to perform Vedic rituals. Second, it facilitates them to observe daily practices like Sandhyavandana (worship of Sun), which purifies the practitioners from Ashaucha and frees them from unintentionally committed Adharma. As noted in previous chapters, menstruation itself acts as an austerity and a purificatory process, which frees women from Ashaucha and Adharma. Thus, the latter purpose of Upanayana is fulfilled in women by menstruation, and hence, the prevalence of the view that women do not need Upanayana. But the other purpose, i.e. imparting competency to perform Vaidika rituals is not accomplished in menstruation or menarche rituals. This, is instead, accomplished in women through Marriage or Vivaha Samskara. It is, for this reason, that texts such as Mnu Smriti (2.67) note that marriage or Vivaha is itself a full-fledged Samskara, wherein the husband takes up the role of a Guru. In other words, menstruation and marriage together accomplish the purposes in girls which Upanayana serves in the case of boys. Menarche rituals, therefore, celebrate the onset of this function of purification in women.

It is a different issue, however, that on the ground, many of these practices today are on the verge of disappearance, with some having picked up highly negative connotations, largely due to the fact that they have been reduced to blind mechanical restrictions that ignorant and ill-informed parents are imparting to their young children by packaging them as 'forbidden practices/superstitions'. This may also be the result of 'modernisation' and 'convent education' that takes on the Christian ideas of taboo[11] subjects and impurity. But if we were to consider the essence of the traditions and the knowledge preserved in them on their own merit, we will see their positive side.

Tantric Tradition and Sacred Menstruation

This association of menstruation with sacredness is further reinforced in Tantric practices such as Yoni Puja (worship of the female Yoni), wherein a ritual worship is carried out not only of a woman, but also of her Yoni or Vagina, which is perceived to be a symbol of the Cosmic Yoni from which the entire universe has emerged. Menstrual blood is, in fact, considered pure and sacred, and plays a very important role in these Tantric rituals.

The Yoni Tantra, for example, notes that the Yoni puja must be carried out only in the Yoni which has started menstruating. It says: What point is there of many words? The yoni which has bled is suitable for worship. Do not worship a yoni which has never bled. Worshipping a yoni which has never bled causes loss of siddhi on every occasion.[12]

Describing the menstrual blood as a pure and eternal substance, *Kaulajnananirnaya* of Matsyendranath (Patala 8), says: 'In Kaula Agama, the five pure and eternal substances are ash, wife's nectar, semen, menstrual blood and ghee mixed together. In occasional rites and in [the] acts of Kama Siddhi, the great discharge is without doubt and most certainly what one should do in Kaula Agama… One should always consume the physical blood and semen. Dearest One, this is the obligation of the Yoginis and the Siddhas.'[13] The same text (Patala 8) further states about the spiritual and medicinal power of menstrual blood, thus: 'A Brahmin goes to heaven by endless washing of the feet and mouth, whereas a person repeatedly making aforehead mark of Kunda, Gola or Udbhava menses destroys various ailments such as leprosy and smallpox and is free from all disease in the same way that a serpent sloughs its skin.'[14] It further notes in Patala 18 that: Blood is the female (Vama) elixir. Mixed with wine and semen, it is the Absolute.[15]

Another text, *Matrikabheda Tantra* (Patala 8) describes different kinds of menses thus: Sri Shankara said: The first menses appearing in a woman who has lost her virginity is Svayambhu blood. In a maiden born of a married woman and begotten by another man, that which arises is Kunda menses, the substance causing the granting of any desire. Deveshi, a maiden begotten by a widow gives rise to Gola menses, which subdues gods. The menses arising in the first period after a virgin becomes a married woman is the all bewildering Svapushpa.[16]

In his introduction to *Kaulavalinirnayah* of Jnanananda Paramahamsa, John Woodroffe, while summarising the contents of chapter 17 of the text writes: The text goes on to say that there are people who regard semen and menstrual fluid with disgust (Vicharayet), but they forget that the body by which they hope to attain Liberation is composed of these two forms of matter; that the marrow, bone and tendons have come from the father, and the skin, flesh and blood from the mother. It further says that there is no reason for man's disgust for excreta or urine, for these are nothing but food or drink which has [sic] undergone some change and contains living creatures and the Brahman substance is not absent therefrom. The purity that man ought to cultivate is that of the mind. All things are pure. It is one's mentality (Vasana) which is evil.[17]

Thus, we have enough evidences in the Tantric textual tradition which shows how menstruation is perceived as pure and sacred, and a central element in certain kind of rituals, especially those which involve the worship of the genitals, and of sexual intercourse.

Yoni Tantra, for example, gives this procedure for how Yoni should be worshipped, in the form of a dialogue between Goddess Parvati and her Lord, Mahadeva, and as noted before, only a Yoni which has bled is worshipped. When Parvati asks her husband in what way should a practitioner worship Yoni, which is the essence of the cosmos, Mahadeva replies thus: A sadhaka wishing to worship a yoni, which is the form of the cosmos, should cause an erection, and insert it into that thing which is Shakti Herself. The vagina is Mahamaya and the penis is Sadashiva. Worshipping them, one becomes liberated while still alive, there is no doubt of it. One should offer bali, flowers and so forth. If incapable of this, worship with wine, O Durga. One should do pranayama and my six-limbed puja in the yoni region. After reciting the mantra [a] hundred times at the base of the yoni, one should rub the linga and the yoni together.[18]

Similarly, the Bauls of Bengal – a syncretic group of mystic singers and dancers, whose religious beliefs are influenced by Vaishnava, Sakta, Tantric Buddhism, Samkhya and Sufi belief systems – practice Deha Sadhana (spiritual practice using the body), a form of sexual yoga, wherein sexual energy is transformed into Prema (divine love) and Spiritual ecstasy. The Bauls believe that men and women are abodes of two different aspects of the Divine. The women's Nir, i.e. sexual fluid (literally water) contains one aspect of the divine, which is believed to descend down in the form of a fish during the monthly periods. Similarly, the men's Kshir, i.e. semen (literally milk) is said to contain the other aspect of the divine. The Bauls believe that through the ritual practice of sexual Yoga during menstruation, the 'fish' (the feminine aspect of the divine) that 'swims' in the menstrual fluid could be united with the Kshir, and a state of Yogic bliss or Ananda can be attained. In other words, the Bauls perform sexual intercourse during menstruation as a means to attain divine bliss and spiritual emancipation. It is important to note that this sexual intercourse indulged as part of Deha Sadhana is purely a devotional act and should not be confused with sexual intercourse indulged in for the sake of sensual pleasure or conception. The importance of menstruation during the Deha Sadhana can also be understood by the fact that the time of monthly periods is called 'Mahayoga' (Great

Yoga) and the first and the third day of menstruation are designated as 'Amavasya' (New Moon) and 'Poornima' (Full Moon) respectively.[19]

Even Yoga-upanishad texts like *Yoga-Shikha Upanishad*, which is among the 108 authentic Upanishads listed in the *Muktika Upanishad*, describes sexual sadhana during menstruation as 'Raja-Yoga'. It says: There abides in the great spot in the middle of the Yonis of creatures: Rajas (menstrual fluid) resembling the Japa and Bandhuka flowers in colour, well-protected and (representing) the Devi (feminine) principle. By the conjunction of the Rajas with the Retas(of the male organ), (i.e., of Shakti with Shiva), there is what is known as Raja-yoga. From Raja-yoga (the Yogin) shines out after attaining the psychic powers of attenuation and the like.[20]

Devipuram is a temple in Andhra Pradesh, which is an important center of Devi worship in the Tantric tradition of Srividya. The temple itself has been built in the form of Sri Chakra – the abode of the Supreme Goddess Lalita Tripurasundari, and it contains a Kamakhya Peetham – a naturally formed Yoni. Speaking to Sinu Joseph of 'Mythri Speaks', Sri Amritananda Natha Saraswati, the founder of Devipuram and a practitioner of Srividya, said that most priests in his temple were women and that they were all free to stay at the temple during their monthly periods. He further said: 'What is pure, we don't touch. And what we don't touch, we call it a Taboo. She (a menstruating woman) was so pure, that she was worshipped as a Goddess. The reason for not having a woman go into a temple is precisely this. She is a living Goddess at that time. The energy of the God or Goddess which is there in the Murti will move over to her, and that (the Murti) becomes lifeless, while this (the menstruating woman) is life. So that's why they were prevented from entering the temple.'[21] Thus, the Guruji of Devipuram, clearly associates purity with menstruation and considers menstruating women as living Goddesses, while also highlighting the fact that the practice of menstruating women not being allowed into temples was rooted in the fact that there will be an imbalance in the energy of the temple.

Therefore, it is clear that in the Tantrika tradition, menstruation is a sacred celebration, which is ritually pure, potent with many positive attributes, and is an inseparable aspect of many Tantrika practices. But it is to be noted that most Tantrika practices and the associated worldview, are highly tailor made and their applicability are limited to a particular place, context, rituals, and to competent practitioners of these rituals; not to general society. Yet, despite this limited application, what the texts like *Yoni tantra*, practices like Deha Sadhana of the Bauls, or the views of the Devipuram Guruji, establish is the fact that Hinduism does not put forward a blanket worldview on any issue. Instead, Hindu tradition and practices are tailor-made based on different situations, goals, competencies, and needs of the people. As a result, menstruation, which is otherwise rightly associated with ritual Ashaucha (because of which sexual intercourse and sacred activities like worship are restricted), becomes associated with ritual Shaucha (purity), sexual intercourse and worship in the case of Yoni puja, Deha Sadhana and similar other Tantric practices.

Deities & Festivals Celebrating Menstruation

The role played by menstruation in spiritual and religious practice, especially of a Tantrika variety, clearly depicts its association with worship and sacredness. Festivals associated with the menstruation of the Hindu Goddesses show how it is celebrated. It is only in these festivals that the full implication of the notion of menstruation as a sacred celebration will become evident.

A number of deities are associated directly or indirectly with menstruation in the Hindu tradition: Parvati, Lajja Gowri, Brahmacharini Durga, Bhuvaneshwari, Kamakhya, Harchandi, and Bhoomi Devi to name a few. These deities, though independent in name and form, are considered to be different aspects or manifestations of the primordial Shakti (power) or Adya (the First), who is considered to be the mother or the originator of the entire universe. Thus, menstruation is associated with the sacred feminine, and is celebrated through the worship of these deities and the festivities associated with such worship.

Lajja Gowri, for example, is specifically associated with sexuality, fertility and childbirth. She is iconographically depicted in a sitting position with the legs open and an exposed vulva. Thus, through fertility and childbirth, she is also indirectly linked to menstruation. A more direct connection can be found in Shakti as Durga. Goddess Durga manifests herself in nine forms and these nine forms are offered special worship during the famous Hindu festival of Navaratri or the festival of nine-nights. The nine forms of Durga are: Shailaputri, Brahmacharini, Chandraghanta, Kushmanda, Skandamata, Katyayini, Kaalratri, Mahagauri and Siddhidhatri. Among the nine, the first five forms are specially associated with different phases in a woman's life. Shailaputri corresponds to childhood, Brahmacharini corresponds to puberty, Chandragantha indicates marriage, Kushmanda and Skandamata correspond to pregnancy and childbirth, respectively. Thus, Brahmacharini Durga presides over puberty and menarche and this form of the deity is worshipped during the second night of Navaratri.

A more intimate correlation with menstruation is found in Goddess Bhuvaneshwari, who is considered as the presiding deity of menstruation in the Dharmashastra tradition. *Dharmasindhu*,[22] a medieval Dharmashastric text written by Kashinatha Upadhyaya, for example, observes that if the menarche commences in certain months, during certain lunar days, or under certain stars, then it is inauspicious. That is, the onset of menstruation during such durations is considered as an indication of some future obstacles, troubles, or disabilities that the girl may face in the future. Months which are considered inauspicious for having menarche includes the Hindu months of Chaitra, Jyeshta, Aashada, Bhadrapada, Kaarthika, and Pushya. Similarly, Dharmasindhu considers Pratipada, Chaturthi, Amavasya, and six other lunar days as inauspicious. Sunday, Tuesday, and Saturday are considered inauspicious. Menarche under ten stars is considered inauspicious. To offset these effects, and to ensure that the indicated future trouble is removed, Dharmasindhu suggests that a particular ritual called 'Bhuvaneshwari Shanti' be performed after marriage but before Garbhadhana Samskara (the rite for conceiving a child). The deity of this ritual is Goddess Bhuvaneshwari, who is worshipped, and whose blessings are sought.

There is also the famous Goddess Kamakhya and her Ambubachi festival celebrated in Assam. Goddess Kamakhya is believed to undergo menstruation for three days every year and the temple is closed for the period to give her rest. The festival is celebrated during the monsoon, in the Assamese month of Ahaar, which falls in June. For three days, the Goddess takes rest. People in the region do not perform any farming activity so as to be able to give Mother Kamakhya, who is also Mother Earth, rest. Daily worship and religious performances are also halted. During this period, Goddess Kamakhya, who exists as a naturally formed Yoni in stone, is covered with a red cloth. On the fourth day, after the Yoni is bathed and ritually worshipped, the temple doors are opened and devotees are given special Prasada – a piece of the red cloth, which was used to cover the Yoni, and which has become moist due to the Mother's bleeding (in the form of natural springs). The special Prasada is considered highly auspicious and purifying in nature and hence thousands of devotees from faraway places come every year to pray to the Mother and partake of her Special Prasada.

The four-day festival is accompanied by huge celebrations in the form of a four-day Mela (fair) called Ameti, wherein Tantric Sadhus and Babas from across India visit, and where rural crafts are exhibited. The Ambubachi festival serves as a practical illustration of how Hinduism harmoniously integrates different nuances associated with various aspects of menstruation – Ashaucha, austerity, rest, and celebration – into one integral festival that is beneficial to everyone.

Another example that illustrates the notion of menstruation as a celebration is the festival of Raja in Odisha, which is also celebrated during June.The Menstruating Goddess (Bhu-devi/ Earth Goddess) who is worshipped here is variously known as Harchandi, Prithibt, Thakurant, Basudha, Draupadi. The festival is celebrated by both men and women. But women consider themselves Amsha (parts) of the Goddess.Therefore, the entire celebration happens around women.

Kartikeya C Patel, in his paper, 'Women, Earth, and the Goddess: A Shākta-Hindu Interpretation of Embodied Religion', quotes an Odiya woman, who participated in a field study on this festival in Odisha conducted by Frederique Apffel-Marglin and Purna Chandra Misra, as saying: Harchandi is at her menses; three days are gone and tomorrow is Thakurant Gadua. After taking bath as the girls will do, so also she will do. Red colour will be thrown on her so it will appear as if she is bleeding. Pouring this red on her they will treat her as if she were menstruating… yes, that cloth on which the red is thrown will be put in a bucket of water so the water will be red. The priest will show it to the pilgrims and say 'this is the blood of Thakurani'. People out of joy and happiness will take that water.[23]

The women in the Federique Apffel-Margin study strongly believed that the 'Stridharma' of the women and the Goddess must be respected, and that they should be allowed to rest during menstruation, so that the process of menstruation, which affects women at multiple levels, and which in the case of the Goddess, affects the cyclical continuity of life in nature and maintains balance, remains undisturbed and unaffected. They also believed that any disturbance to this process will have unpleasant effects.

Regarding how the festival of Raja connects Dharma, Happiness, and menstruation, Patel writes:

Hence, religious (dharmic) happiness is directly linked to the happiness and worship of the feminine. Giving happiness to women, the earth, and the Goddess partly depends on not disturbing them during their menstruation. During the menstruation festival, the earth must not be dug or plowed [sic] and one must not walk on the earth barefoot as that would hurt or disturb her. In the same vein, women should be given rest during their menstruation and should not be disturbed....But giving rest to mother earth or to women during the menstruation period is only one way to make them happy. Another way to make them happy, and thereby make religious (dharmic) life happy, consists in worshipping the female body with offerings. The men at Harchandi offer sacrificial animals to the Goddess to make her happy....Similarly, women are kept happy by being given clothes, ornaments and leisure time.[24]

Thus, the festival of Raja, beautifully weaves various elements of rest, merriment, worship and celebration around Menstruation. Women are treated as manifestations of the Goddess, and menstruation is recognised as a positive 'natural' process that is very vital for women as well as for nature. The seclusion (away from men), resting, and other menstrual practices are meant to ease the menstrual process. Moreover, since the menstrual cycle is associated with fertility and bringing new life into this world, the activity is treated as a sacred celebration and men are obliged to give happiness to the womenfolk.

Chengannur Mahadeva Kshetram[25] in the Southern State of Kerala is yet another place where the Goddess menstruates and her menstruation is celebrated. Every few months, the Murti of Goddess Parvati (Bhagavati), which is present at the temple is believed to menstruate, and during that period, for three days, her Murti is shifted to a separate room and is given rest. Whether the Goddess is menstruating or not is determined by the wife of the Supreme priest of Sabarimala, who regularly inspects the Udayada (the inner skirt) of the Goddess for any blood stains. If any stains of menstrual blood are found, then the temple announces the celebration of the festival – 'Thripputharattu'. For the first three days, the Murti of the Goddess is secluded from the Murti of her husband, Lord Shiva, and is allowed to rest. She undergoes all menstrual practices that women undergo, and temple women sleep outside her room during the night to give her company. On the fourth day, the Goddess is taken on a female elephant to the Pamba River for a ritual bath. She is then dressed in grand clothes and jewelry, and several ceremonies and elaborate rituals are performed. Thousands of people from across Kerala visit the temple to participate in this festival.

The Keddasa festival[26] celebrated in the Dakshina Kannada district of Karnataka is another festival which demonstrates the association of menstruation with notions of rest and sacred celebration. It is celebrated for three days by the Tulu speaking population of the district. The ancient festival is celebrated in honour of the annual initiation of the fertility season (agriculture) of Mother Earth. Tulu people believe that Mother Earth undergoes menstruation like women for three days and thereafter becomes ready to give birth to crops and fruits. The festival is celebrated on the last three days of the Tulu month known as 'Puyintel', which roughly falls in January or February, each year. Farmers give complete rest to the mother earth on all three days. Hence, activities such as digging, trenching and cutting trees are stopped during that period. They worship the land and distribute Navadhanya (a mixture of nine grains) among kith and kin. On the fourth day, they begin sowing activities by first sprinkling turmeric and oil on the ground.

Although these celebrations of menstruation festivals on a grand scale are limited to a few pockets in the country, the notion of menstruation as a celebration itself is widespread across India. Quoting Bhattacharyya, Janet Chawla in her paper, 'The Mythic Origins of the Menstrual Taboo in the Rig Veda' writes: 'According to historian NN Bhattacharyya, different areas of India have had notions of the menstruating goddess. In Punjab, it was believed that Mother Earth ('Dharti Ma') 'slept' for a week each month. In some parts of the Deccan after the 'navaratra', goddess temples are closed from the tenth to the full moon day while she rests and refreshes herself. In [the]Malabar region, Mother Earth was believed to rest during the hot weather until she got the first shower of rain.'[27] Chawla further writes: Bhattarcharyya notes that the auspiciousness of menstruation, representing potential fertility, is symbolised by blood or the colour of blood and is regarded as sacred.... Deities and sacred objects are daubed with red colouring as a part of ritual worship. Within Indian culture, red signifies auspiciousness and potential growth – these ancient religious ideas and symbols are definitely linked to the blood of menstruation.[28]

Therefore, it is quite clear that the Hindu tradition recognises menstruation as a sacred and positive process which must be respected, worshipped, and celebrated. Though women become associated with temporary Ashaucha, this does not degrade them or make them inferior. Instead, the whole process is considered as highly sacred and purifying in nature, which sets women free from Karmic bondage. Women are thus encouraged to perceive menstruation as a privilege available exclusively for them; something that, in fact, facilitates their overall well-being.

Yogic & Ayurvedic perspectives on Menstruation

In the previous sections we examined in detail some of the major notions such as impurity, austerity, rest and sacredness associated with menstruation in the Hindu tradition. In this section let us shift our focus to Yoga and Ayurveda, two independent but interlinked Hindu knowledge systems, and see how they understand menstruation. While Ayurveda is a holistic medical and lifestyle system, Yoga is a comprehensive philosophy and worldview. They are deeply linked since both intimately deal with the individual at the physiological, vital, and psychological levels.

Menstruation & Yoga

Yoga forms an important branch of the Hindu worldview. It is a very vast, diverse, and largely practical system, which aims to free an individual from the bondage of worldly life. *Yogasutra* of Patanjali (1.2-3) defines Yoga as 'Yogash chitta vritti nirodhah. Tada drashtuh svarupe avasthanam',[1] i.e. Yoga is the cessation of all thought modifications of the mind, with the seer dwelling in its true nature. Thus, the ultimate goal of Yoga is 'Self-Abidance'.[2] It aims to remove the thought-patterns of the mind, so that a practitioner can realise his innermost Atman and become established in it. And through this process, it also ends up improving the physical, mental and spiritual health of the individual and the society.[3]

Towards this end, the Yoga tradition deeply explores the various dimensions of individuality, including physiology, functions of the Prana – the life force and the mind. It aims to harmonise the functions of the body, Prana, and the mind with each other and facilitate dawning of greater self-awareness. Therefore, the Yogic analysis of human physiology and the functioning of the Prana within the human body can serve as a useful guide to understand menstruation as a physiological process and its relationship to the functioning of life-force.

In the section on Ashaucha we have dealt with Hinduism which sees an Individual as having five layers of individuality. Yogic literature elaborates on how one should cultivate one's body, mind and the vital force (Prana), so that they facilitate the attainment of the highest state of Samadhi. Hatha Yoga, Patanjali Yoga and Kundalini Yoga aim to harmonise the body, Prana, and the mind. Prana is the life-force that supports the body and connects it to the subtle mind. It is the life-force, which enlivens the body and accomplishes all activity. It is for this reason that a person is considered 'dead' when the life-force leaves the body.

Yogic scriptures perceive this Prana, which makes up the vital body, as having five different functions within the gross human body aimed at accomplishing five different tasks that are necessary to keep a person alive. These tasks are: inhalation, elimination, digestion, deglutition and sound production, and circulation. These are governed by Prana, Apana, Samana, Udana, and Vyana, respectively.

Mahabharata Shanti Parva (Section 184) states: Through the breath called Prana, a living creature is enabled to move. Through that called Vyana, they put forth strength for action. That called Apana moves downwards. That called Samana resides within the heart. Through that called Udana one eructates and is enabled to speak in consequence of its piercing through (the lungs, the throat, and the mouth). These are the five kinds of wind that cause an embodied creature to live and move.[4]

These five are together called Pancha Prana or Pancha Vayu (five airs), and according to *Shiva Samhita* (3.7), a Hatha Yogic text, the seats of the first four Vayus are respectively located at the heart, anus, navel, and throat, and Vyana – the fifth, is all pervading in the body. Shiva Samhita (3.8) further enunciates five more minor aspects of the vital force: Naga, Kurma, Devadatta, Krikala and Dhananjaya, which perform the functions of belching, opening the eyes, hunger and thirst, yawning and hiccupping, respectively. Thus, these ten Pranas play a vital role in the growth and sustenance of the physical body and any imbalance in them will directly result in an imbalance in the physiology of the body.

Menstruation, being a downward process of elimination, is predominated by the Apana Vayu. And hence, during the monthly periods, the Apana Vayu is in an exalted state. On the other hand, any religious and spiritual activity, be it Yoga, meditation, Puja, fire ritual, or visiting temples, causes some degree of upward movement of Apana Vayu.

Yoga, for example, aims to move Apana upwards, so that it merges with Prana and takes an individual to a state of heightened self-awareness. Similarly, Puja and fire ritual, aims to awaken the Kundalini, by first making the Apana move upwards. Temples are basically centers of cosmic energies, which will have a similar effect on individuals as Yoga or Puja. The energy and the environment in a properly consecrated temple will facilitate meditation and stillness of the mind by moving the Apana Vayu upwards. But Apana Vayu is a downward moving force by its very nature. Therefore, any attempt to make it move upwards during menstruation will interfere with the menstruation process and hence create an imbalance.

Rajarshi Nandy, a spiritualist writes in his article 'Sabarimala Discreet, Not Discriminatory' thus:

> In Yogic parlance, the body is ruled by five main vayus or forms of vital air: prana, apana, vyana, samana and udana. Of these, apana vayu rules all downward bodily movements, from defecation to menstruation or orgasm. One of the primary aims of a successful yogic process is to force the apana to move upwards inside the body, synchronise it with the prana, and awaken a state of heightened awareness and concentration, referred to as the kundalini awakening.
>
> It is not that every time a person visits a temple such is going to happen; nevertheless, every time a concentrated attention is diverted into a process or an object, religious or secular, there is always the chance of such a happening. During menstruation, there is a continuous increase or greater prevalence of the Apana vayu inside the body. Hence, trying to concentrate hard on anything would be equivalent to forcefully trying to change the direction of an already aggravated vital air in the body. This can potentially open the individual to the unpleasant prospect of undergoing various physical or psychological problems if such a course of action is deliberately pursued for a sufficient length of time. All successful worship is finally a matter of applied concentration. Therefore, as a precautionary measure, it is traditionally and, if I may add, wisely regarded that entering a shrine during the 'periods' is a bad idea.[5]

Therefore, Yogic literature perceives menstruation as a physiological process that is deeply connected with the Apana Vayu and any hindrances caused to the functioning of the Apana Vayu will result in unpleasant physiological conditions. The advice regarding non-performance of Yoga and other religious activities, including visiting temples during menstruation has to be understood with reference to the impact of these activities on the Apana Vayu, which facilitates menstruation.

Menstruation and Ayurveda

Ayurveda is a health and medicine system, which has been prevalent across India for thousands of years. This indigenous medicine system is intrinsically connected to Hindu philosophy, religion and culture. Thus, the roots of Ayurveda are in Sanatana Dharma and it is considered one of the Upaveda – supplementary systems of knowledge attached to the four Vedas.

Ayurveda recognises menstruation as a physiological process, and like other physiological processes, it is also governed by the actions of the Doshas.

According to Ayurveda,[6] each individual has a particular temperament and constitution (Prakriti), which is formed during the union of sperm and ovum. The Prakriti of an individual depends upon the working of these Doshas. Ayurveda classifies people into different Prakriti categories based on the Dosha, which is predominant in a person. Doshas are three in number: Vata (related to movement), Pitta (related to digestion), and Kapha (related to cumulation).Their mutual action causes various physiological functions within the human body. Based upon the predominance of the Doshas, people are classified into three categories of Prakriti – Vata, Pitta and Kapha. Ayurveda defines the health/illness of a person based on whether there is a balance or imbalance in the working of the Doshas, and whether or not they are in sync with his Prakriti.

Coming to menstruation, Ayurveda divides the monthly cycle into three phases: Ritu-Kala, Ritu-Vyateeta-Kala, and Rajahsrava-Kala. Each phase is predominated by a different Dosha. Ritu-Kala refers to the proliferative phase during which follicles inside the ovaries develop and mature in preparation for ovulation. This phase is for a duration of twelve to sixteen days and is dominated by Kapha Dosha, which governs regeneration and growth. Ritu-Vyateeta-Kala refers to the Secretory

Phase, wherein various hormones and nutrients are secreted in anticipation of nourishing the conceptus (the embryo) if conception were to take place. This phase will exist for a duration of nine to thirteen days and is dominated by Pitta Dosha, which governs all secretion activities in the body. Rajahsrava-Kala is the actual phase of menstruation, wherein the menstrual blood along with the endometrium is shed from the body. This phase exists for three to five days and is predominated by Vata Dosha (and the Apana vayu), which governs all movement within the body.[7]

The workings of these three Doshas will determine whether a woman will undergo a normal or abnormal menstruation process. Ayurvedic texts define normal menstruation[8] as one which is not associated with pain or burning sensation; the excreted blood is not unctuous, not very scanty or excessive in amount, and its colour resembles the red juice of lac or of rabbit's blood. This normal menstruation occurs when the three Doshas exist in balance.

A Vatika menstrual flow, for example, will be accompanied by pain. This is so because the presence of excess Vata will result in its Sheetha and Khara qualities to constrict the blood vessels, which in turn will result in very less menstrual discharge. The free flow of Vata will also be obstructed, thus causing pain. On the other hand, a Paittika menstrual flow will result in heavy bleeding and the Pitta Dosha will cause swollen breasts, acne etc. Kapha Dosha is by nature dull, heavy and sticky. Hence, a Khaphaja menstrual flow will cause heavier flow with clots in the menstrual blood. It is to be noted that all these external symptoms of pain, scanty flow, excess flow etc. are considered signs of abnormal flow.

Sushruta Samhita (Sharirasthana 2.4) says that disturbed Arthavam (i.e. abnormal menstruation) caused by the disturbed Vayu (i.e. Vata), Pittam, Khapha and blood, either severally or in combination of two or more Doshas, will hamper the ability of a woman to conceive. It classifies abnormal menstrual flow as one where the flow is excessive (Asrigdara) and where it is suppressed (Amenorrhoe) and suggests treatment for both conditions (Sharirasthana 2.19-23). It further states that among the various kinds of abnormal menstruation, those which 'smell like a putrid corpse or fetid pus, or that which is clotted, or is thin, or emits the smell of urine or fecal matter, should be deemed as being beyond remedy; the rest being amenable (Sharirasthana 2.4)'.[9]

Further, each person will have her own Prakriti depending upon the predominance of the Doshas. As a result, each woman is susceptible to develop different abnormal conditions due to the imbalance of the Doshas. Thus, a woman with Vata Prakruti is more likely to develop pain during menstruation. One with Pitta Prakruti is more susceptible to mood variations, and a woman with Kapha Prakriti is likely to have more clots in her menstrual blood.[10]

From the above, it is clear that an imbalance in the Doshas will lead to an imbalance in the menstruation process, which in turn affects the health of a woman, including her capacity to conceive. Add to this the fact that the drastic physiological and psychic changes that a menstruating woman experiences makes her more vulnerable to various diseases during her periods. Further, the imbalance of the Doshas may affect the health of the child conceived during Ritu-Kala. Considering all these factors, Ayurveda has prescribed a mode of life to be adopted by menstruating women – a series of Dos and Don'ts – called '*Rajaswala Paricharya*', which aims to protect their health and prevent health defects in the child, in case conception happens after menstruation.

Charaka Samhita (Sharirasthana 8.4) says: After the onset of menstruation, for 3 days and nights, the woman should

Table-1: Dos and Don'ts prescribed in Ayurvedic Rajaswala Paricharya, along with abnormalities in child if prohibitions are not implemented by menstruating women over long period.

SI NO	Dos during menstruation	Don'ts during menstruation	Abnormalities in Child if Don'ts are performed
1.	To observe celibacy during the first three days of menstruation	Sleeping during day time	Over Sleepy
		Use of Collyrium	Blind
		Weeping, Crying	Visual Disturbances
2.	Sleep on Kusha Mattress	Bathing and Annointment	Miserable
		Massage	Skin disorders
3.	Should eat meal made of ghee, Shali rice, and milk; or meal made of barley	Nail Pairing	Deformity in nails
		Running	Reckless, indecisive
4.	To eat food directly taking over palm, or in clay utensils, leaves	Laughing	Discoloration of teeth, lips and tongue
		Indulging in long conversations	Over talkative
5	To take food in less quantity	Listening to various topics	Deaf
		Combing	Bald
6	Concentrate on auspicious things	Nasal instillation of medicine	Menstrual abnormalities in female child
		Exposure to wind, Fatigue work	Mental illness

observe celibacy, should sleep on the ground, take food with hands from an unbroken utensil and should not cleanse her body in any way.[11]

Similarly, Sushruta Samhita (Sharirasthana 2/25) says: A woman in her menses should lie down on a mattress made of Kusha blades (during the first three days), should take her food from her own blended palms or from earthen saucers, or from trays made of leaves. She should live on a course of Habishya diet and forswear during the time, even the sight of her husband. After this period, on the fourth day she should take a ceremonial ablution, put on a new (untorn) garment and ornaments and then visit her husband after having uttered the words of necessary benediction.[12]

The Ayurvedic texts stress that intercourse during menses should be avoided, because if a child is conceived (it's possible,[13] though less likely) from such an intercourse, such a child may suffer intra-uterine death or death within a few days of birth, or if alive, suffer from some deformity.[14] Ayurveda further elaborates on the Dos and Dont's that must be followed during menstruation and how the long-term practice of prohibited elements of Paricharya may have harmful effects on the child conceived during Ritu-Kala. Table-1 summarises the guidelines.[15]

Some of these restrictions may seem odd and we may wonder whether there is a scientific basis for them. We shall, at some point, also look at scientific studies, which examine the practical usage of Rajaswala Paricharya and see how it alleviates menstruation-related problems. But first we must understand the physiological process of menstruation in the context of Paricharya.[16]

A comparison of Rajaswala Paricharya with the Dos and Dont's prescribed during different medical conditions reveals that menstruation is first and foremost a naturally occurring purification (Shodhan) process, which helps purify the body and restore health by removing impurities. Thus, the mode of life prescribed for menstruating women is more or less the same as those prescribed for people who have undergone the Shodhan procedure as mentioned in the Ashta-Mahadoshkar-Bhava. These are eight activities, which are to be avoided during any Shodhan procedure performed in Ayurveda. They include: Talking loudly, travelling in vehicles, excessive walking, sitting in one place for a long time, having food in ajeerna awastha, having non-prescribed food, sleeping during the day and sexual intercourse. These prohibitions will help prevent the vitiation of the Vata and Kapha Doshas, restore the strength of the body, and nourish the Agni (digestive capacity) of the person. These eight prohibited activities during the Shodhan process are similar to the activities that are prohibited for menstruating women (as given in Table-1). Hence, they play a similar function in the case of menstruation as well. Therefore, it can be concluded that Paricharya prescribed for menstruating women will assist in the natural Shodhan process and will restore health to the menstruating women by preventing any imbalance in the Doshas and by nourishing the Agni.

Secondly, menstruation is a state of Agnimandya – a state of weakened internal fire – as a result of which menstruating women experience reduced appetite. This state is common during all Shodhan procedures. To remedy this and to rekindle the digestive fire, certain diets, which are simple and easily digestible, are prescribed. One such diet is a meal made of ghee and Shali rice. Sticking to this diet along with other elements of Rajaswala Paricharya like not sleeping during day time, not doing exercises and activities of physical exertion, not anointing the body etc. will help in rekindling the digestive Agni of the menstruating women and thus prevent unpleasant physiological conditions that may arise due to weakened digestive fire.

Thirdly, a menstruating woman is perceived as a person with a wound. This is because the body sheds the lining of the uterus during menstruation, thus indicating an active wound. As a result, the Paricharya prescribed for menstruating women includes elements that are prescribed during injury (or during surgery), so as to assist in the speedy and uninterrupted healing of the wound. Both menstruating women and injured persons are advised to consume light and easily digestible food, avoid intercourse, avoid sleeping during daytime, and avoid physical exertion.

From the above, it is clear that the purpose of the various Dos and Don'ts of Rajaswala Paricharya is to protect menstruating women (who are susceptible to various diseases) by preventing the vitiation of various Doshas, by re-kindling the internal digestive fire, and by healing the internal injury. If Rajaswala Paricharya is not followed over a long period of time, the imbalance in the Doshas, as well as the conditions like Agnimandya, may become a permanent condition, thus seriously affecting the health of the woman. This, in turn, may also have harmful effects on the children she conceives.

There is a cause and effect relationship between factors like the vitiation of the Doshas and Agnimandya, on the one hand, and the many unpleasant symptoms experienced by women during menstruation, on the other. For example, pain in the abdomen is clearly due to the hindrances to the free flow of Apana Vayu (i.e. Vata), thus causing the uterus to apply more pressure for expelling menstrual blood. This obstruction to the flow of Vata also causes cramps in the calf muscles. Moreover, physical exertion leads to the vitiation of Vata, which in turn leads to weakness. Agnimandya causes increased frequency of motions. The vitiation of Kapha, Vata, and blood causes pimples. Abnormality in Rasa-Dhatu causes irritation, mood swings, and depression during menstruation.[17]

This cause-effect relationship also exists between the vitiation of Doshas in menstruating women and the deformity that one may observe in children conceived by such women. For, example, Rajaswala Paricharya advices menstruating women to not run, laugh loudly, or talk too much, and says that if these Don'ts are not followed, the conceived child will be unsteady, have discolored teeth, or will be over talkative. This is so because running, laughing, and talking too much during menstruation will result in the vitiation of the Vata Dosha, and if women persist with these activities during monthly period after period, this may become a permanent condition, which will in turn affect the health of the conceived child, when it is in the mother's womb. Similarly, if menstruating women sleep during day time, it will cause vitiation of Kapha and Pitta Dosha, which in turn may result in the children developing characteristics like sleepiness and laziness.; if they listen to loud music, it will vitiate Vata Dosha, and if persisted over long periods of time, it may affect the hearing capacity of the child conceived by such women; and if they apply bodily cream, oil etc. which are contra-indicated in Agnimandya, such women may be hurting their internal Agni, which if it persists, may cause skin disorders in children born to such women.[18] But, this does not mean that each and every woman who does not follow Rajaswala Paricharya will end up having children who are either deaf, lazy, or have skin disorder. Instead, the gist is, the children born to such women are more susceptible to developing those unsavory conditions, because of their exposure to the vitiated Doshas, while they were in their mother's womb.

The usefulness of the mode of life prescribed by the Ayurvedic Rajaswala Paricharya in protecting the health of menstruating women and in ensuring that they undergo normal menstruation, without any pain and other unpleasant symptoms, has been scientifically established by at least two studies. The first study titled: 'Rajaswala Paricharya: Effect on Menstrual Cycle and Its Associated Symptoms' was conducted by Dr Pallavi Pai, Dr Sarita Bhutada, and Dr Prasad Pandkar, and was published in IOSR Journal of Dental and Medical Sciences in February 2015.[19]

For the study, a sample of thirty unmarried females between eighteen and twenty four with a regular menstrual cycle was selected. These women were asked to practise Rajaswala Paricharya during the three days of their menstruation over six consecutive cycles. The effect of the practice on the menstrual symptoms experienced by them was noted and appropriate statistical tests were carried out. At the end of six months, the study found that there was not only a drastic reduction in the number of menstrual symptoms experienced by each woman, but there was also a drastic reduction in the number of women who experienced any given symptom.

The evaluation was carried out with respect to thirteen menstrual symptoms: Pain in lower abdomen (28, 3), Lower back ache (24, 2), Pimples (20, 5), Breast tenderness (1, 0), Cramps in calf muscles (13, 1), Loss of appetite (17, 6), Hot flushes (12, 5), Nausea/Vomiting (7, 1), Constipation/Increased bowel movements (8, 2), Increased frequency of micturition (6, 1), Weakness (25, 8), Headache/Migraine (11, 1), Excitability/Irritability/Depression (21, 2). The figures in the bracket denotes the number of people who experienced these symptoms before the study and at the end of the study, respectively.

The above figures clearly show how except for the symptom of breast tenderness, in the case of all other symptoms, there was a drastic reduction in the number of people who experienced those symptoms. The greatest reduction was observed with respect to lower abdomen pain, lower back ache, cramps in calf muscles, depression weakness, and pimples.

Similarly, each subject in the study experienced drastic reductions in the number of symptoms, they were afflicted with. The number of symptoms experienced by a single person before beginning of the study ranged from four to nine. At the end of the study, the maximum number of symptoms experienced by a single subject stood at four. As many as eleven out of the thirty females reported zero symptom at the end of the study. Similarly, nine students reported experiencing one symptom, four students experienced two and three symptoms, and just two students experienced four symptoms.

Thus, a clear relief from menstrual symptoms was experienced by those women in the study within six months of the practice of Rajaswala Paricharya. The fact that the Paricharya was beneficial to these women can also be gauged by the fact that the compliance to its various tenets among these women increased from an average of 76.10 per cent to 86.66 per cent during the study period.

In the second study titled 'Efficiency of Rajaswala Paricharya in Asrigdara (Dysfunctional Uterine Bleeding): A Case Study',[20] a twenty five-year-old female patient who was suffering from heavy menstrual bleeding which lasted five-six days was treated with a regimen of Rajaswala Paricharya for four consecutive cycles. At the end of the treatment, the woman's menstrual bleeding had returned to normal. The case study was conducted by Sonu, Hetal H Dave, and Vipin Kumar, and the criteria used for examination included: Duration of flow, interval of flow, number of sanitary pads used, clots and weakness, abdominal pain and such associated symptoms. The tabulated results were as follows:

Table-2: Results of Rajaswala Paricharya on a 25-year-old female suffering from heavy menstrual bleeding

SI NO	Criteria	Before Treatment	After Treatment
1	**Duration of flow**	8 days	5 days
2	**Interval of flow**	20 days	28-30 days
3	**Pads used**	1st day- 3 pads 2nd day- 5-6pads 3rd and 4th day- 3 pads 5th and 6th day-2 pads 7th and 8th day- 1-2 pads	1st day- 3 pads 2nd day- 2-3 pads 3rd day- 2pads 4th and 5th day- 1 pad
4	**Clots**	Big clots on 1st and 2nd day	Nil
5	**Associated Symptoms**	Weakness, abdominal pain	Nil

These studies show beyond doubt the efficacy and utility of Rajaswala Paricharya and the soundness of the Ayurvedic principles on which the Paricharya is based. What is interesting to note here is the fact that many of these tenets regarding menstruation practices prescribed in Ayurvedic texts, have also been prescribed in various Shruti and Smriti texts, thus establishing how health and medical considerations formed an inseparable aspect of Dharmic practices. It also goes to show how Ayurveda is integral to Sanatana Dharma as an Upaveda, with it highlighting the health aspect, whereas texts like Smritis highlight the Dharmic and social aspect.

Menstruation Restrictions

In the previous sections, we made a thematic examination of the different facets of the Hindu perceptions of menstruation.

We also briefly saw several menstrual practices found in texts like Vedas, Smritis etc. and scientifically explained in the texts of Ayurveda. In this chapter, let us take a more systematic look into these different menstruation restrictions observed by Hindu women.

In his book *The Cochin Tribes and Castes* (Vol 1), LK Anantha Krishna Iyer observes that menstruation practices among the Keralite Kaniyans was true for most communities across India in pre-colonial India. Although under the influence of colonialism, urbanisation and the imposition of western modernity, many of these practices have declined, a significant number is still practised by a large section of Hindu society even today.[1]

Let us now take a deeper look at some of these menstruation restrictions observed by Hindu women.

No sexual intercourse

This is one of the most important counsels given by Hindu scriptures to menstruating women. This advice is found in many texts: Yajurveda Taittiriya Samhita (Verse 2.5.1), Angirasa Smriti (Verse 37), Manu Smriti (4.40), Sushruta Samhita (Sharirasthana 2.31), and *Kashyapa Samhita* (Sharirasthana 5.5), to name a few.

First, Sexual intercourse during menstruation, if it leads to conception (even though the chances are slim), may result in inter-uterine death, or death within a few days of birth, or some form of deformity in the child. This reason is indicated in the Vedas and explicitly stated in the Ayurvedic texts. Second and more important is the fact that sexual intercourse during menstruation causes huge imbalance in the Tri-Doshas. Hence, it is to be avoided. Other reasons indicate that menstruation is a process of austerity and self-purification. Hence, Brahmacharya (celibacy) must be practised, just as it is practised in other austerity practices. Moreover, since menstruating women are in a heightened state of Rajas, sexual activity will not be good for either partner, especially the male.[2] This is because sexual intercourse by its very nature is an intimate process that involves union and the exchange of energies at various levels. Further, since during menstruation any activity involving physical exertion should be avoided to prevent the imbalance of Prakriti Doshas and the resulting adverse effects on health, sexual intercourse should also be avoided.

No running, exercises and household activities

This advice is found in texts such as Angirasa Smriti (Verse 37), Vashishta Dharma Sutras (5.6), and Sushruta Samhita (Sharirasthana 2.24).

The principal reason behind this prescription is the fact that menstruation should be considered as a period of rest. Menstruating women, being in an extremely sensitive physiological condition, should avoidall physically tiring activity. The Ayurvedic texts indicate how excess physical activity may lead to an imbalance in the Doshas, which may have an adverse effect on the health of the woman. Further, if these Doshas persist, due to repeated physical activities during menstruation over a long period of time, it may also negatively impact the children conceived by such women. Taking all this into account, various texts have suggested that menstruating women avoid all household works, running, excessive walking, excessive talking, loud music etc. The texts also advise that cooking should be avoided since food carries energy and the Rajasic condition of menstruating women could be counter-productive.

No bathing, combing, application of collyrium, body anointment and other self-adorning activities

These advices occur in the Yajurveda Taittiriya Samhita (Verse 2.5.1), Vashishta Dharma Sutras (5.6), and in the Ayurvedic text, the Sushruta Samhita (Sharirasthana 2.24).

The principles guiding these prescriptions are two-fold: One, austerity by its very nature demands that all sense-engaging activities like combing, application of collyrium, body anointment and massage, make-up etc. be given up. Two, these activities, including bathing, may result in imbalance of Doshas, and repeated practice during menstruation is bound to have adverse effects on the health of the woman as well as of the children she may conceive.

Segregation

Hindu texts do not explicitly mention segregation for menstruating women. Yet, we find some form of segregation being practiced, including having separate huts for them in some villages. Further, certain tenets of menstruation practices prescribed in the texts - Yajurveda Taittiriya Samhita (Verse 2.5.1), *Brihadaranyaka Upanishad* (6.4.13), Vashishta Dharma Sutras (5.6) and *Charaka Samhita* (Sharirasthana 8.4), require a certain degree of segregation to be implemented.

Apart from the obvious fact that menstruating women often experience pain and mood swings and hence may prefer to be left undisturbed, another aspect to consider is the fact that menstruation involves the management of a lot of blood. Today, with the availability of sanitary pads and tampons, this has become manageable (although not necessarily the best and eco-friendly option[3]), and women can comfortably go out in public. This was not always the case. Thus, some form of segregation was implemented to allow menstruating women to peacefully spend their time without any external disturbances and without any obligation to go out in public and hence become susceptible to embarrassing situations.

Prescriptions like not cooking, not using normal utensils, not touching people, especially the husband, sleeping on ground etc. also involve forms of segregation. Since menstruating women will be in a heightened Rajasic condition (and the associated Ashaucha) and coming in direct physical contact, or eating food cooked by them, will result in Rajasic energy being transferred to others. Such a transfer may not have an immediate, perceptible effect on the receiver, but if such exposure continues over a long period, it may lead to imbalances in the physiological and subtle processes (for example, an imbalance in Prakriti Doshas).

Add to this, the notions of menstruation as being a period of rest, austerity and self-purification. Every person wants to be left undisturbed, while he is taking a rest or sleeping. Similarly, austerity by its very definition is a solitary effort, where the practitioner prefers to be alone and undisturbed. Thus, menstruation being both a period of rest and of austerity, menstruating women do practice some degree of segregation during her monthly periods.

Restrictions related to food

Ayurvedic texts such as the Susruta Samhita (Sharirasthana 2.25) suggest that menstruating women should eat 'Havishya Anna'. Similarly, texts such as the Vashishta Dharma Sutras (5.6) advise menstruating women to avoid eating meat.

'Havishya Anna' refers to the food that is ideal for offering in the Yajna (fire ritual), which flares up the fire slowly and steadily. During menstruation, the women's digestive fire Jathara-Agni is very weak; this condition is called 'Agni-mandya'. Hence, Ayurveda suggests that one should consume food which is fit to be used in Yajna, so that the digestive fire is also flared up. Havishya Anna is basically a combination of ghee, Shali rice and milk. Another dish that is ideal during menstruation is called 'Yawaka'– made from barley and milk. Apart from this, substances like Hing (Asafoetida) and Black Salt, which are good for igniting the digestive fire, should be consumed. More importantly, menstruating women should eat less and eat easily digestible food.

The purpose of these restrictions regarding food is to protect the health of menstruating women. A simple sattvik food consumed in less quantity is the ideal diet for menstruating women.

Restrictions related to performance of religious and spiritual activities, including visiting temples

This is another important advice given to menstruating women. Though widely prevalent even today, many women do not understand the principle behind this. Restriction on the performance of religious and spiritual activities has been explicitly mentioned in the Angirasa Smriti (Verse 37), which asks menstruating women to 'not engage in holy/sacred activities'. Similarly, Vashishta Dharma Sutra (5.6) asks menstruating women to 'not touch fire', which is a reference to not cooking food, as well as not performing fire-ritual-worship.

The principle reason behind this injunction is the fact that menstruating women, due to their heightened state of Rajas, have entered a temporary phase of ritual Ashaucha, which makes them ineligible to perform religious rituals. For performing any ritual, an individual should be physically clean, as well as mentally pure and calm and more importantly, should have Sattvik disposition at physical, vital, and mental levels. But, since, menstruating women have heightened level of Rajas at all the three levels, they become ineligible to perform or participate in any religious activities.

Menstrual blood is also considered as emitting a specific kind of subtle odor, which can potentially disturb the spiritual environment within the temple or at a religious ceremony. Elaborating on this topic, Rajarshi Nandy writes:

> Hindu tradition as followed in various sampradayas and matas, from Smritis to Agamas and other generic localised customs, and specially those that claim to have been derived from the Vaidika traditions are unequivocal in stating that a woman, while menstruating, should not be present during the performance of religious rituals and/or enter temples where deities have been consecrated into the vigrahas. One of the reasons for this is because menstrual blood was/is considered unclean, with a specific kind of subtle odour that emanates from it, which can potentially disturb the environment inside the temple. In any worship, a most basic step is offering of the panchatattwa to the deity. The simplest of this process is the panchopachara puja, which includes making offerings flowers and dhoopas. Gandha, or smell, especially of the variety that has an uplifting effect on the human consciousness, is considered vital for most rituals. Hence, while chandan (sandal) remains one of the favourite ingredients for ritualistic worship across India, women during periods are strongly discouraged from entering into shrines.[4]

Yet another reason is the fact that performing or attending such religious ceremonies and rituals, or entering temples during menstruation over a long period of time may have an adverse effect on the health of the menstruating woman. As explained before, the energy present at a properly consecrated temple, or the energy generated in a properly performed religious ritual, will facilitate spiritual upliftment and calmness of the mind in those who participate, by causing the Apana Vayu to move upwards. This upward movement will interfere with the downward movement of Apana Vayu that is facilitating menstruation. This interference will result in imbalance of the Prakriti Doshas, which in-turn will affect the health of the menstruating woman over a long duration.

Thus, menstruating women have been advised not to take part in any religious activity, including visiting temples, so as to fulfil the dual purpose of: facilitating maintenance of the spiritual atmosphere at the temples and during the religious ceremonies, without any disturbance to its energy and spiritual environment; and more importantly, protecting the menstruating woman from any adverse effects on her health due to interference with her physiological functioning of Doshas.

The importance of observing these menstruating practices in Hindu tradition can be gauged by the fact that Hindu women who fail to observe these practices intentionally or unintentionally are considered to have incurred a Dosha (Karmic fault) called 'Rajaswala Dosha'. Each year, Hindu women observe a festival involving fasting and worship of the Rishis called 'Rishi Panchami' to become free from this Rajaswala Dosha. Rishis are the Seers who are believed to have perceived first-hand the mantras of the Vedas and then revealed archetypes of all branches of knowledge to humanity. Rishis – Kashyapa, Atri, Bharadhvaja, Vishvamitra, Gauthama, Jamadagni and Vashishta – are worshipped on the day, which usually falls during August-September. It is held that worshipping the Rishis in repentance during this particular day frees women from the karmic guilt incurred due to non-observance of menstruation restrictions.

Nevertheless, at this point, it is important to highlight that the practice of most of these menstrual restrictions have been given up by the current generation. Some, however, practice a few restrictions, especially those related to religious practices. According to a study by Dr Jasmine Gujarathi, Dr Dilip Jani and Dr ARV Murthy,[5] which interviewed girls from urban and rural background, the data showed that out of 798 girls interviewed, only 14.16 per cent followed the restriction on cooking. Similarly, restriction on touching others, sleeping on same bed, and on applying turmeric and kajal were followed by 10.90 per cent, 5.89 per cent, and just 2.38 per cent of girls respectively. Adherence to menstrual restrictions was highest with respect to religious practices like not participating in religious activity (41.60 per cent) and not visiting temples (47.62 per cent). Only twenty five girls (3.13 per cent) said that they did not follow any restriction.

The study is very insightful because it reveals that almost half the interviewed girls followed menstrual restrictions with respect to religious practice, but mostly ignored others, especially those given in Ayurvedic Paricharya. This is significant because it denotes that somewhere down the line people forgot the health principles which are as important a guiding principle behind the various tenets of menstrual Dos and Don'ts, as the religious and spiritual principles. This is further reinforced by the fact that out of 676 girls who answered the question about why they followed some of the restrictions, 39.50 per cent girls selected 'culture' as the reason and 44.53 per cent selected 'religion'. The study also revealed that out of 583 girls who answered the question about why they no longer follow restrictions all the time, 24.70 per cent of them said it was due to the exposure to a new, modern culture, whereas 38.25 per cent said it was because these restrictions are no longer practical in today's times. This clearly shows the influence of western modernity which alienates people from their own traditions. This being the case, it may be worth asking whether these restrictions are even practical in today's fast moving society?

The present globalised society with its fast life poses serious obstacles to the traditional way of life. Women may find it very difficult to strictly follow all the restrictions all the time. But contemporary women also struggle with menstrual difficulties. The practices need to be seen not as 'oppressive restrictions' being imposed on them but rather as therapeutic prescriptions. As the study by Dr Pallavi Pai, Dr Sarita Bhutada and Dr Prasad Pandkar, quoted in the sections on Yoga and Ayurveda shows, with little effort, women naturally increased observance of the menstrual restrictions as they practised them and experienced the benefits. The study had shown that the compliancy to various menstruation restrictions among the thirty unmarried woman, who were monitored, increased from an average of 76.10 per cent at the beginning to 86.66 per cent towards the end of the study period.[6] This clearly shows that, when seen as natural, alternative therapy and part of a spiritual practice, women may choose to practise many, if not all of the menstrual restrictions during their monthly periods. This practice of even few tenets of the menstruation Dos and Don'ts can be highly beneficial. As Lord Krishna in the Bhagavad Gita (2.40) says: 'Even a little practice of Dharma saves one from great fear.'

What was followed as ritual in the past needs to be grounded in scientific reason and experience in this age. The Western lens of 'religion' and 'superstition' distorts our understanding of the scientific basis for these rituals. More important than strict adherence to each and every prescription is the inner awareness that menstruation is an austerity, a self-purifying process and the recognition that menstruation practices have been designed for the overall welfare of women. Thus, developing a correct and a positive outlook towards menstruation practices is as important as practising them. With proper understanding, this practice might gain credence naturally, in our times.

Menstruation Notions in Other Indic Traditions

Introduction

APART FROM Hinduism, Buddhism, Jainism and Sikhism are the three religious and spiritual traditions which originated in India. These Indic traditions, though sharing a common basis of Dharma with what is considered mainstream Hinduism (Vaidika, Agamika and Pauranika Hinduism), developed independently and throughout history maintained a distinct identity.

In the traditional Hindu framework of *Darshana*s or worldviews, while Nyaya, Vaisheshika, Samkhya, Yoga, Mimamsa, and Vedanta, which are today identified as 'Hindu', were classified as 'Astika Darshana' (those that upheld the validity of Veda as a valid source of knowledge), Buddhism and Jainism were categorized into 'Nastika Darshana' or worldviews, which did not recognise the Vedas as a valid source of knowledge. Sikhism, owing to its recent origins, was not including in the Darshana framework.

In terms of geographical spread, while Jainism and Sikhism have more or less limited their reach to India alone, Buddhism spread far and wide to Tibet, China, Japan and other South-East Asian nations. Even today, despite losing ground to Islam and Christianity outside India, Buddhism still flourishes and informs the general culture of the people in Tibet, China and Japan.

We will now briefly examine notions regarding menstruation prevalent in these three Indic traditions.

Buddhism in India, China,Tibet, Japan & SE Asia

Considered one of the 'Nastika Darshanas'[1] in the Indic division of different schools of philosophies, Buddhism traces its origins to Gautama Buddha, who is estimated to have lived during the fifth-sixth century BCE. Though it originated in India, and for centuries harmoniously coexisted, mingled and flourished side by side Hinduism or Sanatana Dharma, Buddhism declined here after the Islamic invasions in the twelfth century CE. On the other hand, it was first introduced to China in the first century CE and established a firm footing by the fourth-fifth century CE. Likewise, it entered Sri Lanka by the third century CE, was officially introduced in Japan in the sixth century CE, and actively spread in Tibet between the seventh and ninth centuries. Even today, Buddhism has considerable presence in China, Tibet, Japan, and South East Asian countries.

Menstruation in different Buddhist Traditions

Though it is generally held that in Buddhism, menstruation is seen as 'a natural physical excretion that women have to go through on a monthly basis, nothing more or less',[2] we do find a number of notions, including those of suffering and impurity associated with it in the Buddhist tradition.

Cordia Ming-Yeuk Chu observes that '[the] Chinese have traditionally regarded menstrual blood as unclean and polluting because of its magical power, and the danger it may present. It is very potent when used in magic and counter-magic or in exorcising evil spirits. Gods avoid it and will neither protect nor communicate with anyone contaminated by a menstruating woman. Worst of all, women are condemned to undergo torture in hell for spilling unclean blood on to the earth during menstruation or childbirth. However, its role in procreation makes it vitally important'.[3]

The central tenet of Buddhism is that life is full of suffering. The first of the four Nobel truths of Buddhism designates birth, ageing, illness, death, experiencing of the displeasing, separation from the pleasing, and non-attainment of desired objects as the great sufferings of life. Additionally, for women, it is held that the Buddha enunciated five more sufferings: menstruation, pregnancy, childbirth, having to wait upon a man, and being subjected to the in-laws.[4] Thus, in the Buddhist tradition, while both men and women suffer, women suffer more, and their unique physiological makeup and social conditions, including menstruation, contribute to this additional suffering. As Yeshe Choekyi Lhamo notes: 'such arrangement demonstrates that the very body of a woman was (and still is) seen as a source of suffering'.[5]

Similar to suffering, in the case of pollution as well, Buddhist tradition perceives, all human bodies, not just female bodies, as 'flawed and 'leaking' filthy substances.[6] But even here, there is a difference. The Chinese Buddhist tradition divides a female body into two parts: Upper and Lower. While the upper part with its oozing breast milk is considered pure, the lower abdominal region with its flowing menstrual blood is considered impure.[7] Lhamo notes that while authentic Buddhist sutras do not explicitly represent female body as polluted, there are a number of sutras containing the seeds of such views.[8]

One of the prominent sutras in the Mahayana tradition in China called *Amitabha Sutra* notes that those who recite the sutras are reborn only as men, and in 'Amitabha's Pure Land, the word "woman" is not even heard'.[9] In other words, women are so polluted that even the word is not heard in Amitabha's Pure Land. Similarly, in Akshobya's paradise, it is believed 'women are no longer subjected to menstruation'.[10] Then, there is one sutra which says: The female defects – greed, hate and delusion, and other defilements are greater than the male's... because I wish to be freed from the impurities of the woman's body, I will acquire the beautiful and fresh body of a man.[11]

Therefore, like suffering, with regard to impurity as well, while both male and female bodies are polluted, the latter is seen as more polluted, and menstruation is one of the factors that contributes towards this additional pollution. Lhamo further observes that while in the Buddhist tradition, physical impurity is treated as metaphors for desire, Chinese medicine considers emotions as manifesting physically, with women being considered as 'emotionally unstable'.[12] This conflation of the Chinese medical views with Buddhist views has resulted in further reinforcing the Chinese – Taiwanese Buddhist view of menstruation as impurity.

Not only menstruation, even childbirth is associated with pollution in the Indo-Chinese Buddhist traditions.[13] Taiwanese Buddhists exclude both menstruating and pregnant women from undertaking religious rituals and practices.[14] Menstruating women monks are prohibited from either meditating or participating in communal rituals, as well.[15] Many temples, especially in Thailand, do not allow menstruating women to circumambulate around the Stupas.[16] Summarising the common restrictions practised by menstruating Buddhist women, M Guterman et al. write: Some common taboos include women being banned from participating in folk rituals, and that they must avoid temples. Menstruating women cannot meditate (though some women do, as they feel particularly 'connected'), nor can they have contact with priests. They cannot take part in ceremonies, such as weddings, either.[17]

Lhamo notes that 'Daoism, Chinese medicine and folk wisdom suggest that just as men lose Qi (life-force) through ejaculation, women lose Qi through menstruation'[18] and this is one of the reasons why women are advised not to meditate during monthly periods. Another reason is the Buddhist belief of hungry ghosts, especially prevalent in Taiwanese society. Taiwanese Buddhists, who celebrate the annual Ghost Feeding Festival, also believe that there are hungry ghosts who survive on blood. Lhamo observes: Because hungry ghosts feed on blood, and because menstruating and birthing women lose blood, they are said to attract them. Hence a bleeding woman is – as a source of blood and attraction to ghosts – taken as a threat to herself and others'.[19] Yet another reason for prohibiting menstruating women from entering temples is because 'it is believed that menstruation prevents people who come into contact with it from communicating with the gods, and it is a command of respect to not enter a temple if you are menstruating.[20]

An interesting aspect of Chinese Buddhism is the belief that women stop menstruating as they progress on the path of spirituality, especially when they enter the first level of arhatship. Elaborating on the rationale behind this Buddhist belief, Lhamo writes: Buddhism connects the renunciation of sexual desires with a quest for purity: a good practitioner is supposed to be closer to enlightenment than the average adherent, and we have seen earlier that enlightened persons are able to control bodily functions, including sexuality. Thus, in ceasing to menstruate and ejaculate, practitioners prove their ability to control their bodies. In controlling their natural drives, practitioners eradicate the greatest hindrance to enlightenment: desire, one of the three root-defilements that binds humans to cyclic existence – samsara.[21]

This belief that women undergo physical transformation as they progress further spiritually is particularly prevalent in Taiwan, so much so that nuns routinely attempt to conform to 'physical androcentrism' by concealing their breasts or by addressing fellow nuns as 'Dharma brothers'.[22] Moreover, Buddhist texts such as *Abhidarimakosa* suggest that 'physical as well as mental characteristics of women change as women advance in meditative practice'.[23] However, this belief in physical transformation on the spiritual path is not unique to women. Though less prevalent, some Buddhist texts such as the Vinaya texts also speak about the 'transformation of male sexuality', and hence, strictly prohibit ejaculation for male monks.[24]

The Chinese Buddhist tradition goes a step further. It not only conceives of uterine blood as polluting, but also conceives of a bloody hell into which only women are sent. Popularly called *Blood Bowl Sutra*, despite its origins in Daoism, it is so prevalent in Buddhist traditions that many consider it to be a Buddhist scripture. Lhamo notes that the Blood Bowl Sutra represents women as suffering and ignorant, and infested with worms that inhabit their joints and vaginas,feeding on the blood therein.[25] The Sutra states that this blood hell 'is not something that involves men. It only has to do with women, who every month leak menses, or in childbirth release blood which seeps down and pollutes the earth gods'.[26]

This interesting text was then carried into Japan during the Muromachi period, i.e. between thethirteenth and sixteenth centuries CE,[27] where it was called 'The Buddha's correct sutra on the bowl of blood'. According to Momoko Takemi, the Sutra 'teaches the way of salvation for women who have fallen into

Hell because of the pollution of blood'.[28] Variant accounts of this Sutra are available across Japan, and one popular variant begins with Mokuren, one of the disciples of Buddha, putting forth a question to the Buddha thus:

> Once I went to such-and-such a prefecture, and saw in the middle of a large field there a Hell composed of a pond of menstruation blood. This pond was some 84,000 jujana wide, and in the middle women who were wearing handcuffs and ankle chains were undergoing hardships. The demon who was the lord of this Hell came here three times a day and forced the women sinners to drink the polluted blood; if they refused to do so, he would beat them with an iron rod. Their screams of anguish could be heard from great distances away. The sight of this made me very sad, and so I asked the Lord of the Hell why the women were being forced to undergo such hardships. He replied that the blood the women had shed during the birth of their children had polluted the deity of the earth and that, furthermore, when they washed their polluted garments in the river, that water was gathered up by a number of virtuous men and woman and used to make tea to serve to holy men. Because of these acts of uncleanliness, the women were now forced to undergo sufferings.
>
> Thus, Mokuren used his holy powers to come to the seat of the Buddha and to inform him of what he had seen with his eyes. He asked, then, what he needed to do for the women to be saved from their punishments in the pond of blood.
>
> The Buddha then answered, teaching Mokuren how to save the women. He said it would be necessary for them to respect the three treasures of filial piety, to call on Mokuren, to hold a Blood Pool Liberation service, to hold a Blood Pool Feast, to read [the]sutras, to have an esoteric ceremony, then to make a boat and float it off. At that time a five-colored lotus flower would appear in the middle of the Blood Pond. Then, he said, all of the women sinners would be saved, and reborn in the Buddha's land.[29]

It is interesting to note that while the account given in the Sutra condemning women to blood hell has been largely received by academics as a misogynist text, the purpose of the Sutra itself seems to be to save women from the sufferings of this blood hell. Moreover, Takemi notes a three-fold practical usage of this text in Japan, all of which is intended to protect or help women. Takemi observes that though these practices have more or less died out today, previously the Sutra was used in three prominent ways in Japan: as a Sutra which saved the souls of the dead; as an instrument for obtaining rebirth in Western Paradise; and as a protective amulet, which protected pregnant women and ensured safe birth, and which also acted as a charm against impurity.[30] Takemi notes that various elaborate ceremonies involving the Sutra were practised to attain the above mentioned three goals.

While the notion of impurity associated with menstruation is also prevalent in Tibetan Buddhism, it is interesting to note that in one of the Buddhist myths, menstruation was originally a male process, which was taken away from men by the Buddha as punishment and instead given to women as reward for their cleanliness.[31] There are a number of female Tibetan deities who are intimately connected to menstruation. For example, Dakini, a famous naked deity, is portrayed in Tibetan Buddhism as holding a skull cup filled with menstrual blood.[32] The menstrual blood of another deity, Dorje Phagmo is 'believed to be present in the waters of lake Phodrang Kyomotso in Arunachal Pradesh and is highly valued in tantric ritual'.[33] By associating these deities with menstrual blood, notes Kara Spafford, 'religious Tibetan women can potentially feel empowered and confident through their own menstruation'.[34]

Tibetan culture also promotes a view that women have more bodily enemies in the form of menstruation and childbirth than men that obstructs their pursuit of religious purity,[35]

Spafford observes that though 'it is not explicitly written in Buddhist texts that women cannot enter monasteries or partake in Buddhist rituals while menstruating, yet the concept thrives in [the] Tibetan Buddhist culture'.[36] Spafford adds that the notion that the 'bodily functions' of women can result in ineffectiveness of rituals and endanger entire communities is present not only in Tibetan Buddhism, but also in Japanese Buddhism.[37]

In Tibetan medical literature, which is heavily informed by Tibetan Buddhism, both pollution and the power aspect of menstruation were highlighted. The famous text of embryology titled *The Entering the Womb* states: '[The vagina] is a nauseating swamp hole, extremely foul-smelling like a pack animal's excrement, inhabited by countless hundreds of thousands of worms and dripping with unclean substances, putrid and rotting with reproductive substances, blood and fume—if you see it, you will be repulsed.'[38] On the other hand, there are medical texts which portray menstrual blood as 'both natural and powerful' and 'by accumulating instead of flowing away, menstrual blood literally creates the flesh, blood, and organs of the fetus during conception'.[39] Then, there are Tantric rituals, which utilise menstrual blood to attain various magical powers like 'invisibility, immortality, and telekinesis'.[40] Spafford writes, 'Human wastes are considered to be the 'five nectars' in Indian and Tibetan tantric thought, which are transformed into powerful substances through ritual blessings'.[41]

In short, though it is popularly held that Buddhism perceives menstruation only as a natural process, our examination of various Buddhist traditions reveals that they also associate notions of impurity with menstruation. It is considered a hindrance for women who aim to attain Buddhahood. While Buddhism consider both men and women as impure and in suffering, women are considered to be in a status of greater impurity and suffering due to menstruation. Nevertheless, menstruation is also perceived as being powerful with an ability to provide magical powers, as in Tibetan Budddhism.

Jainism

Jainism or Jain Dharma is one of the ancient religious traditions of India. Being mostly a Shramanic or ascetic tradition, Jainism traces its roots to a line of twenty four liberated teachers known as 'Tirthankaras', with the last Tirthankara, Mahavira, estimated to have lived around 500 BCE. Also considered one of the Nastika schools of philosophy in the Indic system, Jainism has co-existed, mingled and mutually interacted with Hinduism for many thousand years.

Women occupy a central position in Jain society and spiritual practice, constituting two of the four limbs of 'Sangha' the community of the pious, which is an important Jain institution, consisting of a muni (male ascetic), aryika (female ascetic), Sravaka (laymen), and Sravika (laywomen), who continuously practise Dharma. Jains believe that as long as the Sangha endures, Dharma will also endure, and when the Sangha perishes, Dharma will also perish.[1]

In religious and spiritual life, householder Jain women play a key role in activities related to food, worship and ceremonies.[2] Food, its preparation, the dietary rules and fasting are very important to the religious practice of the Jains. The women of the household take responsibility for a number of activities surrounding food; from the preparation of proper food based on Jain ritualistic and dietary requirements to taking care of alms to Jain monks.[3] They must also have thorough knowledge of the traditional calendar and the knowhow about when to eat, what to eat, and when to fast. Fasting is, in fact, considered a way of performing austerity for women.[4] Though women are usually not allowed to 'enter the innermost sanctuary and touch the idols'[5] due to their perceived lack of required ritual purity, they take the lead in performing religious ceremonies and singing devotional hymns; they are also competent to practice internal worship. But menstruating women, owing to their state of impurity, 'should not perform worship or undertake pilgrimages to sacred places'.[6] Also, sects like Kharatara-gaccha sect prohibit 'women of childbearing years' from anointing the 'Jina images with sandalwood paste'.[7]

Now, coming to the practice of ascetism, being primarily an ascetic religious tradition, Jain Dharma facilitates both men and women to renounce the sensory world and adopt a life of renunciation and asceticism and strive to attain Moksha – freedom from the Karmic cycle of birth and death. Arvind Sharma notes that right from Rishabhanatha, the first Tirthankara, many Tirthankaras including Parshvanatha and Mahavira, had a large number of women, both ascetics and laywomen as disciples.[8] *Kalpasutra*, a Svetambara Jain text, in fact, records that during the time of Mahavira, the last Tirthankara, there were around 36,000 female renunciates as compared to 14,000 male ascetics – that is, more than twice the number of women ascetics than their male counterparts.[9] The Svetambara tradition, in fact, recognises Mallinatha, the 19th Tirthankara as a woman, although the Digambara tradition does not subscribe to this view. Nevertheless, both these traditions provide Diksha or initiation into asceticism to men and women. Only two categories of women are barred from taking initiation, according to *Chedasutras*, the Svetambara books of discipline: those who are pregnant and those who are below the age of eight or those who have small children.[10]

Once initiated into asceticism, both male and female monks have similar rules and regulations to follow, though some additional regulations are also stipulated for women. The five great vows (pancha-mahavratas), for example, are common to all ascetics, irrespective of their gender. These vows are: non-injury, truthfulness, non-stealing, celibacy, and non-possession. Then, there are guidelines like the kind of lodgings that the ascetics must avoid, which are common to both genders. *Acharanga Sutra*, the foremost book giving guidelines about monastic conduct, in fact, specifically mentions both male and female monks. In book 2, it says: 'A monk or a nun should not use for religious postures... a lodging where the householder or his wife ...rub or anoint each other's body with oil or ghee or butter or grease; for it is not fit.'[11] Again, 'a monk or a nun should not use for religious postures. . . a lodging where the householder or his wife...rub or shampoo each other's body with perfumes, ground drugs, powder, lodhra ... for it is not fit'.[12] On the other hand, Chedasutras lay down a number of guidelines, which are specific to women ascetics: 'A nun is not allowed to be alone. A nun is not allowed to enter alone the house of a layman for food or drink, or to go out from there alone. A nun is not allowed to enter alone a place to ease nature or a place for stay, or to go out from there alone. A nun is not allowed to wander about alone from one village to the other. A nun is not allowed to be without clothing. A nun is not allowed to be without superior. A nun is not allowed to stand in the ascetic posture called kayotsarga.'[13] Then, there are texts like Brihatkalpabhashya, which prohibit female monks from keeping or using certain vegetables and fruits having elongated shapes, and even objects like handles and knobs, owing to their similarity to the phallus.[14] These additional restrictions appear to be stipulated to protect women ascetics from situations that may lead to the violation of their vows,[15] especially the vows of celibacy. (For example, a lonely woman ascetic could be sexually assaulted, or herself give in to temptation.)

Despite such elaborate and gender-specific stipulations regarding the ascetic life catering to the unique temperaments and capabilities of men and women, the Jain tradition believes that men, in general, are better equipped to attain Moksha than women. While Digambaras believe that women are absolutely incapable of attaining Moksha in their current condition, and hence, have to take rebirth as men; Svetambaras believe that despite being at a disadvantage compared to men, some women can still attain moksha in their lifetime.[16] It is perhaps for this reason that even elderly female ascetics with a very long life of austerity were still considered subordinate to young male renunciates of only a few years of austerity, with a Svetambara ascetic rule going to the extent of stipulating 'even if a nun is ordained for a hundred years she must pay homage to a young monk, even if that monk has been ordained that very day, by going forth to meet him and by greeting him in reverence'.[17] Aravind Sharma comments that this could be the reason why there are no literary records of women Jaina monks attaining high titles of 'Acharya' or 'Suri' like their male counterparts, though, they had their own titles like 'Ganini', 'Pravartini' and 'Mahattara', which were mostly conferred upon them by the male ascetics.[18]

The Jaina tradition, specifically the Digambaras, offers a number of reasons why women are thus disadvantaged compared to men regarding attaining Moksha, the most prominent being a woman's inability to adopt complete nudity.The issue of nudity, is, in fact, so central and controversial to Jaina tradition that it has been among the centerpieces of religious debates between the Digambara and Svetambara sects for centuries.

According to the Digambaras, wearing clothes denotes a state of attachment to the physical body. It also denotes that one is attached to mental conditionings like shame. In other words, they 'lack spiritual maturity' to understand that it is the inner soul and not the outer body which is of 'ultimate significance'.[19] Digambaras note that the reasons why women ascetics cannot fully adopt nudity, and hence, cannot attain Moksha in their current life, is actually two-fold: One, they would be 'vulnerable to sexual assault',[20] Two, nudity will give rise to feelings of 'lajja' (shame), which in-turn implies the presence of unalleviated sexual desires. Hence, non-nudity implies a state of hankering for material pleasures.[21] To this, the Svetambaras, over the centuries, have responded by forwarding the argument that clothes are 'mere aids (upkarana) of mendicant life, akin to the whiskbroom, as opposed to possessions'.[22] Also, to the Digambara retort that wearing clothes also results in 'Himsa' or injury to the many micro-organisms present in the clothes, Svetambaras have responded by arguing that by following the guidelines of conduct stipulated for women ascetics, they will avoid all injury.[23]

This debate and its outcome are beyond the scope of the present discussion. However, what is relevant to us here, is the second prominent reason – that of the female anatomy, especially the presence of menstruation in women – offered by the Digambaras for the disadvantaged position of women ascetics with respect to attaining Moksha. Surprisingly, the Svetambaras either agree with this or are silent. Let us now take a deeper look at the Digambara and Svetambara positions on menstruation and the female anatomy.

Digambara view on menstruation

In her thesis 'Asceticism among Jaina women: power, sexuality and social control in selected districts of north India', Manisha Sethi discusses in detail the debate on female renunciation between the Digambara and Svetambara sects. She notes that the beginning of this debate, which raged for more than a thousand years, can be found in the works of the second century Digambara ascetic, Acharya Kundakunda, and that his work *Sutraprabharta* is the first known text which 'denies women access to spiritual pursuits on account of the prohibition on female nudity and her specific female biology'.[24]

In Sutraprabharta, Kundakunda observes: 'In the genital organs of the woman, in between her breasts, in their navels and armpits, it is said [in the scriptures) that there are very subtle living beings. How can there be the mendicant ordination (pravrqjya) for them?'[25] That is, since the woman's body with its unique biological features is said to cause 'Himsa' or injury to a large number of subtle living organisms, women are unable to fully put into practice the austerities that are required by a Jaina ascetic, most important of which is the vow of Ahimsa. As a result, they are naturally at a disadvantaged position compared to men in the pursuit of Moksha. He further observes that 'Women have no purity of mind; they are by nature fickle-minded. They have menstrual flows. [Therefore] there is no meditation for them free from anxiety',[26] noting how menstrual flow does not allow them to have purity of mind, and hence prevents them from meditating peacefully, without anxiety. Though some believe that the above quote is incorrectly attributed to Kundakunda, it is an interesting observation, for it shows the Jaina view, which connects menstruation to impurity of mind and the inability of women to meditate without anxiety. It could perhaps be a recognition of the fact that during menstruation a lot of women are given to anxiety, irritation and mood swings, which prevent them from indulging in any kind of spiritual activities. Women, in general, are believed to be more emotionally oriented than men, owing to their biological makeup.

Building up on Kundakunda's work, Acharya Jayasena, a twelfth century Digambara monk, in his *Tatparyavritti* writes: 'Women are subject to the sudden oozing of blood [i.e., the menstrual flow]; which brings about both fickleness of mind as well as weakness of body and generates extremely subtle human organisms.'[27] Jayasena also brings up the issue of 'Himsa' caused to subtle organisms in humans during menstruation as another argument for putting women at a disadvantaged position than men regarding ascetism and Moksha. Though he recognises that even male bodies shelter subtle organisms, they are very minimal[28] when compared to those sheltered in women's body, and hence, the injury caused in a woman's body is many times more than in a male's body. Jayasena further reinforces his argument by noting that women lack the first three 'admantine joints of bones that lend sturdiness to the body'.[29]

In short, in the Digambara Jaina view, menstruation makes the body weak, the mind impure, and causes injury to a lot of subtle organisms sheltered in the physical body, placing a woman ascetic at a disadvantaged position regarding the practice of meditation and severe physical austerities, and hence, prevents them from attaining Moksha in their current condition.

Svetambara view on menstruation

While the Svetambara monks have repeatedly offered counter-arguments to the Digambara position that women cannot attain Moksha in their current lives or that they are disadvantaged due to the lack of total nudity, they have not only *not refuted* the Digambara position regarding menstruation and the effects of menstrual impurity on women, some Svetambara ascetics like Meghavijaya have instead offered arguments that reinforce this Digambara view on menstruation.

Meghavijaya was the eighteenth century Svetambara monk, who offered vehement arguments against the Digambara positions on women and ascetism. But on the topic of female anatomy and menstruation, he notes that 'women suffer from constant itching' due to the presence of millions of subtle beings in their body, as a result of which they are unable to attain any 'cessation of desire'.[30] He further argues that menstruation is 'a voluntary act directly connected with a woman's libido, comparable to a man's seminal discharge'.[31] He further approvingly quotes previous authors who have written about how women are 'the site(s) of himsa or injury',[32] since, during sexual intercourse, millions of beings inside the vagina and the uterus perish. But he adds that this injury involved in the flow of menstrual blood in the vagina can be compared to 'excess of phlegm due to a sinus condition; the flow of blood or pus due to wounds or boils'.[33] That is, the injury caused due to menstrual blood and female anatomy is minimal, and hence will not prevent women ascetics from observing their vows of Ahimsa or from attaining Moksha. Further, by framing menstruation in terms of libido as a female counterpart of men's seminal discharges, Meghavijaya effectively argued that like the male seminal discharge, even female menstrual discharge would slowly disappear when female ascetics enter advanced stages of spirituality.[34]

In the words of Manisha Sethi: 'While not disputing that women in general do display the defects highlighted by Digamabars (such as crookedness, excessive sexual desire, falsehood and so on), he (i.e. Meghavijaya) urges for distinguishing the category of nuns who undertake the vows of celibacy from the general population of women.'[35] In other words, the Svetambara view as enunciated by Meghavijaya is that despite the disadvantages related to menstruation and female anatomy listed by the Digambaras as well as Meghavijaya himself, women ascetics can still attain Moksha in their lives.

To summerise, women play a central role in family, social and religious life. While the householder women engage in activities surrounding food and religious worship, those interested to attain Moksha are admitted into ascetic order. While both Digambaras and Svetambaras initiate women into asceticism, they believe that the female anatomy in general and menstruation and women's inability to practice nudity in particular puts women ascetics at a disadvantaged position regarding the attainment of Moksha. While the Digambaras believe that women ascetics can never attain Moksha in their lives and have to be reborn as males, the Svetambaras believe that despite their disadvantages, they can still attain Moksha in their current lives.

Sikhism

Sikhism is an Indic religious tradition which has its origins in fifteenth century Punjab. The teachings of Sikhism are based on the lineage of ten Gurus starting from Guru Nanak Dev and ending with Guru Gobind Singh, who declared the sacred text *Guru Granth Sahib* as his successor. Thus, the life and culture of Sikhs is centered upon the teachings of the Guru Granth Sahib.

Sikh women hold an equal position and share responsibility with men in religious life. They are part of religious congregations, participate in Kirtan, Langar (common kitchen), Akhand Path (non-stop recitation of scriptures) and other religious and cultural activities.[1] The Sikh perception of women can be summed up best in these lines from the Guru Granth Sahib: 'From the woman is our birth, in the woman's womb are we shaped; To the woman we are engaged, to the woman we are wedded; The woman is our friend and from woman is the family; Through the woman are the bonds of the world; Why call woman evil who gives birth to kings and all? From the woman is the woman, without woman there is none.'[2]

Regarding menstruation, Aru Bhartiya notes that 'Menstruating women are allowed to visit Gurudwaras (religious place of Sikhs) and offer prayer. There is no restriction to movement in the house or outside'.[3] Nikky Guninder Kaur-Singh notes that 'The denigration of the female body "expressed in many cultural and religious taboos surrounding menstruation and childbirth" is absent from the Sikh worldview...Guru Nanak openly chides those who attribute pollution to women because of menstruation'.[4]

The rejection of the notion of impurity, especially with respect to childbirth and by extension regarding menstruation can be found in the Guru Granth Sahib itself, which states: 'If one accepts the concept of impurity (regarding birth), then there is impurity everywhere. In cow-dung and wood there are worms. As many as are the grains of corn, none is without life.First, there is life in the water, by which everything else is made green.How can it be protected from impurity? It touches our own kitchen. O Nanak, impurity cannot be removed in this way; it is washed away only by spiritual wisdom.'[5] Further, the futility to perceive pollution with respect to menstruation is highlighted by saying: As a woman has her periods, month after month, so does falsehood dwell in the mouth of the false; they suffer forever, again and again. They are not called pure, who sit down after merely washing their bodies. Only they are pure, O Nanak, within whose minds the Lord abides.[6]

Instead, the Guru traces pollution to the 'heart and mind'[7] of the person and says: The impurity of the mind is greed, and the impurity of the tongue is falsehood. The impurity of the eyes is to gaze upon the beauty of another man's wife, and his wealth. The impurity of the ears is to listen to the slander of others. O Nanak, the mortal's soul goes, bound and gagged, to the city of Death. All impurity comes from doubt and attachment to duality. Birth and death are subject to the command of the Lord's Will; through His will we come and go. Eating and drinking are pure since the Lord gives nourishment to all. O Nanak, the Gurmukhs, who understand the Lord, are not stained by impurity.[8]

Further, the Guru Granth Sahib glorifies the role of menstruation in facilitating childbirth and the continuation of the family by stating: By coming together of mother and father are we created, by union of the mother's blood and the father's semen is the body made. To the Lord is the creature devoted, when hanging head downwards in the womb; He whom he contemplates, for him provides.[9]

In short, while Sikhism perceives menstruation as an important activity related to childbirth and continuation of family, it does not attach any specific notion of impurity to either menstruation or childbirth. Instead, it defines purity and impurity in terms of virtue and vice. As a result, there are no restrictions on menstruating Sikh women, preventing their participation in any religious or cultural events.

Comparison with Hindu Tradition

Being religious traditions which arose out of Hindu culture and society, Buddhism, Jainism, and Sikhism borrow many elements of belief and practise from Hindu Dharma. Even when there is divergence of views, such divergences are often also the outcome of unique social and historical conditions that were prevalent in Hindu society. Buddhism, which spread across Asia, also absorbed and mingled with native traditions in China, Japan, etc. and developed an independent life in those places. Thus, when compared to Hindu religious tradition, these other Indic religious traditions show a number of similar and divergent elements regarding their perception of menstruation.

Buddhism, for example, perceives all bodies as being polluting, although the female body takes the larger burden of impurity. Hindu tradition also perceives different conditions under which both men and women enter Ashaucha or impurity. For a woman, menstruation is a recurring condition of impurity. Just as Buddhist women do not meditate or go to temples during periods, Hindu women also avoid spiritual practices during menstruation. Thus, there is similarity in how both

Buddhism and Hinduism associate menstruation with impurity. A similarity can also be perceived with respect to the celebration of menarche rituals prevalent among Buddhists and Hindus in Sri Lanka.[1]

Scholars have often speculated, with some justification, that Hinduism has influenced Buddhism in its outlook towards menstruation. But Buddhism, which has developed independently in China, Japan and other places has also been influenced, perhaps in a stronger way by the native traditions in those places. Hence, while the Taiwanese believe in ghosts feeding upon menstrual blood, no such belief is prevalent in the Hindu traditions. Similarly, while Hinduism does believe in the presence of different realms of hells (called Narakas) wherein people suffer the consequences of their Adharmic actions, there are no Hindu beliefs of hells specifically made of menstrual blood where all women are bound to suffer, as is believed in Buddhism. Nor do Hindu traditions necessarily believe that as women progress spiritually, their menstruation will stop.

One interesting aspect which comes up while comparing Buddhist views to Hindu views is the perception regarding Qi. Chinese Buddhist tradition believes that just as men lose Qi through ejaculation, women lose Qi through menstruation. Qi is the Chinese equivalent of Hindu Prana Shakti as well as the Yogic concept of Ojas. Like the Buddhists, the Yogic-Tantric tradition does perceive any ejaculation, whether it is through sexual coitus or through menstruation as a loss of Ojas. At the same time, menstruation is also considered a heightened condition of Rajas, wherein the Apana Vayu is very strong. Menstruation is perceived as a self-purification process which removes this excess Rajas, thus bringing a balance to the Pranas. Thus, while the Buddhists concentrate only on the loss of Qi and advise women not to meditate, Hindu traditions concentrate more prominently on the heightened Rajas, which has caused an imbalance of Prana, which makes women vulnerable and also incompetent for meditation and other spiritual activities.

Coming to Jainism, there is one aspect, which is shared by both Buddhists and Jains regarding women. Both have easily accepted women into ascetic orders, but both consider women as being at a disadvantage with regard to final liberation or Buddhahood, as the case may be. While Buddhists consider women as being at a disadvantaged position due to their being at a greater stage of suffering and impurity, Jainism perceives women as being at a greater state of Himsa (injury); both views areinfluenced by menstruation. Hindu traditions, on the other hand, while generally restricting the ascetic orders to mostly men, do not consider women as being incapable or even at a disadvantage for attaining Moksha. Hindu spiritual traditions have conceived of a large number of spiritual paths catering to different people with different tendencies and capacities. While men owing to their physiological and psychological make-up have been considered more suitable to the path of austerities and renunciation, women have been considered more suitable for the path of devotion, again owing to the make-up of their body-mind complex, including menstruation. As a result, while women are considered less capable for the path of renunciation, they are considered more capable for the path of devotion and thus having the ability to attain Moksha or final liberation just like men. It is interesting to note that despite this recognition of the difference in the biological nature of the two genders, even Hindu traditions have admitted many women ascetics, especially in their Tantric and Bhakti traditions. Even Vedic traditions have seen female ascetics like Rishika Sulabha. Thus, while Hinduism has provided several options for women to pursue spiritual progress, this has not been possible for Buddhist and Jaina traditions, since they are basically ascetic orders. Nevertheless, at least the Svetambara tradition holds that despite the disadvantage, women nuns can attain Moksha.

Sikhism takes an explicitly opposed position to the Hindu traditional view on menstruation. As noted before, the Guru Granth Sahib clearly disregards the discourse of purity-impurity prevalent in the Hindu tradition and instead adopts a moralistic view of life, promoting a discourse based on virtue and vice. While scholars have often held this change in perspective as radical and reformist in nature, it is also worth noting that Sikhism developed at a very crucial and troublesome time in Indian history when the country was overrun by Islamic invaders. The presence of an aggressor meant that people could no longer practise their life the way they did during normal times. It was what the Hindu Dharmashastras call 'Apad Dharma' or the time of emergency, when all Dharmic rules and regulations applicable otherwise were disbanded. It is possible that the Sikh gurus, having perceived the difficulty of people in practicing the prescribed rules regarding Shaucha-Ashaucha during such troubled times, may have deliberately adopted a discourse based on virtue-vice, while condemning the purity-impurity discourse as being futile and impractical at that time.

One can find hints of this in the Guru Granth Sahib itself. On page 472, it says: 'Wearing blue robes, they seek the approval of the Muslim rulers. Accepting bread from the Muslim rulers, they still worship the Puraanas. They eat the meat of the goats, killed after the Muslim prayers are read over them, but they do not allow anyone else to enter their kitchen areas. They draw lines around them, plastering the ground with cow-dung. The false come and sit within them. They cry out, "Do not touch our food, or it will be polluted!" But with their polluted bodies, they commit evil deeds. With filthy minds, they try to cleanse their mouths. Says Nanak, meditate on the True Lord. If you are pure, you will obtain the True Lord.'[2] Then, again it says in the same page: As a woman has her periods, month after month, so does falsehood dwell in the mouth of the false; they suffer forever, again and again. They are not called pure, who sit down after merely washing their bodies. Only they are pure, O Nanak, within whose minds the Lord abides.[3]

The first quote is about the troubled times of Islamic invasions. It also shows how Guru Nanak counseled those who had adopted Adharmic ways of living in their mind and actions, all the time selectively only adhering to purity considerations that were convenient for them, while forgetting the core essence of Dharma. The second quote is even more interesting because it does not reject the Hindu perception of menstruation as being a temporary state of impurity, but only changes the narrative by noting how speaking falsehood is a greater Adharma and hence a greater impurity. Here again, Guru Nanak is urging people to return to the first principle, which in essence is what Apad-Dharma or Dharma in an emergency is all about. Nevertheless, it is possible that considerations of Apad Dharma could only be one of the many factors that influenced Sikhism to take a completely contrary position regarding menstruation. The other possible reason could of course be the need for defining self-identity by othering the mainstream community, which was Hinduism. We see such attempts of defining oneself by othering the rival community more prominently in Jewish-Christian interaction, which we shall look into later.

Menstruation Notions in Abrahamic Religions

Introduction

OFTEN RELIGION is considered to be derived from the Latin term 'Religare', which means 'to bind'. Despite doubts expressed by some scholars regarding this etymological derivation, to bind or unite appears to be one of the defining traits of all Abrahamic monotheistic religions, which believe in one God, one Book and one path to salvation.

Though the term 'religion' is loosely used today to refer to all spiritual and religious traditions, a proper enquiry into its meaning and implication would denote that the term is most correctly applied to only Abrahamic monotheistic religions and not to other traditions such as the Dharmic traditions of Hinduism, Buddhism and Jainism (or even to Pre-Christian Pagan traditions), which are multifaceted, with religious, spiritual, philosophical and civilisational facets to them.

Hence, we would limit the discussion in this section to menstruation notions prevalent in the three Abrahamic religions: Judaism, Christianity and Islam.

Judaism

The Jews trace the origins of their religion as well their own ancestry to Abraham, Isaac and Jacob, who are known as 'Patriarchs'.[1] Abraham, who was father to Isaac and grandfather to Jacob is supposed to have been born in the year 1948 from Creation i.e. 1800 BCE and the covenant he made with God is believed by the Jews to be the origin of Judaism and the Jewish people.[2] In fact, according to the Jewish tradition, Jacob was given the name 'Israel' by the God and his twelve sons founded the twelve tribes of Israel, making the Jews 'Children of Israel'.[3] Historically, though, Judaism can be traced back to the Iron Age Kingdom of Judah and Second Temple Judaism.[4]

Judaism can be understood as having three defining features: God, Torah and Israel.[5] While God refers to the God of Israel- the Jewish conception of a monotheistic God of all creation, the Torah forms the foundational religious text of the Jewish people, and Israel is a reference to Jewish culture as a historical culture of a particular people. *Torah*, in turn, can be divided into written Torah and oral Torah, with the former including the five books of Moses and the entire Hebrew literature, and the latter being the interpretive tradition later compiled in the *Talmud* and Rabbinic commentaries.

With this brief background into Judaism, let us now turn our attention to how Judaism perceives menstruation.

General Beliefs and Practices regarding Menstruation

William E Phipps observes that 'Throughout Judeo-Christian history the taboo (related to menstruation) has been a main cause for excluding women from positions of authority'.[6] This is because in the Judeo-Christian scheme of the world, women were associated with 'the fall from grace'[7] and the process of menstruation itself was considered a 'state of sin'.[8]

Despite what appears to be a clear negative connotation of menstruation in the Judeo-Christian tradition, in Judaism itself, menstruation attained a very central role in the medieval times, and the observance of menstrual laws became a 'defining criteria of Jewishness',[9] one that was used by the Jews to set themselves apart from the Christians, according to Sharon Faye Koren.

She observes: Jews believed that they were pure and holy because they maintained Levitical purity laws, while Christians were impure and idolatrous because they engaged in sexual relations with menstruant women. Jesus was 'the son of a menstruous woman', whereas the Jewish communities of the Rhineland likened themselves to later-day high priests. In thirteenth-century Kabbalah, Edom, the standard medieval representation of Christians, is said to be as impure as a niddah, for, like menstruants, Gentiles belong to the demonic side. Sexual relations with both menstruants and Gentiles were considered idolatrous acts that had led to the exile of the Shekhinah.[10]

Thus, Niddah and the laws associated with Niddah became a central element of not only the Jewish lifestyle, but also of the Jewish identity during the medieval period and to this day, it continues to be so.

According to Jewish tradition, Niddah refers to a state of ritual impurity into which a woman enters when she experiences uterine bleeding, especially after she becomes aware of that bleeding. While the blood flow from the womb may be caused due to multiple reasons, one enters a state of Niddah only when the bleeding is due to causes other than injury. Thus, a woman in menstruation has entered a state of Niddah. Similarly, childbirth, sexually transmitted disease or other non-injury reasons can cause Niddah.

A menstruating woman is not only considered to be under Niddah for the time she is bleeding, but also for seven days after the bleeding stops, called 'clean days'. Also, the menstruating days are counted for a minimum of five days. Hence, Niddah lasts for at least twelve days, at the end of which, the woman in Niddah is expected to immerse herself completely in the ritual bath of Mikveh, after which she is considered as having entered a state of purity again.

The practice of Niddah by Jewish women entails their adhering to certain dos and don'ts during that period. According to Harold M Kamsler, the guiding principles of Niddah can be divided into three parts: complete separation of husband and wife during the bleeding days; practice of sexual abstinence during the seven clean days after menses; and examination and cleansing during the clean days ending with final purification in Mikvah.[11] Thus, sexual abstinence forms the central tenet of the observation of Niddah.

M Guterman, et al, note in their paper that sexual abstinence not only involves avoidance of sexual intercourse, but also abstinence from 'any physical contact between males and females during the days of menstruation and for a week thereafter', including 'passing objects between each other, sharing a bed, sitting together on the same cushion of a couch, eating directly from the wife's leftovers, smelling her perfume, gazing upon her clothing (whether or not it has been worn), or listening to her sing'.[12] Highlighting the centrality of sexual abstinence among husband and wife during Niddah, Sharon Faye Koren quotes Ketubot 61b (a special type of Jewish prenuptial agreement) of Babylonian Talmud, as stating that a 'menstruating woman is permitted to engage in all the same activities as a non-menstruating woman, with three exceptions: making her husband's bed, washing his feet and pouring him wine – acts that might lead him to transgress the Levitical prohibition against engaging in sexual relations with a menstruant'.[13]

The importance of Niddah in a Jewish woman's life can be gauged by how each Sabbath evening, Jewish families read this warning from *Mishna*, Treatise Sabbath, Chapter II: 'For three transgressions, women die in childbirth! Because they have been negligent in regard to their periods of separation at the time of their menses, in respect to the consecration of the first cake of the dough and in the lighting of the Sabbath lamps.'[14] Further, we have from Leviticus, the third book of the Jewish Bible, a prescription of the highest punishment of excommunication for couples who violate the guidelines of Niddah: 'And if a man shall lie with a woman having her sickness and shall uncover her nakedness, he hath discovered her fountain, and she hath uncovered the fountain of her blood; and both of them shall be cut off from their people (Leviticus 20: 18).'[15] Jewish traditions consider excommunication the greatest punishment because 'it was an excommunication by God, a divine punishment which would result in premature or sudden death'.[16] In *Zohar* (2:111a), an important text of Jewish mystical tradition of Kabbalah, we find the voice of the evil serpent attached to two kinds of women: those who do not observe the laws of Niddah during their bleeding and clean days and hence pollute their husbands by engaging in sexual intercourse with them and women who delay going to the ritual bath of Mikvah causing distress to their husbands.[17]

The primary source of Jewish beliefs and practices around menstruation is Halaka, the Jewish code of law, which has elaborate rules regarding every aspect of Jewish life. These laws have their origin in the Laws of Family Purity enunciated in the *Leviticus*, the third book of the Jewish Bible. Thus, to understand Niddah, it becomes imperative that we have a closer look at these injunctions from Leviticus. There are three sections in Leviticus, which are most relevant to our present discussion. They are Section 15:16-33, Section 18:19 and Section 20:18.

Leviticus 15:16-33 says:

> A man from whom there is a discharge of semen, shall immerse all his flesh in water, and he shall remain unclean until evening. And any garment or any leather [object] which has semen on it, shall be immersed in water, and shall remain unclean until evening. A woman with whom a man cohabits, whereby there was [a discharge of] semen, they shall immerse in water, and they shall remain unclean until evening. If a woman has a discharge, her flesh discharging blood, she shall remain in her state of menstrual separation for seven days, and whoever touches her shall become unclean until evening. And whatever she lies on during her menstrual separation, shall become unclean, and whatever she sits on, shall become unclean. And anyone who touches her bedding, shall immerse his garments and immerse [himself] in water, and he shall remain unclean until evening. And anyone who touches any object upon which she will sit, shall immerse his garments and immerse himself in water, and he shall remain unclean until evening. And if he is on the bedding or on the object, upon which she is sitting, when he touches it, he becomes unclean until evening. If a man cohabits with her, [the uncleanness of] her menstruation shall be upon him, and he shall be unclean for seven days, and any bedding he lies upon, shall become unclean. And a woman whose flow of blood flows for many days, outside of the time of her menstrual separation, or she has a discharge after her menstrual separation, then all the days she has her unclean discharge, she shall be unclean just like the days of her menstrual separation. Any bedding upon which she lies during all the time of her discharge, will have the same [uncleanness] for her, as the bedding of her menstruation. And any object upon which she will sit, shall become unclean like her menstrual uncleanness. And anyone who touches them shall become unclean; he shall immerse his garments and immerse

> [himself] in water, and he shall remain unclean until evening. And if she becomes clean of her discharge, she shall count for herself seven days, and after this, she may be cleansed. And on the eighth day, she shall take for herself two turtle doves or two young doves, and bring them to the kohen, to the entrance of the Tent of Meeting. And the kohen shall make one into a sin offering and one into a burnt offering, and the kohen shall effect atonement for her, before the Lord, from the uncleanness of her discharge. And you shall separate the children of Israel from their uncleanness, so that they will not die on account of their uncleanness, if they defile My Sanctuary which is in their midst. This is the law for one who has a discharge, and one from whom semen issues, through which he becomes unclean. And for a woman who has her menstrual flow, and for one who has a discharge, whether male or female, and a man who cohabits with an unclean woman.[18]

Leviticus 18:19 says: 'Do not approach a woman to have sexual relations during the uncleanness of her monthly period.'

Leviticus 20:18, says: 'And if a man lie with a menstruating woman and reveal her nakedness, and she revealed the fountain of her blood, both of them will be cut off from among their people.'

To summarise, while Leviticus 15:16-33 enunciates how a Jewish man becomes unclean through the discharge of semen, while a Jewish woman becomes unclean when she has menstruation and how a menstruating woman and her husband must conduct themselves during menstruation, Leviticus 18:19 includes sexual intercourse with a woman in her menses in its list of different kinds of prohibited sexual relationships, such as incest and bestiality. Leviticus 20:18 similarly censures sexual intercourse with menstruating women and says such couples must be excommunicated. It is interesting to note that while the injunction about impurity in 15:16-33 is with respect to the

Jewish Temple/Sanctuary, the other two injunctions are related to prohibited sexual practices. This, we will explore in detail in the next section.

Though, from the above, it is clear that the tenets of sexual abstinence are mainly to be observed between husband and wife, M Guterman, et al note how 'any form of physical contact with pleasurable intent (including holding hands, hugging, andkissing) is prohibited with any menstrual woman who has not yet immersed in the Mikvah'.[19] Thus, all unmarried women, after they start menstruating, are considered to be in a state of Niddah, since they perform Mikvah for the first time just before their marriages, and hence any kind of physical contact with them is prohibited.

Guterman, et al further opine that during the Middle ages, Jewish society used fear of physical danger and disgust as a means to induce the Jewish people to practise these laws related to Niddah. They write: 'When a woman was menstruating, she was seen as a physical and spiritual danger to all men. Nahmanides states that her breath is harmful, and her gaze is detrimental. A woman was instructed not to walk between two men, because if she did so at the end of her period, she would cause strife between them, and if she passed between them at the beginning of her period, she would cause one of them to die. This shows that the "danger" of the menstrual woman is not simply the blood, but even the atmosphere around her. Additionally, a woman is instructed to be careful when cutting her toenails during her menses, for fear that her toenail clippings would spread infection to anyone who stepped on them.'[20] Medieval Judaism, in fact, traced menstruation to one of the ten curses that Eve was punished with for her transgressions[21] and in Orthodox Judaism, to this day, menstruating women are excluded from religious ceremonies owing to this curse considered still valid.[22]

Coming to Jewish scriptures, in the Talmud, we find the uterus described as a 'place of rot'.[23] In Shabbat 110a of the Babylonian Talmud, we find a reference to how 'announcing oneself as a menstruant will deter the sexual advances of snakes'.[24] In non-Pentateuchal books of the Bible, menstruation has been used as an allegory of evil.[25] Yet, menstrual blood was also recognised for its magical powers, and rags soaked in menstrual blood were traded.[26]

In the rabbinic literature tradition, we find a text called *Baraita de-Niddah* enunciating on the laws of Niddah, how their practise is beneficial and their non-compliance harmful. Explaining the dangers of non-compliance, the text states:

> She who observes the laws of niddah neither cooks nor bakes for her husband. And she does not dance nor shake out the bed, nor draw water for him from an earthenware container. Why? Because she is impure, and she pollutes by necessity. Rabbi Hanina said, 'even the saliva that she spits out onto the mattress [pollutes her] husband and sons'. They (menstruating women) are forbidden entrance to the synagogue until they immerse themselves.
>
> She who has relations with her husband while a niddah will cause her sonsnot to inherit the Torah; and that is not all, for she will cause them to beafflicted with leprosy for one hundred generations.
>
> A woman who is menstruating may not separate hallah [i.e., remove and set aside a portion of the dough, by biblical law, for the priests], nor may she light Sabbath candles. Why? Because she would be blameworthy and would make her household blameworthy.[27]

Among the Jewish mystic traditions of the Middle Ages, we find women being perceived as becoming possessed by 'Sitra Ahra', the evil Other Side, during their monthly flow and thus were considered as a danger to human beings.[28] Women during menstruation were in fact perceived as an 'incarnation of Lilith/Samael', the opposite of the holy and were placed at 'the opposite extreme' from the holy Heikhal, the sefirotic realm (i.e. God's realm) in the Kabbalah tradition.[29] This understanding of Niddah was as being impure and dangerous owing to women becoming possessed by the evil, This Other Side, was then extended to Gentiles, especially Christians, who were considered as being as impure as a Niddah because they belonged to the demonic side.[30] This perception led the Kabbalists to prohibit sexual relationships with both Niddah and Gentile women, since they considered these actions to be idolatrous ones, which had caused the expulsion of Shekhinah, the female aspect of God.[31]

One of the central tenets of Kabbalist practice is the prohibition of sexual intercourse with four kinds of women: Niddah [a menstruant], Shifah [a maidservant], Goyah [a Gentile woman] and Zonah [a harlot]. Among the four, sexual abstention from Niddah is considered most important, for Zorah, the foundational text of Kabbalah tradition, says: 'While abstention from all four is essential to the maintenance of the sefrotic realm, only those who avoid menstruating women merit visions of the Shekhinah.'[32] And since maidservants, Gentile women, and harlots did not observe the laws of Niddah and other family purity laws, the rabbinic tradition considered all of them as being menstruants and hence impure and possessed by the Other Side.

This was then used by the Jewish traditions of the Middle Ages to define a unique Jewish identity for themselves by othering the Gentiles, especially Christians as being possessed by the evil Other side. Highlighting this aspect, Moses de Leon writes: Since Israel is the sole holy nation, it is incumbent upon it to remain holy. The nations of the world come from the side of impurity, from the side of the serpent and his polluted consort. He who has sexual relations with a Gentile is guilty of bowing down to a foreign God. In addition, he is guilty of profaning the sister of the Place [i.e., God] by causing her to be bound to foreign Gods in a polluted place. He who engages in relations with such a woman transgresses the words of the Sages, who warned against sleeping with NaSHGaZ, a menstruant, servant, gentile woman and harlot. He who has sexual relations with a Gentile therefore commits idolatry, denies the existence of God, causes the sister of God to consort with foreign gods, sleeps with a niddah, and is guilty of spilling his semen in vain.[33]

Interestingly, the same menstruation was also used by Christians during the Middle Ages to define their own identity by othering the Jews. Sharon Faye Koren, who in her seminal work 'The Menstruant as "Other" in Medieval Judaism and Christianity' compares how Jews and Christians utilised menstruation for othering each other, concludes her observations thus:

> Jews and Christians derived prejudices against menstruants and menstrual blood from the Bible and from Greco-Roman scientifc tradition, and they used these prejudices to vilify each other. In the Pentateuch, menstruants are denied access to the Temple, and sexual relations with them are prohibited; in Greco-Roman medicine, biology is invoked to underscore women's perceived inferiority; and in classical natural philosophy, menstruants are said to pose dangers to others. Jews and Christians contextualised these received symbols in ways that reflected their importance to each culture.
>
> Menstrual purity was a quotidian aspect of Jewish family life and a powerful religious symbol throughout the Middle Ages. In medieval Jewish mysticism, menstruation took on a symbolic significance, undergirded by the Levitical purity system. Thirteenth-century Kabbalists expatiated on the dangers of menstruation to reinforce the need to separate menstruants from the holy. Casting Gentiles as menstruants similarly protected the holy from the impure, creating an

> impermeable boundary between polluted Gentiles and the holy seed of Israel.
>
> Twelfth and thirteenth-century Christian theologians, by contrast, generally did not refer to menstrual impurity, but rather emphasised the medical dangers of contact with menstruants. Where some rabbinic sources had taken Gentiles as being literally afflicted with flux impurity, Christian exegetes understood Levitical menstrual impurity as signifying the ways of the Gentiles and idolators. This metaphorical association, ironically, led to the symbol's reification in the thirteenth century: Jewish men, perceived as greedy, sinful unbelievers, were believed to suffer a quasi-menstrual flow. This new biological understanding of Jews corresponds with the trend in the thirteenth-century Church of seeing outsiders in biological terms; heretics, lepers, homosexuals and Jews were all infectious to the organic body of the Church. As this imagery of infection justified the expulsion of Jews in Western Europe, the slander of menstruation fed into the blood libel and justified putting them to death. The perceived powers of menstruation escalated throughout the Middle Ages, to the detriment of the Other.[34]

Contemporary Jewish sources, however, note M Guterman et al, perceive menstruation and the laws of Niddah as a 'blessing', which focusses on intimacy and companionship between couples.[35] Similarly, Charlotte Elisheva Fonrobert notes, 'A more apologetic position emphasises the positive aspect of the ritualisation of womens' bodies and its affirmation of women's physiology. This position classically focuses on the psychological health inherent to the ritualisation of menstruation. By requiring a married couple to abstain from marital intimacy for a certain amount of time, the sexual life of a couple is affirmed and regulated. The periods of withdrawal that are created teach a couple to fall in love with each other regularly'.[36]

Thus, we can see that the Jewish practice of Niddah is deeply associated with the concept of impurity, but its primary focus has remained limited to regulating the sexual activities between the couples. Though associated with impurity, even danger, which made the adherence to the laws of Niddah a central tenet of Jewish identity during the Middle Ages, Modern Orthodoxy has often stressed the aspect of increased intimacy and enriched relationship that the observance of the laws of Niddah imparts to the couple.

Let us now briefly explore the concept of Niddah and the deeper nuances associated with the practice in the rabbinic tradition.

Etymology and Meaning of Niddah

We already noted that Niddah refers to the state of uterine bleeding experienced by women during menstruation, childbirth etc. But to have a deeper understanding of the practice, it is important to enquire into the etymology of the term and how it is interpreted in the Jewish tradition.

In her book, *Menstrual Purity*,[37] Charlotte Elisheva Fonrobert makes a detailed exploration ofthe concept of Niddah, its multiple etymologies, and how it evolved in the rabbinic tradition. In this section and the next three sections, we will be exploring her research to have an in-depth understanding of the practice of Niddah.

Regarding the etymological meaning of Niddah, Fonrobert notes that 'there are two choices as to the verbal root of the word and two choices as to the referent of the action described by the verb'.[38] While some scholars like Rachel Adler have determined the verbal root to be n-d-d, meaning 'abhorrence and repulsion',[39] others have traced it to n-d-h, which means 'to cast away'.[40] Some other scholars like Barukh Levine trace the meaning to the root n-z-h, which means 'to spatter or sprinkle',[41] while Jacob Milgrom suggests a meaning of 'expulsion or elimination'[42] for the term Niddah. Thus, while the root n-d-d conveys a meaning of impurity, the root n-d-h conveys a meaning of expulsion. Regarding the referent of the action of expulsion described by the term Niddah, while Levine opines that it 'describes the physiological process of the flow of blood'[43] and to 'one who is spilling blood',[44] Milgrom points out how it can also refer to menstruants themselves who became excluded from society and confined to separate quarters.[45]

But Fonrobert notes that this meaning for Niddah, i.e. of expulsion or segregation of menstruants from the society is not supported by the Jewish textual sources.[46] She points out how the rabbinic tradition makes a clear distinction between expulsion from society and the segregation of the wife from her husband with respect to sexual intimacy and how in the case of Niddah there is only a separation of the wife and husband.[47] Fonrobert further quotes a passage from the Babylonian Talmud, which calls a Niddah 'galmudah' and explains the term as 'She who is weaned from (gemulah da) her husband'.[48] Thus, she rightly observes that 'the term niddah does not have an inherent meaning, in and by itself, of the ostracised "woman" or "abhorrence and repulsion", nor can we reconstruct its original meaning. Rather, it acquires different meanings and connotations in different contexts'.[49] For example, in the context of the impurity of genital discharges in the biblical texts, niddah has the meaning of 'menstrual impurity', whereas in post-biblical usages, specifically in Mishnaic texts, it simply means 'menstruants'.[50]

Summing up her discussion on the etymological meanings of Niddah, Fonrobert writes: In sum, the context of rabbinic literature as the primary semantic field of the term niddah does not support the meaning of ostracism and banning. The literature does not reflect or even allude to a practice of excluding menstruating women from social life. On the contrary, some of the texts indicate or even emphasise that menstruating women are not to be excluded from social life. In rabbinic literature, therefore, the primary range of meaning of the term niddah seems to be simply 'the woman who is menstruating.[51]

Framing of Niddah in Rabbinic tradition

One of the interesting aspects of the framing of Niddah is that while the Biblical texts speak about sexual abstinence and the ritual impurity associated with menstruation as two conceptually independent aspects, the post-Temple Jewish practice seems to have predominantly retained only the sexual abstinence aspect, while employing the language of impurity to refer to sexual abstinence itself, thus merging two conceptually and halakhically different aspects into a single framework.

We already saw how while Leviticus 15 speaks about ritual impurity associated with menstruation in the context of the impurity of genital discharges, Leviticus 18 lists sexual intercourse with menstruating women in its list of prohibited sexual relationships. Leviticus 15, in fact, makes a detailed discussion on how 'a person with a certain kind of genital discharge could transfer a status of impurity to a thing or to any other person, not just to his or her spouse'[52] and how this transfer of impurity can also happen through touch or sexual intercourse. But, the context of this entire discussion in Leviticus 15 is the requirement of certain purity conditions on the part of Jewish people for entering the Temple of Jerusalem. Those who had contracted impurity had to undergo purification rituals, including an offering of a bird at the Temple. But, with the destruction of the Temple in 70 CE, these impurity stipulations enunciated in Leviticus 15 are no longer applicable to people. On the other hand, the prohibition on sexual intercourse with menstruating women mentioned in Leviticus 18 and 20 remains valid even today owing to their non-connection to the Temple of Jerusalem. Highlighting this, Fonrobert notes: In post-Temple times, most of the halakhic regulations and observances still practised today concern the prevention of sexual relations between husband and wife during the wife's menstrual period. For example, the prohibition on a man touching his wife is not based on the fear of her menstrual impurity, but on the notion that touching her will lead to sexual relations at a time when they are biblically prohibited to each other. Similarly, a man may not touch any woman other than his wife, again not because of her potential impurity, but because of rabbinic concepts of touch and the loss of male sexual self-control.[53]

Thus, in the Biblical texts, ritual impurity and sexual abstinence associated with Niddah are conceptually two distinct notions. But the rabbinic tradition introduces a linguistic slippage, which obscures the distinction between the two notions. Fonrobert observes that while the rabbinic texts continue to recognise the distinction between these two notions at a conceptual level, there is a 'sliding of the two conceptual frameworks into each other, primarily on a linguistic level'[54] by employing 'the language of impurity as an expression describing the woman's condition in which she is prohibited from having sexual relations'.[55] She quotes anecdotal evidences from the Talmudic literature dealing with sexual abstinence wherein the language of impurity has been employed to refer to prohibition on sexual intimacy. For example, in the Tractate Niddah of the Babylonian Talmud, to the question why a menstruating wife is prohibited for her husband by Torah, it is answered that 'the Torah said that she will be in the status of impurity for seven days, so that she will be beloved to her husband as in the hour of her entering the Huppah [the wedding canopy]'.[56] Fonrobert notes that the reference to impurity in this passage has no ritual connotation and instead is merely a reference to menstruant's condition of sexual abstinence. Another example Fonrobert cites is a conversation between Shmu'el and his wife as found in the Palestinian Talmud:[57]

> *'Shmu'el wanted to sleep with his wife.*
> *She said to him: I am in the status of impurity.*
> *But the next day she said: I am in the status of purity…'*

Here, impurity/purity clearly refers to sexual inaccessibility/accessibility. In other words, while the tenets of ritual impurity as enunciated in Leviticus 15 became inapplicable in the post-Temple scenario, the rabbinic tradition continued to employ the language of impurity to refer to even the tenets of sexual abstinence derived from Leviticus 18 and 20. This is important because as Fonrobert notes: 'This obfuscation allows for the coining of the phrase *taharat hamishpaha* or "family purity" in popular literature on Jewish law, as an umbrella term for the laws regulating sexual relations between husband and wife during her menstrual period',[58] though the term 'family purity' is actually a misnomer since it does not concern the ritual impurity connected to the Temple of Jerusalem, but to sexual prohibition laws.

Thus, contrary to popular perception, wherein the laws of Niddah are traced back to the Leviticus 15 on ritual impurity and thus considered demeaning to women, the current practices of Niddah, despite bearing the designation of 'impurity' do not have any direct connection to the ritual contexts of impurity enunciated in Leviticus 15 (which have in any case become redundant in the post-Temple scenario) and instead must be traced to the list of prohibited sexual relationships in Leviticus 18 and 20. This also explains why, unlike other civilisations like Greek, Roman or Babylonian, the Jewish Niddah practices limit themselves only to concerns of sexual abstinence between husband and wife and not to the workings of Ashaucha/

Miasma energies. However, Fonrobert cautions that 'the opposite reading' that focuses only on the sexual prohibitions between menstruating wife and her husband and ignores all considerations of impurity will be 'no more correct'.[59]

Mitzvat Niddah as a punishment for Eve's 'sin'

Though Biblical texts themselves do not provide reasons for the prescription of sexual abstinence during menstruation (called *mitzvat niddah*), we can find in the rabbinic tradition some attempts at constructing an etiological myth to account for it.[60]

We have already noted how each Sabbath evening, Jewish families read this warning related to *mitzvat niddah*, *mitzvat challah* and *mitzvat tier shel-shabbath* (taken from Mishna, Treatise Sabbath, Chapter II): For three transgressions women die in childbirth! Because they have been negligent in regard to their periods of separation at the time of their menses, in respect to the consecration of the first cake of the dough and in the lighting of the Sabbath lamps.[61]

In a midrashic text attributed to a Palestinian Rabbi, Yehoshua from second century, we find this following passage forwarding a divine reason for these three practices viz. *mitzvat niddah, mitzvat challah* and *mitzvat tier shel-shabbath*:

> [the students asked him:] and why was she [the generic woman] given the 'commandment of niddah'? [Rabbi Yehoshua answered] because she spilled the blood of the first *adam*, therefore she was given the 'commandment of niddah'. Why was she [the generic woman] given the 'commandment of challah'? [Rabbi Yehoshua answered] because she spoiled the first adam, who was the 'challah' of the world [at creation]. Therefore, she was given the 'commandment of challah'. And why was she given the 'commandment of lighting the sabbath lamp'? [Rabbi Yehoshua] answered: on account of the extinction of the soul of the first adam, therefore she was given the 'commandment of lighting the sabbath lamp'.[62]

That is, in the opinion of Rabbi Yehoshua, mitzvat niddah has been prescribed for all Jewish women as a 'divine punishment for the first woman's act of disobedience'[63] that resulted in the death of the first man. Explaining the nuances involved in this midrashic etiological myth, Fonrobert writes:

> The midrash reasons by analogy. The first woman committed a transgression by disobeying the Creator, the consequence of which was the expulsion of the first man and woman from the Garden. This expulsion brought about the introduction of death ('spilling of blood') into human life. Therefore, God punished her with a commandment having to do with blood.[64]

A more pronounced reasoning is found in a midrash offered by the Palestinian Talmud, which states: Eve caused his [the first adam's] death, therefore he [God] gave the 'commandment of niddah' to the woman.[65] Then, we have this passage from *Tanhuma*, which considers the prescription of sexual abstinence as women's penance for 'Eve's act of murder'.[66] 'And why are women given these commandments (the triad of niddah, challah and lighting the shabbat light)? Since our sages said that Adam was the beginning of the creation of the world and [then] Eve came and spilled his blood . . . and the Holy One Blessed Be He said: She shall be given the commandment of the blood of niddah so that it canserve as her expiation for the same blood which she spilled.'[67]

Thus, we see the rabbinic tradition constructing the prohibition of sexual intercourse during menstruation as a divine punishment and expiation for the first woman Eve's sin of disobedience that led to the fall from grace and removal from the Garden of Eden. This correlation perhaps also holds the answer to why the rabbinic tradition continued to use the terminology of impurity for referring to *mitzvat niddah*, although the two had distinct conceptual origins. Since, women entered *mitzvat niddah* owing to Eve's sin, menstruating women were considered to be impure due to their entering the state of sin they inherited from Eve, from which they would emerge purified only at the end of Mikveh. This entering of the state of sin perhaps impelled the rabbinic tradition to employ the language of 'impurity' to describe *mitzvat niddah*.

In any case, we also find a more positive etiological myth to account for *mitzvat niddah* in the rabbinic tradition. In the Babylonian Talmud, we find the following passage: 'As a certain Galilean expounded in front of Rav Hisda: The Holy One Blessed Be He said: I have put into you [plural] a quarter of a log of blood. [By analogy] I have cautioned you [plural] in matter shaving to do with blood. I have called you 'firstling'. [By analogy] I have cautioned you [plural] in matters having to do with the first[portion of the dough]. The soul which I have given you is calledlamp. [By analogy] I have cautioned you [plural] in matters having to do with a lamp.[68]

Contrary to the previous etiological myth of divine punishment, this passage portrays the three *mitzvat*s as human obligations towards God in return for His gift of life to humans. Fonrobert writes: These commandments, which interestingly the Babylonian Talmud understands, at least conceptually – as incumbent upon the community as a whole and not just upon the woman or women, are interpreted as reminders that life is God-given. Therefore, the Galilean constructs them as an expression of the positively defined relationship between the divine as creator and the human as the created, embodied being.[69]

Rabbinic Architecture of the Woman's body[70]

> Rabbi Eleazar says: just as there are hinges for a house, so are there hinges for a woman, as it is said: 'and she [Elis, daughter-in-law] bent down and gave birth, since her labour pains came upon her' (1 Sam. 4:19).

> Rabbi Yehoshu'a says: just as there are doors to a house, so there are doors to a woman, since it is said: '[Cursed be the day on which I was born] since it did not shut up the doors of my mother's womb' (Job 3:10).
>
> Rabbi Aqiva says: just as there is a key to a house, so there is to a woman, since it is said 'and he [God] opened her [Rachel's] womb' (Gen. 30:22). (bBekh 45a)[71]

The above passages from Biblical texts and the midrashic readings of them give a good glimpse into the rabbinic construction of the architecture of a woman's body as a house with different parts of her body correlated to doors, bolts, and hinges. Though the exact referents of these metaphors in the above passages are not clear, in the words of Fonrobert, 'what is striking, however, is the insistence on comparison between the woman and the house: just as a house, so the woman'.[72] Then, there are many passages wherein metaphors like 'open door', 'door and bolt' have been used with an explicit reference to a woman's sexual status. In Babylonian Talmud, for example, the metaphor 'open door' is often used singularly to refer to a woman's 'suspected loss of virginity'[73] or simply to the non-virgin status of a woman. In one of the texts, we find this passage:

> There are those who say that this is how [Rabban Gamliel] answered him: Perhaps you intentionally moved it aside and thus tore away the door and the bolt. I will tell you a parable: To what can this matter be compared? To a man who walks in the deepest darkness of the night, and if he moves aside intentionally he finds it opened, if he does notmove aside intentionally he finds it closed.[74]

In the above passage, the phrase 'the door and the bolt' is an explicit reference to vagina and hymen. The man in the story apparently complains about not finding his wife a virgin when he approached her and the Rabban Gamliel counsels him that perhaps he himself accidently tore away the hymen!

While this rabbinic metaphorical construction of a woman's body as a house, with its androcentric underpinnings, can give many insights into the gender dynamics prevalent in the Jewish tradition, our primary concern in this section is to understand how this metaphorical construction was utilised by the rabbinic tradition in its enunciation of menstrual impurity. From this perspective, the metaphorical construction of the woman's body as a house and the rabbinic usage of phrase 'my house'[75] to refer to 'my wife', indicates not only a correlation between interiority and the woman, but that 'she is the interior'; it is as if the woman herself has become 'house'.[76] This association of interiority with women and the construction of the interiors of women's body as different parts of the house has played a prominent role in the Jewish understanding of menstrual impurity and the practice of Niddah.

We already saw how Leviticus 15 enunciates about men and women entering a state of impurity due to genital discharges. But what we did not note before, however, is how the language employed by the Leviticus with respect to menstrual impurity of women utilises the architecture of 'interiority' and hence significantly differs from its treatment of men's impurity due to genital discharges wherein it upholds men's 'exteriority'. Regarding this, Fonrobert observes: the rabbinic conceptualisation of the difference between male and female bodies quite literally hinges on a single letter in the biblical text, or, one could say, on the difference between two letters in the text.[77]

While enunciating about men's genital impurity, Leviticus 15.2 says: 'When any man has a discharge, his discharge [being] *from his body*, he is in the status of impurity.' On the other hand, regarding women's menstrual impurity, it says in verse 15.19: 'When a woman has a discharge, her discharge [being] blood *in her body*, she shall remain in her status of separation for seven days.'[78] Though, at a first glance, there appears to be a symmetry regarding impurity among both genders, there is a difference in how the text phrases the location of discharge that results in impurity. While with respect to men, they enter the state of impurity when there is a discharge 'from the body', women enter impurity even when the menstrual blood is 'in her body'. This distinction is made even in *Sifra*, the Halakhic Midrash on Leviticus, which notes that 'From his body' refers to when impurity of a man appears outside his body (Sifra 1, 75 a), whereas 'In her body' implies that a woman is in impurity not only when the blood is outside, but also when the blood is inside (Sifra 4, 78a).[79] In the Hebrew text, the difference is merely that of two letters, as Fonrobert notes: It is the difference between these two letters, or prepositions in the English translation, which to the rabbinic sages establishes the male body in terms of surface, as exteriority, and the female body in terms of space, as interiority.[80]

Highlighting the far-reaching consequence of the rabbinic structuring of menstrual impurity as 'in the body', Fonrobert writes: 'Why does the midrashic commentary make this fundamental distinction, one that engenders far-reaching consequences in rabbinic halakhic discussions? For if we hold that the woman enters a status of impurity when the blood is still inside her body, it will be difficult to determine the chronological beginning of her status of impurity. When the blood exits from her body, it has already been inside her body. How long? Where? How far back in time from the point that the blood appears "outside her body" has she been in the status of impurity?'[81] It is to answer these and other questions that arise from this conceptual structuring of impurity that the rabbinic tradition embarked upon enunciating women's interiority in terms of chambers of a house and then speculating regarding the presence of blood in which chambers cause impurity and which does not.

In the Mishnah, we find the following passage regarding the inner compartments of a woman:

The sages crafted a metaphor concerning the woman: '[there is in her] a chamber, a vestibule and an upper chamber. Blood from the chamber is in the status of impurity. If it is located in the vestibule, it is in the status of impurity if there is a doubt, since the assumption is that it derives from the source (mNid 2:5).'[82] In the Palestinian Talmud, we find this passage: 'This is [what] the Mishnah [implies]: The blood of the chamber is in the status of impurity, but the blood of the upper chamber is in the status of purity (pNid 2:4, 50a).'[83] That is, while the blood in the chamber is definitely menstrual blood and hence is impure and the blood in the upper chamber is definitely not menstrual blood and hence pure, the blood in the vestibule has the halakhic status of 'doubtful impurity'. The Palestinian Talmud, further mentions: 'The chamber lies more inside than the vestibule. The upper chamber is located on top of the chamber [reaching] towards half of the vestibule, and an opening of the upper chamber opens into the vestibule (pNid 2:4, 50a).'[84] Then, the text further discusses the purity/impurity status of blood in the vestibule based on whether it is present in the external half of the vestibule or in the internal half with the midpoint being marked by the opening of the upper chamber into the vestibule. The text notes that while the blood in the interior half is definitely impure owing to it being derived from inner chamber, the status of blood in the outer half of the vestibule remains doubtful.

Many scholars have attempted to recognise the biological organs that these metaphorical chambers and vestibule refer to. The Meiri, a medieval commentator, writes: 'The chamber is the space of the womb where the embryo is formed, and the blood of niddah or of zivah come[s] out from there, and it is its origin. It is called the chamber because it is the innermost of all of these, and the vestibule is the neck of the womb which is an elongated place. Its top shrinks at the time of pregnancy so that the embryo does not fall out, and at the hour of birth it opens widely...And close to it, between the two, is a place called upper chamber where the two eggs of the women are. The ejaculated semen is cooked there, in the two channels in it.'[85] That is, The Meiri formulates the uterus, the vagina, and the cavity that contains ovaries as the chamber, vestibule and the upper chamber, respectively. On the other hand, modern commentators like Albeck identify uterus, vulva and vagina as the chamber, vestibule and the upper chamber.[86] Another scholar Meacham suggests bladder as a possible referent of upper chamber.[87] Fonrobert notes that the 'only agreement between all these commentators is that the chamber refers to the womb or the uterus'.[88]

It is important to note that *Tosefta*, which acts as a supplement to the Mishnah, explains that the 'doubtful impurity' mentioned in the passages cited above with respect to blood in vestibule has a 'practical consequence' only with respect to Temple practices. It says: 'On account of the blood which is located in the vestibule they burn the terumah and they declare in its case a liability with respect to the purity of the Temple and things related to the Temple (tNid 3:9).'[89] In other words, in the post-Temple scenario, not only the issue of doubtful impurity in the vestibule, but the entire discussion on the purity/impurity of blood in different compartments within a woman's body has no direct practical consequence. Despite this loss of direct practical consequence, the impurity/purity analysis based on the metaphorical construction of women's internal architecture has continued to remain relevant in the post-Temple scenario in a secondary sense.

A parallel could be drawn here to bring about this secondary relevance. The mishnaic tractate enunciates on bloodstains, their colours, shapes, locations, and how to determine impurity based on them. For example, five colours of blood have been classified as causing impurity in women, and this has been mentioned at one place.[90] Another passage mentions how the blood on the flesh, if near genitalia causes impurity, if far from genitalia, a woman remains pure.[91] These injunctions are applicable only in the context of the Temple, and hence, in the post-Temple scenario, they became redundant. Yet, they have continued to remain relevant in the contemporary Jewish handbooks in a secondary sense. Fonrobert writes: Their secondary meaning is that certain colours of blood or certain stains indicate that the blood is most likely uterine or menstrual and therefore prohibits the woman having sexual relations with her husband. In other words, the above-mentioned phrase – 'five colours of blood are impure in a woman' – comes to also mean – 'five colours of [genital] blood indicate that she has her menstruation, and therefore cannot engage in sexual relations with her husband'.[92]

Similar to the case of colours of blood, the rabbinic construction of the woman's internal architecture has continued to operate even in the post-Temple scenario. The construction of purity/impurity status of the blood with reference to their origins in different rooms of the woman's house has remained relevant in determining whether the woman remains accessible or becomes inaccessible to her husband.

In short, while the discourse on constructing purity/impurity of blood have actually become redundant in Post Temple scenario (i.e. after the Jewish temple was destroyed), yet the discourse has remained relevant in a secondary sense to indicate when women should abstain from sexual intercourse.

Purity & Impurity in Jewish Mysticism

In previous sections, we briefly looked into how menstruation is considered as a state of impurity and what its practical consequences were in pre-Temple and post-Temple scenarios. But, before we conclude our analysis of Jewish perceptions of menstruation, we need to examine how Jewish Mysticism treat the subject of purity and impurity.

Impurity and purity, known as *tum'ah* and *taharah* are among the important elements of Jewish mysticism, including in the medieval twelfth-thirteenth century originated Kabbahlic and eighteenth century Chassidic traditions, which devote considerable attention to these elements, especially in the context of Niddah.

While tum'ah and taharah are normally understood as impurity and purity either in the sense of hygiene or in the context of a ritual, the Chassidic teaching defines them as spiritual conditions to be understood in terms of 'absence' or 'presence' of holiness.[93] In an interview, Rivkah Slonim, education director at the Chabad Center for Jewish Student Life at Binghamton University, notes: It is crucial to dispel the myth that purity is the religious term for clean, and impurity, the concomitant term for dirty. Impurity is neither tangible nor discernible; it is a spiritual condition. When we open the text, we see that the Torah clearly makes spiritual purity a requisite to entrance [sic] into the realm of the holy. In biblical times, and through the Second Temple period, the interplay of purity and impurity took center stage in Jewish life. Entrance to holy space – first the tabernacle and later the Holy Temples – was contingent on spiritual purity. Today, it is in sacred union alone that this law is enforced. For now-until the Holy Temple is rebuilt – it is in our bedrooms that we build the most hallowed of all hallowed shrines.[94]

In short, the absence of holiness is 'spiritual impurity', and its presence is 'spiritual purity'. This holiness is again defined in terms of whether the person or entity is in union with the Creator or not. In *Tanya*, an early work of Chassidic philosophy, Rabbi Shneur Zalman of Liadi states: 'For the holy side is nothing but the indwelling and extension of the holiness of the Holy One, blessed be He, and He dwells only on such a thing that abnegates itself (batel) completely to Him ....'[95] That is, holiness or purity is defined as nullification or abnegation of one's own independent existence with respect to God, who is the Creator, the source. On the other hand, the opposite of this, i.e. a person or entity, which is separated or far from its source is impurity. In the Kabbahlic tradition, this presence of unholiness or impurity is called as *sitra ahra*, the 'other side'. Regarding sitra ahra, Susan Handelman writes:

They are what is 'outside', what is far from G-d's presence and holiness. They flourish in the realm where He is most concealed and least felt, where there is least holiness. In a place where G-d [i.e. God] is least felt, there is naturally more room for 'opposition' to Him. Spiritually speaking, what is most evil and most impure in a person is, above all, the assertion of self: one pushes G-d's presence away and creates a void, a vacuum where His presence should be.[96]

This dichotomy of purity and impurity or holiness and unholiness is also understood in terms of life and death with death considered the primary cause for tum'ah and almost all cases of tum'ah being directly or indirectly connected to death or at least to an absence of life. The contact with a dead body is of course a cause for impurity. A person with a leprosy-like disease called *tzoraaswas* is also considered tum'ah. Menstruation and childbirth are other important periods of impurity. It is interesting to note that even these two situations are considered related to death. While menstruation is connected to death due to its obvious connection to non-fertilisation of the egg causing, as it were, the death of the potential life,[97] the case of childbirth, the connection is more indirect. During pregnancy, the mother's body is understood to be the home to two lives, but upon childbirth, there will be an absence of one life within the mother. This loss of one life from the standpoint of the mother causes her to enter a state of impurity.[98]

Apart from this connection to death, the other reason why menstruation and childbirth are associated with tum'ah is because just prior to attaining these conditions, women are in a heightened condition of purity. Handelman observes: 'Every month, this great potential for holiness, a woman's potential to engage in the sublime power of creation, reaches a peak in her body (an 'ascent'). When the potential is not fulfilled and the holiness departs, the now-lifeless remnants leave the body. And this 'descent' is susceptible to tum'ah. It is precisely because of the high level of G-dliness involved in the procreative process that tum'ah can occur at all.'[99] Similarly, in the case of childbirth, Handelman notes that since according to Talmud, God is directly involved in the birth of every child, childbirth is considered as a very heightened condition of purity and holiness and 'after birth, this intense holiness, this powerful force of G-d, "departs" and there is greater potential for tum'ah'.[100]

At this juncture, it is important to differentiate between two kinds of tum'ah: one created by God Himself as part of his Creation and one that a person willingly enters by committing sin. The Chassidic tradition believes that whatever is there in the realm of holiness has a counterpart in the 'other side' and God has created this dichotomy so that people may have free choice to 'reject the evil and choose the good'[101] and, further transform the evil into good. Thus, the first kind of tum'ah or the descent into the other side has been created by God so as to facilitate even higher ascent to holiness. Rabbi Menachem

Mendel Schneerson, the Lubavitcher Rebbe, notes that this descent is only a preparation for the further ascent and is in fact only a part of it.[102] On the other hand, the tum'ah that a person willingly commits takes a person farther and farther from God.

This distinction is significant for understanding the laws of Niddah and its association with impurity. Handelman writes:

> The tum'ah, the impurity that attaches to a sin, is a void we create and by which we degrade ourselves. The tum'ah of niddah, however, is a built-in part of a woman's natural monthly cycle. Her 'descent' from a peak level of potential holiness (i.e., where the creation of a new life is possible) does not mean that she is, G-d forbid, 'sinful' or 'degraded,' 'inferior' or 'stigmatized.' On the contrary, precisely because there is such holiness involved in a woman's possession of the G-dly power to create, as if ex nihilo, a new life within her body, there is the possibility for greater tum'ah – but also a great elevation.[103]

However, while the 'other side' in general was built into the very Creation, this tum'ah of niddah was brought into the creation after the fall of Adam and Eve when Eve committed the first sin, as we saw before. This sin, which is also called the sin of the Tree of Knowledge resulted in an intermingling of the good and the evil, which were completely distinct prior to Eve's sin. While the sin of Eve caused the fall from spiritual plane into physical plane and as a repentance the women were given the tum'ah of niddah, this very tum'ah can also act as a facilitator for woman's future ascent when she adheres to the laws of niddah. Thus, this descent, according to Chassidic tradition, is only a preparation and a part of the ultimate ascent and the observance of the laws of niddah, including Mikveh, acts as a purification process that prepares one for the ultimate ascent. This association of niddah with purification is nowhere more explicit than in its connection to moon and Shechinah – the feminine aspect of God.

Shechinah, Moon and Menstruation

Though Judaism is a monotheistic religion, Jewish mystic traditions recognise that this One God has many aspects and manifestations. In the medieval Kabbahlic tradition, this God–the Creator is called Ein Sof, the infinite, who is beyond the creation and beyond human understanding. From Ein Sof emanate ten lower sefirots or aspects of God into the realm of being. The last of the ten sefirots is 'Shechinah', the female aspect of God, which is closest to human existence and who manifests here as the 'dweller within'.

The term Shechinah literally means 'dwelling' and denotes the dwelling of the presence of God in this world. Though the term is not found in the Bible, it is found in rabbinic traditions and it evolved into the Divine feminine in the Kabbahlic tradition. While the infinite transcendent aspect of God was considered masculine, the immanent 'indwelling' aspect became the female Shechinah.Jill Hammer notes that 'She is a mystical embodiment of the feminine, earth-centered presence of God, and was also called the bride of God, the Sabbath, the Torah, the moon, the earth and the apple orchard'.[104]

According to Sharon Koren: Thirteenth century Kabbalists believed that when the Children of Israel braved the agonies of slavery and the ten displays of divine might that devastated Egypt, they did not do so alone. Rather, the Israelites knew that the Shechinah, the pre-eminent feminine aspect of God, dwelled alongside them in Egypt. Medieval Kabbalists often portrayed the feminine Shechinah as a loving mother who suffers along with her children of Israel in exile. She toils with her children while they are slaves in Egypt and protects them in the wilderness after they are liberated.[105]

Koren further notes that since the Bible mentions that humans were created in God's image, Kabbahlics believe that God in His aspects must also have bodies like humans and by corollary human biological processes must also reflect a divine reality.[106] Thus, for example, Kabbahlics believe that human sexual union between male and female is a reflection of union between two sefirot, Tiferet and Shechinah, who are often called King and Queen or groom and bride, respectively. Similarly, menstruation and childbirth are also correlated with Shechinah. While Kabbahlics trace women's monthly periods to Shechinah herself menstruating 'when she comes under the influence of the demonic "other side",[107] the sitra achra; women's pregnancy and childbirth is traced to Shechinah['s] ability to receive the emanations from the higher sefirot'.[108]

Elaborating on this connection between Shechinah, menstruation and the laws of Niddah that prohibits sexual intercourse during menstruation, Koren writes: Medieval halacha (Jewish law) required women to separate from their husbands for 12 to 14 days every month: the five to seven-day period of menstruation plus another seven 'clean' days. The Zohar traces the source of this halacha to the myth of the Shechinah. The Zohar considers Egypt to be the ultimate symbol of the sitra achra. When the Shechinah dwells with the Children of Israel in Goshen, She becomes influenced by the 'other side' and begins to menstruate. Therefore, she must separate from her husband, Tiftret, for the duration of her blood flow; as a consequence, she is exiled or banished (literally) from the forces of the Holy. Although her flow ends as soon as the Children of Israel flee Egypt, the Shechinah is not ritually pure yet. In keeping with the dictates of halacha, she must separate from her husband for another seven clean days.[109]

Shechinah is also intimately associated with the moon, especially the new moon. The moon is almost always associated with menstruation across the world. Writing about the intimate connection between Judaism, the moon and menstruation, Handelman observes:

> The Talmud compares the Jewish people to the moon, for just as the moon waxes and wanes every month, so too do the Jews undergo phases of concealment and renewal in exile and redemption. The appearance of the new moon, Rosh Chodesh, is a minor holiday, marking the beginning of a new month. And this day is also a special holiday for women…A woman's body, of course, also follows a monthly cycle, and Chassidic teaching illumines a deeper correspondence between the cycle of niddah and the new moon.

The third Lubavitcher Rebbe (the 'Tzemach Tzedek') explains that on Rosh Chodesh the moon is renewed, 'purified', and again 'unites' with the sun; it again receives its reflection. This union of the sun and the moon on Rosh Chodesh corresponds to the union of man and woman after the days of niddah are over. And in the same way that a woman is renewed monthly, so will the Jewish people be renewed at the time of their redemption, which will culminate in their higher union with G-d.[110]

It is interesting to note that despite being a monotheistic religion, Judaism, at least the mystic traditions within Judaism like Kabbalah and Chassidism associated Shechinah, a feminine aspect of God, with the moon and menstruation. This association not only highlights the purification aspect of Niddah, but also renders a kind of sacredness to the entire process.

Niddah or menstruation is one of the important times in a Jewish woman's life. The laws of Niddah, which have their roots in the Jewish Bible, became the defining criteria of Jewishness in the medieval period. There are two prominent biblical principles that govern the practice of Niddah: Impurity and Sexual abstinence.

On the one hand, the impurity considerations, which were primarily with respect to the Temple of Jerusalem, have become non-functional in the aftermath of the destruction of the temple in 70 CE. On the other hand, the principle of sexual abstinence during Niddah has not only survived till date but is also considered an important tenet of Jewish practice even today. Jewish couples are expected to practice sexual abstinence for a total of twelve-fourteen days, five days during menstruation and seven 'clean' days thereafter. Only after the twelve day period, when women purify themselves in the ritual immersion of Mikveh will they become 'pure' and accessible again for sexual intimacy.

Jewish tradition traces these laws of Niddah to the first woman Eve's sin of the Tree of Knowledge that resulted in the fall and death of Adam.The Jewish mystical traditions like Kabbalah, on the other hand, try to understand menstruation in its relationship to Shechinah, the feminine aspect of God.

Christianity

Christianity is an outgrowth of Judaism[1] whose origins can be dated to the mid-first century after Christ. Like Judaism, it is also a monotheistic Abrahamic religion, but its religious beliefs are centered on the life and teachings of Jesus Christ. While the Hebrew Bible is the central scripture of the Jewish people, Christians consider it the Old Testament, and add a New Testament, a collection of twenty seven books, including the Gospels, which chart out the life and teachings of Jesus Christ, to their Bible.

Though Christianity shares its basic scriptures and many tenets of its beliefs and worldview with Judaism, owing to the fact that it developed as a breakaway from Judaism, Christians, throughout their history, have attempted to define their identity by 'othering' Judaism. Menstruation was used as one of the tools towards this end. Christianity also used menstruation to 'other' idol-worshipping pagans. Of course, this use of menstruation for 'othering' a rival community was not unique to Christianity.

In the previous section, we saw how even Judaism, especially during the Middle Ages, employed the same with respect to Christianity. However, while Judaism used Niddah practices to define itself as distinct from Christians, menstruation has been defined/used by the Christains rather diversely.

General Beliefs and Practices regarding Menstruation

We have already noted how in the Judeo-Christian world, menstruation, especially its association with Eve's sin and the resultant curse, has been one of the main reasons for keeping women away from positions of authority.[2] And like Judaism, even Christianity derives its primary views about menstruation from Leviticus, which is part of the Old Testament of the Christian Bible. But unlike Judaism, Christians do not follow any particular menstruation practices like Niddah and Mikveh. On the other hand, this non-observance of Niddah regulations and the belief that Baptism, the Christian rite of purification and admission into Christianity, itself frees women from all impurities formed the basis of defining unique Christian identity during Early Christianity.

Despite this, Christians, for the most part of their history, have considered menstruation as dangerous and have observed a number of restrictions and taboos. Many Christian homes also observe sexual abstinence during menstruation.[3] The notion about danger has been so prevalent and widespread that even as late as 1878, we find the British Medical Journal publishing that menstruating women could cause bacon to putrefy.[4] William E Phipps observes that 'The taboo is so alive that menstruation is customarily spoken of in hushed tones and only in woman-to-woman talk. Because of embarrassment, many mothers still fail to provide their daughters with adequate advance briefing about their first menstruation'.[5] M Guterman, et al. note that 'there are some Christian denominations, including many authorities of the Orthodox Church, who will not allow women to receive communion during their menstrual period. Menstruation taboos are also responsible for the belief of many Catholics that a woman should not have intercourse during her monthly period. Catholic canon law refuses to allow women or girls to be in any semi-sacerdotal roles, such as altar server'.[6] They further write about how the Russian Orthodox Christian women live in secluded huts, do not attend church services, do not touch food, or have contact with men during menstruation.[7] The air around such women is believed to be polluting and especially dangerous for 'young hunters', the weather is believed to be affected negatively by the gaze of such women and they are also believed to 'repel fish and game'.[8] Sister Vassa Larin, a nun in the Russian Orthodox Church notes in an article: 'When I entered a convent of the Russian Orthodox Church Abroad in France, I was introduced to the restrictions imposed on a nun when she has her [monthly] period. Although she was allowed to go to church and pray, she was not to go to Communion; she could not kiss the icons or touch the Antidoron; she could not help bake prosphoras or handle them, nor could she help clean the church; she could not even light the lampada or icon lamp that hung before the icons in her own cell: this last rule was explained to me when I noticed an unlighted lampada in the icon-corner of another sister. I do not remember that anyone attempted either to question or justify these strictures; we simply presumed that menstruation was a form of "impurity", and we had to stay away from things holy so as not to somehow defile them.'[9] She adds that 'there are different regulations in the Russian Orthodox Church based on the concept of "ritual impurity", varying from parish to parish, usually depending on the local priest.[10]

Such apprehensions regarding menstruation are not unique to Russian Christians. Noting how fear and anxiety exist throughout the Mediterranean region, especially in the rural areas, David D Gilmore writes: Among the Orthodox Sarakatsani, mountain shepherds of Epirus in northern Greece, for example, a menstruating woman must avoid approaching a lactating sheep or else it will stop giving milk. Throughout rural Greece, menstrual or postpartum blood is so powerfully baleful that it "weakens even God". A menstruating woman in Greece may not, therefore, enter a church, make a meal, or visit the sick. Women's bodily functions are said to be polluted before God, and woman is the epitome of pollution, equal in sinfulness to a murderer. Indeed, there is something truly malignant, even demonic, about women's bodies in this culture, where women are called "devils", and their "shame" (specifically, their genitals) must be concealed and periodically purified, as in ancient times, by ritual bathing, not in a mikvah bath, but in the sea.[11]

After examining Greece, Gilmore takes up Spain and summarises the Spanish situation thus: Brandes says that in Monteros, in Catholic Spain, men consider menstrual blood to be polluted for the specific reason that it carries away the filth that inevitably accumulates over the course of a woman's cycle. In neighbouring Portugal, a woman having her period must keep away from vulnerable farm animals and cannot participate in sausage making or other food preparation for fear that the food will become poisonous and the people who eat it will become sick'.[12] Gilmore adds that menstrual disgust can be found even in 'contemporary United States' and quotes a report that notes how young men among college students found menstruation 'unsanitary, repugnant, or otherwise distasteful.'[13]

Menstruation, Baptism and Early Christianity

Early Christianity represents a period prior to the First Council of Nicaea in 325 CE and is usually divided into the Apostolic

Age and the Ante-Nicene Period. Writing about Christianity vis-à-vis Judaism during this phase, Sister Vassa Larin observes:

> Neither Judaism nor Christianity was a clearly separate, developed identity in the first centuries: they shared a common approach to certain things. The Church clearly acknowledged the Old Testament as divinely-inspired Scripture, while at the same time distancing herself since the Council of the Apostles (Acts 15) from the prescriptions of the Mosaic Law. While the Apostolic Fathers, the first generation of church writers after the Apostles, barely touch upon the Mosaic laws concerning 'ritual impurity,' these restrictions are widely discussed somewhat later, from the middle of the 2nd century.[14]

During this period, i.e. the period prior to the First Council of Nicaea in 325 CE, there were attempts to posit Baptism, the rite of admission into Christianity, as a one-time purification process for all impurities including those associated with Menstruation. Methodius of Olympus, for example, writes: 'It is clear that he who has once been cleansed through the New Birth [baptism], can no longer be stained by that which is mentioned in the Law....'[15] Similarly, Clement of Alexandria notes that since, 'the Lord has cleansed the faithful through baptism for all marital relations', the couples were no longer required to take a bath after sexual union, something which was prescribed in the Mosaic Law.[16] However, this trend is nowhere as instructive as in the case of Syriac *Didaskalia*, a third century text by an anonymous Christian authority, which nevertheless claims to have apostolic authorship,[17] and contains a strong reprimand for women who avoid prayer or scripture lessons during menstruation.

The text locates itself in third century Syria and addresses women, whom it has identified as those who 'have been converted from the (Jewish) people to believe in God our Savior Jesus Christ'.[18] Charlotte Elisheva Fonrobert notes that it is the 'only document in premodern history of Judaism and Christianity in which we find women developing an argument for why they wish to practice menstrual separation'.[19] The points of contention addressed in the text were actually two issues: One, the continued observance of menstrual separation and Niddah by women converts; Two, the continued observance of Sabbath, despite the Christian replacement of Sunday for Sabbath. While the Didascalia's arguments against Sabbath are beyond the scope of this book, suffice to say that the anonymous author 'enters an elaborate discussion of biblical exegesis, to "prove" that the first day of the week is indeed more important than the Sabbath'.[20]

Regarding the continued practise of menstrual separation for seven days by women converts to Christianity, Didascalia notes that they offered two reasons: One, that they were void of the Holy Spirit during the seven days of menstruation; Two, they were in a state of impurity because the Biblical scriptures, i.e. the Leviticus prescribed so and that they believed those injunctions as being applicable to them. Against the first position, the Didascalia[21] argues thus:

> *For if you think, O woman, that in the seven days of your flux you are void of the Holy Spirit, if you die in those days, you will depart empty-handed and without hope.*
>
> *But if the Holy Spirit is always in you, without (any real) hindrance you keep yourself from prayer and from the Scriptures and the eucharist. Indeed, think and see that prayer also is heard through the Holy Spirit, and the eucharist is accepted and sanctified through the Holy Spirit. And the Scriptures are the utterances of the Holy Spirit and are holy. For if the Holy Spirit is in you, why do you keep yourself from approaching the works of the Holy Spirit?*[22]

That is, against the women converts' assertion that they think they become void of the Holy Spirit during menstruation, Didascalia argues that their position is untenable since the Holy

Spirit is always in them. Hence, they have no legitimate reason to observe menstrual separation or not practise prayer or scripture reading or the eucharist. In other words, their observations of menstruation restrictions are merely 'empty observances'.[23] That the Holy Spirit is always in them is a reference to the rite of Baptism through which a non-Christian becomes a Christian and gains entry into the 'catholic church which is the receptacle of the Holy Spirit'.[24] Didascalia, thus, notes:

> *A believer is filled with the Holy Spirit, and he [sic] who does not believe, with an unclean spirit...He therefore who has departed and abides afar and has departed from the unclean spirit by baptism, he is filled with the Holy Spirit. And if he does good works, the Holy Spirit stays with him, and he remains fulfilled, and the unclean spirit finds no place in him.... Indeed, there is also no other power whereby the unclean spirit may depart except though the pure and holy Spirit of God*.[25]

Stressing on the centrality given to the Baptism rite in the Didascalia, Fonrobert quotes from the text regarding how it posits Baptism as imparting forgiveness to everyone for all their previous sins,[26] including to the Jews and gentiles who have chosen to believe and get baptised.[27] But, the Baptism's imparting of forgiveness is contingent upon the baptised not indulging in 'the abominable and defiled works of the wicked heathens'.[28] That is, if the baptised were to continue observing practices that they did previously, in this case, the observance of menstrual separation etc., then they will fall from the forgiveness received by baptism and the Holy Spirit will leave them and they will instead be filled with unclean spirits.

Fonrobert summarises the Didascalia's position against the first argument of women converts thus: 'The rite of baptism signifies the endowment of the Holy Spirit, the replacement of the pre- and extra-baptismal unclean spirit once and for all. The person can only be filled by either the Holy Spirit or an unclean spirit... Both are exclusive of the other. The "possession" of the Holy Spirit, though received with baptism, remains contingent upon "good works". According to the Didascalia's explanation of the significance of baptism, therefore, the women's pneumatology is inadequate, for they will not only be void duringtheir period of menstrual separation, as they claim, but that void will be filled with unclean spirits, which leads to a battle between spirits, and to the ultimate replacement of the Holy Spirit with unclean spirits, which reverses the baptismal gift.'[29]

The second argument that the women converts offered was regarding the Biblical injunctions of the *Old Testament* which prescribe Niddah. The women argued that in practising menstrual separation, they were only following the Biblical injunctions, since even the Old Testament is considered a Scripture of Christianity. Countering this, the author of Didascalia says: But again I say to you, O woman; (if) in the seven days of your flux you regard yourself impure according to the second legislation – after seven days, therefore, how can you be purified without baptism? But if you shall bathe yourself, through that which you suppose, that you are purified, you shall abrogate the perfect baptism of God which completely forgave you your sins, and you will be found in the evils of your former sins, and you shall be delivered over to the fire eternal. But if you be not bathed, according to your own imaginings you remain unclean, and the empty observance of the seven days has helped you nothing, but it will rather harm you – for according to your opinion you are unclean, and as one unclean you shall be condemned.[30]

Elaborating on the arguments forwarded by the author of Didascalia, Fonrobert writes: He constructs a no-win situation for the women: if you women consider yourselves to be in the status of impurity during your menstrual period, how is the end of this period to be marked? If you immerse, you question the validity of your baptism, which was to symbolise that purification – in the spiritual sense – has been achieved once and for all. But if you don't mark the end of your period and uphold the community's once andfor all understanding of the purification in baptism you will remain wedded to your status of impurity. The apparent acceptance of their impurity here seems to be only a rhetorical one in the development of his argumentative refutation. All of which is to say that you should not consider yourselves to be in a status of impurity during your menstrual period in the first place, inspite of this being based on biblical legislation.[31]

Thus, Didascalia posits Baptism as 'the only legitimate rite of purification for Christians',[32] who become purified of all their sins including those associated with menstruation.

Some scholars trace Didascalia's positing of Baptism as freeing women from menstrual impurity to Jesus Christ himself and note how they are among the few exceptions to the otherwise negative views regarding menstruating women that is prevalent in Christianity. William E Phipps, for example, notes: 'In the course of Christianity there have been several notable exceptions to the disdain expressed by males toward menstruants. Jesus was remembered in the Gospels for his criticism of the levitical purification laws with respect to foods, leprosy, and women. In defiance of his Hebrew code, he touched and was touched by a "leper" and by "a woman with a flow of blood" both untouchables. His body language confirmed his words of acceptance of the manstigmatised because of a dermatological disease and the woman frightened by prolonged irregular vaginal bleeding.'[33] The author of Didascalia himself resorts to quoting Gospel as his third and final argument against the women converts and uses the reported conduct of Jesus Christ as the scriptural authority. He writes:

> *And again you shall not separate those (women) who are in the habit. For she also who had the flow of blood when she touched the border of our Saviour's cloak, was not censured but was even esteemed worthy for the forgiveness of all her sins. And when (your wives have) those issues which are according to nature, take care, as is right, that you cleave to them, for you know that they are your members.*[34]

Here, Didascalia is actually speaking against the levitical prohibition of sexual intercourse during menstruation and is instead urging husbands to not deny sexual intimacy to their menstruating wives. To establish his point, the author takes a 'recourse to a source of authority that could be shared by any Christian, the authority of Jesus, as reported in the gospels'.[35] When he writes, 'For she also who had the flow of blood when she touched the border of our Saviour's cloak, was not censured but was even esteemed worthy for the forgiveness of all her sins', he is making a reference to a famous account found in synoptic Gospels of Mark (5:25-34), Matthew (9:20-22) and Luke (8:42-48). But, Fonrobert notes that the story in the Gospel is 'significantly transformed' in the Didascalia's presentation with 'significant omission and addition' made to the original story.

The story in the Gospels[36] speaks about a woman who had continuous blood flow for twelve years and despite her best efforts and consultation with numerous doctors, the flow had not stopped. The woman comes from behind and touches the garment of Jesus, which instantly heals her. Noticing that his energy suddenly drained out of him, Jesus asked who touched him. The woman comes forward but is trembling with fear. Jesus addresses her as daughter and assures her that her faith has made her well.

Many modern scholars of the *New Testament*, much like the author of the Didascalia, have interpreted the Gospel account as a rejection of notions of menstrual impurity and Niddah practices by Jesus Christ. Selvidge, for example, describes the story as being written 'to free early Christian women from the social bonds of niddah, "banishment" during a woman's menstrual period'.[37] But there are some serious issues with such an interpretation. First, the Gospel account does not refer to a menstruating woman, but to a woman having a medical condition of abnormal flow of blood for twelve years. Second, the primary focus of the account is the healing powers of Jesus Christ and makes no reference to Niddah practices as such. Third, whether the woman's touching of the robe of Jesus Christ really constituted a transfer of impurity according to Biblical laws is debatable and as a result, whether Jesus' assurance to the woman denotes his rejection of Niddah is also debatable.

Regarding the first and second issues in the interpretation adopted in Didascalia, Fonrobert notes:

> The omission lies in the fact that in the original story in the synoptic gospels the narrative starting point is that a woman suffers from a blood flow for twelve years, while in the Didascalia she appears as a woman with merely (any kind of) a blood flow. At first sight this omission might appear insignificant, for presumably the narrative device in the gospel story is only a symbolic enhancement or a dramatic exaggeration. However, the twelve years in the original story emphasise the severity of the illness, of which the woman is healed by Jesus. In the gospel narrative the question is about a pathological blood flow as opposed to niddah. The emphasis lies on the miraculous event of healing. In the summary in the Didascalia, on the other hand, the emphasis of the story shifts away from the narrative enhancement of Jesus' miraculous healing to the touching of Jesus' garment as a transgression of biblical impurity regulations. Hence, Jesus appears to take on the biblical tradition of menstrual separation, since by praising the woman he transforms her act from transgression to exemplary behavior.[38]

Emphasising how the healing power of Jesus Christ is central to the story, Fonrobert further observes: 'This story is one among the many in which Jesus appears as a miraculous healer. It underlines the contrast between Jesus' power to heal and that of regular doctors...The semantic weight of the woman's touching of Jesus' garment lies in the healing power of his touch after the doctors have tried their medical treatments, a mere touch of Jesus suffices to heal her'.[39]

Regarding the question whether the woman's touch really formed a transfer of impurity according to Biblical laws, Fonrobert observes: 'The woman in the gospel story commits no transgression when she touches Jesus' garment. Neither biblical nor mishnaic law consider[s] the case of a person in a status of impurity who deliberately touches somebody else. Rabbinically speaking, the woman of our narrative would only have committed a transgression had she done anything that might lead to or initiate sexual contact, which is clearly not the point of the story.'[40] As a corollary, we can see how the story is neither about menstrual impurity and Niddah practices, nor about Jesus Christ speaking against them. As Fonrobert rightly concludes: 'The case for impurity according to either biblical or rabbinic law as a primary concern of the narrative cannot therefore be consistently argued. The attempt to read this story as an abrogation of biblical traditions concerning menstruation and irregular discharges of blood remains unsuccessful. The Jesus of this narrative appears as someone who has the power to heal a woman with a severe sickness, where others have failed.'[41]

That the Didascalia's interpretation of the Gospel story was not widely accepted even during Early Christianity can be known from the fact that the same story was interpreted in a completely opposite manner at about the same period as Didascalia. In mid-third century, Dionysius, the bishop of Alexandria, writes in a letter thus: 'The question concerning women in the time of their [menstrual] separation, whether it is proper for them when in such a condition to enter the house of God, I consider a superfluous inquiry. For I do not think, that, if they are believing and pious women, they will themselves be rash enough in such a condition either to approach the holy table or to touch the body and blood of the Lord. Certainly the woman who had the discharge of blood of twelve years' standing did not touch (the Lord) Himself, but only the hem of His garment, with a view to her cure.'[42]

From this, we can conclude that Didascalia's attempts to portray Christian women as not being subjected to sin and impurity during menstruation, since they have already become purified by Baptism, was not a widely prevalent doctrine even during Early Christianity. Instead, it was a localised phenomenon, which was perhaps necessitated by the presence of a significant population of Jews, necessitating Christians to define their identity as different from the Jews. As Sister Vassa Larin notes: 'The situation was different in the Syrian capital of Antioch, where a strong Jewish presence posed a tangible threat to Christian identity.'[43] The fact that the 'Councils of the church in subsequent centuries upheld Dionysius' judgment as authoritative'[44] and that by fourth century, both the Greek and the Latin components of the Church had adopted the Levitical laws[45] regarding menstruation, shows how the notion of impurity and sin, and not Didascalia's positioning of Baptism as an antidote of menstrual impurity was the majoritarian view during the early centuries of Christianity. And it is this majoritarian view, which ultimately ended up in associating women with idolatry, sin and witchcraft during the Middle Ages.

Medieval Christianity & Medical Dangers of Menstruation

Christianity during the middle ages displayed 'an overt loathing and fear of women',[46] especially towards those that were menstruating. Apart from notions equating menstruation to idolatry, witchcraft etc., which we will examine in subsequent sections, Christian theologians also highlighted the medical dangers of menstruation. The Western Catholic Church, in fact, made use of Pliny's views on the powers of menstrual blood to 'vilify women'.[47]

Thomas Aquinas, the famous Catholic priest and the Doctor of the Church, who lived in 13th century Europe, writes thus about women: 'As regards the individual nature, woman is defective and misbegotten for the active power in the male seed tends to the production of a perfect likeness according to the masculine sex; while the production of woman comes from defect in the active power or from some material indisposition, or even from external influence, such as that of a south wind, which is moist.'[48] Quoting approvingly a comment by Jerome, a 4th century priest and theologian, Aquinas further writes: 'Men ought to keep away from their wives during menstruation because it is then that deformed, blind, lame, and leprous offspring can be conceived.'[49]

Aquinas was not the first to speak about the medical dangers of menstruation, nor the last. Sharon Faye Koren traces the sources of Christian prejudices against menstruation into two sources: Biblical Metaphors and Greko-Roman medicine.[50] She writes that 'even before Aristotelian medical views reached both Jews and Christians in the Latin West during the twelfth century, Christian scholars in late antiquity had inherited fears of menstruants from such Greco-Roman natural philosophers as Pliny, Aelian and Solinus, as recorded in Latin encyclopedias'.[51] Isidore, the bishop of Seville, who lived in the sixth-seventh century for example, calls menstrual blood as 'a woman's superfluous blood',[52] which, according to him, was called as 'muliebria' or 'womanlies', since, women alone are 'menstruating animals'.[53] He writes that when there is contact with such menstrual blood, 'crops do not germinate, new wines go sour, grasses die, trees lose their fruit, iron is corrupted by rust, air and copper are blackened; which should dogs eat of it, they are made rabid. Even bituminous glue, which is dissolved neither by iron norby [strong] waters, polluted by this gore, falls apart by itself'.[54] Isidore's primary concern in his writings about women was the promotion of celibacy and he discouraged conjugal desire even among married couples, since he saw sexuality as a 'by-product of original sin'.[55]

The re-introduction of the Aristotelian natural philosophy in the middle ages further 'exacerbated'[56] the prevalent notions about dangers of menstruation, especially of sexual union with menstruating women. To illustrate this, Koren quotes one cannon lawyer Rufinas, who in the twelfth century, appealed to the then newly discovered classical works on medicine to justify his support for menstrual separation. He declared in his *Summa Decretorum* thus: 'That blood is so execrable and impure, as already Julius Solinus has written in the book about the miracles of the world, that through its contacts fruits do not mature, plants wither, the grass dies, the trees lose their fruits, the air becomes dark, if dogs eat it they are afflicted with rabies. . . And intercourse at the time of the monthly period is very risky. Not only because of the uncleanness of the blood has the desire to be restrained from contacting a menstruating woman: from such an intercourse a spoiled fetus could be born.'[57] Similarly, Robert of Flamborough in his manual for priests titled *Liber Peonitentialis* (the Book of Penance), written in 1210, notes: 'Each month the heavy and torpid bodies of women are lightened by the flowing of unclean blood. And if a man has intercourse with a woman at this time, those conceived by this union are said to carry the vice of the seed with them, and so lepers and those afflicted with elephantiasis are born from this conception, and soundness degenerates, having been by the enormity of limbs and the baseness in the bodies of them'[58] and adds that even married couple must observe menstrual separation. Such views were prevalent even till the 19th century and in 1878, we find the *British Medical Journal* claiming how menstruating women would cause bacon to putrefy.[59]

It is interesting to note that while scholars have rightly pointed out the reintroduction of Greco-Roman philosophy and medicine as the cause of medieval Christian fears about the medical dangers of menstruation, what is often not highlighted is the fact that the concept of miasma was on one hand de-rooted from the Greco-Roman philosophical context, and on the other, it was reformulated to fit into Biblical worldview. While Greco-Roman society was a miasma-katharsis based society, Christian society was a sin-virtue based society. As a result, the notions of Miasma or impurity, which were connected to lack of vitality and the incompetence to enter the sacred space were reformulated to fit into the Biblical concept of Original Sin. We already saw how Isidore, the bishop of Seville, introduced the Greco-Roman elements of Miasma regarding how menstruation affects crops etc. to reinforce his Biblical views about sexuality as a by-product of Original sin. Rabanus of Mainz, who lived in 8th-9th century, further reformulated Isidore's scientific formulation regarding menstruation to connect it to idolatry and errors.[60] Glenda Lewin Hufnagel[61] mentions an interesting discussion on the life-expectancy of women in the medieval Europe, which is very illustrative to understand the reformulation of Greco-Roman ideas to fit into Biblical society. While Aristotle advocated that men had greater life expectancy than women (due to men being the warmer of the two sexes), medieval Europe saw that women on an average lived longer than men. To resolve this discrepancy, St Albertus Magnus, the teacher of St Thomas Aquinas and St Gregory the Great, enunciated two unique suggestions. Magnus explained that 'it was very likely that the Greek sage had been referring not to men and women as they existed in the thirteenth century, but rather as they had been in their perfect natures before the fall'.[62] That is, the Aristotelian view of men having greater life-expectancy refers to an age before the fall of mankind due to Eve's sin and hence, his view did not correspond to the ground reality of medieval Europe. St Gregory the Great, on the other hand, while also connecting menstruation to the Original Sin, explained the increased life expectancy of women as a positive by-product of the women's fall. He notes: '...Eve, and all her female descendants began to menstruate. On the one hand, of course, this was her – and their – curse, God's punishment of our first mother for having gotten the human race into its present sinful predicament, yet on the other, ...in this punishment there was also a secondary benefit...because of [the] menstruation – consequence of the fall though it may be [that] women alone are enabled periodically to purge the poisons from their humours in a monthly effusion of blood... therefore the curse now allows them *per accidens* to live longer than men... Aristotle becomes both right and wrong; and [the] reason is neatly reconciled with revelation, reality with authority is a perfect thirteenth-century synthesis.'[63]

This introduction of such reformulated Greco-Roman ideas about menstruation into medieval Christian society had inimical consequences for Christian women. This is because, the Greco-Roman notions about menstruation, which were a complex culture-specific formulation deeply related to Miasma on the one hand and sacred celebration on the other, became reduced to mere bodily dangers when they were appropriated and digested into Christian society, since Greco-Roman notions were uprooted from their cultural contexts. Then, the reformulation of such uprooted and reductive notions of impurity as bodily dangers by connecting it to the Original Sin and idolatry ultimately resulted in the othering of the Jews and the persecution of women under the pretext of witchcraft.

Menstruation, Idolatry and the 'Othering' of Jews

In her paper 'The Menstruant as "Other" in Medieval Judaism and Christianity',[64] after noting how the Greco-Roman ideas about the medical dangers of menstruation were reintroduced into Christian society in the middle ages, Sharon Faye Koren elaborates on two other significant notions regarding menstruation that became prevalent in the medieval Christian society resulting in a very unsavory consequence. One was the branding of menstruation as idolatry and the other was the usage of menstruation for 'othering' the Jews.

Koren notes that Rabanus of Mainz, the abbot of Fulda and the bishop of Mainz, who lived in the eighth-ninth century was one of the most prominent Christian exegetes who equated menstruation with idolatry by adopting a moralistic interpretation of the Levitical laws of menstruation in contrast to the rational interpretation of the Jewish exegetes or the Cosmic interpretation of the Kabbalists. In his work, *De Rerum Naturis*, Rabanus writes thus: 'By allegory the flow of blood can be understood as the obscenity of idolatry and the pollution of errors. And in this way the time of menstruation is to be understood to be that time in which the entire world was involved in error and idolatry. And it is not permitted to approach a menstruating woman, nor to have intercourse with her; because neither is it permitted to Catholic men to have commerce with the idolatry of pagans or the heresy of heretics.'[65] Thus, for Rabanus, the impurity associated with menstruation was neither miasma as understood by Greco-Romans, nor medical danger as was understood by Isidore. Instead, he enunciated it as an 'internal, spiritual state of being',[66] as a 'symbol of idolatry'.[67] Koren notes that this interpretation later became very popular during the renaissance in the twelfth century CE, when texts like *Glossa Ordinaria*, the medieval commentary on Bible, interprets the Leviticus (20.18) prohibition against sexual intercourse during menstruation as a ruling against the 'whole error of idolatry and sacrifices' and 'the wisdom of the Gentiles'.[68] The *Glossa Ordinaria* further notes how just as the couple who engage in sexual intercourse during menstruation are to be punished by cutting them off from the community, those who engage in idolatry must be punished by killing them amidst people.[69] This equation of menstruation with idolatry, on the one hand, led to further demonisation of the pagans, who have been persecuted throughout Christian history, and on the other hand, led to the demonisation of women as sinners and their further marginalisation in Christian society.

Regarding the othering of the Jews, Koren notes how the Christian exegetes interpreted the Biblical prohibitions as 'alluding to the feminisation of the sinner' with one interpreter interpreting niddah as 'men effeminate by women' and zavah as a 'man who does not reign in his passion'.[70] *Glossa Ordinaria* reinterprets the Biblical story of Rachel and Laban to 'feminise the sinner by attributing an allegorical menstrual flow to Laban'.[71] In the Biblical story, which appears in the *Genesis*, Rachel hides the idols of her father, Laban, by sitting on it, while Laban greedily searches everywhere for it. At a time, when it was the convention for the children to rise up to greet the elders, Rachel excuses herself by saying that she was menstruating. The authors of the *Glossa* praise Rachel for suppressing the idols by sitting on them just as the Christian Church covers 'vice of terrestrial concupiscence' and censures Laban for following the 'uncleanness of avarice as if menstruating'.[72]

Koren notes that this interpretation of Rachel and Laban's story may have been the 'earliest sources for the medieval slander of Jewish male menstruation', since, menstruation was no longer a 'female physiological state, but a potential moral condition of both men and women' and 'Jewish men, often slandered as effeminate, greedy unbelievers, would therefore be the most likely to display it'.[73] This Christian notion of Jewish male menstruation did not remain limited to allegorical rhetoric about the moral degradation of the Jews. Instead, it was literalised by conceiving a notion of 'Jewish male flux' excessive flow of blood from the anus of Jewish men – and then rationalising it using theology and humoral science.[74] Koren observes: 'Medieval scientists noted that Jews, like women, were by nature pale because they suffered from an excess of cold and wet humors. These excess humors settled in the lower abdomen and were transformed into blood. In order to maintain homeostasis, Jewish men purged themselves of this excess blood through hemorrhoidal bleeding. In medieval medicine, this Jewish anal flux was analogous to menstruation; both were the body's means of expelling noxious humors.'[75]

This notion of the Jewish male flux, which became widely prevalent across Christian societies, had dire consequences on Jewish communities. Since Christians began to believe that Jews killed Christians, as that was the only way they could overcome their blood flux, the Jewish community was persecuted and banished from many Christian states. Koren notes: The belief that Jews suffered from moral impurity physically manifest as the Jewish male flux had powerful consequences for Jewish communities throughout Ashkenaz. The Fourth Lateran Council confined Jews to their homes during the Holy Week in order to protect Christian children from bloodthirsty Jews. In 1235, Christian religious leaders cited the medicinal value of Christian blood as proof for the blood libel at Fulda. Jews were expelled from Thuringia in 1400 because of 'their need for human blood to heal a wound that flowed in them perpetually'. And in Tyrnau in 1494, twelve Jewish men and two women were accused of killing a Christian child. They were forced to confess that 'men and women among them suffer equally from menstruation... The blood of a Christian is the specific medicine for it, when drunk'. All fourteen were burned.[76]

Menstruation, Witchcraft and Persecution of Women

One of the most horrifying aspects of Christian history was the persecution of women under the pretext of witchcraft in early modern Europe. Between 1450 and 1750, for three hundred years, both Christian and secular authorities across Europe employed enormous resources to identify and execute witches.[77] Tens of thousands of people perished under witchcraft persecution. Glenda Lewin Hufnagel notes: 'Estimates of the actual numbers of European women killed varies from scholar to scholar with the range from a high of nine million (Armstrong & Pettigrew, 1993) to approximately 50,000 (Briggs, 2007, 1996a, 1996b; Behringer, 2004; Canwell & Sutherland, 2007: Gaskill, 2005; Oldridge, 2008; Pavlac, 2009; Robisheaux, 2009; Roper, 2004;), with recorded attributions to 26,000 in Germany, 10,000 in France, 1,000 in England and four in Ireland. Persecution was repeated on a small scale in 1692 in the Massachusetts Bay Colony (Baker, 2007; Demos, 2008; Godbeer, 2005; Hill, 2002; LeBeau, 2009; LePlante, 2008; Norton, 2002; Roach, 2002, 1996; Roper, 2004; Rosenthal & Adams, 2009).'[78] Among the victims, women constituted around 80% of those who were accused of witchcraft and 85% of those who were executed for it.[79] The persecutions were so severe that 'after the Church executed individuals accused of practising witchcraft in many German villages, the female population was drastically reduced', with two villages in 1585 being left with only one female inhabitant after the witch-trials.[80] Further, both witch-hunters as well as the informers were paid handsomely.[81]

The horror of this persecution has been graphically described by Miriam Simos in *The Spiral Dance: A Rebirth of the Ancient Religion of the Great Goddess*. She writes: 'The terror was indescribable. Once denounced, by anyone from a spiteful neighbour to a fretful child, a suspected witch was arrested suddenly, without warning, and not allowed to return home again. She was considered guilty until proven innocent. Common practice was to strip the suspect naked, shave her completely in hopes of finding the devil's "marks", which might be moles or freckles...In England, "legal torture" was not allowed, but suspects were deprived of sleep and subjected to slow starvation, before hanging. On the continent, every imaginable atrocity was practiced – the rack, the thumbscrew, "boots" that broke the bones in the legs, vicious beatings – the full roster of the inquisition's horrors...The accused were tortured until they signed confessions prepared by the inquisitors....Most cruelly, they were tortured until they named others, until a full coven quota of thirteen were taken. Recalcitrant suspects, who maintained their innocence, were burned alive.'[82]

At the heart of these witchhunts were the medieval Christian blood beliefs, especially those regarding menstruation. Francesca Matteoni notes that 'theories regarding the body played an important part in the complex of witchcraft beliefs which nourished the period of the trials and persecutions in Europe'.[83] Both the commoners and the educated perceived the witch-body as 'the evidence of a dangerous power' with blood being considered 'the means of exchange between a supernatural force and the physical world'.[84] Matteoni further notes that blood was at the center of 'a discrimination process, which catalysed religious and social conflicts, individuating the ideal enemy in different kinds of social groups: the Jews and then women, old or poor people, categories which were ascribed to the witch-stereotype'.[85] It was in this context that menstruation was used as a 'vehicle for blaming women for all that was believed to be evil in the world'.[86]

The Western Christian Church, which introduced the reformulated Greco-Roman ideas of menstruation into Christian society used these reformulated ideas, especially those from Pliny etc. to disparage women. Shuttle and Redgrove, who made a comparative study of folklore descriptions of witches and Pliny's description of menstruating women, found many similarities between them, especially in how both of them were believed to have the power to cause sickness in cattle or cause destruction of crops through rains or hailstorms.[87] They note that the image of the witch is an 'image of the transforming and changing menstrual cycle; it occurs all over the world because women occur all over the world', and these images are 'very, very old in human history because menstruation is as old as Eve; it is thought to be evil because men fear the powers and abilities of women'.[88] This equation of menstruation to witchcraft contributed to further vilification of women as an embodiment of sin in medieval Europe. As Monica Sjoo and Mor Barbara observe, such beliefs led to 'the myth of "feminine evil" which dominated the Western world for over two thousand years, led logically to the religiously targeted murder of women as witches during the Great Inquisition of Europe'.[89]

It is important to note that the notion of witches or witchcraft as such was not unique to medieval Europe, but instead can be found across almost all cultures and traditions across the world. But, it was the persecution of those believed to have practised witchcraft which was a new development during the late medieval period. As Matteoni observes: The witch itself was not an original invention of the early modern period. Witches or sorcerers accused of maleficium, that is the capacity to harm other individuals by supernatural means, had operated in the known world since antiquity, but the presence of such people did not imply their persecution. It is during the late medieval period, that the witch started to be seen as the personification of the theological evil, becoming not just a single malevolent person, but the member of a sect of devil worshippers, which through and beyond the physical body of society, attempted to destroy its spiritual order. Even if the Catholic Church was primarily responsible for creating the diabolic witch, consequently both Catholics and Protestants fought witches in the attempt to Christianise Europe, and especially its rural people, among whom magic and ancient pagan beliefs still diffused and mingled with Christiani deas.[90]

Thus, in his *The Satanizing of Women,* Savramis rightly calls the medieval witchhunters 'representatives of a theology that satanises sexuality as such, equates women with sexuality, and seeks to destroy the female sex in order to eliminate "wicked" sexuality in favour of a man-ruled Christian world'.[91]

Situation in India

Christianity is the third dominant religion in India with 28 million followers constituting around 2.3 per cent of the population according to the 2011 census. Large denominations of Christians are present (many, for several centuries) across the country.

Like Christian communities elsewhere, Indian Christians also associate some notion of sin and pollution with menstruation. Even today, there are young girls who associate menstruation with God's curse.[92] Christian women in India, like their counterparts in the rest of the world, have historically avoided going to Church or receiving communion during menstruation.

Writing about the notions of pollution prevalent among Christian communities in India, Surinder S Jodhka notes: Practices relating to birth, menstrual and death pollution have been recorded among the Syrian Christians of Kerala in the last century, but they are much rarer today. Tamil Nadu Christians, both rural and urban, also appear to have retained such ideas, if with modifications. Among Chennai Protestants, for instance, many women are still reluctant to enter a church or, in particular, to receive communion when they are menstruating. However, they are not segregated during menstruation and do not avoid cooking. Some traces of pollution practices also appear to exist among Christians in central India.[93]

It must be pointed out, though, that a large number of Christian women have given up many of these practices as can be seen from a 2016 study wherein none of the seventeen Christian girls interviewed for the study practised any kind of taboo or restriction .[94] Nevertheless, a significant section of the Christian population in India continues to adhere to its religious notions and the accompanied practices on menstruation, much like its counterparts in other religious traditions, as can be seen from numerous studies on the issue.[95]

Both, Christianity and Judaism have associated menstruation with Eve's sin and the fall of women from grace. Though, during early Christianity, Baptism was posited as an alternative to Niddah of the Jews and hence was used to define Christianity as separate from Judaism, the perception of menstruation as dangerous has prevailed throughout the history of Christianity. This notion of menstruation as dangerous has led to the observance of certain taboos including avoidance of sexual intercourse and non-eligibility to receive communion during the monthly periods.

During the middle ages, the negative attitudes towards menstruation became intensified, after the Greco-Roman notions of menstruation, including their medical notions were reformulated and reintroduced into Christian society. The notions of miasma associated with menstruation in the Greco-Roman society became reformulated to fit into the Biblical concept of Original Sin. As a result, menstruation became associated with idolatry and sin and was used for othering and persecuting all those who were considered menstruating: heretics, Jews and women accused of witchcraft.

Islam

Islam is another monotheistic Abrahamic religion built around the core beliefs that there is only one God called Allah and Muhammad is His prophet and messenger to the people. Though Islam traces its roots to Judaism and Christianity, and recognises Adam, Abraham, Moses and Jesus as messengers of God, Prophet Mohammad is held as the final messenger, the 'seal of prophesy',[1] whose teachings supersede all other previous teachings. Islam is thus held by believers as the 'perfection of the religion',[2] which was first revealed to Abraham.

Historically, Islam was founded by Muhammad during the early seventh century in Mecca and was later spread across Arabia and beyond by the Caliphate. Owing to its common origins in Abrahamic monotheism, Islam derives many elements of its worldview from Christianity and Judaism, while also defining its separate identity by 'othering' both Christianity and Judaism. Christians and Jews, though considered as the People of the Book and hence, better than pagans, idolaters and unbelievers; they are still held as having strayed from God's true faith, a status which is allotted only to Islam.

Nevertheless, the Islamic views on menstruation heavily borrow from Judaism and Christianity, including their notions of impurity and original sin.

Menstruation and Impurity

The notions of purity and impurity are vital elements of Islam, which consider menstruating women as 'vulnerable, weakened, and polluted'.[3] The Muslim community uses a number of terms to refer to menstruation like *Dam al Haid* (a combination of blood, the place and the time), *A'ad al-Shariah* (habit of the month), *Haq Shar* (right of the month) and *Ana Manakish* (I am not clean).[4] Of these terms, the last one, *Ana Manakish*, which is a dialectical Moroccan Arabic phrase, is especially significant since, 'I am not clean' is how women communicate with their friends that they are undergoing monthly menses.[5] Thus, we can see that menstruation as impurity is deeply ingrained even in the vocabulary itself.

Purity and Impurity, which are called '*Tahara*' and '*Najasa*' are important aspects of Islamic life. The Quran (2.222) itself notes that Allah 'loves those who keep themselve spure and clean'.[6] Water is among the prominent tools used for purification. Islam prescribes two kinds of ablution rituals for purification: *Wudu* and *Ghusl*. Wudu is an obligatory component of daily Islamic prayer, which is to be carried out before each of the five daily prayers. Ghusl, on the other hand, is a full ablution, a lengthier purification process, which is performed during special occasions. Nitzan Ziv notes that there are three such special occasions: 1) after a new Muslim takes shahada (witnessing prayer) for the first time 2) after sexual intercourse where there has been discharge of semen or sexual fluids 3) after a woman completes her menstrual cycle.[7] He further notes: 'In the Qur'an there are two types of blood that are distinguished from regular blood, which require a full ablution; dam al haid and dam al nifas, menstrual and the post-natal bleeding. These categories of blood are considered impure, in contrast to the blood that may emerge from other parts of the body resulting from a cut or nosebleed, for example.'[8]

Thus, menstruation was clearly considered an impure condition, with menstrual bleeding being 'both sexual and dirty, [and] unacceptable while performing religious duties'.[9] As a result, Islamic texts and different schools of Islamic law have articulated various restrictions for women to follow during menstruation.

M Guterman et al. observe: 'There are two main prohibitions placed upon the menstruating woman. First, she may not enter any shrine or mosque. In fact, she may not pray or fast during Ramadan while she is menstruating. She may not touch the Qur'anic codex or even recite its contents. Secondly, she is not allowed to have sexual intercourse for seven full days (beginning when the bleeding starts). She is "exempted" from rituals such as daily prayers and fasting, although she is not given the option of performing these rituals, even if she wants to.'[10] The Hanafi School of Islamic Law recognises eight such prohibited activities. They are: Alaat (ritual prayer), Fasting (obligatory or otherwise), Recitation of even a single verse of the Holy Quran, Touching Quran, Entering the Masjid, Circumambulation (awaaf) of the Holy Kaaba, Sexual intercourse, and Sexual enjoyment from the navel to below the knees of a menstruating woman.[11] Other schools, more or less, follow the same list.

Prohibition on fasting implies that Muslim women cannot fast even during Ramadan, on days when they are having the monthly menses, and they have to instead make up later. On the other hand, the prohibition of entry into Masjids does not imply a prohibition regarding entering the 'musalla' or temporary prayer room. Menstruating women can enter prayer rooms, which are not Masjids.[12] Though there is a prohibition on reciting even a single verse of the Quran, they can read out a few words or a half verse if needed.[13]

Regarding sexual intercourse, the prohibition is present in the Quran itself. Verse 2.222 says: 'They ask thee concerning women's courses. Say: They are a hurt and a pollution: So keep away from women in their courses, and do not approach them until they are clean. But when they have purified themselves, ye may approach them in any manner, time, or place ordained for you by Allah. For Allah loves those who turn to Him constantly and He loves those who keep themselves pure and clean.'[14] This is perhaps the only prohibition directly mentioned in the Quran itself, while others are derived from Hadiths or mandated by Islamic law. It is interesting to note that prohibition of sexual intercourse does not imply prohibition of any interaction between the husband and wife. As the eighth prohibited activity mentioned before shows, only sexual enjoyment below the navel is prohibited. One of the Hadiths, belonging to the Maliki school of thought, says: 'Aisha, wife of the Prophet (may peace be upon him), reported: I used to comb the hair of the head of Allah's Messenger (may peace be upon him) while menstruating.'[15] Another Hadith reports that when Mohammad's wife Aisha suddenly started bleeding during the night, he said: 'Put on a skirt and come and lie down there again.'[16] Thus, it is clear that only sexual enjoyment, including intercourse below the navel, is prohibited for menstruating women. And the reason for such a prohibition is clear from the Quranic verse: impurity and harm. It is for this reason that a full-fledged ritual bath is suggested at the end of menstruation, which is considered to last a maximum of ten days. This is suggested for the purification of the menstruant. Only after thus ritually cleansed is the Muslim woman allowed to resume her prayers, fast, or enter a mosque.

Menstruation and Coming of Age

Despite menstruation being associated with impurity, menarche or the on-set of menstruation itself is considered a very crucial event in a Muslim woman's life. While menarche marks the coming of age in almost all cultures and societies, in Islamic society, it also marks that the girl is now 'mature enough to assume the duties expected of every practising Muslim'.[17] That is, menarche acts as a formal entry into Islamic life and she will now be expected to pray five times a day and fast during

Ramadan, among other Islamic duties. Interestingly, Muslim boys also begin to pray and fast only after they have had their first emission of semen.[18] Thus, menarche has a positive role in the life of a Muslim woman.

Menstruation and the 'fall of Eve' in Islamic texts

Much like Christianity and Judaism, Islamic tradition, especially post-Quranic traditions have associated menstruation with the fall of Eve and have reinterpreted the concept of impurity in terms of sin and fall. While in the Quranic account of Adam and Eve, they are consistently addressed as a couple, with God warning them about the tree, Satan approaching both of them together and then their eating of the forbidden fruit together resulting in their fall; the post-Quranic texts drastically change the narrative by emphasising the role of Eve and connecting it to the fall of women as a whole.

DA Spellberg notes, 'The themes that feature Eve in these earliest hadith collections reveal aspects of her depiction that are not present in the Quran. They include her name, the precedent she set in spousal deceit, her creation from a rib, ritual purity, and motherhood'.[19] Al-Bukhari, the celebrated author of the hadith collection known as *Sahih al-Bukhari*, for example, writes about Eve in his section called 'al-anbiya' (the prophets): 'Were it not for Hawwa (Eve), the female would not deceive her husband.'[20] Al-Bukhari, thus, equates Eve's behavior with all women, and considers her deception of the husband as being inherent to all females. Spellberg rightly asks: 'Yet where in the Qur'an did Eve deceive Adam? Indeed, where in the Quran is she named 'Hawwa'/Eve at all? Implicit in this account is an already assimilated biography of the first woman. Both of the oral relaters, the codifier, and the reader assumedly already knew that Adam's wife was named Eve, and that she was the first transgressor in the Fall, a clear borrowing from pre-Islamicmaterials, specifically Genesis 3:20 and 3:13, now cast in the Prophet's words.'[21] Thus, the post-Quranic traditions heavily borrowed from the Judeo-Christian tradition, and in doing so, they borrowed the reformulated narrative of purity/impurity, which, as we saw under the section on Christianity, was delinked from the Greco-Roman miasma and was instead interpreted using Eve's fall and the Original Sin.

Detailed information about the prevalent Islamic understanding of Eve in the late ninth and early tenth centuries is available in the tenth century historian and exegete al-Tabari's multi-volume *Ta'rikh al-Rusul wa'l-Muluk* (History of the Prophets and Kings). Spellberg summarises al-Tabari's account of the fall of Adam and Eve, thus:

> We learn from al-Tabari that Adam refuses to eat of the tree that Allah had forbidden them, but his resolve is weakened by his wife...Hawwa's determination to eat of the tree is, in al-Tabari, a direct result of her dealing with Iblis, the fallen angel whose sin of pride conveys on him the alias al-Shaytan (Satan). Eve cannot take an active role in the human expulsion from paradise without linkage to Satan. Thus, both the first woman and Satan work together to influence Adam, who, increasingly, demonstrates marked passivity before the suggestions of his mate. Iblis entered into the belly of the snake, the only animal who would allow herself to be used as a disguise for Satan's re-entry into the Garden...Once inside his snake accomplice and the Garden, Iblis picks the fruit of the forbidden tree. Then he describes the delights of the fruit to Hawwa. Whereupon, 'Eve took and ate some of it. Then she went with it to Adam.' Hawwa's words to Adam mimic those of Iblis to her. Adam takes the fruit from his mate and eats. The snake/Satan-woman-man trajectory of Genesis 3:4-733 is here entered into the Islamic account of the Fall....The trajectory of blame in Genesis 3:12-14, implicitly alluded to in al-Bukhari's 9th-century hadith, is here both affixed and detailed within Islamic history.[22]

Spellberg further observes: Al-Tabari's account explains the origin of menstruation in terms of sacred biology as a divine punishment meted out to Eve for her role in the corruption of Adam. The expulsion from paradise serves to define and condemn female biology forever after. The Islamic Eve is condemned by Allah "to bleed once every month – as she caused this tree to bleed".[23]

While noting the Prophet's instructions in his collection of Hadiths, Ibn Maja, who belonged to the ninth century quotes the famed Islamic Jurist Al-Shafi, 'I, who was approached by some Muslims for an explanation of one of the instructions of the Prophet regarding ritual purity. In answer to their question, Al-Shafi said, "I enunciated about the link between ritual purity and Adam and Eve and stated that while Adam was 'made from clay and water', female infants, who are descendants of Eve are composed of 'flesh and blood'".[24] Writing about the far reaching but negative consequences of such a comparison, Spellberg observes: Eve's placement in a section dedicated to ritual purity seems to signal implicitly that women are born ritually unclean and that they are made of different substances than men. Blood may also signal menses, which will indeed eventually render the female infant ritually impure in Islamic practice on a monthly basis and link her to the physiological punishments meted out to Eve in post-Quranic sources. Once again, Eve provides the impetus for the leap from the specific to the general indictment of all women, enforcing key differences in biology and gender definition.[25]

Spellberg notes that the divine punishment for the sin of Eve was not limited to physical functions, but Allah also diminished 'her mental capacity and character because of her role in the Fall'.[26] Thus, the post-Quranic Islamic traditions use the fall of Eve and the resulting menstruation as a reason to sideline women by considering them 'foolish'. It is no wonder then we hear Al-Tabari writing thus: If it were not for the misfortune which befell Eve, women on Earth would not menstruate and they would be good-natured and would have easy pregnancies and births.'[27]

Ghusl, Henna & Jinns

We already saw how menstruating women were expected to undergo an elaborate purificatory ritual called Ghusl at the end of their monthly bleeding. One important aspect of this purification is the application of henna. Catherine Cartwright Jones notes that henna was frequently part of post-menstrual Ghusl, the purification bath, applied in patterns and techniques varying according to local taste.[28]

Henna in the Semetic language refers to the plant, 'Lawsonia Inermis' as well as to the paste made out of its leaves, which is then used to create body art.[29] Muslim women, especially in North Africa and Middle East, applied henna to their nails, hands, feet and hair, during Hamam, the traditional public bath taken at the end of monthly menses.[30] During Hamam, women bathed in running water and their body was thoroughly scrubbed. The hair, feet, and fingertips were applied with henna. The hair in the pubic region was also removed and henna was applied to the vulva extending it up to the navel.[31]

Though the practice of applying Henna predates Islam, henna application became an integral part of Islamic life, with Prophet Muhammad himself reportedly supporting the practice. The Prophet is said to have 'dyed his beard with henna and applied henna to cuts and scratches'.[32] According to Sunan Abu Dawud, Muhammad said to a woman 'if you were a woman, you would make a difference to your nails, meaning with henna'.[33]

Stressing on the significance of Henna application in a Muslim woman's life in the context of menstruation, Catherine Cartwright Jones writes: When a woman marks her hands and feet with henna, she can be identified as pure, from a distance; the stains last for about three weeks, the duration of her sexual availability prior to her next menstrual cycle, or pregnancy. Henna stains communicate that she is pure, worthy of human and supernatural approval, and an appropriate sexual partner. The fresh dark henna stains denote her readiness, and worthiness, for sexual intercourse. Since henna stains last about three weeks, the demise of the henna stain is complete about the time of her next menstrual cycle, and she enters menstruation without the mark of sexual availability. Bright, dark henna stains, then are a marker of the sexual, available, pure, woman. Absence of henna stain is the mark of a woman who is menstruous, or an otherwise inappropriate sexual partner'[34]

Thus, the use of Henna during Ghusl not only served the purpose of purification, but also served the purpose of displaying to others, especially to the husband that she is pure and available for sexual intimacy. More importantly, Henna application also fulfills a supernatural purpose.

Catherine Cartwright Jones writes:

> Islamic menstrual taboos were based on a concept of pollution and vulnerability versus purity and strength. Menstruating women were vulnerable to jinn and the Evil Eye, irresistibly drawn to blood, particularly reproductive blood. These evil forces caused fitna, or disorder, which manifested as disease, inappropriate conduct, and tragedy. Henna contained baraka, or blessedness, which protected the wearer from misfortune. Women used henna and protective patterns drawn with henna to purify their bodies, to preserve the health of their skin and hair, and to protect their souls and minds from attack by malevolent spirits. Women negotiated their menstrual and reproductive vulnerability through henna, wearing visible symbols to show that they were pure, strong, in good spiritual standing, as well as in emotional and physical health.[35]

She further adds that 'Ghusl and henna do not only protect the person from unpleasant smells, excreta and residue; ritual cleanliness protects the person from the malevolent sprits attracted to filth and menstrual blood, and from the damage caused by these spirits, Jinn'.[36]

According to Islam, Jinns are an order of spirits created from smokeless fire, who are lower than angels. The malevolent ones among them are attracted to urine, feces, foul odors, semen and blood. They were especially attracted to genital blood from menstruation, childbirth, miscarriage, or circumcision. Hence, cleanliness was crucial in keeping them at bay.[37] It was also believed that 'if [a] Jinn attacked a woman during her menstrual period, she may become infertile, argue with her husband, have severe headaches, depression, and lose her husband's affection, even become ill or die'.[38] Similarly, the 'Evil Eye was often considered the cause of lost fertility, lost love, lost health'[39] as well. Hence, to wash off these Jinns and Evil Eyes, Muslim women are expected to purify themselves using Ghusl and the application of Henna patterns at the end of their monthly periods. The most widely prevalent patterns drawn for protection are diamonds and stars, with the diamond shapes having a dot at the center being considered most potent against the effects of Evil Eye.

Situation in India

The practice of menstruation restrictions and allied observations is widely prevalent among Indian Muslims. Based on her discussions with Muslim women in India, Aru Bhartiya observes: From what I gathered after interviewing a few people is, that in Islam, menstruating women aren't supposed to touch the Quran, enter the mosque, offer the ritual prayer or have sex with her husband for seven full days. The woman is exempted from rituals such as daily prayers and fasting, although she is not given the option of performing these rituals, even if she wants to.[40]

A 2015 study involving 100 Muslim adolescent girls and 50 mothers conducted in Banihal, Jammu and Kashmir by Sarika Manhas and Rabia Salem revealed that 'All of them faced restrictions related to dietary intake whereby they were prohibited for taking some specific foods during their monthly menstrual cycle. All of them also faced prohibitions related to religious activities such as praying, reading Quran, fasting, going to shrine (dargah). Both the adolescent girls as well as their mothers reported facing religious restrictions during their monthly period once they attain menarche. 74% of sample females faced restrictions related to food during menstruation. Certain specific physical activities were also tabooed and hence the menstruating women couldn't participate in those activities. The sample Muslim females also faced restrictions related to their physical hygiene, and further, these restrictions were followed more by the mothers than the girls'.[41]

Similarly, a study conducted by Suneela Garg, Nandini Sharma and Ragini Sahay in an urban slum in Delhi notes: 'The avoidance of bathing during menstruation is commonly observed among Muslims in the study area whereas Hindus do not practise this. Muslims believe that a bath with cold water during menstruation leads to swelling of the fallopian tubes (nalon) and abdominal pain.'[42] They further added that religious practices like visiting holy places or touching holy texts were avoided by Muslim women for their study area.[43]

Thus, we can see that Muslim women in India like their counterparts in the rest of the world strictly practise various menstrual restrictions, especially those related to religious activities.

To summarise, Islam locates itself in the Semetic tradition. Hence, it inherits the Judeo-Christian view on Menstruation, which connects it to the original sin and the fall of Eve. Menstruating women are considered vulnerable and impure and are expected to undertake an elaborate purificatory bath called Ghusl at the end of menstruation. One important aspect of Ghusl is the application of Henna dye on fingertips, hands and feet, which not only serves to announce the purity status of Muslim women, but also is believed to keep away the influences of malevolent Jinns and the effects of the Evil Eye. While menarche denotes the coming of age of Muslim girls, wherein they become eligible to practise religious duties like praying five times or fasting during Ramadan, they are prohibited from indulging in these duties during their monthly menses. Sexual abstinence is likewise expected of menstruants.

Comparison with Hindu Tradition

In the previous sections, we reviewed various menstruation perceptions and practices prevalent among Abrahamic religions of Judaism, Christianity and Islam. In this section, let us do a comparative analysis of perceptions and practices of these religions with those of Sanatana Dharma aka Hinduism.

When we compare Judaism with Hinduism, we find many parallels regarding their menstrual notions and practices. The most striking of them is the association of impurity with menstruation, the lifestyle regimen that women are expected to inculcate during their periods and the element of 'curse' which forms a central part in the etiological accounts behind these practices. Like Hindu women, Jewish women are also expected to avoid sexual intercourse during menstruation; like Hindu women, even Jewish women are believed to have become pure after ritual bathing of Mikveh at the end of menstruation; and similar to Hindu life-regimen for menstruating women in the form of Rajaswala Paricharya, even Jewish women have to adhere to the laws of Niddah. Yet, a closer examination of these tenets reveals very interesting and significant differences in how they have been formulated and the underlying principles governing them.

Consider the notion of impurity, for example. The Hindu understanding of Ashaucha is governed by a deep understanding of human individuality at physical, vital and mental sheaths and it is the excess of Rajasic energy and the imbalance in these layers of individuality which makes menstruating women enter a temporary period of ritual impurity. This in turn makes her ineligible for sacred activities, sexual intercourse, or physical contact with others. On the other hand, the Jewish laws of Niddah are exclusively focused on sexual abstinence between husband and wife and derive from the Leviticus laws related to sexual abstinence. Though termed 'impurity', the Niddah laws are not related to ritual impurity sections of the Levictus, which have in any case become inapplicable in the post-Temple scenario, as we saw in detail under the section on Judaism. Therefore, while in the Hindu context, menstrual impurity implies a condition of heightened Rajas and the ineligibility for certain actions like sacred activities, household works and sexual intercourse, menstrual impurity in the Jewish context simply means 'non-availability' for sexual union and does not directly refer to any ritual impurity.

Nevertheless, the Chassidic traditions of Judaism define menstrual impurity in terms of the 'absence of holiness' and connect it to death in the form of the non-fertilisation of the egg. An interesting parallel here can be seen in how even in Hinduism, one of the reasons behind menstruating women being in Ashaucha is the non-fertilisation of the egg, which incurs 1/3rd Brahmahatya. Though menstruation is not considered 'absence of holiness' in Hinduism and on the contrary, it is considered 'pure' and 'sacred' in certain Tantrika traditions, both Hinduism and Judaism in general, recognise the principle of purification ingrained in the process of menstruation. For the mystic traditions of Judaism, menstruation is a preparation for greater ascension towards God, while for Hindu traditions, menstruation is a natural purification process, which frees women from not only bodily toxins and excess energies, but also frees them from many Adharmas (unrighteous actions), thus taking them close to the divine and to liberation.

Now, coming to the respective etiological accounts behind their beliefs and practices. We find that both use the principle of 'curse' or 'punishment' to convey their teachings, and in both cases, menstruation is supposed to act as a process of purification, yet the very content of the respective etiological accounts, as well as its implication, is prominently different. In the Hindu etiological account, as we have seen before, it is Lord Indra who commits the Adharmic act of Brahmahatya and becomes associated with its guilt. Out of compassion, women help Indra by taking $1/3^{rd}$ magnitude of his Adharma upon themselves. In the Jeweish etiological account, on the other hand, it is Eve, the first woman who committed the sin. Often called the First Sin, Eve not only disobeyed God's command, but also made Adam, the first man, disobey God, leading to their expulsion from the Garden of Eden, which brought death into human life. Therefore, God punished her with a commandment having to do with blood i.e. menstruation, and the prohibition of sexual intercourse during menstruation is a woman's expiation for Eve's sin. Though both stories contain the element of punishment and expiation, in the case of Judaism, it is women who are portrayed guilty, while in the case of Hinduism, women only take upon the Indra's guilt willingly and out of compassion. While the former condemns women as sinners, which would later lead to the severe oppression of women in medieval Christianity, which also shares the belief in this etiological account, the latter elevates women to the position of divinity. In any case, the respective etiological accounts play an important role in these two systems framing their menstrual laws. Just as the Story of Indra informs us of the Hindu association of the notions of impurity, austerity, purification and celebration with menstruation, the Story of Eve informs us of the Jewish association of menstruation with the 'absence of holiness', since each month, women are considered to enter the state of sin that they inherited from Eve. The difference in life-style regimens prescribed for menstruating women also owes to this etiological difference. While abstinence from sexual intimacy alone is the most important tenet of the Jewish laws of Niddah, with other observances like not cooking for husband being a derivative of this sexual abstinence, the Hindu Rajaswala Paricharya takes into account a number of principles like Ashaucha, austerity, purification, rest, and the health of the woman into consideration.

Another prominent element common to both religious systems is the association of the Divine Feminine with menstruation. While Hinduism associates a number of female Goddesses with menstruation and with deities themselves menstruating as well, even Judaism, especially the Hassidic traditions, despite being monotheistic, associate the feminine Shechinah with the moon and menstruation. Though both believe that human sexual union is a reflection of divine union (of Shiva-Shakti in the Hindu case and of Tiferet-Shechinah in the Jewish case) and human menstruation is a reflection of the Divine Goddess' menstruation, the Chassidic tradition connects it into Shechinah coming under the influence of the demonic Other Side as the cause of menstruation, while Hindu tradition celebrates the Divine as well as human menstruation as a celebration of nature and cosmic order (Rta).

Now, coming to Christianity and Islam, since both locate themselves in the Semetic tradition, they inherit the Abrahamic view on Menstruation, which connects it to the original sin and the fall of Eve. Both Christianity and Islam derive notions of purity-impurity from Greco-Roman civilisation, but reformulate them to fit into Biblical concept of Original Sin. As a result, what was connected to vitality and incompetence in Greco-Roman as well as in Hindu tradition becomes reformulated into virtue-sin categories. Thus, while both Christians and Muslims observe many menstruation practices similar to Hinduism, like Christian women not undertaking communion or Muslim women not fasting or praying during menstruation, the underlying principle which guides these practices is fundamentally different from those observed in Hinduism or in other non-Abrahamic traditions like the Greco-Roman. As we saw in the earlier sections, this reformulation of the Greco-Roman views of menstruation into a biblical categories has resulted in Christianity committing great horrors upon women in the form of witchcraft persecution in the Middle ages, or Islam sidelining women by considering them to be of diminished mental capacity. Such othering of women on the account of menstruation is almost absent in non-Abrahamic traditions, including Hinduism. Though, some modern academics have tried to read negatively the association of menstruation with the notion of impurity in Hinduism, most such views do not have a factual basis and are instead an outcome of pre-conceived bias and an ignorance about the nuanced definition of the category of Ashaucha. In any case, there is no evidence in Hindu history, which is comparable to witch burning in Christianity or the severe restrictions placed on women in Islam. Instead, we have enormous evidence regarding the celebration of menstruation among different Hindu communities. Coming to celebration, while neither Christianity nor Islam associates any sacredness or feminine divinity with menstruation (Judaism at least associates a feminine divinity with menstruation), nevertheless, menarche is considered very important as it represents the transition into adulthood. This is especially true among Muslims, who consider menarche as a sign of the girl' smaturity, enough for her to assume the duties expected of every practising Muslim. This notion is very similar to traditional Hindu society, wherein menarche marked the transition of a girl into adulthood wherein she becomes eligible for shouldering the duties of Grihasta-Ashrama (Stage of householder).

Thus, we can see that the Judeo-Christian treatment (including Islamic) of menstruation is fundamentally different from the Non-Abrahamic traditions. Though all of them subscribe to the categories of purity-impurity and all of them do observe many menstrual restrictions, which are similar to practices observed in Hinduism or the Greco-Roman tradition, the foundational principles governing these practices as well as the very definition of purity-impurity categories is quite different. While Hinduism associates menstruation with a heightened state of rajas in physical, vital and mental sheaths, Abrahamic worldview associates menstruation with Original Sin and Eve's fall from grace. While purity-impurity is understood as a reference to vitality and incompetence in Hinduism, the Abrahamic religions associate it with virtue and sin. There are thus, some prominent irreconcilable elements between the Hindu and the Abrahamic view of menstruation.

Menstruation Notions in Ancient Western Civilisations

Introduction

WHILE INDIA and China were the cradles of civilisation in the East, major civilisations in the West flourished in Greece, Rome, Babylon and Egypt. The ancient Greek Civilisation has been dated to have started around the eighth century BCE in the Archaic Period and is said to have lasted till the end of Antiquity in the sixth century CE. However, it reached its zenith during the Classical period between the fifth and fourth century BCE and the subsequent Ḥellenistic period, which lasted till around the first century BCE. Similarly, the ancient Roman civilisation had its origins around the eighth century BCE in the Italian peninsula and lasted till around the sixth Century CE. After the decline of the Hellenistic period, the Roman and Greek cultural elements merged and made way for a Greco-Roman world till the end of Antiquity.

The Mesopotamian Civilisation originated in Central-Southern Mesopotamia, between the Tigris and the Euphrates rivers. Mesopotamia is one of the oldest cradles of civilisation, which saw the dawn of civilisation around 12,000 BCE. Between 3,500 BCE and 2,000 BCE, the region saw the emergence of two important civilisations: Sumerian and Akkadian. But it was during the reign of the Amorite Dynasty from Babylonia between 2,000 BCE and 1,600 BCE that the Mesopotamian civilisation was transformed into the Babylonian Civilisation and reached its zenith. Similarly, Ancient Egypt saw the dawn of civilisation around 10,000 BCE in the proximity of the River Nile. The Egyptian civilisation reached its zenith during the Pharaonic period, which started around 3,200 BCE, when Upper and Lower Egypt were unified,and lasted till the region was occupied by Alexander III of Macedon in 332 BCE.

Now, let us briefly look at how these ancient civilisations of Greece, Rome, Mesopotamia and Egypt perceived Menstruation.

Greek Civilisation

The ancient Greek civilisation reached its zenith during the Classical age, when it emerged as a source of flourishing knowledge in almost all areas of arts and sciences. We can trace the roots of medicine, biology, philosophy, physics and politics of the western world to this Greek Classical period, which saw the emergence of great thinking minds like Hippocrates, Socrates, Plato, Aristotle and Archimedes, to name a few.

In Classical Greek medicine, menstruation was well recognised as being beneficial to women. In fact, menstruation was perceived as a phenomenon, which differentiated women from men. Lesley Dean-Jones in her book, *Women's bodies in Classical Greek Science* calls menstrual blood the 'linchpin' of both the Hippocratic and the Aristotelian understanding about how women differed from men.[1] She further adds: whether a woman was healthy, diseased, pregnant, or nursing, in classical Greece her body was defined scientifically in terms of blood hydraulics.[2]

Despite this overwhelming recognition of the importance of menstruation in the classical medical texts, it appears that the topic is seldom mentioned in Classical Greek Literature, including the Greek comedies, which have otherwise utilised almost every human biological function as fodder. Even Classical Greek Mythology does not have an explicit account about the origins of menstruation. Lesley Dean-Jones, thus, rightly observes that, 'even the genres of Greek literature that deal quite openly with the most intimate areas of human experience are silent on the subject of menstruation'.[3]

Scholars have expressed varied opinions to account for this lack of any extensive literature regarding menstruation in Classical Greece. Phillip Slater, for example, opines that the Greeks must have perceived menstruation as a normal aspect of women's life, and hence, no evidence of menstruation restrictions could be found imposed on menstruating women.[4] Scholars such as Shuttle and Redgrove, on the other hand, have held that the lack of discussion about menstruation only points to tabooing by 'avoidance and ignorance'.[5] It is also possible that the lack of extensive treatment of menstruation in Greek literature was due to a combination of multiple factors, including those expressed by the above authors. That, menstruation is a unique and a very intimate personal experience exclusive to women, may have also played a role in its scanty reference in literature. As Dean-Jones writes: 'menstruation is one of the exclusively female bodily experience[s], and unlike others, happens to every woman whether she has any contact with a man or not.'[6] This realisation of the intimate nature of the experience may have prevented men from openly writing about or discussing menstruation, except for those in the field of medicine.

Whatever be the exact reason for this lack of extensive literature about menstruation, we have to make do with whatever is available to us for an overview on the Greek perception of menstruation.

General Attitudes towards Menstruation

As already noted, Menstruation was well recognised as that which differentiates women from men in Greek medical literatures. Further, the medical literatures noted that young girls, on an average, start menstruating at the age of fourteen, although there could be variations. Rufus of Ephesus, the ancient Greek Physician, writes: 'those who are of a ruddy complexion and fleshy around the hips and loins reach puberty earlier than those who are pale and flat-hipped.'[7] The variations in the onset age of menstruation was common knowledge. We know this since the legal age of marriage for girls was set at twelve (it was fourteen for boys), two years earlier than the average age of menarche, to account for the variations in the exact age.

In the cultural sphere, the Greeks perceived the onset of menstruation, which marked the phase of female maturation as a process of taming and ripening.[8] Children were perceived as being wild and untamed by nature. As a result, at the onset of menarche, when a young girl would become ready to be married off, she was required to be tamed; and menarche and the associated rituals acted as the taming procedure. For example, Athenian girls participated in the menarche rituals dedicated to goddess Artemis at Brauron, wherein they danced as a bear and were considered tamed after such a dance.[9] Similarly, in Thessaly, young girls imitated fawns in the menarche rituals.[10] Though, the term 'taming' may suggest an element of violence or force, the ritual itself does not appear to have involved any force. Instead, it appears the rituals served as a medium for young girls to understand their future responsibilities and hence, prepare themselves to embrace their adult marital life in a spontaneous manner. Susan Guettel Cole, in her *Domesticating Artemis*, writes: 'These roles were considered to be a preparation for the experience of pregnancy and childbirth.'[11] That the onset of menstruation was largely perceived as a positive natural process can also be gauged by the fact that girls who started bleeding were considered as 'tender ripe fruit', while those who were yet to were considered 'unripe'.[12]

Regarding the perception of menstruation itself, scholars have pointed towards an apparent dichotomy among the ancient Greeks. On the one hand, menstruation was revered as a sacred life-giving force associated with fertility and motherhood and was deeply connected with the worship of Greek goddess Artemis. On the other hand, there was a recognition of the kind of energies associated with menstruation (and menstrual blood), which resulted in unfavorable effects in certain situations. Demokritos, for example, states that if menstruating women were to walk three times on the field, with bare feet and flowing hair, all insects and worms in the field would be destroyed.[13] A similar view was expressed by ancient Roman historian Pliny, who based his research largely on earlier Greek works.

This apparent dichotomy between Menstruation as a sacred process, and Menstruation as being associated with energies having unfavorable effects (i.e. pollution), has often been explained by the scholars as an outcome of the shift in Greek society from matriarchy to patriarchy. In her *The Battle between the Moon and Sun*, Jenny Kien suggests that this dichotomy must be understood in the context of the mythical battle between the Moon and the Sun. The Sun represented the changes in physical properties, whereas the moon was associated with the different phases of life and with the seasonal changes in nature, with both of them being symbols of the Mother Goddess. The moon, in matriarchal cultures with moon-womb religions, was especially perceived as the womb of the Goddess. Additionally, the Moon also had a male aspect, which caused the monthly bleeding in women, by having intercourse with them. Thus, the Moon was associated with both the male and the feminine aspects. Kien suggests that during the mythical battle between the Moon and the Sun, the male aspect of the Moon became dominant, causing the feminine aspect to be slowly discarded. As a result, the connection of the moon with the female womb and menstruation was discarded, resulting in the positive association of menstruation with fertility and motherhood being replaced by taboos that caused the isolation of women. In other words, during the movement of society from matriarchy to patriarchy (wherein the male god gave birth to other gods), the sacredness of menstruation diminished, and it began to be identified with the 'otherness' of women.[14] Echoing a similar view, Glenda Lewin Hufnagel, writes: 'Central to the Classical Greek and Roman concept of menarche and menstruation is the fact that the Greek and Roman period marked a religious paradigm shift from a position in which the powers of female fertility and menstrual blood were revered as sacred, to one of a religious order in which only male gods could give birth to female deities. This shift in religious order coincided with a shift in societal relationships; what had been a matriarchal society was overtaken by patriarchal rule.'[15]

But it is also possible that the perceptions regarding menstruation were not connected to this shift in the social setup from matriarchy to patriarchy. In decentralised and open cultures like Hinduism, both the notions of Ashaucha (impurity) and sacred-celebration have simultaneously existed with regard to menstruation, with both of them being complementary, not contradictory to each other. It is quite possible that Greek paganism, which has many similarities with Hinduism, may have had a similar perception of menstruation as well. This is augmented by the fact that both Hinduism and Classical Greece share similar notions of Shaucha-Ashaucha or Miasma-Katharsis – the concept of purity and pollution. Bharat Gupt writes: 'There is no feature of the Indo-European culture more distinctive than its preoccupation with pollution and purity.'[16] He further adds that the elements of Miasma-Katharsis could be found in the earliest of Greek Muthois (oral traditions), with Miasma associated with impotence (i.e. incompetence/pollution) and Katharsis associated with vitality (competence/strength). To the Greeks, impurity, not profane, was the opposite of Sacred. They associated menstruation, death and child-birth with impurity.[17] They held that to approach the sacred, it was required that impurity be eliminated, and that an object or person is made pure through a process of purification.[18] Therefore, impurity was as much related to purity and hygiene, as it was related to the competency to approach the sacred. Thus, Andreas Bendlin rightly observes:

> Purity and pollution are two religious categories by means of which Greek religion enforces areligious world-view upon the daily lives of ordinary Greeks. Whenever they access the realm of the sacred (which is said to be pure), and when ever they return from a state of pollution to their ordinary lives, religion requires purification of them. Religious scruple about purity limits access to the divine; religious scruple interprets childbirth and death, menstruation, certain foods, or sexual inter course as ritually polluting.[19]

The importance of purity-impurity in Greek society, including with respect to menstruation, can also be seen from epigraphic evidences, citing which, Robin Osborne in his, *Women and Sacrifice in Classical Greece* writes:

> In fourth century Cyrene, in [the]late second-century Delos, and in [the] third-century Lindos, a man's sexual contact with a woman, or contact with a woman giving birth, carried

> impurity; a sacrifice had to be made for [the] newly-wed women at Cyrene. Concern for impurity resulting from contact with other people seems in the Delian case entirely centred on women, with menstruation and miscarriage as the other polluting factors mentioned (along with eating fish and pork), but this is not always the case, for contact with dead relatives of either sex is considered a problem at Lindos and Cyrene.[20]

Thus, Ancient Greece was well aware of the concept of Shaucha and Ashaucha and this could easily explain the dual perception of Menstruation: in its vitality aspect, as a positive life-giving phenomenon, and in its impotence/impurity aspect, as having unfavorable results. It is also possible that the apparent shift in the perception regarding Menstruation, which is today attributed to a shift from Matriarchy to Patriarchy, may simply have been a shift from recognition of only the Katharsis/Shaucha aspect of menstruation to a recognition of both the Katharsis and the Miamsa aspects of menstruation.

Whether there was really a shift in the perception of menstruation or not, whether the assumed shift happened due to social changes, or due to better understanding of the principles underlying menstruation, what is undeniable is that there was a recognition that menstruation was vital in the life of women and that it was both a vitality imparting phenomenon and a Miasma causing phenomenon in Ancient Greece, with the recognition of the latter perhaps being a necessary aspect of the former itself.

Greek Goddess Artemis and Menstruation

Among the deities in the Greek pantheon, it is the goddess Artemis, who was most intimately associated with the lifestages of women. She was particularly associated with young girls, whose transformation she guided, to adulthood, and marriage and motherhood. She was perceived as presiding over all the physical, psychological, social and cultural changes in a woman's life.

In other words, ancient Greeks perceived goddess Artemis as the personification of the force and the energy that brought about various biological transformations in women. Thus, they worshipped her to facilitate these transitions into adulthood, marriage, and motherhood, all the while recognising that offending the goddess would lead to problems associated with menstruation, fertility, and motherhood.

The best example that illustrates this is the bear dance ceremony. Most of the worship of the goddess Artemis through bear dance ceremonies was carried out on the physical margins of the polis. In this particular menarche ceremony, young girls enacted a dance in dedication to the goddess, wherein they imitated 'she-bears'. According to the story associated with this ritual, 'a young girl was supposed to have teased a bear, sacred to Artemis. The bear scratched her in retaliation, and when her brothers responded by killing the bear, the whole community suffered from infectious disease (loimodes nosos). This plague was brought to an end only when the community established a regularly scheduled ritual, the arkteia, where young girls called arktoi, "she-bears", played the part of the bear and performed dances for Artemis'.[21]

Scholars have tried to interpret this story in numerous ways, but it is clear that the bear dance ceremony marks the on-set of menstruation, and hence the transition of young girls from childhood to adulthood, from being virgin maidens to coming of marriageable age. The ceremony was not only designed to sensitise young girls to the biological, mental and cultural transformations they would undergo, but also to prepare them to handle corresponding responsibilities in an organic manner. More importantly, the ceremony shows that Artemis is the goddess, who not only facilitates this transformation in a safe and smooth manner but that she is also the personification of the very process of this transformation.

Add to this, the fact that Artemis was perceived as the goddess of protection.[22] Various myths and accounts were written down about how those interfering with the rituals would face punishments, be it the men who molested the female participants in the rituals, or the participants themselves, who failed to control their own bodies by adhering to stipulated restrictions. Even cities, which housed such people would be penalised. Kallimochos,[23] who was a noted poet and scholar and a native of Greece, notes in one of his hymns to Artemis that people with whom the goddess is pleased, will have both riches and a long life; whereas the goddess frowns upon those who are unjust, making them suffer through plague and frost, with their women dying during childbirth, or giving birth to deformed babies. Kallimochus, in fact, cites a long tradition that associates various unpleasant conditions that women suffer such as deformed children and stillborn babies with an offence/insult towards Artemis. Thus, Artemis, as the personification of menstruation, was perceived to facilitate, nurture and protect women through their transformations, when properly invoked and worshipped; whereas non-performance, improper performance, or any interference in the offering of worship to her resulted in punishments in the form of various obstacles and complications in the process.

This dual-aspect of protection and punishment by Artemis and its relationship to the proper performance of the rituals hints that the Greeks, like the Hindus, may have recognised the presence of various subtle and Pranic (vital) energies, which accompany and facilitate these female transformations. They must have also observed that any obstruction or imbalance in these energies would result in an imbalance of the biological process. These underlying energies appear to have been personified as goddess Artemis by the ancient Greeks, whom they referred to by the epithet 'Apankhomenê' – the 'Strangled Lady', with strangulation being a reference to menstruation.

In Ancient Greece, strangulation or choking represented a condition of 'shedding no blood'.[24] Artemis was considered to be a goddess who would never undergo menarche and would never bleed, hence the name Apankhomenê – Strangulated Lady or Lady who never bleeds.

There is an interesting story behind this epithet of the goddess. According to Pausanias,[25] a Greek traveler and geographer, once, a group of children playfully strangled a statue of Artemis by putting a noose around its neck and called her the strangled lady. The adults, who perceived this as sacrilege, stoned these children to death. The goddess, who became angry at this insensitive and inhuman behaviour shown by the grownups towards those innocent children, punished the entire community in the form of a disease, which caused the death of infants inside the womb itself. In other words, for stoning innocent children, the goddess took away the ability and privilege of becoming parents from the entire community. The disease withdrew from the community only after its members consulted Delphi, who suggested that they give the children a decent burial, and that they conduct an annual sacrifice to honour them since they were wrongly killed. She began to be referred to as 'Artemis Apankhomenê' after this incident.

What is insightful in the story is the kind of punishment that the goddess gives. It is not a normal everyday kind of disease. Instead, it specifically targeted the biological process of menstruation and reproduction in women, causing the infants to die in the womb. From the specific kind of punishment given by Artemis, it appears that it was delivered not only because the innocent children were stoned, but also because the children were right in calling her Strangulated, and the adults stoned them without understanding this. Thus, Artemis, despite being a goddess who never menstruates, is the one, who facilitates and controls menstruation in young girls.

This story and the epitaph of the goddess has a medical meaning as well. Helen King has dealt with this medical aspect in depth in her books *Bound to bleed: Artemis and Greek women* and *Hippocrates Women: Reading the female body in Ancient Greece*. Summarising this, Susan Guettel Cole writes:[26]

> Helen King has pointed out that the crucial element in this particular story is the medical meaning of the epithet 'strangled', relevant here to the nature of the disease sent by the goddess.... King explains the choking of the goddess in terms of Greek theories of female physiology. Hippocratic medical writers assumed a symmetry between lower and upper body entrances and exits, and they interpreted problems with breathing and swallowing as symptoms of reproductive distress. Strangulation or choking would have been an indication that menstrual bleeding was impeded. Female bleeding was considered a sign of health. Bleeding marked the important transitions in a woman's life: at menarche, at the first experience of sexual intercourse and at childbirth. Strangulation or choking would therefore have been a sign that an important female transition was incomplete.

In other words, Artemis represents the state of impeded menstruation, which again goes to show that Artemis is the personification of the principle and the energy, which causes, controls, and hence, can also impede menstruation. Helen King, thus, rightly observes: 'Artemis does not bleed, but she sheds the blood of others, both as huntress and as director of the process by which a parthenos becomes a gynê.'[27] Parthenos represents a virgin maiden, whereas gynê represents an adult woman. According to Greeks, a parthenos transforms into a gynê only after successfully completing menarche, marriage (i.e. first sexual encounter) and childbirth, each of which is accompanied by bleeding[28] and Artemis, who presides over all the three processes, has the power to either facilitate smooth transformation or impede the process by causing obstructions in the bleeding. It is for this reason that the Greeks considered bleeding to be a sign of health, and non-bleeding a sign of sickness in women.[29]

The association of Artemis with the biological process of menarche, first sexual encounter and childbirth, can not only be known from her association with bleeding, but also from the series of ritual worship and the kind of offerings that Greek girls made to her at the various stages of their lives. Susan Guettel Cole, thus, writes:

> Service to the goddess required a cycle of rituals celebrated at each stage of the female maturation process: before puberty, before marriage, between marriage and first pregnancy, during pregnancy, at time of childbirth, and for mothers, at important stages in their own children's developmental cycle. No single ceremony, however, stood out as more important than others… Artemis presided over each of these transitions. The critical series of transitions began even before the first signs of sexual development, was punctuated by the onset of menstruation, marked by the first experience of sexual intercourse, and lasted until the birth of the first child.[30] During these rituals, among other things like objects in the shape of wombs, vulva and breasts, which are clearly the symbols of womanhood and motherhood, Artemis was also offered clothing and girdles. The offering of girdles seems to be most important, since, one of the epithets of Artemis is 'Lysizonos', meaning 'she who loosens the girdle'.

Girdle was an important part of female clothing in ancient Greece. It was deeply associated with the various stages of a woman's life. Children did not use girdles.Hence, young girls were 'ungirdled'. Upon the onset of menstruation, however, they were given girdles to wear. This girdle, worn by the virgin, was later untied and offered in ritual worship to goddess Artemis as part of the marriage ceremony. She was then given a special ritualised girdle for her wedding night, which was untied by her husband. A married woman, later unties her girdle during childbirth.[31]

Thus, all the important stages in a Greek woman's life were associated with untying the girdle, and goddess Artemis, who 'unties the girdles', presided over the smooth functioning of these stages.

Menstruation and Moon

Menstruation and the moon have been intimately linked in almost all cultures across the world. Ancient Greece was no exception. Artemis was also considered the goddess of the moon, with one of her epithets being 'Phoebe' – the bright one. Her symbols included the bow, arrows, stags, the hunting dog and the moon. As a moon goddess, she was often portrayed as wearing a long robe and a veil covering the head. Though Artemis was generally associated with all the three phases of the lunar cycle (as conceived by the Greeks), her specific association was with the Crescent moon – the first phase of the lunar cycle, which symbolised the 'emergent life force'.[32] It is for this reason that she was sometimes depicted in classical art with the crown of the Crescent moon. This association of Artemis with the Crescent moon on the one hand, and with menarche on the other, shows how the Greeks linked the phases of the moon to the biological phases in a woman's life. The Crescent moon, which symbolically represented 'emergent life force', shows that the Greeks perceived the onset of menstruation as a positive transition into a stage of marriage and motherhood that facilitated women to bring new life into the world.

The association between the moon and menstruation was not limited to Artemis, who presided over both the processes. But there was a general consensus that the lunar cycle influenced menstruation. Thus, one of the Greek medical texts states: 'In healthy women the menses appear every month, because the month has a particular power over the body.'[33] Commenting on the above quote, Lesley Dean-Jones writes: 'The statement… on the month's particular power over the body would seem to suggest the correspondence of a woman's menstrual period to a particular phase of the moon.'[34] Further, the ancient Greeks seem to have believed that women in general menstruated during the waning phase of the moon. Thus, Soranus, a Greek physician from Ephesus, in his *Gynecology*,[35] quotes Diocles, another physician and Empedocles, a pre-Socrates philosopher, as saying that all women menstruated during the waning moon (though Soranus himself did not subscribe to the belief). Similarly, Aristotle writes: 'And the fact that the menses tend to occur naturally during the waning moon is attributable to the same cause. For this time of the month is colder and more humid because of the wasting and disappearance of the moon.'[36] On the other hand, few Hippocratic authors took the first day of menstrual bleeding as the first day of the menstrual cycle and as the first day of the lunar month. Hence, they opined that menstruation happened during the waxing phase of the moon.[37] Though the former was the more prevalent opinion, both these view show one thing: the Greeks recognised the subtle relationship between the moon and menstruation, so much so that some believed that the moon itself was a female form[38] and hence worshipped Artemis, the goddess who presided over both.

Menstruation and Animal Sacrifice

In the medical texts of ancient Greece, we come across an interesting comparison between menstrual bleeding and animal sacrifice.

The Hippocratic text *Diseases of Women* (1.6), for example, states: 'If a woman is healthy, her blood flows like that from a sacrificial animal and it speedily coagulates. Those women who habitually menstruate for longer than four days and whose menses flow in great abundance, are delicate and their embryos are delicate and waste away. But those women whose menstruation is less than three days or is meagre, are robust, with a healthy complexion and a masculine appearance; yet they are not concerned about bearing children nor do they become pregnant.' Similarly, another Hippocratic text *On the Nature of the Child (18.4)*, compares lochia bleeding to that of a sacrificial animal, using words identical to the description of menstrual bleeding in *Diseases of Women* (1.6). Aristotle in *Historia Animalium (581b1–2)*, on the other hand, compares the menstrual blood of a young girl to that of a freshly slaughtered beast.

From the above descriptions, it is apparent that the analogy has been made to convey the symptoms of normal menstruation. As the *Diseases of Women* (1.6) shows, in healthy women (i.e. having a normal menstruation), the bleeding should neither be excessive, nor scanty; and hence the flow should be in a clear, unobstructed manner in sufficient quantity, like those of sacrificed or slaughtered animals. This analogy has parallels in Ayurvedic texts,[39] which describe normal menstruation as one wherein the blood flow is neither excessive, nor scanty, and resembles the blood of a rabbit.

However, some scholars like Helen King, have argued that the analogy has a deeper culture meaning related to 'ideas about gender and society which can be found outside medical sources' and in particular in the 'overlapping contexts' provided by the role of sacrifice in Ancient Greece.[40]

Animal sacrifice occupied an important place in Greek culture and society. It had a religious and spiritual significance as a part of a divinely ordained social order and as a medium for communicating with the gods. It was also closely linked with agriculture, marriage, reproduction and other important activities of a common man.

Regarding the meaning of the analogy comparing menstrual bleeding and the bleeding of sacrificial animals, on the one hand, there are scholars such as Detienne, who argued that the analogy, when combined with the fact that Greek women were excluded from 'shedding of the blood' during sacrifices, points to the exclusion of women from politics and religious activities, and thus their having an inferior status. On the other hand, we have scholars such as Helen King, who have opined that the analogy points towards how menstruation played a more fundamental role, similar to that of animal sacrifice, in the Greek conception of the Cosmic order.

In his *The violence of wellborn ladies: women in the Thesmophoria,* Detienne[41] writes: 'Just as women are without the political rights reserved for male citizens, they are kept apart from the altars, meat, and blood.' He further quotes Aristotle's comparison of menstrual bleeding with that of slaughtered animals, and opines that the reason for women's exclusion from the shedding of the blood in sacrifices is that they themselves bleed, and that this implies their general exclusion from sacrifices as a whole. In other words, he places menstrual bleeding at the centre of women's exclusion from both political and religious (sacrificial) rights in Ancient Greece. However, questioning Detienne's assertions, Robin Osborne in his, *Women and Sacrifice in Classical Greece,* has shown using epigraphic evidences that women's inclusion, not exclusion from sacrifices, was the norm, since, 'In the corpus of sacred laws, cases of specific exclusion of women are much more numerous than specific inclusions'.[42]

Osborne further questions Detienne's attempts to arrange different activities involved in an animal sacrifice into hierarchical levels, with shedding of the blood forming the central portion. Detinne implies that since women are excluded from the portion involving shedding of the blood of the sacrificial animal, they must have been sidelined and normally excluded at all levels as well. Osborne asserts that such hierarchical levels have no basis, since, the verb used for slaughtering – 'thuein' – actually covers the entire sacrificial ceremony and not just the killing part.[43] Another point that Osborne raises is the fact that sex-specific regulations in many cults, and even otherwise, were unconnected to political circumstances.[44] Also, scholars such as Burkert[45] have shown how men and women play distinct roles during a sacrificial ceremony, with women performing roles like kanephoroi (leading the procession to the ceremony) and ololygê (ritual cry), and men cutting hair and wielding the axe. This shows that women were as much a part of the sacrificial ceremony as men. Thus, Osborne rightly concludes: Greek cult practices must both be seen not to be closely linked to day-to-day politics as carried on in the Assembly, and also not treated as simply a product of the rationalising of natural process.[46]

Helen King, in her *Hippocrates' Women: Reading the female body in Ancient Greece* compares menarche and marriage to an act of sacrifice, with menstruating women donning the role of the sacrificial animal, menstrual and lochial blood being the sacrificial blood and the fetal membranes acting as the sacrificial bowl, where the blood is collected.

Writing about women donning the role of the sacrificial victim, Helen King writes: 'In myth and tragedy it is most commonly a parthenos of the age for marriage, rather than a mature, married and childbearing gynê, who becomes the sacrifice. Many elements of the Greek wedding evoke the preparation of a beast for sacrifice; for example, cutting hair, washing, giving a sign of consent and wearing a garland….It is implied that the bride is being prepared to be a "sacrificial victim", that is, to shed her blood. Blood and sacrifice thus separate humans from gods, and men from women.'[47] She further points out how though the bowl used to collect blood from the sacrificed animal is called 'sphageion', in the Homeric description of the blood sacrifice, the bowl is called 'amnion', a term, which in many Greek works also refers to fetal membrane that covers the fetus. Also, just as the sacrificial bowl collects the blood in the sacrifice, the 'membranes around the fetus collect blood as the fetus draws it from all over the body'.[48]

Thus, there is a clear evidence of how the Ancient Greeks perceived menstruation and related activities such as marriage and childbirth as a religious/spiritual sacrifice. It is important to note that the comparison of women with sacrificial animals does not necessarily imply a negative connotation as may be assumed. In this connection it may be useful to draw a parallel with the Hindu concept of Yajna since the Greeks share similar perceptions about sacrifice as the Hindus. For example, the purpose of the sacrifices, according to the Greek philosopher Theophrastus, were three-fold: to honour them, to thank them, or to request a favour from them.[49] Likewise, all Karmas, including Yajnas, are broadly classified into Kamya and Nishkamya, i.e. those performed with some desires to be fulfilled and those performed out of love, devotion and in honour of the deities, respectively.

Now, to understand the essence of a sacrifice and the role of the sacrificial animal, let us look into the Purusha Sukta of the Rigveda. The hymn describes how the Devas (gods) create the entire universe using a grand Yajna (sacrifice), in which Purusha or the transcendental reality (God) is used as the sacrificial animal.[50] In other words, Purusha himself transforms and becomes the Universe, with Yajna or sacrifice being not only the facilitator of this transformation, but the very process of transformation itself. Applying this understanding to the Greek comparison of menstruation to a sacrifice, we can see that this is a reference to a woman's transformation from a child into an adult, from a young maiden into a wife and a mother. More importantly, it places menstruation and women themselves at the centre of not only spiritual and religious life, but also of the cosmic order. Helen King rightly concludes: 'For an ancient Greek woman, "health" is to bleed like a sacrificial victim; but this analogy proposed that menstruation was not only a sign of health, but also something as fundamental as animal sacrifice to the maintenance of the present order.'[51]

Greek Medicine on Menstruation

Medical writers in Ancient Greece dealt extensively with menstruation, and recognised menstrual bleeding as a sign of the health of a woman. Hippocrates, who is considered the father of western medicine, was the first to recognise the beneficial nature of menstruation. He considered it 'nature's way of getting rid of the bad humors' that were responsiblefor these maladies (premenstrual headaches, swelling, and nervousness).[52]

Among the Greek medical works, *Corpus Hippocraticum,* or the 'Corpus of Hippocrates' and the works of Aristotle are the most important sources of our knowledge about the Greek understanding of menstruation. Though 'Corpus Hippocraticum' has been named after Hippocrates, it is so 'diverse in style and subject matter and opinions expressed contradictory enough to make it impossible for the corpus to represent the work of a single medical writer'.[53] In other words, it is a compilation of medical works of a large number of Greek physicians, Hippocrates being most important among them.

It is interesting to note that Greek medical texts use different names[54] to refer to menstruation based on their context. 'Hê physis', for example, means 'nature', and perhaps refers to the menstrual period being the unique nature of women.

Similarly, 'Gynaikeia' means 'woman's things' and can refer to any menstrual period. But, importantly, when gynaikeia is used with 'proton' (first), it refers to menarche. 'Ta hôraia', on the other hand, also refers to menarche, but implies a meaning of 'ripeness'. 'Hôrê gamou' is another term, which means 'ripe for marriage'. These terms are instructive for they allow us to have a glimpse into the width of knowledge of the ancient Greeks about menstruation.

'In Hippocratic gynecology', says Helen King, 'to be a woman is to menstruate. This poses the problem of women who do not menstruate: they may be ill, in which case drugs or mechanical procedures can be used to induce menstruation; they may be pregnant, in which case there is no danger to their health because the excess blood is contributing to the foetus; or they may be past the menopause, that natural process of 'drying out' which transforms even a wet and spongy female body into something that 'does not need to bleed'.[55]

We have already seen how the Greek medical texts speak about healthy women menstruating every month and how their blood flow resembled the blood flow from a sacrificial animal. In *Disease of Women*-I,[56] which is an important text from the Hippocratic corpus, the Greek medical writer writes: 'An average menses for any healthy woman is about two Attic cotyls – or a little more or a little less – and this appears, moreover, for two or three days.' He further says the bleeding will be dense in consistency and abundant during the middle, while it is sparse and thin in consistency during the beginning and the end. Though this (the two Attic cotyls quantity) blood flow, which amounts to around one pint, is at least eight times more than the actual blood loss during menstruation (as has been determined in recent times), it still highlights the keen interest for minute details in Ancient Greece. Moreover, medical writers such as Soranos[57] have observed that the quantity refers to absolute maximum flux (Gynecology 1.20) and hence, normal quantity was understood to be much less. Also, some scholars have attributed the error to inaccurate methods of measuring the quantity of menstrual flow.

The author of the *Diseases of Women*-1 further points out menstruating for more than four days and in very huge quantities indicate how those women are delicate and their wombs waste way, whereas those who menstruate very less and in meager quantity are susceptible to not becoming pregnant ever. The author further writes: 'Whenever in a woman who has never given birth, the menses are suppressed, and cannot find a way out, illness results', and lists out how when menstruation is suppressed for a long time, it will lead such women to suffer from suffocation, fever, and lower back ache during the third monthly period; increased suffering from suffocation, etc. along with loss of appetite and sleep during the fourth monthly period, and if menstruation is suppressed further, then it would cause, severe pain, vomiting, fever, body ache, violent thirst etc., which may severely hamper her health.

Speculating on the reasons behind why women menstruate and men don't, the author of *Diseases of Women*-1 writes:

> I say that a woman's flesh is more sponge like and softer than a man's: since this is so, the woman's body draws moisture both with more speed and in greater quantity from the belly than does the body of a man. For if anyone should set clean wool and a piece of cloth which is clean, thickly-woven, and equal in weight to the wool, over water or on top of a damp place for two days and two nights, when he takes them off and weighs them, he will discover that the wool is much heavier than the cloth. The reason this happens is that water in a wide-mouthed jar always escapes in an upward direction. Now the wool, on the one hand, because it is both porous and soft, receives more of the escaping water, while the cloth, because it is solid

> and thickly woven, will be filled up, although it does not take on much of the escaping water. It is in this way, then, that a woman, because she is more porous, draws more moisture and draws it with greater speed from her belly to her body than does a man.
>
> And when the body of a woman whose flesh full of blood and if that blood does not go off occurs, then her flesh is full and becomes heated. A woman has warmer blood and therefore she is warmer than a man. If the existing surplus of blood should go off, no pain results from the blood. Because a man has more solid flesh than a woman, he is never so totally overfilled with blood that pain results if some of his blood does not exit each month. He draws whatever quantity of blood is needed for his body's nourishment; since his body is not soft, it does not become overstrained nor is it heated up by fullness, as in the case of a woman. The fact that a man works harder than a woman contributes greatly to this; for hard work draws off some of the fluid.

Aristotle,[58] on the other hand, has argued in his works such as *De Generatione Animalium* that women and men belonged to the same species, and that the only difference between them was that women did not have sufficient heat in their principle to convert nourishment from their blood into semen (GA 725a 11-727a 1). Though he does not mention the volume of menstrual discharge, he believed that among all animals, human females discharged the largest quantity of menstrual blood (GA 728b 15). He further observed: 'For the most part, women do not suffer from hemorrhoids, nosebleeds or any other such discharge unless the menses are suppressed; and if any of these discharges do take place, the menstrual flow is less in quantity, as if the secretion is being re-routed to these (GA 727a 12 16).' He believed that most women menstruated regularly at monthly intervals because nature measured everything by periods like days, months, and years (GA 777b 17-30) and that they menstruated during the waning phase of the moon (GA 767a 2-6).

It is to be noted that many of the observations of the Greek medical writers are incorrect and contradictory to modern findings. This is mainly because the ancient Greeks did not dissect human bodies and much of Hippocratic and Aristotelian understanding of the woman's interior space 'were inferred from observable phenomena such as menses and breasts, and [an] analogy with such things as sponges and cupping instruments'.[59] It was also because of 'wrong inferences stemming from presuppositions which the individual never thought to challenge, rather than a wilful neglect of the facts before his eyes'.[60] But what is important to note is that despite many huge gaps, the ancient Greek physicians had thoroughly investigated menstruation and examined the biological transformations that affected women. In the process, they laid the foundation for future research and understanding.

One can say in summary, ancient Greek medicine had thoroughly investigated menstruation and had rightly arrived at the conclusion that it was vital for the overall health of women. For the Greeks, it was menstruation, which set women apart from men. Hence, in medicine, as well as in culture, it played a central role in the Greek woman's life. Greek society perceived menstruation as a positive sacred transformative process, which had a religious and spiritual standing similar to that of animal sacrifice, and it worshipped goddess Artemis for protection and the facilitation of this sacred process. Though a notion of Miasma (impurity) was associated with menstruation, its role was more complementary than contradictory to sacredness. Moreover, considerations for Miasma may have been a necessary aspect of sacredness itself. Young girls worshipped goddess Artemis by enacting a bear dance at the onset of menstruation and invoked her protection through menarche, marriage and child-birth.

Roman Civilisation

If there was one civilisation which could be considered the civilisational inheritor of Ancient Greece, it was Ancient Rome. Much of Greek knowledge, culture, beliefs, and attitudes were not only inherited by the Romans, they were further built upon and expanded. This applied to their knowledge of menstruation, as well.

Physicians in the Roman Empire, like the larger Roman society, inherited a rich medical tradition from the Greeks with respect to the female anatomy, women's health and menstruation. Galen, for example, who was perhaps the most notable Roman physician, started his research on menstruation and women's health by first collecting the available material from Greek physicians and medical writers like Hippocrates and Aristotle.[1] And then, there was Soranus of Ephesus, a Greek physician, who settled in Rome and practised medicine there. He is often considered the 'greatest physician of antiquity'[2] and he not only documented how menstruation was inevitable for pregnancy, but also correctly described all the female reproductive organs, including the external genitalia and the clitoris.[3]

But apart from the medical accounts, there is a scarcity of evidence regarding menstruation in the primary literary sources of the Romans, as it was with the Greeks. Yet, even with this minimal evidence, we can see that the Romans, like the Greeks, on the one hand, associated menstruation with impurity, and on the other hand, perceived its sacred aspect, and worshipped goddess Diana, the Roman counterpart of the Greek goddess, Artemis, as the deity of menstruation. The Romans went further and examined how the subtle energies, especially those causing impurity (Greek Miasma or Hindu Ashaucha), affected various day-to-day activities.

From the writings of Roman scholars such as Pliny the Elder and Lucius Junius Moderatus Columella, we not only get an exaggerated account of the impurity associated with menstruation, but also an exaggerated account of what scholars term as the 'magical powers' associated with menstruation. These 'magical powers', as we shall see later, can be more properly understood as the physical effects that could likely be manifested by the subtle energies associated with menstruation. Despite these exaggerations, what these accounts establish is the fact that the Roman understanding of menstruation, like that of the Greeks, was not limited to the physical aspect. Instead, there was also a recognition of the Miasma-Katharsis aspect of menstruation, albeit with exaggerations.

Menstruation and Impurity

The Romans inherited the concept of 'impurity' or Miasma from the Greeks. But scholars opine that the Roman perception of impurity was in some ways different.

Bernhard Linke, in his chapter: 'Sacral Purity and Social Order in Ancient Rome' contributed to the book, *Purity and the Forming of Religious Traditions in the Ancient Mediterranean World and Ancient Judaism*, deals with this difference in perception. Summarising the observations put forward by Linke, book editors Christian Frevel and Christophe Nihan in their Introduction write:[4]

> Linke argues that in ancient Greece, purity is inseparable from the attempt to secure the presence of deities within human society through the delineation of spatially distinct areas, whose 'marked-off' character (i.e. their sacrality) was highlighted by physical markers (such as, especially, boundary stones) as well as by distinctive codes of conduct. Such marked-off spaces were, however, always 'precarious', which accounts for the importance given to the performance of rituals of purification in Greek sanctuaries. Compliance with the rules of purity defined by local sanctuaries establishes the appropriate behavior of a person entering a sacred precinct to

> engage in an interaction with the Greek gods. In the case of ancient Rome, however, the general function of purification rituals appears to have been different, especially in the case of those rituals performed on a regular basis (and not only in exceptional circumstances); furthermore, Linke argues that this basic difference should be related to a more general distinction in the perception of sacred space in Greece and Rome. In the case of ancient Greece, the general function of purity rules can be defined as an attempt to increase the 'densification' of the sacral within the human sphere. The Romans, in contrast, had a much more intense perception of the presence of such sacral forces among them, and that perception significantly influenced their social, political and religious organisation. Accordingly, in Roman society, the central function of purification rituals was much more oriented towards the preservation of a state of 'harmony' and stability, whenever that state was considered to be potentially endangered. Linke shows in detail how this basic difference applies at the level not only of the main purification rituals that were performed in Rome, but also of the roles ascribed to Roman ritual specialists (i.e. priests), in contrast to Greek ones.

Thus, according to Linke, the perception of purity and impurity in Ancient Rome had attained a more general character than in Ancient Greece and was no longer specifically confined to the worship of deities at the temples. Instead, purity and impurity were perceived as connected to harmony and to the stability of society as a whole. But this did not mean that purity-impurity became irrelevant to the worship at temples. Linke notes: 'In Rome, there were also numerous occasions, in which the warranty or the restitution of ritual purity played a significant role. This applied to critical situations that might be caused by the death of a member of the community or by violations against sacral regulations and procedures. In such cases, purification rituals had to be performed. These expiatory actions were termed *piacula* and were designated to heal any breach of the sacral regulations. Possible offenses to be expiated by a *piaculam* were disruptions of prayers or sacrifices as well as violations of a feast day or neglect by a priest.'[5] Thus, the concept of purification was still relevant to temple worship, but the scope of purity-impurity had been expanded.

Linke provides numerous examples to show how the notion of purity-impurity was expanded in Roman society, and how various rituals were periodically performed 'to ensure the fertility of the fields and to prevent any pollution or sacral impairment'.[6] One such example, he quotes, is the rituals called 'lustrationes'. 'Lustratio' refers to a ritual of purification by sacrifice. It was a simple ritual, in which the performer carried a sacrificial animal in a circular procession around an object or a plot (most likely an agricultural plot) and the animal was then sacrificed at the end of the ritual. Similar lustrationes were done circling the Palatine (high royal officials) or the city of Rome. The ritual's primary purpose appears to be ensuring the fertility of the fields by preventing any pollution or impurity that may endanger them. Another example of lustrationes that Linke provides was the ritual performed at the end of the Roman census. After the census was completed and the real estate properties were registered anew, the newly constituted community of citizens was assembled and the censor would circumambulate them along with a pig, a sheep, and a cow, which would then be sacrificed to Mars. The ritual not only aimed to revive the community's connection with Mars, it also meant to protect the fertility of the fields and attain future prosperity.'[6]

Thus, there was a clear expansion of the notion of purity-impurity into such mundane activities. This general expansion was perhaps also the reason behind the Roman exploration (which was mostly absent among the Greeks) of the effects of Miasma energies associated with menstruation on mundane objects and activities and their formulations of often exaggerated effects.

Though scholars such as R Beck have opined that the Roman culture was: 'relatively free of the sense that there exists a class of naturally occurring things that pollute in and of themselves, for example, certain types of food source, menstruation and childbirth',[7] this view has been satisfactorily rebutted by scholars such as Jack Lennon, who, in his paper 'Menstrual Blood in Rome: An Unspeakable Impurity?' makes an interesting observation about the connection between menstruation and impurity. He quotes Sextus Pompeius Festus, a Roman grammarian, who lived in the latter half of the second century who comments: 'Ancunulentae refer to women during the time of menstruation, from which we derive the word inquinamentum.'[8] Inquinamentum means 'impurity', especially in the sexual context. This connection between the terms used for menstruation and impurity is a clear pointer towards the Roman association of impurity with menstruation. Thus, after examining the available evidences from the Roman period, Lennon concludes: 'What are we to make, then, of Beck's suggestion that natural pollutions, such as those of childbirth and menstruation were not present in ancient Rome? The answer must surely be divided between those official regulations dictated by religious rituals, and those more changeable ideas that existed in wider society and Italian folklore. In terms of religious prohibitions, Beck may be correct in noting the absence of restrictions on menstruating women. However, this does not take into account the frequent allusions made in the ancient evidence to the infectious and dangerous properties of menstruation. Menstrual blood did, indeed, pollute in and of itself in a number of contexts, and remained a consistent source of danger, whether to a man, an insect, a plant or even a magic spell.'[9] Perhaps, the best evidence regarding this association is provided by Pliny the Elder.

He was a Roman author and naturalist, who lived around 23–79 AD and wrote an encyclopedic work *Natural History*, comprising thirty seven books. In Natural History, among other things, he writes in detail about the Roman perception of menstruation, menstruation's association with impurity, and its effects on mundane activities. He dedicates two chapters, one in book 7 and one in book 28, to the subject of menstruation.[10]

In book 7, in the chapter titled 'Remarkable Circumstances Connected with the Menstrual Discharge', he writes thus (translation by John Bostock):

> Among the whole range of animated beings, the human female is the only one that has the monthly discharge….It would indeed be a difficult matter to find anything, which is productive of more marvellous effects than the menstrual discharge. On the approach of a woman in this state, milk will become sour, seeds which are touched by her become sterile, grafts wither away, garden plants are parched up, and the fruit will fall from the tree beneath which she sits. Her very look, even, will dim the brightness of mirrors, blunt the edge of steel, and take away the polish from ivory. A swarm of bees, if looked upon by her, will die immediately; brass and iron will instantly become rusty, and emit an offensive odour; while dogs which may have tasted of the matter so discharged are seized with madness, and their bite is venomous and incurable….It is said that the ant, even an insect so extremely minute, is sensible of its presence, and rejects the grains which it has been carrying, and will not return to them again. This discharge, which is productive of such great and singular effects, occurs in women every thirty days, and in a greater degree, every three months. In some individuals it occurs oftener than once a month, and in others, again, it never takes place. Women of this nature, however, are not capable of bearing children, because it is of this substance that the infant is formed….

Again in book 28 which deals with remedies derived from living creatures, in the chapter titled 'Facts Connected with the Menstrual Discharge', Pliny writes (translation by John Bostock):

> Over and above these particulars, there is no limit to the marvellous powers attributed to females. For, in the first place, hailstorms, they say, whirlwinds, and lightning even, will be scared away by a woman uncovering her body while her monthly courses are upon her....As to the menstrual discharge itself, a thing that in other respects, as already stated on a more appropriate occasion, is productive of the most monstrous effects, there are some ravings about it of a most dreadful and unutterable nature. Of these particulars, however, I do not feel so much shocked at mentioning the following. If the menstrual discharge coincides with an eclipse of the moon or sun, the evils resulting from it are irremediable; and no less so, when it happens while the moon is in conjunction with the sun; the congress with a woman at such a period being noxious, and attended with fatal effects to the man. At this period also, the lustre of purple is tarnished by the touch of a woman: so much more baneful is her influence at this time than at any other. At any other time, also, if a woman strips herself naked while she is menstruating, and walks round a field of wheat, the caterpillars, worms, beetles, and other vermin, will fall from off the ears of corn. Metrodorus of Scepsos tells us that this discovery was first made in Cappadocia; and that, in consequence of such multitudes of cantharides being found to breed there, it is the practice for women to walk through the middle of the fields with their garments tucked up above the thighs.In other places, again, it is the usage for women to go barefoot, with the hair dishevelled and the girdle loose: due precaution must be taken, however, that this is not done at sun-rise, for if so, the crop will wither and dry up. Young vines, too, it is said, are injured irremediably by the touch of a woman in this state; and both rue and ivy, plants possessed of highly medicinal virtues, will die instantly upon being touched by her.

Much as I have already stated on the virulent effects of this discharge, I have to state, in addition, that bees, it is a well-known fact, will forsake their hives if touched by a menstruous woman; that linen boiling in the cauldron will turn black, that the edge of a razor will become blunted, and that copper vessels will contract a fetid smell and become covered with verdigrease, on coming in contact with her. A mare big with foal, if touched by a woman in this state, will be sure to miscarry; nay, even more than this, at the very sight of a woman, though seen at a distance even, should she happen to be menstruating for the first time after the loss of her virginity, or for the first time, while in a state of virginity. The bitumen that is found in Judaea, will yield to nothing but the menstrual discharge; its tenacity being overcome, as already stated, by the agency of a thread from a garment which has been brought in contact with this fluid. Fire itself even, an element which triumphs over every other substance, is unable to conquer this; for if reduced to ashes and then sprinkled upon garments when about to be scoured, it will change their purple tint, and tarnish the brightness of the colours. Indeed so pernicious are its properties, that women themselves, the source from which it is derived, are far from being proof against its effects; a pregnant woman, for instance, if touched with it, or indeed if she so much as steps over it, will be liable to miscarry.

Laïs and Elephantis have given statements quite at variance, on the subject of abortives; they mention the efficacy for that purpose of charcoal of cabbage root, myrtle root, or tamarisk root, quenched in the menstrual discharge; they say that she-asses will be barren for as many years as they have eaten barley-corns steeped in this fluid; and they have enumerated various other monstrous and irreconcilable properties, the one telling us, for instance, that fruitfulness may be ensured by the very same methods, which, according to the statement of the other, are productive of barrenness; to all which stories it is the best plan to refuse credit altogether. Bithus of Dyrrhachium informs us that a mirror which has been tarnished by the gaze of a menstruous female, will recover its brightness if the same woman looks steadily upon the back of it; he states, also, that all evil influences of this nature will be entirely neutralised, if the woman carries the fish known as the sur mullet about her person.

On the other hand, again, many writers say that, baneful as it is, there are certain remedial properties in this fluid; that it is a good plan, for instance, to use it as a topical application for gout, and that women, while menstruating, can give relief by touching scrofulous sores and imposthumes of the parotid glands, inflamed tumours, erysipelas, boils, and defluxions of the eyes. According to Laïs and Salpe, the bite of a mad dog, as well as tertian or quartan fevers, may be cured by putting some menstruous blood in the wool of a black ram and enclosing it in a silver bracelet; and we learn from Diotimus of Thebes that the smallest portion will suffice of any kind of cloth that has been stained therewith, a thread even, if inserted and worn in a bracelet. The midwife Sotira informs us that the most efficient cure for tertian and quartan fevers is to rub the soles of the patient's feet therewith, the result being still more successful if the operation is performed by the woman herself, without the patient being aware of it; she says, too, that this is an excellent method for reviving persons when attacked with epilepsy.

Icetidas the physician pledges his word that quartan fever may be cured by sexual intercourse, provided the woman is just beginning to menstruate. It is universally agreed, too, that when a person has been bitten by a dog and manifests a dread of water and of all kinds of drink, it will be quite sufficient to put under his clip a strip of cloth that has been dipped in this fluid; the result being that the hydrophobia will immediately disappear. This arises, no doubt, from that powerful sympathy which has been so much spoken of by the Greeks, and the existence of which is proved by the fact, already mentioned, that dogs become mad upon tasting this fluid. It is a well-known fact, too, that the menstruous discharge, reduced to ashes, and applied with furnace soot and wax, is a cure for ulcers

> upon all kinds of beasts of burden; and that stains made upon a garment with it can only be removed by the agency of the urine of the same female. Equally certain it is, too, that this fluid, reduced to ashes and mixed with oil of roses, is very useful, applied to the forehead, for allaying head-ache, in women more particularly; as also that the nature of the discharge is most virulent in females whose virginity has been destroyed solely by the lapse of time…

In these two chapters, Pliny provides a very vivid account of both the favorable and the unfavorable effects of miasma energies associated with menstruation on human activities and the surrounding environment. Favourable effects include their remedial usage in treating certain medical conditions, and their usage in farming. Unfavourable effects include their effects on various plants and other non-human life forms, their effects during eclipse and on human activities. But it is important to note that Pliny's account should not be always taken literally. For one, it is obvious that it is an exaggeration to state that menstruation causes brass and iron to become rusty or that menstruating women will scare away hailstorms and lightening. Even while ignoring these obvious exaggerations, one must be careful while literally interpreting the text. Since scientific tools can neither confirm nor deny the workings of the miasma energies associated with menstruation, it will be very difficult to correlate literally all the instances mentioned by Pliny with menstruation. Thus, the importance of Pliny's work is neither in its vivid accounts, nor in literal interpretations nor their scientific validations. Instead, it is in the fact that Pliny shows how Romans had deeply explored and documented the workings of the miasma aspect of menstruation and how they were aware that subtle miasma energies affect even the smallest of non-human life. Pliny himself captures this essence of his message when he says: 'It is said that the ant, even an insect so extremely minute, is sensible of its (menstrual blood's) presence.'

Accounts similar to Pliny's can also be found in the works composed by Lucius Junius Moderatus Columella,[11] who lived in the first century and who was the most important writer on Agriculture in Ancient Rome. In book 10 of his twelve books on agriculture, he writes about how menstruating women can get rid of pests in farms:

> *But if no medicine can the pest repel,*
> *Let the Dardanian arts be called to aid,*
> *A maiden then, who the first time obeys*
> *Her youth's fixed law, bare-footed and ashamed*
> *Of the foul blood which flows, with bosom bare*
> *And hair disheveled, thrice about the beds*
> *And garden-hedge is led. What wondrous sight,*
> *When she with gentle pace her course has run!*
> *E'en as when from a shaken tree rains down*
> *A shower of shapely apples or of mast*
> *Sheathed in soft shells, so roll in twisted shapes*
> *To earth the caterpillars.*

In book 11, he adds: 'Care, however, must be taken that a woman is admitted as little as possible to the place where the cucumbers and gourds are planted; for usually the growth of green-stuff is checked by contact with a woman; indeed if she is also in the period of menstruation, she will kill the young produce merely by looking at it.' These views are very similar to Pliny's and go to show how they were widely prevalent across the Ancient Roman civilisation.

The Roman accounts of menstruation, especially those of Pliny's, have often been interpreted as evidence of the negative connotations attached to menstruation in the Ancient Roman society. Jack Lennon, who quotes extensively from Pliny in his paper, writes: 'the evidence examined throughout this paper will show categorically that fear of the polluting power of menstrual blood and the process of menstruation itself is demonstrated by our surviving sources.'[12] He further concludes: 'Menstrual blood did, indeed, pollute in and of itself in a number of contexts, and remained a consistent source of danger, whether to a man, an insect, a plant or even a magic spell.'[13] Lennon's conclusions can be summed up thus:

1. Romans feared menstruation, especially its miasma aspect.
2. Menstruation was perceived as a constant source of danger to everyone.
3. Menstruation was polluting in and of itself.

This perception of the miasma or Ashaucha associated with menstruation is neither unique to Lennon, nor applied only regarding the Roman people. In fact, much of the academic analysis on the subject across cultures often perceives the Ashaucha aspect with its restrictions on certain activities as a symbol of fear, danger; a negative connotation. But in the case of the Greeks, we have already seen that this is not true. Similarly, in the chapter on the Hindu views of Menstruation, we have seen that menstruation is neither feared nor does it have negative connotations attached to it in Hinduism, despite its association with Ashaucha. This likely is true of the Ancient Romans as well, who, like the Greeks, shared a polytheistic heritage with the Indians.

Regarding the issue of Roman fear towards menstruation, the argument rests on the fact that the Romans associated impurity with menstruation and believed that the subtle energies associated with this impurity could have unfavorable effects on human activities, plants, insects etc. But how correct is such a conclusion, considering how Pliny himself does not appear to express any fear towards menstruation. On the other hand, Pliny writes about menstruation thus: 'It would indeed be a difficult matter to find anything, which is productive of more marvellous effects than the menstrual discharge' in his book 7. Similarly in book 9, he writes:'there is no limit to the marvellous powers attributed to females.' Hence, if anything, Pliny was awestruck with menstruation. How does one explain all the exaggerations in his account? We do not know whether these exaggerated accounts of menstruation's effects on the mundane environment were imagined as a result of fear based on superstition. Or, were they due to incomplete knowledge? Or, were they deliberately exaggerated to stress upon the effect of the miasma associated with menstruation on the common people? Perhaps, all three factors played a role. In any case, this shows that menstruation was not a source of fear as is often understood. Similarly, the view that menstruation was perceived as a constant danger to everyone is also not correct, since, Pliny highlights the many favourable and useful benefits of the miasma energies associated with menstruation. Thus, the Romans clearly did not associate menstruation with danger alone. Finally, the view that menstruation was polluting in and of itself, ignores the account of Macrobius, who lived around the fifth century and who in his book, *The Saturnalia*, describes menstruation as the process of removal of harmful material from the body.[14] Though Lennon himself quotes Macrobius, he ignores his views while calling menstruation impure in and of itself in Ancient Rome. From Macrobius' account, it is clear that although menstruation involved the removal of harmful substances from the body and hence the menstrual blood flow was associated with subtle miasma energies, the process itself was a purification process. This view has a clear parallel with the Hindu view, which perceives menstruation as not only associated with Ashaucha, but also as an austerity and self-purification process. Add to this the fact that the Romans also associated menstruation with sacredness and worshipped goddess Diana as the goddess of menstruation.

In other words, associating the Roman perception of menstruation with fear, danger, or impurity alone ignores many other aspects of the Roman view. A more holistic and balanced view would be to recognise how the Romans, despite their exaggerated and at times incorrect accounts of the effects of menstruation, had recognised the miasma energies associated with menstruation and had continuously explored their physical effects in day-to-day life. Their classification of the effects of menstruation into favourable and unfavourable effects was more a practical classification to act as guide in day-to-day life, than a result of any fear. Additionally, miasma or impurity was only one aspect of menstruation, as they, like the Greeks and the Hindus, also associated sacredness with menstruation.

Menstruation and 'Magical powers'

Scholars have written extensively about the association of menstruation with magical powers. Glenda Lewin Hufnagel, for example, quotes various scholars, and writes in her book *A History of Women's Menstruation From Ancient Greece to the Twenty-First Century*, thus: 'Shuttle and Redgrove compare Pliny's description of menstruation with historical and folklore description of the witches and discovered that they are strikingly similar. Witches and menstruating women, both had the power to "make cattle sicken and die or cause hailstorms or unreasonable rain to ruin the crops". Margaret Mead made a similar connection between the universal image of the witch, which she believed is common in all cultures. Shuttle Redgrove explains: The image of the witch is consistent, because it is an image of the transforming and changing menstrual cycle; it occurs all over the world because women occur all over the world, and if they didn't, we wouldn't be here…'[15] That is, one can perceive a parallel between the description of witches and their magical power and the magical powers associated with menstruation. But, what exactly are these magical powers?

Let us return to Pliny. As already noted, he attributes the powers to control nature to women, in general, and to menstruating women, in particular, in his book 28, and writes thus: 'For, in the first place, hailstorms, they say, whirlwinds, and lightning even, will be scared away by a woman uncovering her body while her monthly courses are upon her. The same, too, with all other kinds of tempestuous weather; and out at sea, a storm may be lulled by a woman uncovering her body merely, even though not menstruating at the time.' Pliny further adds that menstrual blood could be used to neutralise any magical spells cast upon a family by those who indulge in magic. He writes:

> Another thing universally acknowledged and one which I am ready to believe with the greatest pleasure, is the fact, that if the door-posts are only touched with the menstruous fluid all spells of the magicians will be neutralised – a set of men the most lying in existence, as any one may ascertain. I will give an example of one of the most reasonable of their prescriptions – take the parings of the toe-nails and finger-nails of a sick person, and mix them up with wax, the party saying that he is seeking a remedy for a tertian, quartan, or quotidian fever, as the case may be; then stick this wax, before sunrise, upon the door of another person – such is the prescription they give for these diseases! What deceitful persons they must be if there is no truth in it! And how highly criminal, if they really do thus transfer diseases from one person to another…'

The above descriptions by Pliny, along with the other descriptions we saw before, show that the 'magical powers' were nothing but the subtle workings of the energies associated with menstruation. Though we may discard specific examples like scaring away hailstorms as exaggerations, the description shows that menstruation is a period of heightened energy, and if utilised, its subtle energies can have a considerable impact on the surrounding environment. Utilising menstrual blood to ward of negative 'magical spells' must be understood in that context. In this context, it will be worthy to draw knowledge from Hindu traditions, as well.

Hindu traditions consider women to be the embodiment and the very manifestation of Shakti or cosmic energy. Hindu texts recognise how during menstruation, women are in a heightened state of Rajas, wherein the Prana Shakti has a specific character. Such conditions not only have subtle and physical effects on the surrounding environment, they can also be utilised in a different manner. In fact, women can heighten their Prana Shakti and utilise them even when not menstruating by performing appropriate rituals, Sadhana (spiritual procedures) and Yoga. Perhaps it is this heightened Prana Shakti that the Romans recognised as being capable of impacting nature and removing magical spells. After all, what is called 'magic' in academia is nothing but a play of various subtle energies, especially at the Pranic level. The comparison between menstruating women and witches further reinforces this possibility. Witches were those women with some powers, and as stated above, Hindu texts mention how super-normal strength and power can be attained using Yoga and Sadhana. Thus, the similarities between witches and menstruating women, when perceived in the light of the information revealed by the Hindu traditions, is nothing but a similarity caused by the workings of the same Prana Shakti in both a menstruating woman and women involved in rituals and spiritual practices (i.e. witches).

Thus, despite exaggerations and certain incorrect conclusions, the ancient Romans not only knew of impurity and its association with menstruation, they also understood to some extent about how these subtle energies impacted the surroundings.

Goddess Diana and Menstruation

No account of the Roman perception of menstruation is complete without a discussion of its sacredness and its relationship to goddess Diana.

Just as the Greeks worshipped Artemis as the goddess of menstruation, the Romans associated goddess Diana with menstruation. Though Diana is said to have originated as an independent forest goddess in Aricia in Italy, it is scholarly consensus that she subsequently became identified with the Greek goddess Artemis, and like her, she also became the goddess of hunt, the moon, menstruation, and childbirth.

Among of the coins unearthed from Ancient Rome, there are some depicting the cult image of Diana from the grove. In one such coin,[16] Diana is shown as three figures, with each representing a different aspect: as huntress (called Diana), as the goddess of the underworld (Hecate) and as the goddess of the Moon. This triple form also illustrates Diana's association with the three phases of the moon. As huntress, Diana is associated with the crescent moon like Artemis; as Luna, or the goddess of the moon, she is associated with the full moon phase, and as Hecate, she is associated with the dark moon. With an epithet of Trivia, Diana was worshipped at a point where three roads met (hence the name Trivia: tri- three, via-way[17]) and was sometimes depicted as a creature with three heads.[18] In her huntress form, she was depicted with her skirt tucked up high, while at Ephesus, she is 'loaded with breasts and teats'.[19] In her aspect as Lucina, she is associated with childbirth. Diana, the name, is from the root 'di', which was often taken to mean bright, and hence, was associated with the moon. Cicero, the Roman philosopher and politician, says that the moon governed birth, death, growth and decline. Hence, Diana was invoked at the birth of a child.[20] But, it was in her aspect of huntress that Diana was most favoured by her devotees.[21] In this role, like Artemis, Diana was associated not only with nature and wild animals, but also with virgins. She presided over the process of menarche and menstruation that transformed young girls into adults. At Philippi, for example, Diana was the most prominent deity for women's religious and spiritual practices.[22] Portefaix, who examined the importance of goddess Diana to women at Philippi concludes that her role was reflected in activities such as midwifery, puberty rites, healing processes and funerary preparations performed by her devotees.[23]

Therefore, like Artemis, Diana was clearly associated with all the three phases of the moon and hence presided over all aspects of women's biological activity from the onset of menstruation, and childbirth to menopause and death. CMC Green rightly concludes: Thus, there was no time among the Latins when the moon goddess was not also a hunting goddess, or when the hunting goddess Diana was not also the moon. There is no either-or, no decision we must make between Diana the moon goddess and Diana the huntress. Diana was worshipped in the wild, in a crater beside a lake, because that was where her elements – the moon, the wild, the water – could be worshipped together.[24]

This shows that in Ancient Rome, menstruation was not perceived only in terms of miasma or the magical powers it held, but also as a sacred act, which was presided over by Goddess Diana.

Roman Physicians on Menstruation

Roman physicians inherited a huge corpus of medical knowledge from the Greeks. As noted before, Galen began his research by collecting medical information from Aristotle, Hippocrates and other Greek doctors such as Rufus. He was the most notable physician of Roman times, who was the first to identify that oviducts convey ova (which he had considered to be 'female sperm') to the uterus.[25] He had also showed how the 'vessels carrying menstrual blood to the uterus end in crypts'.[26] He perceived menstruation as an evacuation of excess bodily humours from the female body. He wrote: 'I imagine that the female sex, in asmuchas they heap up a great quantity of humours, by living continually at home, and not being used to hard labour, or exposed to the sun, should receive a discharge of this fullness as a remedy given by nature.'[27] Similarly, Soranus of Ephesus, another famous physician during Ancient Rome, remarks that women remove surplus matter through menses, just as men through athletics.[28] He further perceived menstruation as a bodily catharsis, which was natural to women and which 'needed to be monitored, but not feared, unless it failed to occur'.[29] He had counseled virgin women like the Vestal Virgins – the virgin priestesses of the Roman goddess Vesta – that though virginity was accompanied by menstruation and menstrual difficulties, it did not cause any unfavourable effect on women's health.[30] It is interesting to note that the Humourism system of medicine prevalent in Ancient Greece and Rome had many parallels with the Ayurvedic medicine system of India, including in the perception of menstruation as a purification process, which removes toxins and excess matter from the body.

Soranus was perhaps the greatest gynecologist of his times. Summarising his contribution to gynecology of his times, Elsimar M Coutinho and Sheldon J Segal write: 'In his textbook, he gave the position and size of the uterus and quite accurately described all the female reproductive organs, including the external genitalia. He included the clitoris but did not explain its function. Like others of his time, he recognised that menstruation was necessary for conception but mistakenly believed that immediately after menstruation was the most fertile time.'[31] They add that Soranus did not exhibit any fear of amenorrhea and instead, he recognised it as common phenomenon among those who engaged in sports, singing etc. He advised such women wanting to conceive to do so after changing their lifestyle suitably.[32]

In his treatise *Gynaecology*,[33] Soranus writes:

> One has to infer approaching menstruation from the fact that at the expected time of the period it becomes trying to move and there develops heaviness of the loins, sometimes pain as well, sluggishness, continual yawning, and tension of the limbs, sometimes also a flush of the cheeks which either remains or, having been dispersed, reappears after an interval; and in some cases approaching menstruation must be inferred from the fact that the stomach is prone to nausea and it lacks appetite. Menstruation which is about to occur for the first time must be inferred from the same signs but above all from the growth of the breasts which, broadly, takes place around the fourteenth year, and from the heaviness, irritation and pubescence in the region of the lower abdomen. (1.24)

Regarding menarche and menopause, he further writes:

> In women who have already menstruated often, each must be allowed to do according to her own custom. For some habitually take a rest, while others go on with moderate activities. But it is safer to rest and not to bathe especially on the first day. But in women who are about to menstruate no longer, their time for menstruation having passed, one must take care that the stoppage of the menses does not occur suddenly. For in regard to alteration, even if the body be changed for the better, all abruptness disturbs it through discomfort; for that which is unaccustomed is not tolerated but is like some unfamiliar malaise. The methods we employ at the approach of the first menstruation must now be marshalled forth during the time when menstruation is about to cease; for that which is able to evoke the as yet absent excretion is even more able to preserve for some time menstruation which is still present. In addition, vaginal suppositories capable of softening and injections which

> have the [same] effect should be employed, together with all the remedies capable of rendering hardened bodies soft. But if the menstruation is too much for the strength of the patient, or again, if it is impeded by abnormal factors, then there is need for therapeutic measures. (1.26)

The writings of Soranus and Galen show extensive knowledge regarding menstruation and women's biological functions among the Ancient Roman physicians. In spite of the fact that not everything they believed was correct it shows their extensive investigation on the subject and their attempts to perfect their understanding and build upon previous works, just like their counterparts from Greece.

Briefly, the Ancient Romans built upon the knowledge they had inherited from the Ancient Greeks, be it in the cultural sphere or in medicine. Roman physicians, like their Greek counterparts, had correctly recognised that menstruation was vital for female health. Soranus had advised women to not fear it. In the cultural sphere, the Romans, like the Greeks, recognised both the sacred and the miasma aspect of menstruation. They went a step further and investigated the subtle energies associated with miasma and their effects on human activities. Though some of these observations were quite exaggerated and their knowledge of the workings of these energies very basic, compared to the Hindu traditions, they still appear to have correctly understood the general effects of miasma energies. On the sacred front, they worshipped goddess Diana, the Roman counterpart of the Greek goddess, Artemis, as the deity of the moon, menstruation and childbirth, and invoked her protection during midwifery, puberty rites, and healing processes.

Mesopotamian Civilisation

When we speak of Mesopotamia, we actually speak of four different empires and the cultures and traditions associated with them. The Sumerians, Akkadians, Assyrians and Babylonians, who flourished in the region that is known today as Iraq and Kuwait, including some parts of Syria and Turkey.

The information we have about their civilisation has been reconstructed mostly from the thousands of written documents left by them as clay tablets written in cuneiform writing. Though, as M Stol says, 'The documentary evidence on women in Mesopotamia is quite impressive',[1] the reference to menstruation itself appears to be quite scanty. For example, Erica Reiner[2] points out that not a single term has been found in the Babylonian medical texts specifically referring to menses. Similarly, there are no elaborate discussions about menstruation in any of the Babylonian writings.[3] Nevertheless, we do have references to female bleeding, especially in the therapeutic texts dealing with recipes and incantations and some information about the association of deities such as Ishtar and Inanna with menstruation, from which we are able to fairly reconstruct how Mesopotamians perceived menstruation.

Social condition of Mesopotamian women

Women in Mesopotamia were generally associated with 'left', while the men folk were associated with 'right'.[4] Thus, the female protective deity walked towards the left of a person, the girl fetus was considered to be on the left side of the mother's womb, and women were said to wear the clothes on their left.[5] Women used to adorn their eyes with guhlu (a lead product) and their bodies with ornaments like golden earrings, silver rings on arms and feet, nose rings and necklaces.[6] The Sumerian language had a special dialect called 'Emesal' exclusively used by women in their conversations as revealed by the literary texts.[7]

Marriage was considered very important in women's lives and they were married early between the age of fourteen and twenty, while men married much later between twenty six and thirty two.[8] In one of the hymns dedicated to the Mesopotamian goddess of healing, Guha, important stages in a woman's life are described thus: 'I am a daughter, I am a bride, I am a spouse, I am a housekeeper.'[9] Marriage was not just between the groom and the bride, but instead was a family relationship between the groom and the leading male (mostly the father) in the bride's family.[10] Virginity before marriage played an important role in a woman's life as it was considered an asset to the bride and her father, since it would ease the task of finding a groom for her.[11] Strict punishments were prescribed for the violation of the betrothed girl's chastity, as well as for casting unsubstantiated doubts regarding a girl's virginity.[12] Virginity had ritual value as well, with some ritual procedures being stipulated to be done only by the virgins.[13] Child-bearing was considered the most important duty of a married woman.[14] Sons were preferred, since they were supposed to support the parents in their old age and perform the final rites after their deaths.[15] Both daughters and sons lived at their parent's home till they got married and started their independent family.[16] Those who remained unmarried and did not bear children were censured.

Summarising the social condition of women and its impact on menstruation in Mesopotamia, Elsimar M Coutinho and Sheldon J Segal write:

> Under the ruling Syrians, over three thousand years BC, decrees governing mating were established and marriage was introduced as an official recognition of a union of woman and man. Considering the high mortality of the time because of epidemics and violent wars, childbearing was a goal of great social consequence. The youth who did not marry and have children was criticized, as was the young girl who remained a virgin and did not become pregnant.
>
> Marriages were arranged by parents when the future bride and groom were still children, or sometimes even before they were

> born. When a young girl reached puberty, she would leave her family and live with the family of her husband, where she would remain until her death. If she did not conceive she could be returned to her family or treated even more harshly. Encouraged by community leaders and aware of the high rate of child mortality, women married in this way would have successive pregnancies, menstruating only rarely. Only those who could not have children experienced menstruating regularly for many years. Rejected by their husbands and stigmatised by the community, many had no choice but to turn to prostitution. The study of hundreds of thousands of documents describing more than three thousand years of civilization in Mesopotamia reveals this pattern of marriage, childbearing, and the relationship between childlessness and prostitution. While these documents hold no specific references to menstruation, we can surmise its rarity in women other than the childless. Since pregnancy and lactation were associated with amenorrhea and not having children meant menstruating, it can be concluded that menstruating regularly was undesirable.[17]

Thus, due to the prevalence of high mortality of children and the resultant stress placed on childbearing, menstruation in Mesopotamian women appears to have been less prevalent, if not scanty. This perhaps also explains the scarcity of materials detailing Mesopotamian attitudes to menstruation when compared to the Greeks or Romans.

Let us now see what the little evidence available about menstruation tells us about the Mesopotamian perception of the process.

Female Bleeding in Mesopotamia[18]

According to Ulrike Steinert,[19] Mesopotamians associated blood with both life and vulnerability. On the one hand, blood was associated with life and creation, with Babylonian creation myths like those in the *Atramhasis Epic* speaking about how 'the flesh and blood of a slain god served as vital components for the "mixture", from which the first human being or prototype was shaped', and on the other hand, having blood denoted physical vulnerability and human mortality, which also served as a means to differentiate a humans from a demon or a spirit, which could not be wounded by a weapon. Since the bodies of all men and women were made from blood, bleeding was considered unavoidable, and was common to both the genders in the Mesopotamian worldview.

Contrasting the menstrual notions prevalent in Mesopotamian medicine with Greek medicine, Ulrike Steinert further writes: While in Greek medicine, the menses are tied up with ideas of regularity and humoural balance, as well as with beliefs about the "natural" constitution of the female body, comparable gender-specific theories of menstruation seem to be lacking in the Mesopotamian sources.[20]

Though no specific term for menstruation is available from the cuneiform texts concerning medical recipes and incantations, we do find different terms referring to female bleeding in various contexts:

1. 'Blood' (Akkadian: ***damu***; Sumerian: **múd**)
2. 'A woman's blood' (as in: **K. 263+10934: 1**:[21] '**[diš munus múd-*šá* du-*k]u?*** *nu tar-su a-na tar-si*' meaning '**[If a woman's blood flow]**s (and) does not stop, to stop it'; **BM 45736: 13**:'[22] '[KA.inim].ma? munus múd. me-*šú at-ru-ma nak-da-a*[*t*]' meaning '[Incantation] for a woman whose (menstrual?) blood is excessive in quantity so that she is in critical condition'.
3. Bleeding during pregnancy: **BM 42313+ rev. 12**:[23] '**diš munus *šá* 3 iti múd-*šú*** du-*ak ana šà šà-šà* [nu šub]' meaning '**If a woman who is three months (pregnant) bleeds**, (remedy) so that she does [not abort] her foetus'.
4. Bleeding during childbirth: **SpTU 4, No. 153: 7**:[24] 'munus *šá*! (šú)ù.tu-*ma*múd.meš *la ip-par-ra-su* sum-*s[u]*' meaning

'You administer (it) to a woman who? gives birth and subsequently her blood does not stop.'

5. 'Vaginal discharge' (as in **BAM 237 iv 44:**[25] '[diš munus a.m]eš *ina šà gal4.la-šá* du-*[ku …]*' meaning 'If [fluid]s flow from [a woman's] vagina'; **BAM 241 ii 12:**[26] 'munus *ta-ti-ka-at ú-ri-ša* gig[……]' meaning '(If) a woman suffers from **vaginal discharges** (lit. dribbling from her vagina).
6. Blood of a women in childbed i.e. lochia- '***dam harišti***': **BAM 240: 39'f:**[27] 'diš munus ù.tu-*ma kúm er-ri* tuk-*ši i-ár-ru šà ši […]* / **múd** ***a-riš-ti šá ina šà-šá it-te-[es]-ke-ru*** munus bi *ina ù.tu-š[á …]*' meaning 'If a woman has given birth and subsequently she has intestinal fever, vomits, […]: (it is) **the blood of the woman in childbed, which has been blocked/detained in her womb**; this woman […] during h[er] labour […].'
7. 'Flow (of blood)'- '***sagû***': **BM 38624 obv. ii 28'-30':**[28] '*ana* **munus** ***sa-gu-šá ana*** *kul-lu-mu šal-šú ú.KU.nu.[lu.a …]* suuš giš.nam.tar nita *ina* illu šim. bulu i.i *[…]* ***sa-gu-šá im-mar*** *u-ub-tú šá ar-x[…]*' meaning '(A remedy) for a **woman to make her (menstrual) flow (sagû) appear**: you mix one third of tj [atu-plant, …], root of male pillû-plant (mandrake?) with baluu-resin, […], she will have (lit. see) **her (menstrual) flow** (sagûša immar). A remedy of… […]'; **BM 54587+ obv. 6':**[29] '[… *ina*]síg.àka *ana šà.tùr-šú* gar-*ma* ***sa-gu-šú*** tar-*s[u?]*' meaning '[…] you insert (it) in her womb [in] a wad of wool and **her flow (*sagû*) will stop**'.

From the above list, we can see that while terms like ***damu*** or **múd** simply refer to blood, the examples given in 3 and 4 refer to female bleeding during pregnancy and delivery. The example, 6 refers to female lochia and the 'vaginal discharge' spoken of, examples mentioned in 5 refer to pathological discharges.[30] That leaves us with 2 and 7, which calls the bleeding 'woman's blood' and 'flow'. From the context of the examples cited in 7, it is clear that the reference is to the menstrual flow itself and not to other kinds of female bleeding. The reference to the insertion of a wad of wool may further indicate the usage of tampons[31] by Mesopotamian women. Thus, Ulrike Steinert rightly concludes: 'The rare term *sagû* could be a word for menstruation.'[32]

Now, coming to the usage of 'a woman's blood' in 2, K. 263+10934 and other tablets refer to excessive bleeding. But the context does not tell us whether it is a reference to abnormally heavy menstrual bleeding or to bleeding due to abnormal hemorrhage. Stating that it could easily be applicable to both, Ulrike Steinert writes:

> Because the expression 'blood of a woman' in K. 263+ and other gynaecological texts is very general and because no specific Akkadian term for 'menstruation' is known so far (in contrast to Egyptian and Greek), it seems that the Mesopotamian healers did not discriminate between abnormally excessive menstrual discharge and the pathological flow of blood due to [the] internal ailments of the uterus e.g. tumors, uterine fibroids. Yet, from intercultural parallels it can be concluded that the Mesopotamian recipes under discussion indeed refer to stopping either excessive menstrual flow or, in medical parlance, gynaecolgical haemorrhage (abnormal bleeding). Thus, recipes designed for this purpose can also be found in earlier, roughly contemporary and much younger sources: in Egyptian medical papyri, in the Hippocratic Corpus and in Medieval Jewish texts on women's healthcare.... Moreover, the similarities in the ways of treatment and agreements in the use of materia medica in texts of four different cultures and periods hint at the existence and stability over long periods of time of a common medical tradition, which can be described as recipe-based and partially grounded in folk medicine.[33]

Thus, though the usage of 'a woman's blood' does not specifically refer to menstruation, it does include it under its broad definition.

Among the various gynecological conditions, Mesopotamian tablets appear to have given special attention to stopping abnormal flow of women's blood, which includes as stated before both menorrhagia and bleeding due to abnormal hemorrhage. K. 263+10934,[34] for example, provides many recipes for stopping abnormal flow. It is a one-column-tablet from the Nineveh collection belonging to the early Neo-Babylonian period and written in the Neo-Babylonian script. The front side (obverse) of the tablet contains 23 lines, while the reverse contains 25 lines, i.e. a total of 48 lines. The obverse is further divided into three sections: Lines 1-5 forming the first section, lines 6-10 forming the second section and lines 11-23 forming the third section. The reverse of the tablet contains eight sections, with Lines (24-31), (32), (33-36), (37), (38-39), (40), (41), and (42-48), respectively forming the seven sections.

The first section on the obverse side speaks about two recipes, one plant and one mineral, which are to be administered into the vagina as a suppository to stop the bleeding. In the mineral recipe, the text instructs the medical practitioner to pound a yellow mineral and a reddish mineral, mix them together, wrap it in a red wool and insert into the womb. The plant recipe only replaces the mineral ingredients with the plant extracts (one extract being Cedar resin, the other not known) and the procedure remains the same. The second section on the obverse side speaks about three recipes, with the two of them being a suppository, but using only one ingredient. The third recipe, on the other hand involves the preparation of a potion from the blood of the male partridge bird, which is collected in a vessel and kept overnight. It is to be drunk by the patient the next morning on an empty stomach. The third section on the obverse side prescribes thirteen single ingredient treatments, which involve one extract from a plant or a mineral to be drunk in beer.

On the reverse, the first section consists of five recipes for potions to be drunk in beer. No clear information is available regarding the first three recipes given in lines 24-27, since, that portion of the tablet is damaged. However, the other two recipes given in lines 28-31 are clear. One of these is a complex potion containing three ingredients, two of them being plant based and the third lost in the lacuna. The fifth recipe combines a plant extract with an ingredient from the horn of an animal. And, as before, these ingredients are to be soaked in beer overnight to be consumed the next morning. The second section on the reverse contains a one-line recipe for a suppository and has magnetite as its ingredient. The third section also contains a single recipe for a complex mineral based potion, which involves mixing three powdered minerals (one of them being magnetite) with beer, keeping them overnight and drinking them the next morning. The fourth section consists of a single line (line 37), which is a reminder to the medical specialist to chant an incantation in conjunction with the previous recipe to stop the bleeding. The fifth section prescribes two recipes, one to be administered as a suppository, and the other as a potion. Both have magnetite as the ingredient. The sixth and seventh sections are again single line recipes, one for a suppository, which uses iron stone as the ingredient and the other for a potion, whose ingredients are lost in the lacuna, but which needs to be mixed with water. The final section on the reverse prescribes a ritual that could be employed to stop the bleeding. The ritual appears to involve digging up a hole and burying a waterskin filled with some liquid inside the hole. The mouth of the waterskin is then closed with clay and chaff and sealed with a carnelian seal before sunrise. The ritual ends with recitations of three incantations thrice. The incantations, though not completely clear, involve the invoking of the Mesopotamian gods of incantations and magic: Asallui and Ea, while uttering 'I have sealed your mouth'. It is obvious from the ritual imagery that it has been designed in imitation of the woman's medical condition that the ritual is supposed to treat. The waterskin represents the womb, its neck and mouth represent the cervix and the vaginal opening, and the closing of the mouth represents the stopping of the bleeding. The use of incantations with the ritual imitation of the internal process indicates that the Mesopotamian specialists hoped to direct the energy associated with the incantations to be utilised to stop the blood flow by performing the said ritual. This perhaps also indicates that Mesopotamian specialists knew of the play of energies and their harnessing through ritual. While this ritual prescription appears as a standalone recipe to be used for stopping a woman's bleeding, it is nevertheless worth investigating whether this ritual prescription was meant to be used in conjunction with other recipes, like those that prescribe potions. One element which appears to point in this direction is that the ritual stipulates that the opening is sealed before sunrise, i.e. during the night. In the case of potions as well, they are to be prepared during the evening or night by soaking the ingredients in beer and keeping that overnight under the 'goat-star' (i.e. constellation Lyra) and consuming them only in the morning. Thus, it is worth investigating whether the potions prescribed in the recipes were kept overnight by burying them in waterskin using the rituals and incantations mentioned in the last section of the reverse of the tablet or were they kept overnight by placing them openly under the night sky, perhaps to receive the positive energy from the celestial bodies, as suggested by some scholars?

In any case, from the above discussion it is clear that the medical practitioners of Mesopotamia had a keen interest in this subject and that they spent considerable time and effort to research and experiment about abnormal blood flow and other discharges in women. This is reinforced by the wide variety of ingredients from plant, animal and mineral sources used in different recipes. Suppository recipes used plant ingredients like cedar resin; mineral ingredients like magnetite, iron stone, *kalû*, and *kalgukku*; and animal substance like red wool. Potion recipes had an even more impressive list of ingredients. Plant ingredients include: *elikulla*-plant, *illru, imur-lm, karn šlibi* (fox-vine), *kirbn eqli* (field clod) plant, *maštakal* (a soapwort plant), *nnû, nu urtu, puquttu* (a thorny plant), tamarisk (*bnu*) seed and *tarmuš*. Mineral ingredients include: *gabû/aban gabî* (alum), *bir atni*-shell, *kapu*-shell, *kakkusakku*-stone, šadânu bitu (magnetite), šubû-stone and *urzu*-stone. Animal ingredients include: dove's egg, gazelle horn, and male partridge's blood.

Apart from the above mentioned thirty recipes available from a single tablet- K. 263+10934, many other tablets like BAM 235, 236 and 237 from Assur and tablets – BM 38624 and BM 40152 from Neo-Babylonian period also provide many recipes for stopping abnormal female bleeding.

Another condition, which similarly receives attention from the Mesopotamian medical specialists is the abnormal retention of fluids in the womb, which is just the opposite of the case discussed above. Abnormal retention of the fluids or 'locked fluids' as they are called by Steinert, refers to all cases of 'locked fluids', including Amenorrhea (blocked menses) and retained lochia. This becomes clear from tablet BM 38624, which says: 'You prepare (this) mixture for a woman [..., or] for a woman who is locked (lit. turned back) regarding her fluids, [or for a woman who] does not get (lit. see) [her menstrual period?], to make it appear (BM 38624 ii 19'ff[35]).' Another tablet, BAM 240: 67' says: 'If a woman ditto (i.e. gives birth) and subsequently her womb [gives her a stinging pain (and) her hip]s become shrunken more and more, concerning that woman, locked fluids are present.'[36] Mesopotamian texts prescribe different treatments like fumigation from below, suppositories, salves, lotions and bandages to treat this condition. We have already discussed suppositories and potions with respect to abnormal bleeding. Let us now briefly discuss the 'fumigation from below'[37] treatment, before moving further.

Fumigation is basically a process in which hot and dry vapours are directed all over the body or over specific body parts. In the Mesopotamian prescriptions, aromatic substances were burned in fire or on charcoals, and their fumes were directed to the body. In the case of fumigation from below, the patient's genitals and lower abdomen were exposed to the fumes. The Babylonian tablet from Nineveh, K. 8678+ rev. 9'-12'[38] describes the process thus:

> 'If ditto (i.e. a woman is locked regarding the fluids): you dig a hole, you make it two fingers [deep], […],
>
> […] you cover (it). You throw flour? into it, one tenth of a litre of *ka[mnu*-spice?],
>
> […] solid pieces? of resin, one thirtieth of a litre of *ru*-aromatic […],
>
> […] you spread on coals; you make the woman sit down above it.'

Another tablet BAM 237 i 26'-27'[39] suggests scattering human bone over charcoal in the context of prescribing fumigation from below for stopping hemorrhage. Yet another recipe for releasing postpartum blood prescribes thus: '(If) a woman gives birth and subsequently she has intestinal trouble, her excrement? […], her intestines are blocked, her fluids and [her] blood are (b)locked [in her belly?], to make her release (it): *kukru*-aromatic, juniper, *at'išu*-plant, *umlalû*-aromatic, 'sweet reed', *ballukku*-aromatic, myrrh, *ru*-aromatic, *abukattu* resin, *balu u*-aromatic resin, root of *at'išu*-plant. These eleven drugs you mix together. You gather charcoals of *aš gu*-thorn into a *kirru*-vessel, you throw these drugs into it, you have that woman sit down above it, you wrap her with cloth(s).'[40]

It is interesting to note that this process in the Mesopotamian tablets finds a parallel in the Greek Hippocratic texts as well. One procedure in the Greek texts describes fumigation thus: 'it is necessary to dig a hole and to roast grape stones, in the amount of two Attic choinikes; let him throw some of this ash in the hole, continuously dropping sweet-smelling wine. Seating herself around <the hole> and taking her legs apart, let her be fumigated.'[41]

Though, we are not in a position to verify whether these recipes (fumigation, potions and suppositories) begot the desired results, especially since we are not aware of all the ingredients used in them; nevertheless, it is safe to assume the presence of at least some desired results. There would have been no need for medical specialists to record them on tablets, if that were not the case.

Apart from the treatments for locked fluids and hemorrhages, Mesopotamian texts prescribe recipes for the treatment of conception, to give relief from pain after childbirth, to provoke monthly menses, contraception, abortion, infertility, to prevent miscarriage, Urological complaints, Rectal and Gastrointestinal complaints, and many other gynecological conditions. Comparing and contrasting the focus of Mesopotamian medical texts with their counterparts in Chinese and Greco-Roman medicine, Ulrike Steinert writes: 'Mesopotamian gynaecology seems to possess a (non-exclusive) focus, which is similar to the view of women's diseases as the conditions 'below the girdle' found in Chinese treatises. Especially in comparison with Greco-Roman writers, a lack of attention regarding the breasts and lactation seems noticeable in the Mesopotamian texts, but this impression could be related to the fragmentary nature of our sources and is likely to be corrected in the future.'[42]

Thus, there is a clear evidence that Mesopotamian medical specialists showed deep concern for the gynecological problems of women, including those related to menstruation. They have additionally prescribed several treatments using many ingredients drawn from plant, animal, and mineral sources. This also indicates that there was a thriving medical tradition in the Mesopotamian civilisation.

The cuneiform medical texts of Mesopotamia not only help us understand the thriving medical tradition of the ancient civilisation they also serve as our most important source for reconstructing the culture and worldview of the Mesopotamian people as a whole. Thus, even in the case of menstruation, these medical texts have proven to be valuable resource that have enabled us to understand, to some extent, the prevalent notions regarding menstruation.

Using a linguistic and contextual-interpretative approach, Ulrike Steinert has identified a number of different but related facets of how Mesopotamian society perceived female bleeding. She writes: 'The facets that evolve from the analysis reflect in culture-specific ways how views of women's bodily processes are infused with social meaning, in regard to women's biological and social roles. In short, female blood is seen in contradictory and context-dependent ways: as an unavoidable "ill", as a potential danger to a woman's (or her foetus') life and health, as the counterpart to male warriors' shedding of blood in battle, but sometimes also as a source of female power posing a threat to men's bodies, health and control, which (ironically) can be harnessed to serve socially sanctified ends, i.e. to get rid of (even greater) evil and to fight illness.'[43]

Let us now look into some of these aspects of female bleeding in more detail.

Menstruation as 'illness'

A late Babylonian tablet SpTU 1, 59: 12'-13' from Uruk dated to around 5th-4th century BCE refers to menstruation as 'illness'.

It states: '[So that a woman] who does not see her 'illness', will see her 'illness': You crush *imur-ešra*-plant, [....]-root, [......] (and) *aumtu*-plant together, in oil, beer and/or vinegar [...].'[44] Similarly, Diagnostic Handbook (SA.GIG) Tablet 36: 94, 95, 98 states: 'If a childbearing woman in the middle of her 'trouble' steps to the right: she is pregnant with a 'sleeping one'. If she steps to the left: she is pregnant with a female...'[45] From this we can gather that Mesopotamians attached a notion of 'unavoidable illness or trouble' with menstruation. This notion is widely prevalent across the world. Though illness is often associated with a negative connotation, the reference given in the tablet SpTU 1, 59: 12'-13', hints that it may not have been so. For one, it is clearly a recipe to help women who are experiencing trouble with their periods. It purports to cause it to happen in women whose periods are blocked or delayed. Thus, the existence of such a recipe denotes that Mesopotamian women in general, and medical practitioners in particular, understood the importance of regular periods for the health of women. This view was reflected in Greco-Roman medicine as well. If menstruation was perceived as 'illness' in the negative sense, why would there be a recipe to bring about monthly periods? Hence, it appears that the association of illness or trouble with menstruation may have been a reference to the inconvenience caused during periods due to continuous bleeding as well as weakness, irritation, and stomach cramps that accompany menstruation. Though this is merely a conjecture at this stage, it is worth exploring further.

Another interesting reference to female bleeding, especially from the genitals, is found in BAM 235 obverse 4-5, which is a Neo-Assyrian tablet from Assur, dated to the seventh century BCE. It refers to the bleeding as 'to be struck by a weapon' and says: 'If a woman 'is struck by a weapon', you crush blood of a par[tridge, ...], (and) *nu urtu*-plant together, you have her drink (it) in beer, [...].'[46] Though the tablet does not refer to menstruation in particular, since menstruation is one of the most frequent states when a woman bleeds, the reference appears to be equally applicable to menstruation as well, or perhaps at least to the state of excessive menstrual bleeding. In any case, the phrase 'to be struck by a weapon' is very interesting because it implies an injury. To understand the possible implication of this reference, let us draw a parallel with Ayurveda.

Ayurveda, as we saw before, prescribes a life-style to be adopted by menstruating women called Rajaswala Paricharya, so that they stay healthy, and to prevent imbalance in the internal Doshas. Among the many tenets which govern the life-style practices suggested by Ayurvedic texts, one is the perception of a menstruating woman as a person with an injury. The fact that the body sheds the lining of the uterus during menstruation is taken as an indication of an active wound, and hence, the Ayurvedic texts advise menstruating women to avoid physical exertion, including indulging in sexual intercourse, and to consume light and easily digestible foods. The same practices have been prescribed by Ayurvedic texts in the treatment of people, both men and women, with serious wounds.

From the above discussion, it is clear that one of the ways in which menstruation was perceived, at least in the Indian medical tradition, was as a condition of injury. We find a similar description in the Mesopotamian tablets calling female bleeding 'to be struck by a weapon'. Is it possible that Mesopotamian medical practitioners likewise considered the shedding of the uterus lining as an injury? Was it also one of the reasons why they considered menstruation as a period of 'trouble'? This needs to be further investigated. One pointer in this direction is the comparison of male bleeding from genitals or anus to the females being 'struck by a weapon' in some of the tablets. BAM 159 i 9-11 (MJ Geller, Renal and Rectal Disease Texts (BAM VII), No. 1), for example, mentions: 'If a man passes blood from his penis, like a woman he is struck by a weapon.'[47] Similarly, BAM 99: 27-29 (MJ Geller, Renal and Rectal Disease Texts (BAM VII), No. 35: 27ff) mentions: 'If a man passes blood from his anus, like a woman he is struck by a weapon'.[48] These comparisons of female bleeding with men's injuries resulting in bleeding from the phallus or the anus, do reinforce the view that female bleeding, including menstruation, was perceived as a wound or injury.

Female bleeding as a source of impurity

From the available primary sources, we come to know that the notions of purity and impurity were prevalent in Mesopotamia. While the terms 'kug/kù' and 'dadag' referred to purity in the Sumerian language, the Akkadian terms for purity included the adjectives *ellu* and *ebbu*. Impurity, on the other hand, was referred to by the terms *lu'û* and *(w)aršu/maršu*.

According to Yitzhaq Feder,[49] there are three main aspects of purity/impurity in the sociolinguistic context, which provide an experiential basis for the Mesopotamian notions on the subject. The first is the legal context, wherein purity stands for innocence and impurity for guilt, both to be detected by divine judgment. The second is the ritual context, wherein purity is being free of metaphysical threats, while impurity is being afflicted with metaphysical threats that causes illness and calamity. The third is the context of cult/sacrificial offering, where purity means sacred and eligible for participation in sacrificial offering and the divine space, while impurity means being disqualified from sacrificial offering and the sacred domain. Highlighting the importance of context and the nuance involved in the Mesopotamian view of purity-impurity, Erica Couto-Ferreira and Agnes Garcia-Ventura, write: First, those Sumerian and Akkadian terms usually translated as 'to purify', 'purity', 'pure', etc. show a broad range of semantic nuances that go beyond the ethical, theological, moral and religious sense implied by modern translations of 'purity'. Most verbs and nouns are used in the context of washing (the body, clothing), cleaning (objects of different type), or in the descriptions of the shining nature of an object's properties or material. Most terms referring to cleanliness also show the nuance 'in order, proper'. Second, it is the context rather than the individual or the object *per se* that usually determines when something can be considered 'impure', 'improper', 'unacceptable' or 'disagreeable'. Third, many of these terms can be, and are, applied to both men and women.[50]

Regarding the terms used for purity in Sumerian and Akkadian (and Biblical Hebrew, Ugaritic and Hittite), Yitzhaq Feder writes, 'The primary terms for purity in all of these languages are etymologically related to radiance.'[51] The Sumerian term 'kug/kù', for example, though translated as 'holy' or 'pure' in cultic context, actually means 'shiny' or the quality of shininess.[52] For this reason, the term was used with respect to metal, as in 'kug-sig' meaning yellow metal (i.e. gold).[53] The term 'dadag' can be read as the verb 'zalag', which means 'to shine'.[54] The Akkadian term *ellu*, which is often translated as pure, clean, holy, etc. is likewise also related to 'radiance', since it appears as 'a term for a class of high quality gold and silver' and is also used with reference to high quality precious stone.[55] Further '*ellu*' is used to refer to light and to describe the radiance of the sky as well as the radiance of the face of god Aššu.[56] The term *ebbu*, used to denote cultic purity, is also used to refer to the radiance and brightness of substances.[57] This shows that the Mesopotamian notion of purity, be it with respect to mundane cleanliness or with respect to ritual purity and sacredness, was deeply rooted in the concept of radiance.

Regarding the concept of impurity, Feder stresses: 'From the outset, it is worth emphasizing that there is no Akkadian term for pollution designating a metaphysical force comparable to Hebrew *umah* or Hittite *papratar*.'[58] In the Hittite texts, when the term *papratar* is used in the ritual context, it refers to 'a metaphysical threat which causes illness and other types of misfortune'.[59] In other words, the usage represents an awareness of the concept of miasma or Ashaucha among the Hittites. On the other hand, Feder opines that such a specific term for pollution denoting the metaphysical function of miasma does not exist in the Akkadian language. Nevertheless, as Feder himself adds: 'several expressions can be identified which signify an unclean state.'[60] One such term is the adjective '*lu'û*', which means 'soiled or dirty'.[61] The term is used with reference to the spread of disease in many texts. Another term '*(w)aršu/maršu*', which means 'dirty or unclean' has been often associated with 'the unclean wool of the fuller',[62] which is yet to be processed into a pure wool. This term has also been used in the cultic context as a designation for a state which defiles or desecrates.[63] Then, we have *urruštu*, a derivative of *(w)aršu/maršu*, which is used as a designation for 'unclean women, both parturients and menstruants'.[64] Thus, we have two kinds of impurity, one designated by *lu'û* and the other designated by *aršu*. Contrasting the two, Feder writes that while the former indicates a state of infection caused by ingestion or contact, the latter refers to 'unclean garments' and indicates 'benign uncleanness that must be distanced from the cult'.[65] That is, while '*lu'û*' indicates a condition of serious disease, '*aršu*' indicates a state of impurity in the cultic or religious context. Feder summarises the difference thus: 'synchronic analysis of texts from the Neo-Assyrian period indicates that *aršu* is used to designate the experiential scheme of Uncleanness, whereas *lu'û* is also used in relation to infection.'[66] Another Mesopotamian term that is significant here is *l ellu*, which signifies a condition that makes 'a person or sacrifice unfit for cultic or divinatory use, hence fitting the scheme of Uncleanness'.[67] This concept of *l ellu* has a clear parallel in the Hindu concept of Ashaucha, which is not only related to impurity at various levels, but also refers to the incompetency of a person to perform a certain sacred task owing to this impurity. This is significant, because it points to the fact that Mesopotamian society was aware of at least some aspects of miasma or Ashaucha. Thus, the notions of purity and impurity was widely prevalent in Mesopotamian society and they were also aware about some aspects of miasma, including those relating to ritual and worship, though they did not have a specific term to refer to the metaphysical effects of miasma.

Now coming to the association of impurity with female bleeding, scholars such as Erica Couto-Ferreira and Agnes Garcia-Ventura[68] have pointed out how 'the relationship between menstruation and impurity is assumed by most scholars to be universal and self-evident' and how 'the phrasing of "impurity", when linked with "woman" and "menstruation", triggers a mechanism of knowledge production based in biblical and Christian concepts that contributes to the perpetuation of the dominant patriarchal model'. They add: 'In fact, the specific history of Assyriology as a discipline that derived from the search for confirmation of biblical narratives lies at the basis of many traditional positions adopted in Assyriology.' This is a very significant observation, which holds true as much about Assyriology as with the study of Greek and other ancient civilisations. The association of miasma with menstruation prevalent in many ancient civilisations is often perceived as a degradation of women, all the while sidelining or completely ignoring the sacred aspects of menstruation. This one-sided treatment of menstruation and impurity can be observed in the case of Hinduism as well. One of the probable reasons for this is the prevalence of the Abrahamic worldview in western academia, which either directly through theological frameworks or indirectly through various non-theological frameworks (for example, feminism), influences how scholars understand and interpret ancient civilisations. The absence of female divinity in the Abrahamic worldview has resulted in the sidelining of pagan goddess traditions that were associated with female biological experiences starting from menstruation to menopause. As a result, the miasma or impurity aspect has come to be associated with negative connotations, instead of being perceived as complementary to the sacred aspect of menstruation. Another factor is the separation of the sacred and the profane, which is the basis of the predominant worldview in the West today. This has also resulted in the perception of impurity as non-sacred, instead of being viewed as the other side of the same coin.

Moving on, among the corpus of cuneiform texts related to female bleeding, we find at least two terminologies: *urruštu* and *(m)usukkatu*, which associate female bleeding, including menstruation with impurity. *Urruštu* as mentioned before is a reference to both parturients and menstruants. It literally means 'dirty woman' or 'unclean woman'. Feder opines that the term may reflect a 'substantivised usage of the D-stem verbal adjective: "the stained (one)", referring directly to the sullied garments of these women'.[69] *Musukkatu*, on the other hand, is the feminine form of *musukku*. *Musukku* means an unclean person and included all those who were disallowed from participating in some collective activity, presumably because of their incompetency due to impurity. *Musukkatu*, like *urruštu*, referred to both parturients and menstruants. Feder writes: 'Contact with the *musukkatu* disqualifies objects and personnel from ritual use. Furthermore, these women are to be secluded and are presumably prohibited from having sexual relations.'[70] In other words, there was a clear association of female bleeding with impurity.

For example, in one of the tablets (Hunger, SpTU 1, No. 44: 69ff. //) it is mentioned: 'May they draw water from the

Ulai river (and) from the wide sea, in which an *urruštu* (impure woman) has not washed her hands, in which a *musukkatu* woman has not washed her clothing!'[71] Another tablet says: 'may they draw water from the Ajabba, the wide sea, water from the Tigris (and) water from the Euphrates, over which an *urrutštu* woman has not bent down, [in whi]ch a *musuk [katu*-woman has not washed herself]!'[72] In both the tablets, both *urruštu* and *musukkatu* have been used, perhaps one referring to menstruating women and the other to parturient, and both kinds of women have been associated with a notion of impurity. Also, the injunction not to bathe in the water used by menstruants and parturients seems to point towards the prevalence of some awareness about the workings of miasma energies. Such awareness can also be understood from references to 'dirty women' in incantations against child-snatching Lamaštu, a malevolent goddess in Mesopotamian lore. One such incantation says: '…I have conjured you (lit. made your swear) by the power (lit. oath) of the angry heart and (anger)-darkened head, by the power of well and ditch, by the power of garbage pile and its dust, by the power of the clothing of a dirty woman, by the power of the road and those who travel on it…',[73] and thus, clearly referring to the 'power of the clothing of dirty woman' i.e. the energy associated with the female blood, which has been perhaps shed during menstruation. Further, one of the Mesopotamian omens says, 'If a man touches a *musukkatu* woman passing by, [he will] not [be pure?] for six days'.[74] Another Sumerian proverb says: 'The goat spoke in the manner of a wise old woman but acted in the manner of an impure woman.'[75] There is a regulation from an Assyrian harem, where women 'who may not be approached' (i.e. menstruating women) were temporarily excluded from coming before the king.[76] Also, there was a prohibition against touching an 'unclean woman' at the end of ritual aimed at obtaining the favour of a deity for a man.[77] From this, we can gather that Mesopotamian society did associate a notion of impurity to menstruation and also appears to have understood to some extent the workings of miasma energies associated with menstruation.

It is interesting to note that it was not female bleeding alone which was associated with impurity. We find interesting references to even male genital discharges being designated as impure. In one of the rituals to remove impurity, it is mentioned: 'If a man's limbs are "poured out" like (those of) a sick person, [...], his feet and a his ...are weak, he talks (about doing something), but does not achieve (anything), his potency is taken away, he is always angry, his semen flows like one who has illicit sex with a woman, either with his urine or spontaneously: that man is impure, god and goddess have turned away from him, his word does not find acceptance.'[78] In another ritual, this time against witchcraft, it is mentioned: 'If a man is bewitched so that his body is "poured out", his semen flows whether he is walking, standing or lying down or when he is urinating, like (those of) a woman his seminal emissions are impure.'[79] Thus, there is a clear association of impurity with male genital discharge as well. This shows that Mesopotamians associated impurity with all genital discharges, be it menstrual blood in women or seminal discharge in men.

Medical Use of Female Body Substances

Mesopotamian physicians appear to have utilised various body substances from women in impure condition for medical treatments. For example, the milk of *musukkatu* women was used as an ingredient in the treatments for the eyes.[80] Similarly, the urine of a woman who had just given birth to a boy was used in a recipe for a leather pouch to remove epilepsy.[81] Then, there was 'soiled rag' i.e. the menstrual bandage that was also widely used in various medical recipes.

One of the tablets, BAM 183: 6-7, says: 'In order for illness not to approach a baby: cornel(?) seed, tamarisk seed, *papparhû* seed and soiled rag you roast, crush and mix with oil. Before (the baby) is given the breast to suckle, you anoint him (with the mixture), and he will stay healthy.'[82] Another tablet, BAM 183: 10-15 // K. 3628+: 19'-24', gives the following recipe: 'For ditto (so that the *lilû*-demon does not come close to a baby): You fumigate (var. anoint) him with snake skin, "mother scorpion" (i.e. the back shield of a scorpion?), cress, soiled rag, combed-out hair, and horned alkali.'[83] Yet another recipe from the tablet- AMT 93/1: 10'-12' //, says: 'If a ghost afflicts a man, to cure him: you fumigate him with pig dung, dog dung, wolf dung, fox dung, gazelle dung, *nnû* plant, horned alkali, stag horn, sulphur, bitumen, human bone and dirty rag (burned) over embers.'[84]

From the above illustrations, it is obvious that the medical usage of substances from parturients and menstruants, be it the milk or the menstrual bandage, not only shows an awareness about medical properties associated with substances from *musukkatu* women, but also an awareness about the usefulness of the miasma energies with respect to certain illness and psychological and metaphysical conditions. Whether these medical recipes were really effective or not is difficult to say today since only fragments of information are now available. Nevertheless, the medical usage of menstrual bandages, for example, reinforces the view that Mesopotamians had some knowledge about the association of miasma with menstruation and how these miasma energies functioned.

Inanna and Ishtar: Sacred aspect of Menstruation

As is the case with the Greeks and the Romans, an account of menstruation in the Mesopotamian civilisation is incomplete without a discussion about its sacred aspect. This is depicted by Inanna and Ishtar, prominent goddesses of Mesopotamia, both of whom preside over love, fertility, beauty, sexual desire, war and power.

Though Inanna and Ishtar are two independent goddesses, they are in reality one deity worshipped by two different names with similar functions and sharing similar mythologies. While Inanna was a Sumerian goddess, early attested and widely worshipped among Sumerians with the city of Uruk as her main cult center, Ishtar was a later counterpart of Inanna, who was prominently worshipped in the Akkadian and Babylonian Empires until the spread of Christianity around first-fifth century that resulted in the decline and eventual extinction of Mesopotamian religions. In other words, to speak of one will automatically include the other.

Though Inanna/Ishtar is mostly associated with love and war, she is also associated with the moon and menstruation. To begin with, Inanna was often described as the daughter of the moon god 'Nanna-Suen' and his wife Ningal.[85] Across the world cultures, the moon has been consistently associated with menstruation, and as the daughter of the moon-god, she was also associated with menstruation. Also, Inanna was rarely referred to as 'mother' or 'old woman' in the cuneiform texts. Instead, she was most predominantly associated with maidens – young girls between menarche and marriage.[86] She was further described as Morning Star and Evening Star[87] and models of vulvas representing her have been found in many excavated sites.[88] She was also intimately associated with the planet Venus.[89] These give strong indications of the association of Inanna/Ishtar with menstruation.

Describing the intimate nature of this association, Judy Grahn writes: This is a deity for whom menstruation, sexuality, and other functions of her vulva are at the heart of her sacrality (Meador, 1992; Wolkstein & Kramer, 1983).This surely explains why the laws of the cosmos are woven into a holy loincloth that binds her loins. One of her other names, Ishtar, contains the syllables indicating menses (Meador, 2000, p. 56). The inner sanctum of her temple, the giparu, is the women's secluded section. The Sumerians were people who celebrated Inanna at the new moon by holding a parade for her, and who reveled in sacred blood: they sprinkled drops of blood when they walked in procession to her, and they poured the red liquid of blood on to the dais where she would stand, or seat herself (Black et al., 1998-2001a; Wolkstein & Kramer, 1983).[90]

Another scholar, Sandra Bart Heimann, points out that Inanna 'represents women's blood power, menstruation, especially the first maiden's menses'.[91] She further writes that as the moon-goddess, Inanna 'appears and disappears', and how this disappearance is a reference to the 'menstruation seclusion' of both the women and the goddess. In one text, Inanna leaves the battlefield and retires to her temple house for menstruation seclusion but is then persuaded to return. In another poem, a mortal man who had gone to meet the goddess, looks through her window and finds Inanna sitting nude on a cushion. Regarding the symbolism of this imagery, Sandra Bart Heimann writes: 'The window is the very same window of goddess and woman alike. They peer from the sanctity of the women's quarters.... The cushion Inanna sits upon is the menstrual seat that evolves into the seat of power of rulers.'[92] Later, in another place, Heimann adds: Inanna rules her planet and emerges as the new crescent moon, her disappearance as planet and dark moon is menstrual seclusion. Any cyclic seclusion is equivalent to menstruation, women's blood power. Inanna's association with new moon and blood reveal her as goddess of menstruation. Though that particular epithet is not stated in poems, it is implied and underlies her fertile potency.[93]

Thus, as the daughter of the moon god, Inanna/Ishtar was a goddess of menstruation, who not only presided over menarche, but also governed the transition of young maidens from menarche to marriage. At the dark moon, she disappeared into her menstruation seclusion, and presided over such menstruation seclusions of mortal women. Goddess Inanna imparted sacredness to the entire phenomenon of menstruation and facilitated young girls to smoothly blossom from being children into maidens and then into brides.

To conclude, Mesopotamians associated blood with both life and vulnerability. Menstruation and other female bleeding were referred by a number of terms, prominent among them being 'women's blood'. Though the cuneiform texts do not have a specific word for menstruation, the term 'sagû' appears to have been used only in the context of menstruation.

Mesopotamian society appears to have been aware about both impurity (miasma) and the sacred aspects of menstruation. On the miasma front, they variously perceived menstruation as an illness, as a source of miasma with polluting power, which also had useful benefits. On the sacred front, menstruation was presided by goddess Inanna/Ishtar, who made the entire process fulfilling for young girls. On the medical front, Mesopotamian gynecological texts extensively dealt with various ailments unique to women and proposed a number of recipes to counter conditions like abnormally excessive menstrual discharge.

Egyptian Civilisation

Ancient Egyptians perceived life as a cycle of birth, death and rebirth,[1] and in this cycle, menstruation, marriage and pregnancy played a very important role. They, in fact, identified menstruation with the Nile Flood, one of the most important symbols in Egyptian theology, and like it, menstruation was perceived as a 'symbol of renewal and fertility',[2] despite also being a 'dangerous time'.[3] To them, much like their counterparts in Mesopotamia, Greece and latter Rome, menstruation had both 'Miasma' and sacred elements. But, it appears, it was the Egyptians alone, apart from the ancient Hindus of India, who had recognised menstruation as a purificatory process.

Social Condition of Women in Ancient Egypt

Women in ancient Egypt appear to have enjoyed far more freedom than their counterparts in the Greco-Roman civilisations. They enjoyed the same legal and financial rights as their male counterparts. They could own and sell property, including money, land, goods, servants etc. They could sign contracts and conclude legal agreements. They could adopt children, initiate divorce, remarry, free the slaves; they were also entitled to sue at law.

As in most societies, old and new, husbands were considered the heads of their household. Yet, in Egypt, we find women enjoying enormous liberty, love and affection both at home and outside. Prince Ptah-hotep, the author of *Papyrus Prisse*, who probably lived about 3,350 BCE, advises thus to menfolk: If you are wise, you will take proper care of your house and love your wife in all honor. Nourish, clothe and adorn her, as this is the joy of her limbs. Provide her with pleasing odours; make her glad and happy as long as you live, because she is a gift that shall be worthy of its owner. Don't be a tyrant. By friendly conduct you will attain much more than by rough force. Then her breath will be merry and her eyes bright. Gladly she will live in your house and will work in it with affection and to her heart's content.[4]

Egyptologist Barbara Watterson observes:

> In ancient Egypt a woman enjoyed the same rights under the law as a man. What her *de jure* [rightful entitlement] rights were

> depended upon her social class not her sex. All landed property descended in the female line, from mother to daughter, on the assumption, perhaps, that maternity is a matter of fact, paternity a matter of opinion. A woman was entitled to administer her own property and dispose of it as she wished. She could buy, sell, be a partner in legal contracts, be executor in wills and witness to legal documents, bring an action at court, and adopt children in her own name. An ancient Egyptian woman was legally capax [competent, capable]. In contrast, an ancient Greek woman was supervised by a kyrios [male guardian] and many Greek women who lived in Egypt during the Ptolemaic Period, observing Egyptian women acting without kyrioi, were encouraged to do so themselves. In short, an ancient Egyptian woman enjoyed greater social standing than many women of other societies, both ancient and modern.[5]

Professionally, men and women were largely involved in different kinds of tasks. While men waged wars, managed political administration and looked after the day-to-day activities of the farm; women shouldered overall responsibility of the house, including cooking, sewing etc.[6] They were also free to pursue careers as doctors, scribes, and priests. In fact, female doctors were highly respected.[7] Other professions in which women engaged themselves with, included brewing, weaving, baking etc.

Although we do not find mention of aspecific marriage ceremony, marriage was the 'natural state for people of all classes'.[8] Paintings, inscriptions and reliefs have portrayed 'husbands and wives eating together, dancing, drinking, and working the fields with one another',[9] signifying the importance of marriage in ancient Egypt. There was no fixed age for marriage, but girls usually got married after the onset of menstruation, which was usually around the age of twelve to fourteen years. In fact, unlike today, when an arbitrary age of sixteen or eighteen is considered as threshold between childhood and adulthood, Egyptian girls appear to have been considered adult upon entering menarche and marriage. A passage from an Egyptian text titled 'Instructions of Ani' considered belonging to the eighteenth dynasty of the New Kingdom, urges a man to marry and teach his spouse to be 'human', suggesting a direct correlation between marriage (and menarche) and adulthood.[10] Though there is no mention of menarche rituals or rites of passages in the Egyptian sources, we do have enough evidence about menarche (combined with marriage) as being a threshold of maturity on crossing which, girls became women. Tomb paintings, for example, differentiated female children from adult married women using markers like hairstyles and clothing.[11] While young girls were depicted with a hairstyle called 'sidelock of youth', adult women were depicted with a different hairstyle.[12] Similarly, adolescent girls at banquets have been shown wearing only a girdle, while mature women appear more clothed.[13] Grown-up women have also been associated with a V-necked dress.[14] Carolyn Graves-Brown in her book *Dancing For Hathor: Women in Ancient Egypt*, rightly concludes: 'While we cannot be sure of any formal rite of passage, girls do seem to have been differentiated from women by their clothes, hairstyles and titles.'[15] Thus, the onset of menstruation, followed by marriage, were important events of transformation in women's lives in ancient Egypt.

Pregnancy was another important event, which gave Egyptian women 'respect of society, approval from their husbands, and the admiration of their less-fortunate sisters and sterile friends'.[16] In fact, Egyptian husbands were allowed to divorce their spouses if they were unable to become pregnant. Yet, the choice for birth control and abortion were also available for women,[17] though we do not know how widespread they were, especially considering the fact that fertility was held in esteem and children were regarded as 'gifts of the gods'.[18] But, we do find prescriptions for contraception and records about abortion techniques in the *Ebers Medical Papyrus*, which has been dated to 1550 BCE.[19]

In short, Egyptian women enjoyed far more favourable conditions in their daily life than their counterparts in Ancient Greece or Ancient Rome. Since fertility was held in high esteem, menarche, marriage, and pregnancy, all played a significant role in an Egyptian woman's life.

Conception of Purity in Ancient Egypt

While our understanding of the notion of purity and impurity in the Greco-Roman or Mesopotamian civilisations has been limited due to scarcity of primary sources, it is quite the opposite in the case of Ancient Egypt.

Joachim Friedrich Quack, in his work *Conceptions of Purity in Egyptian Religion*,[20] which is a thorough survey of how purity was practised by Ancient Egyptians, notes how the research on what constitutes purity in Ancient Egypt has not reached the same levels as other cultures because, 'it almost seems that one is threatened with drowning in the vast sea of relevant texts and images'.[21] Further, a very few of the large number of available sources are actually 'substantial, normative and explicit at the same time'.[22] He adds that as a result of the research into Egyptian notions of purity being in a very preliminary stage, we would have to reconstruct the Egyptian attitudes towards purity based on only the 'isolated traces that it has left here and there'.[23]

Despite these severe limitations to understanding the Egyptian notions of purity, Quack has covered large grounds in his reconstruction. His work is divided into nine sections, including the introduction and the final remarks, and each of those sections focus on the concept of purity and how it was practised on the ground, with respect to a different aspect of Egyptian society.

In section two, Quack focuses on the notion of purity in connection to temples, their rituals, and with respect to access to them. The daily temple ritual, for example, was basically a morning ritual for purification and clothing the deity's idol. The very first act of this ritual – 'striking fire' was intimately associated with purity. Another illustrative example is the 'Ritual of Amenophis', widely attested from the New Kingdom onward. In this ritual, purification acts occur at the beginning, then during the preparation and serving of food offerings, and finally as 'a burning of incense and libation to Re'.[24] Similarly, purification acts with water and incense are inevitable parts in the consecration of divine idols through rituals such as the Ritual of Opening the Mouth. Quack observes: 'purification scenes are usually placed at the beginning of a ritual, in order to define the place, persons and objects involved as being pure'.[25] Quack then notes how the 'Egyptian temple is a system with zones of increasingly limited access',[26] with purity being one of the factors governing it. According to the *Book of the Temple*, only high-ranking priests were allowed entry into the interior parts of the temple, and the last of the interior rooms housed the gate-keepers. Similarly, the Osirian part of the temple was accessible to very few ritual specialists. Moreover, trespassers, if caught, were executed. An inscription in the temple of Esna[27] stipulates that those who want to enter the temple must have shaved, clipped their nails and combed their hair. It further says that only women who have become pure, nine days from menstruation, and who have not eaten anything taboo during the four days of menstruation could enter the temple.

These have interesting parallels with Hinduism. The rituals dedicated to deities in Hinduism, be it their consecration or their daily worship, are accompanied with strict rules of 'Shaucha' (purity). The priests, the temple and its surroundings, and the entire temple set-up are subjected to various purity measures.

Further, the innermost part of the temple where the deity has been established called *Garbha Griha* is to be accessed only by the priests performing puja (worship) and not by lay people. We already know that menstruating women are obliged to not enter Hindu temples during their monthly periods. These commonalities point towards an intimate knowledge among the Ancient Egyptians regarding the working of Shaucha-Ashaucha or Katharsis-Miasma energies.

Another common element between the Hindus and the Ancient Egyptians is with respect to purity requirements attached to temple priests, which Quack takes up in section three of his study. Hindu temple priests,[28] who are called *Archakas*, one who performs *archana* (a kind of worship) forms a subset of Brahmanas, who cater to the spiritual and religious needs of Hindu society. They are subjected to a very strict code of purity in their conduct and their food habits, and are obliged to perform a water-based purificatory ritual called *Sandhyavandana* twice or thrice a day. They must also adhere to the ethical values like truth, non-stealing etc. Ancient Egyptians, it appears, had similar strict purity requirements for their temple priests. The very term for priest in the Egyptian texts is *w'b*, which is derived from a root with the meaning 'to be pure'.[29] They were allowed to wear only a certain kind of clothing for entering the temple and were also expected to follow food restrictions. Quack notes[30] that while some priests used to abstain from all foods derived from living creatures, others did not consume animals with cloven hoofs, meat-eating birds, and some other animals like female cows. From temple reliefs,[31] like those at the bark sanctuary of Hatschepsut from the eighteenth dynasty, we come to know that the priests were also supposed to perform a purification ritual with water in connection to their access to the temple sanctuary, a striking parallel with the *Sandhyavandana* rituals of the Hindu archakas. Egyptian priests were also supposed to adhere to strict ethical codes, including adhering to tenets like truth, non-stealing etc. In one of the hieroglyphic temple-access texts from the temples of Edfu and Kom Ombo, the priests are asked to follow these guidelines:[32]

Do not introduce in trespassing!
Do not enter in a state of grime!
Do not tell lies in his house!
Do not snatch through calumny!
Do not accept any list(?)
In being partisan against the small for the great!
Do not add to the weight and to the measuring rope,
And you shall not detract from them!
Do not change arbitrarily in the grain measure!
Do not hurt the bushel of the eye of Re!
Do not reveal what you have seen in privacy
Of all secrets of the gods and goddesses!
Do not stretch out your arm for possession in his temple!
Do not take any liberty to steal his possession!
Beware lest a fool says in is heart:
'One lives by the food of the gods'!
One designates as 'food' what is coming from the offering altar in circulation,
After the god has satisfied himself with it.
He sails in heaven; he crosses the celestial vault,
While his eyes lie on his possessions at their location.
Do not do anything bad against the servant of his house!
He loves his servants very much!
Do not have any sexual intercourse under pressure!
Do not impose any condemnation!
Do not exert any violence against the people in the fields and in the city,

Because they came out of his eyes,
They originated from him!
His heart is very sad about injustice in punishing,
If there is no witness (?).
Do not run with your soles,
Do not be short-tempered in a moment!
Do not give your mouth free run in a discussion!
Do not react with loud voice against the voice of somebody else!
Do not impose any oath over something!
Do not prefer the lies against the truth in a complaint!
Beware that you are not (too) big when passing your service times(?)!
There is none who complains against him
Who is free of being punished for something.
Do not sing in his house in the inner part of the temple at the location of the women!
Do not do anything at a place where it should not be done,
So that there is not a party taking place in his house,
But only at the place in front of which it is allowed to sing
By the entity(?) of the staff(?)!
Do not open the jar in the inner part of the temple,
So that you will not be drunk from it!
Do not anything according to your heart,
But you should look at the old writings!
Pass the directions of the temple in your hands
As an instruction for your children!

Thus, we see a well-established notion of purity and its connection to sacredness in the context of temple worship among the Ancient Egyptians.

In section four, five and six, Quack covers the Egyptian notions of purity with respect to the King, the Elite, and the Commoners, respectively. While the elite, especially the King, were subjected to elaborate purification rituals and restrictions, the commoners had leeway, in some cases reduced to only a notional adherence.

Quack notes that the King was strongly linked to the concerns of Purity.[33] In fact, royal purification rituals for the King have been recorded in a number of Egyptian sources. These rituals were often linked with the Sun god and the morning purification was supposed to have been performed before sunrise.[34] This is yet another parallel with Hinduism, wherein Kings and other Kshatriyas (people belonging to the military and to the administration) were supposed to perform Sandhyavandana, a purificatory ritual dedicated to the Sun, that was to be performed at dawn before sunrise (as well as at dusk). In any case, this purification of the king is a widely prevalent motif across Egypt.[35] We find it in the Old and Middle Kingdoms, though only in fragments. On the other hand, this motif is well attested in the New Kingdom. The oldest complete attestation goes back to the eighteenth dynasty. Regarding how this motif was represented in the New Kingdom, Quack writes: 'Afterward, from the New Kingdom until the Greco-Roman period, the motif of the king being purified by two or four gods is quite well attested. The stylisation of the scene is notable: The water streaming out of the jars of the gods is constituted in most cases by hieroglyphic signs in the shape of "life" (*"nh*) and "dominion" (*w*s*). The positive effects that the purification should produce are made quite obvious thereby. The specific location of this scene is the area of entry into the temple, thus they are mostly engraved in the outer passageways of a temple.'[36] Quack, in fact, reproduces in full, a detailed royal ritual containing thirteen spells for the purification of the King. Though, it is beyond the scope of this book to look into these spells in detail, we reproduce here a few excerpts:[37]

O Water, may you abolish all bad defilement of the pharaoh,
O inundation, may you wash off his errant demons.
May you wash the face of Horus,
May you rub the face of Seth,
May you wash the face of Neith,
May you rub the face of her spinners,
May you yourself rub the face of the pharaoh
As the face of the king when he bedecks his crown!
Loosened are the bands of the pharaoh through Horus,
Opened are his bands through Seth.
His purity is the purity of his god.
He shall not fall on some evil obstacle!
A king's offering, Pharaoh is pure. (Third spell)
Pharaoh has [purified himself] with the great waters
Which come forth from Elephantine, which originate from the [primeval ocean].
He has [purified] himself with the eye of Horus,
He has purified himself with its own substance.
Isis has purified him as she has purified her son Horus in Chemmis.
[He] is the one, prestigious in his dignity (?) in truth,
He is Thot who purified himself with his own substance,
[as] Re purified himself with his own substance.
He has perfumed himself with incense, natron is adhering to his limbs.
Pharaoh is Horus in Chemmis.
To be spoken on four pellets of incense, four pellets of natron, putting them
into water in a new bowl, to put a falcon of wax into it and some [...]
that means [...]. (Eighth spell)
May you awake in peace,
May the ore awake in peace!

Homs purifies himself with him,
Seth purifies himself with him,
Thot purifies himself with him,
Dun-Awi purifies himself with him,
The Djed-pillar purifies himself with him.
May they abolish with it the evil adhering to themselves!
Pharaoh purifies himself with him,
May he abolish with it the evil adhering to him!
He enters into it with the cast-off (garment),
He comes out from it with his jaded (garment).
You have dressed what is at his head,
You have clothed what is at his feet,
You have clothed what is at his bottom,
You have clothed what is at his arms,
You have clothed what is in all his dreams,
In that night when he saw himself at this his place.
Pharaoh is purified with this water which came out from Osiris,
He has provided his bones with what belongs to him.
A king's offering; Pharaoh is pure.
Words spoken over a papyms amulet of ore, put into water, purifying the
King with it. (An excerpt from Ninth spell)
Pharaoh now is 'Osiris who satisfies Re with his truth',
He is pure, purified on his portico(?).
Pharaoh now is 'Tatenen',
He is pure, purified on his elevation.
Pharaoh now is 'The light in its perfection',
He is pure, purified on his hill.
Pharaoh now is 'He has taken hold of himself',
He is pure, purified on his shore.
Pharaoh has crossed the things(?) in the primeval ocean,
He has purified himself in the primeval ocean.

Water is on pharaoh,

No dead man's spirit(?) can encroach on him.

His impurity does not exist.

A king's offering, pharaoh is pure.

To recite upon four figures of the inundation god, in their shape (bs) and

their form (kms) during f...], liquid of every [...] in them. To go around

the king, [every single one...], purify on all limbs(?) of the king. To speak

words, to abolish impurity, abolishing of impurity, male and female dead

man's spirits, male and female enemies, male and female opponents.

This book has been made by the Lord of All when he purified his limbs(?)

after the evil impurity of men, gods, glorified and dead ones. (An excerpt from Tenth spell)

Apart from these royal rituals, the Egyptian Kings may have also had to undergo special ceremonies around the turn of the year for purification.[38] Also, entry into the King's palace was subjected to certain restrictions in terms of purity with people indulging in certain sexual activities or consuming certain food items being barred from entering the palace right after those activities.[39]

While the Kings were thus subjected to elaborate purification rituals and regimens, commoners appear to have been subjected to more relaxed purity regulations. Quack writes: 'Purity in the domains we have explored hitherto is clearly a concern for the elites, not for the population at large. The purity rules in place for entering a temple were not continuously enforced in daily life and for obvious reasons could not have been. This is especially clear with regard to the sexual taboo, which would have led, with perpetual use, to the extinction of the Egyptian population within one or two generations. Likewise, in the case of food taboos it is clear that the fish, pigs and small livestock mentioned explicitly in the relevant texts were actually eaten in Ancient Egypt – only a few members of the elite could have covered their daily protein needs through cattle, geese and desert game.'[40] He further cites the regulations in Esna that imposed special purity periods for those who wanted to enter the temples or wanted to work there as craftsmen, to show how purity in general was not excepted to be followed strictly by the ordinary people. But, this also shows that during certain special periods, when maintaining purity was perceived as most necessary, even common people were expected to adhere to it. More importantly, there appears to have been at least three areas in the social life of the ancient Egyptians, where purity seems to have played an important role even for the commoners: menstruation, childbirth, and death.

While we shall look into the issue of menstruation indepth in the succeeding sections, regarding purity concerns associated with childbirth, we have an interesting reference from *Westcar Papyrus*, an ancient Egyptian text belonging to the Hyksos period, around eighteenth-sixteenth century BCE. In a story it recounts about Ruddjedet and how she gave birth to three sons, who would go on to become kings, it narrates that Ruddjedet 'became pure in a purification of fourteen days'[41] after childbirth. After her purification, Ruddjedet asks her maid about the wellbeing of her household. While this has led some scholars to speculate whether childbirths took place in special buildings outside dwelling houses due to purity considerations, Quack rightly points out that Westcar Papyrus itself does not make any mention to any special building for childbirth.[42] Nevertheless, the fact that Ruddjedet was away from household activities for fourteen days after childbirth due to purity considerations points towards some kind of rest and isolation, perhaps confined to a special room within the house. Considerations of purity, it seems, have been associated with childbirth.

Regarding the dead, while the purity of the corpse itself was maintained and purifications were performed during mummification, the people who mourned the dead entered a temporary period of impurity. This is visible from certain mourning customs, which clearly violated the normal considerations of purity.[43] For example, while shaving the head completely was preferred under normal purity considerations, the mourners used to let their hair grow long during the mourning period.[44] Then, we have the decree of Canopus belonging to 238 BCE, which calls the end of the mourning period as a time for the purification of the mourning hairs. The Egyptian word used is *sw'b snm.t*, which means 'to purify the mourning hairs',[45] thus denoting the period of mourning as a period of impurity, from which one emerges after purification. There was a general non-involvement from the daily conveniences of life which were integral to normal notions of purity like the use of good clothes, ointments, scents etc. as a mark of mourning for the dead. Quack rightly observes: Thus we can see that the mourning period required abstention from the usual condition of purity as a sign of personal pain and sympathy, accepting impurity as a mortification. This in turn provides an opportunity to end the mourning period with a final purification and to reenter the usual state of purity.[46]

Thus, we see a well-developed concept of purity in ancient Egypt. They not only observed strict purity requirements regarding temples and tombs, they were also aware about impurity aspects connected to life events like child-birth and death. While the elite, especially the kings and the priests, were subjected to the maximum regimen of purification owing to their greater responsibility towards society, commoners also observed some notions of purity and impurity in their daily life, despite there being no strict imposition of purity regulations on them, except during special occasions.

Menstruation and Purification

While the elements of both Miasma or impurity and sacredness being associated with menstruation can be witnessed across most ancient civilisations, it is perhaps only in ancient Egypt that we witness an association of purification with menstruation. The only other exception, to this writer's knowledge, is the Hindu civilisation which has flourished in the Indian subcontinent for at least 6,000 years. One does not have to go beyond the term used for menstruation by the ancient Egyptians to establish this connection between menstruation and purification. The Egyptian term *hsmn*, which has been used to refer to menstruation, has been often translated as 'purification'. In fact, *hsmn* has been used for *natron*, the principle purificatory agent.[47]

While scholars such as JJ Janssen have rejected the meaning of menstruation and have instead suggested post-childbirth purification[48] as the meaning of *hsmn*, others such as KA Kitchen have associated *hsmn* with being 'sick'.[49] Yet others have suggested abortion[50] as a plausible meaning. Despite these reservations expressed by a number of scholars regarding the association of *hsmn* with menstruation, there is 'substantial proof that the traditional rendering (i.e. *hsmn* as menstruation) is correct,' writes Paul John Frandsen in his *The Menstrual Taboo in Ancient Egypt*.

Frandsen quotes a number of medical and other texts from the second millennium BCE to corroborate his assertion. They have been reproduced below:[50]

> *If you examine a woman having pain in her stomach while hsmn does not come for her (n ỉy.n n–s {m} hsmn), and you find (. . .), then you shall say concerning it: this is a case of obstruction of the blood in her uterus (Papyrus Edwin Smith, verso 20, 13–15).*

> *If you examine a woman who has spent many years while hsmn does not come for her (n ¡y.n n–s hsmn), she habitually spews up something like water, her stomach being like that which is under fire, but it stops when she has spewed up, then you shall say concerning it: this is an accumulation of blood in her uterus because she is bewitched (Papyrus Ebers 833 = 97, 1–4).*
>
> *If you examine a woman having pain in one side of her vulva, you should say concerning it: this means that her hsmn has lost its regularity (tm m·ºw–s pw ¡n hsmn–s). When it (i.e., the hsmn) has started, you shall make for her: smashed garlic, cider and sawdust of fir tree. Her pubic region is to be bandaged with it (Papyrus Ebers 832 = 96, 20–97, 1).*
>
> *I was taken as a wife to the house of Naneferkaptah (...). He slept with me that night and found me [pleasing. He slept with] again and again, and we loved each other. When my time of hsmn came, I made no more hsmn [Demotic literary text Setne I, from late period].*

From the above texts, it is clear that '*hsmn*' can only refer to menstruation. As Frandsen rightly concludes: 'The accumulated evidence for the term *hsmn* excludes any interpretation other than "menstruation."'[51] In other words, ancient Egyptians perceived menstruation as 'purification' and thus called it *hsmn*. While Frandsen is hesitant to draw a direct correlation between menstruation and purification with respect to *hsmn*, and instead suggests the possibility of the usage of the term meaning purification for menstruation as being only a euphemism or a taboo word,[52] nevertheless, even he concedes that the 'interrelationship of the terminology for menstruation and purification is suggestive'.[53] Noting that the Egyptian usage of the term *hsmn* could indeed denote their perception of its function as purification, Terry G Wilfong writes: 'Indeed, it has been suggested that this usage of "purification" for "menstruation" was an ancient Egyptian euphemism, although it could also be understood as evidence of the Egyptian understanding of the function of menstruation.'[54] Then, we have textual evidence from the Middle Kingdom Lahun in the form of a letter from a Mistress of the House, which points towards a possible purification ritual to be performed after the monthly menses. Ire, the Mistress of the House, writes about her servant visiting the temple 'on day twenty for monthly purification'.[55] Regarding this, Carolyn Graves-Brown observes that 'The need for purification might suggest her monthly period was considered impure. However, one might interpret the passage more positively as meaning that menstruation itself was a purification necessitating a celebratory trip to the temple'.[56] While Brown posits the possibility of a purification ritual at the end of monthly periods as being opposed to or contradictory to the possibility of menstruation itself being purification, with the latter being considered a more positive perception, this need not be the case. A parallel with Hindu tradition can be instructive in this matter, wherein menstruation is considered a self-purifying process wherein various unwanted materials and toxins are removed from the body, as a result of which, it is also associated with Ashaucha or impurity and hence needs a purificatory bath on the fourth day. Thus, the association of impurity with menstruation requiring a purification ritual towards the end, and considering menstruation itself as a purification process, is not mutually contradictory. Instead, it is complementary. It is worth investigating whether such was the case with the ancient Egyptians as well. Prima facie, this appears to be so. Even otherwise, what is clear from the usage of the term *hsmn* for menstruation is that the ancient Egyptians strongly identified menstruation with some notion of purification.

Menstruation as a bwt

Another notion, which appears to have been widely prevalent among ancient Egyptians, is that of menstruation being a *bwt*. A '*bwt*' is an Egyptian term 'designating both the *evil* and the interdiction against it'.[57]

Elaborating on the relevance of *bwt* in Egyptian cosmology, Frandsen[58] observes how Egyptians perceived forty two distinct cosmos with each having its own creator god and extensive cult monographs. These contained detailed descriptions of the 'names of the gods of the cosmos, the name of the hill on which creation took place, the name of the temple, the names of the priests/priestesses, the names of the holy barque (boat), the holy lakes, the holy trees, the festivals, the holy snake',[59] and a list of elements considered *bwt*. Sixteenth Upper Egyptian Nome,[60] for example, includes 'head' and 'bleeding woman' as elements of*bwt*. Seventeenth Upper Egyptian Nome[61] includes 'menstruation woman' and 'breast' under *bwt*. Similarly, Tenth Lower Egyptian Nome[62] calls 'black bull', 'black cow' and 'menstruating woman' as *bwt*.

Frandsen explains that the inclusion of *bwt* in the cult monographs indicates that for the Egyptians, at least of the Late Period, 'evil was a necessary element of all creation'.[63] He notes: The evidence of the cult-monographs shows that these prohibitions, by virtue of being classified as *bwt*, formed an essential part of the cosmological framework of the Egyptians. Violating a *bwt* was essentially an act with cosmological and lethal personal consequences.[64]

Thus, we see that *bwt* as a concept was not just interdictions, it was central to Egyptian cosmology and sacredness. Its violation was an affront to nature and to the cosmos itself. Menstruating women were inevitable parts of many such lists of *bwt*.

While the above quoted nomes mention only a handful of *bwt*-s, there is a list of 20 *bwt*-s from *Papyrus Jumilhac*, a kind of cult monograph of the Seventeenth and Eighteenth Upper Egyptian Nomes. Reproducing the same from Frandsen:[65]

1. The *hstt*-dog of its (i.e., Anubis, the god of the Seventeenth Nome) god, that is, the jackal and the *tsm*-dog
2. The mouth of the ¡w¡w-dog

3. Its *bwt* is the menstruating woman
4. He who does injustice
5. The grunting of the pig
6. To raise the voice before [him or god]
7. To take big steps in his house
8. The furious ones of his city
9. To diminish the (surveying) cord of his fields
10. To falsify the circumference (lit., mouth) of his granary's measure
11. To steal the grain of his fields
12. To diminish the offerings of his temple
13. To attack a son on the seat of his father in his house
14. To kill anyone (lit., eye) from his city
15. To testify against the people of his city
16. To encroach on the rights of the city in his presence (?)
17. The greedy who violates the boundaries of his fields
18. To eat the meat of any animal to be sacrificed
19. To attack the *wedjat*-eye
20. To remove a man from a *semdet* in order to transfer him to another *semdet*

From the above list, we can see that a variety of activities or objects have been termed *bwt*, ranging from criminal activities such as killing someone or stealing grains; non-ethical conducts such as greed and speaking falsehood; to objects like a dog's mouth or people like menstruating women, who can at best be associated with a notion of Miasma or impurity, but are otherwise harmless. This begets the question – should we really perceive these diverse interdictions as being 'evil' in the normal sense of the word? Is the term 'evil', which has strong connections with Christian theology, even suitable to interpret *bwt*-s? Were menstruating women, who appear in many lists of *bwt*-s considered 'evil' in the sense of being inherently bad, wicked, undivine or sinful by the ancient Egyptians?

To answer this, let us return to Egyptian cosmology. Ancient Egyptians believed that the world was created and sustained using what they called *maat*. *Maat* is often translated as 'world order' or 'truth'. It has several contextual meanings including justice, harmony, righteousness and true witness. Siegfried Morenz explains the wide-ranging meanings of the term *maat* thus: '*Maat* is right order in nature and society, as established by the act of creation, and hence means, according to the context, what is right, what is correct, law, order, justice and truth. This state of righteousness needs to be preserved or established, in great matters as in small. *Maat* is, therefore, not only right order but also the object of human activity. *Maat* is both the task which a man sets himself and also, as righteousness, the promise and reward that await him on fulfilling it.'[66] And opposite of this *maat* was *isfet* or *bwt*, which represented disorder, disharmony, or chaos. In the Egyptian worldview, the world was permeated by this duality, with one balancing the other, and the people were expected to always overcome *bwt*, using *maat*.

In *Religions of the Ancient World: A Guide*, Sarah Iles Johnston makes an important observation about the Egyptian understanding of *bwt*. She writes:

> Egyptian has no word for sin in the Christian sense of the term… *Bwt* is a complex category. It denotes both the evil itself and the sin committed when doing – or merely having contact with – something classified as *bwt*. During the almost three millennium of pharaonic history a steadily increasing number of phenomena were included in the category of things *bwt*. The entire catalogue of phenomena classified as *bwt* shows a wide selection of sins, ranging from 'social evils' (or ordinary crimes), such as killing and theft, to violation of ethical norms

> (partiality) and to numerous cultic offenses, such as breaking rules of purity related to contact with the holy. The treatises known as Cult Monographs…always included one or several *bwts*, such as certain species of animals (mammals, reptiles, fish) or parts thereof, members of the body, diseases, miscellaneous substances, people who momentarily or permanently were at the border of the social values of *ma'at* (menstruating women, homosexuals), and proscribed forms of sexual behavior or contact with forbidden food.[67]

From the above discussion, it is clear that the Egyptian perception of *bwt* was very different from how we normally understand terms like sin and evil, which are rooted in Christian theology. As Johnston rightly notes: 'Those in western culture tend to be more familiar with "sin-based" rather than "pollution-based" religions, due to the now-noncultic traditions of Christianity and Judaism'.[68] So, is there a better framework for understanding and drawing parallels with the Egyptian concept of *bwt*? The answer is Yes. We can indeed find a parallel framework in the Dharmic traditions of Hinduism, which is one of the last surviving civilisations with a civilisational continuity of at least 6000 years.

The Hindu concept of *rta* and *dharma* are perfect counterparts for the Egyptian *maat*. The *rta* denotes a cosmic order and harmony, and *dharma* denotes the duties and actions that help one to live in harmony with that cosmic order. *Dharma* literally means 'that which upholds' and has a variety of contextual meanings like truth, order, duties, law, righteousness, and justice.[69] The opposite of *Dharma* is *Adharma*, which may denote disorder, chaos, unrighteousness etc., and which causes the descent of an individual into greater ignorance and sorrow. In short, *Dharma* imparts happiness, and *Adharma* brings sorrow. Hence, the performance of *Dharma* is considered *punya* or a meritorious act, while indulging in *Adharma* is *paapa* or an unmeritorious action. The practise of truth, purity and non-injury is *Dharma,* which begets *punya. Paapa* is associated with several actions ranging from social crimes to unethical activities and the violation of purity. This is because the violation of *Dharma* by indulging in *paapa* results in sorrow, pain and abysmal ignorance.

Thus, while *maat* could be considered the Egyptian counterpart of *Dharma, bwt*, especially in its aspect of interdictions, can be equated with *Adharma* or more precisely with *paapa* or unmeritorious actions, which bring sorrow and lead to disharmony.

Analysing from this perspective, the inclusion of menstruating women in the list of *bwt*-s in the cult monographs could have not been because it was considered evil or sinful in the sense of social crime, inherent wickedness, or immoral activity in the ancient Egyptian society. Instead, it appears, *bwt* in this case was due to the association of impurity or *Miasma* with menstruation. A plausible reason for this could be the Egyptian perception of menstruation as a purification process, which would imply that there was a removal of impurity during the process, thus making it a *bwt* due to this association with impurity. Though, it must be pointed out that Egyptian scholars, at large, have noted in recent years that there was no universal interdiction against menstruating women in ancient Egypt. Instead, the interdictions were context and region specific. Frandsen,[70] for example, notes how 'taboo' is used very loosely with reference to ancient Egypt, and what is usually designated as taboo is either too context specific (related to particular region or a site) or too vague. Terry G Wilfong[71] notes: 'An explicit interdiction against menstruating women does not appear in Egyptian texts until the Graeco-Roman period, and even then, only in specific and limited religious contexts'. He concludes that 'Taking into account the Egyptian understanding of menstruation…it is not surprising to find no evidence for a formal, universal taboo against women in menstruation.'

This application of bwt with respect to menstruation in a highly context specific manner only reinforces the possibility that the ancient Egyptians knew more about the working of the *is fet/ bwt* forces than we give them credit for.

Menstruation and Seclusion

An ostracon designated OIM. 13512 has been considered as definite evidence by Egyptian scholars regarding the seclusion of women during menstruation. The said ostracon, though without known provenance, has been tentatively dated to year 9 of Merenptah i.e. around 1204 BCE using paleontology, grammar and other circumstantial evidences.

The ostracon OIM. 13512 is a piece of white limestone of about 13.2 X 9.1 cm in size, most likely belonging to Deir el-Medina, and inscribed with three lines in hieratic. It records a single event about menstruating women and despite short gaps in the text, the meaning is pretty straightforward. It reads:[72]

> *(Line1)*
>
> *Year 9, fourth month of the season of Inundation, day 13: the day when these eight women came out [to/from*
>
> *(Line 2)*
>
> *the] place of women while they were menstruating. They got as far as the rear of the house which [...*
>
> *(Line 3)*
>
> *...] the three walls.*

From this, it is very clear that women in menstruation used to leave their homes and go to the 'place of women', which was probably outside their villages. The usage of the phrase 'the place of women' suggests that menstruating women did not stay at their homes during menstruation and instead stayed at this 'place of women'. This provides definitive evidence for at least some menstruating women, if not all, practising seclusion in ancient Egypt. That eight women menstruated together as attested in this ostracon also serves as an ancient evidence for menstrual synchrony,[73] as well as its awareness among Egyptians. Evidences have also come from the post-pharaonic Egypt, wherein menstruating women often retired to a specific women's space within the house, usually under the stairs in a multi-storey building. This space has been mentioned in documents concerning the transfer of houses at Thebes, often dated to 267 BCE, which include a clause stating 'You/your women shall menstruate in the women's space.'[74]

Seclusion and purification were also practised after childbirth and perhaps after abortion as well, wherein small rooms within large houses and roofs in small houses were used for this purpose.[75] These spaces could have also served as the retiring place for menstruating women.

An interesting occurrence, though only tangentially related to the issue of seclusion, is the absentee list of workmen from Deir el-Medina citing the menstruation of female relatives as a reason. Wilfong[76] argues that since there weren't frequent absentees citing this reason, it follows that workmen took a day off from work only under special conditions. From the list of absentees and the reasons cited therein, it is clear that workmen mostly took leave when there were some events or happenings at home that caused disruption in the functioning of the household. Thus, Wilfong concludes: 'the Deir el-Medina workmen would have been absent from work for a female relative only on such occasions when their wives and/or daughters were in some way absent from home or were unable to do necessary work in the house'.[77] He gives two probable causes for disruption at home: menstruating women going to the 'place of women' or menstruating wives/daughters experiencing dysmenorrhea. While the latter could indeed have been a valid reason, regarding the former, Frandsen[78] notes that if menstruating women were to go to the 'place of women' every menses causing the husbands to stay at home, there should have been frequent, monthly absences citing menstruation as a reason in the absentee list, which is not the case. Instead, absences are infrequent and without a pattern. While this is true, it is also possible that though menstruating women in a household did visit the 'place of women', as we have seen from ostracon OIM. 13512, there may have been other family members such as a sister, a mother, or a father, who could have taken over the responsibility. It was probably only in the absence of such an arrangement that the husband would take leave from work to manage household affairs. According to Graves-Brown,[79] a probable reason for the absence of the workmen could also be the necessity to carry out rites concerned with menarche of their female relatives, perhaps, of daughters. Frandsen concludes his analysis by linking the absence of workmen with their having come into contact with their female menstruating relatives before these women could enter the 'places of women'. He writes: 'One way of making sense out of the evidence is to interpret the behavior of men and women as interconnected; menstruating women should ideally leave the village before their men were "contaminated", and men stayed at home only if the women failed to reach the "women's place" in time.'[80]

Whether it was to manage the households in the absence of female relatives who have gone to the place of women due to menstruation, or whether it was due to impurity considerations arising out of contact of the workmen with their menstruating relatives, what the absentee list points to is the fact that ancient Egyptian society did recognise the importance of menstruation not only in a woman's life but also in family and society as a whole, and thus had made allowance for the workmen to remain absent from their jobs to manage the household and help their womenfolk spend their period of menstruation in comfort and seclusion.

Thus, there is clear evidence that menstruating women indeed practised seclusion in ancient Egypt. What is not clear, however, is whether this seclusion was due to concerns of impurity alone, or was it also considered as a time for resting and celebrating womanhood. Considering how ancient Egyptians perceived menstruation as both a purification process and as a *bwt* with respect to cult worship, it is possible that the seclusion was practised owing to both concerns.

Menstruation and Birth

In his *The Menstrual Taboo in Ancient Egypt*, Frandsen argues that menstruation and birth were perceived in ancient Egypt as essentially being opposed to one another. He notes how women and tombs were perceived as 'instruments of regeneration'[81] with both being endowed with the capacity to 'transform potential into actualised existence'.[82] While women gave birth to new life by carrying and nourishing babies in their wombs, tombs were considered the body of the sky goddess, wherein the dead underwent the process of rebirth. Thus, for ancient Egyptians, the womb and the tomb were essentially performing the same function: creating life.

Since menstruation implied an 'absence of pregnancy and thus the lack of fertility',[83] it was perceived as opposed to birth, be it human birth or the regeneration within the tomb. Another example which reinforces this idea is the prescription found in one of the medical texts for preventing the drooping of the breasts among new mothers due to too much milk. The text, *Papyrus Ebers*,[84] prescribes an application of menstrual blood from a girl who has just attained menarche on the breasts, belly and thighs of the new mother. The reasoning behind such a prescription appears to be the understanding that menstruation being opposed to pregnancy and birth will counteract the effects of birth. Frandsen notes: Blood from a menstruating woman has a negative impact on someone who has just given birth because menstruation indicates the absence of pregnancy and thus the lack of fertility. Blood from a menstruating woman would then counteract the vital processes associated with creation.[85]

Frandsen, then, makes another interesting observation. He notes that it was not only the tomb, which was perceived to be violated by menstruating women, but even they and their fertility were perceived as being under threat due to the tomb. Noting that this two-way influence between menstruating women and the tomb could be a likely factor for the workmen who took occasional leave from work in the tombs citing menstruation as the reason, Fransen writes: '…we may therefore posit that as long as the men stayed at the Tomb, they were not polluted by contact with their menstruating women and were no threat to the construction work nor did the Tomb, through them, threaten the fertility of their absent womenfolk. During menstruation the latter were both vulnerable to harm from vicarious contact to the Tomb and a menace to the potential cosmic fertility intended for that sacred construction.'[86]

In short, menstruation as being opposed to birth and hence to the tomb accounts for the Egyptian perception of menstruating women as *bwt*, especially with respect to tombs; they could harm the sanctity of the tomb and the processes taking place inside it. Morever, the tomb could also negatively influence the fertility of menstruating women.

Deities of Menstruation

Ancient Egypt had a number of deities who were directly or indirectly associated with menstruation. Prominent among them were Isis, Hathor and Sekhmet.

Isis was among the more prominent deities of the Egyptian pantheon, whose worship spread to the Roman Empire and from there to the greater Greco-Roman world. The earliest mention of this deity appears in the *Pyramid Texts of Unas*[87] dated to 2400 BCE. She was often depicted together with her sister Nephthys. Isis was the daughter of Nut, the sky-goddess and Geb, the earth god. Along with her sister Nephthys, she facilitated the rebirth and revival of her brother and husband Osiris, the deity of afterlife after he was killed by Set. Egyptians thus considered Isis as pivotal to rebirth rites. She was a protector of the dead and of children, and she helped cure animal bites. RE Witt describes her as the 'friend of slaves and sinners, of the artisans and the downtrodden, at the same time she heard the prayers of the wealthy, the unblemished maidens, and the aristocrat and the emperor'.[88] She was also associated with magic and nature. But it was in her role as wife and mother that she was most adored and worshipped.

Isis's association with menstruation is best revealed by the ancient Egyptian amulet of the Tiet, which is popularly known as the 'Knot of Isis' or 'Blood of Isis'. The amulet was red in colour, usually made of blood-red jasper, carnelian, or red glass.[89] It was basically an 'open loop of material, tied with a sash that hangs down below the loop on two sides'.[90] In the famous *Book of Coming Forth by Day (Book of the Dead)*, there is a spell related to this amulet made of red jasper, which makes a direct connection between Isis, her blood and the amulet. Spell 156 states: 'You have your blood, O Isis; you have your power, O Isis; you have your magic, O Isis.'[91] Elaborating on the symbolism of the amulet and its connection to blood, M Isidora Forrest writes:[92]

> The tiet first appears in Egyptian iconography in the third dynasty. It was frequently used in association with the djed pillar of Osiris and so became almost exclusively associated

> with Isis. Used together, the two symbols could refer to the power of the Goddess and God to engender Life. Because of this, the symbols may also be seen as sexual symbols; the pillar referring to the phallus of the God and the knot to the vulva and womb of the Goddess.
>
> It may have been the combination of the tiet's connection with life and its association with Isis' sexuality that led to it being called the Blood of Isis and so being made of red jasper, carnelian, or even red glass. It might represent the red lifeblood a mother sheds while giving birth. On the other hand, it might represent menstrual blood. Some say the amulet is shaped like the cloth worn by women during menstruation. Others have interpreted it as a representation of a ritual tampon that could be inserted in the vagina to prevent miscarriage. In this case, it would have been the amulet Isis used to protect Horus while He was still within Her womb. In addition to blood, the amulet's red color could represent fire and the Sun – and the living, regenerative properties of Isis the Flame, the Radiant Solar Goddess and Lady of Rebirth.

Thus, the Knot of Isis was intimately connected with menstruation, birth and miscarriage. From this we can conclude that Isis herself was perceived in ancient Egypt as a goddess presiding over these important biological processes that women experience, be it menstruation or childbirth.

Hathor was another popular deity in Egypt, who personified 'love, beauty and rebirth'.[93] According to Carolyn Graves-Brown, 'there were more temples to Hathor than any other goddess'.[94] Hathor was often associated with childbirth and sexuality related to it. By the Eighteenth Dynasty, she became associated with the epithet 'Lady of the Vulva', which was originally an epithet of goddess Nebethetep.[95] She was also considered as the Eye of the Universe, the carrier of the ankh, the Cow of Heaven, and as the Great Serpent.[96] Pointing to her connection with menstruation, David Leeming and Jake Page write in their book

Goddess: Myths of the Female Divine that 'Hathor is associated with one of the many stories of the Egyptian beer flood of the Nile and with the blood of menstruation'.[97]

Closely related to Hathor was another goddess called 'Sekhmet', who was considered her solar aspect. The goddess Bast was considered Hathor's lunar aspect. In *Sekhmet, Bast and Hathor*',[98] Normandi Ellis elaborates on this dual nature of Hathor, and the unique attributes associated with each of these forms. Ellis writes: 'Bast is the sensual, purring, nurturing aspect, while Sekhmet is the roaring lion, a goddess with a temple. Bast reveals [herself as]the nurturing mother of her kittens; Sekhmet shows herself the protector of her pride and her cubs. When Hathor's solar qualities are the focal point, the goddess assumes Sekhmet's lion form, and when her lunar qualities are at play, she appears as Bast, the cat.'[99] It is interesting to note that despite being two aspects of Hathor, Sekhmet and Bast existed as independent deities as well. In fact, the three goddesses were considered to be the presiding deities of the three stages in a woman's life. While Hathor was associated with maidenhood, Bast and Sekhmet were respectively associated with motherhood and old age. In these roles, each deity assisted women through their different stages of biological and psychological transformations from menarche and marriage to motherhood and menopause. Sekhmet was particularly associated with menstruation and the cyclical flow of blood. Ellis notes: 'Sekhmet embodies the cyclical blood that flows at birth and death; the blood that flows from mother to child in the womb; the blood on the battlefields, and the menstrual blood or the blood of circumcision that separates the budding young adult from childhood. It is the cyclical red flood of the River Nile that became equated with the red, renewing menstrual blood that cleanses and prepares the way for renewal and regenesis'.[100]

Highlighting Sekhmet's association with menopause, Ellis further writes: 'Blood held within was called the "wise blood", and menopause marked a time for women in ancient Egypt when the inner Sekhmet produced divisions and created magic. The red henna...that adorned the heads of women in Egypt was a tribute to her and was said to be her "magic blood"'.[101]

Thus, we see that the trio of Hathor, Sekhmet and Bast being intimately associated with the different stages in a woman's life, including menstruation, motherhood, and menopause.

Thus, in Ancient Egypt, we witness a complex attitude towards menstruation, which had elements of purification, impurity, seclusion and sacredness, all at the same time. While menstruation was referred to by the name *hsmn* meaning 'purification' indicating the Egyptian perception of menstruation as a purification process; it was also categorised under *bwt* i.e. an interdiction in the cult monographs preventing the entry of women in their menses to tombs and places of cult worship. *Bwt* could be considered the Egyptian counterpart of the Hindu concept of *Paapa* (unmeritorious actions), and in the context of menstruation, it was related to *miasma* or *Ashaucha* (impurity). While there is evidence of women practising seclusion during menstruation, this could have been due to a number of factors including impurity, rest, and the protection of menstruating women. On the sacred front, Isis, Hathor, Sekhmet and Bast were prominent deities who were associated with the different biological phases experienced by women.

Comparison with Hindu Tradition

In the previous sections, we reviewed various menstruation perceptions and practices prevalent in the major western civilisations of the ancient world, namely: Greece, Rome, Mesopotamia and Egypt. In this section, we shall undertake a comparative analysis of the perceptions and practices of these civilisations with those prevalent in the Hindu traditions. Such an analysis could be fruitful at many levels. One, these ancient western civilisations share with the Hindu traditions a number of similar values owing to their similar worldviews. Two, these western civilisations ended long ago. What we understand of them has been reconstructed using a diverse set of evidences, including literary and archeological. Hence, there are gaps in our understanding; there are alsomultiple interpretations of the same evidence; The Hindu tradition is , however, the only living spiritual and religious tradition, which is as old, if not more, as its western counterparts, and yet, with an intact core. Its basic foundation remains as it was despite undergoing many mutations externally. Thus, a comparative study of these civilisations with the Hindu traditions could not only lead to interesting insights, but also help fill up the gaps. Our comparative analysis will be restricted to two elements: purity/impurity considerations and the sacred aspect of menstruation.

We have already noted that the Hindu traditions perceive menstruation as being Ashaucha, austerity, a self-purification process and a period of rest and sacred celebration at the same time. Ashaucha is a complex technical term which goes beyond the normal sense of impurity. It not only refers to impurity at the physical level, which in the case of menstruation is a reference to the removal of blood etc., it also refers to impurity at the level of the pranic (vital) body (due to the removal of excess Rajasic energy) and the mind (due to pain, distraction, irritation etc.). It is the impurity at the pranic and the mental level, which makes menstruating women incompetent to perform certain spiritual practices or enter sacred places of worship. Thus, Ashaucha also becomes a reference to Adhikara or competency and not just to uncleanliness. But, as far as women themselves are concerned, they are called to understand menstruation as a very personal, positive, and sacred experience, with elements of self-purification and austerity.

Thus, as a complex category, Ashaucha cannot be perceived in isolation in its application to menstruation, nor can it be reduced to mere impurity or unhygienic conditions. The simultaneous association of the elements of sacredness, austerity and self-purification imply that the association of Ashaucha with menstruation does not carry a negative connotation, nor does it degrade women. On the other hand, it is precisely because menstruation is a purification process removing impurities at multiple levels that it became associated with Ashaucha. The categorisation of menstruation as Ashaucha implies two things: One, it is a positive process of purification as a result of which menstruating women must take rest, not be involved in hard work, and practise sacred austerity in calm and peaceful isolation, which also protects their physical health and fertility; Two, due to the removal of Rajasic energies and other elements of impurity associated with the physical body and the mind, they are incompetent to take part in spiritual and sacred ceremonies or enter sacred places because of the polluting nature of those energies i.e. their power to cause imbalance to the spiritual energies. It is due to menstruation's role in purifying women and protecting their health and fertility that it becomes associated with divinity and sacred celebration. In the case of the Hindu traditions, this divinity is Goddess Uma or Durga and her multiple forms.

In our review of menstruation notions and practices of the ancient western civilisations, we found the association of impurity with menstruation in one form or the other. While in the Greco-Roman world menstruation was associated with 'miasma', in Egypt, it was categorised as a 'bwt'. Mesopotamians used a number of terms like *urruštu* and *(m)usukkatu* for menstruating women indicating their association with impurity.

Though scholars have often perceived this association and the resulting interdictions in a negative light and have called it taboo, it is possible to have a more balanced understanding of this phenomenon using the framework of Ashaucha found in the Hindu traditions as summarised above.

Take for example, the Greco-Roman concept of Miasma-Katharsis, which has been described as the most distinctive feature of the Indo-European culture.[1] Similar to the Hindu pair of Shaucha-Ashaucha, the Greco-Roman Miasma-Khatharsis is also not only a concept related to purity and pollution, but also to vitality and impotence. Similarly, Mesopotamians associated purity with 'radiance'. The Sumerian term *kug/kù*, as well as the Akkadian term '*ellu*', used for purity, actually indicates radiance. On the other hand, there are a number of terms for impurity in the cultic or religious context like *aršu* and *la ellu*, the latter of which explicitly refers to a person who is unfit for cultic use. Thus, while Katharsis or kug/ellu, like Shaucha, granted competence to enter sacred spaces or perform sacred actions, the Miasma or *aršu/la ellu*, like Ashaucha, prevented such an entry.

In Egypt, though, this prevention of certain people or objects from accessing the cultic sacred place or a tomb took the form of 'bwt', which can more properly be compared to the Hindu tenet of 'paapam' related to Adharma. A point to note is 'paapam' is a reference to an unmeritorious act, which brings sorrow. It is different from the Abrahamic concept of eternal sin. Similar to the Hindu principles of Dharma-Adharma, and Punya-Paapa, the Egyptians conceived of maat-bwt; the former upheld the universe, the latter caused disorder and chaos. There is also the association of impurity with biological activities such as menstruation, birth and death, which are common to most ancient civilisations regardless of whether they originated in the East or the West.

Thus, we see how purity considerations formed an important aspect in the perception of menstruation across ancient western civilisations. They not only shared common elements regarding purity and impurity with each other, but there are many significant parallels, with the Shaucha-Ashaucha understandings prevalent in the Hindu Dharmic traditions.

But, no discussion of impurity with respect to menstruation is complete without a reference to the sacred aspects associated by these civilisations to this process. And, interestingly, there are significant parallels here, as well. We have already noted how all the major civilisations of the West – Greek, Roman, Mesopotamia and Egypt – associate menstruation with a number of female deities. While Artemis and Diana are the presiding deities of menstruation in the Greco-Roman world, Ishtar-Inanna take up that role in Mesopotamia. The ancient Egyptians had Isis, Hathor, and Sekhmet. Among the Hindus, the primordial Mother Goddess, Uma or Parvati, also called Durga, is associated with menstruation. Moreover, there are deities such as Kamakhya and Bhagavati, who are different manifestations of the primordial Shakti, and who are believed to undergo menstruation themselves.

Interestingly, Artemis is not only associated with menstruation or menarche, but also with other aspects of women's life like marriage and motherhood. She presides over all the important transformations in a woman's life. Diana of the Romans, in her triple form as trivia, shared these qualities with Artemis. Inanna in Mesopotamia, likewise, also presided over the transformation of girls from maidenhood to marriage. In Egypt, while Hathor presided over maidenhood, her twin manifestations – Bast and Sekhmet – presided over marriage and menopause, respectively. On the Hindu side, Goddess Parvati in her manifestation as Durga is often perceived in nine forms called 'Nava Durga-s', of which, the first five forms can be specifically associated with the different stages in a woman's life. While Shailaputri represents the young child, Brahmacharini represents the stage of Brahmacharya or maidenhood. Goddess Chandraghanta represents the stage of marriage, while Kushmanda and Skanda-mata are associated with pregnancy and motherhood, respectively. Thus, there is an instructive parallel between how each of the ancient western civilisations perceives of a deity or deities presiding over the different stages of a woman's life, and how Goddess Parvati manifests the different forms towards the same end. There is also the parallel between Kamakhya or Bhoomi of the Hindu tradition resting during menstruation, which happens once a year with Inanna entering menstruation seclusion through her disappearance dark moon.

Though the rituals associated with onset of menstruation like the bear dance dedicated to Artemis, are different in their form and celebration in different civilisations, the fact that menarche was celebrated is in itself another common element shared by these ancient western civilisations with Hindu civilisation.

These commonalities between ancient western civilisations and living Hindu traditions present many interesting possibilities. Though, it must be pointed out that there were many dissimilar elements as well. The understanding of the impurity considerations and miasma energies, be it in the Greco-Roman world or in other civilisations appears to be more informed from the understanding of the effects rather than an understanding of the causes. Thus, while the Greco-Romans held similar views regarding miasma/Ashaucha considerations like the Hindus, there is an exaggerated account of the effects of miasma in the accounts of Pliny. This may have been due to their insufficient understanding of the cause and the working of the miasma aspects. It also appears that the Hindu understanding of human physiology and psychology like those of Panchakoshas, the Yogic workings of the Pranas was either not understood or comprehended only partially. Of course, there is a definite parallel between Ayurvedic Tri-Dosha and Greco-Roman humours, and this may have influenced their understanding of menstruation as well, though to what extent, is difficult to speculate.

This comparative study shows that, contrary to the prevalent academic view, which often assumes that menstruation was perceived in a negative light, by concentrating on the impurity considerations in isolation, we see that for women, these transformations were a positive sacred process, presided over by deities, who protected them, and ensured smooth transformation. Thus, far from degrading menstruating women, as it is often assumed, the impurity considerations when understood in conjunction to sacred elements, give a wholesome form to menstruation notions.

Menstruation Notions among Indigenous Communities

IN THE previous chapters, we examined menstruation notions prevalent in Hinduism and other Indic Traditions, Abrahamic Religions and major Ancient Western Civilisations. Let us now survey the prevalent menstruation notions among the different indigenous cultures and communities of the world. We shall limit our examination to two aspects: Impurity and Sacredness, since these aspects have prevailed in most cultures. Unless specified otherwise, we will rely on evidences presented by Robert Briffault in his *The Mothers*, extracts from which have been compiled in booklet form, titled: *The Moon and Menstruation: A Taboo Subject*, edited by Hilary Alton.

Association with Impurity

The notion of menstruation as a state of impurity which could be communicated to others has been prevalent among most communities across the globe.

North America

Robert Briffault notes that the seclusion of menstruating women in separate huts was practised by all the tribes of North America. Women belonging to Pima Indians, for example, retired to a shelter built in the bushes during menstruation. Canadian tribes follow a similar seclusion; and women are expected to not touch utensils or use the same paths as men during their menses. Women belonging to the Beaver Indian tribe were expected to 'drop, now and then, branches upon the road',[1] as a warning to the men to avoid travelling through those roads. Mohawk Indian women keep a separate set of utensils to be used only during their monthly periods. They are expected to not touch the food and provisions of their husbands nor eat from their utensils during that time. Captain Carver writes thus about Naudowessies, the members of the North American Dakota Tribe: 'The Indian women are remarkably decent during their menstrual illness. In every camp or town there is an apartment appropriated for their retirement at those times to which both single and married retreat and seclude themselves with the utmost strictness during the periods from all society. The men on these occasions most carefully avoid having any commerce with them, and the Naudowessies are so rigid in that observance that they will not suffer any belonging to them to fetch such things as are necessary, even fire, from these female lunar retreats, though the want is attended with the greatest inconvenience'.[2]

Briffault writes that among the Eskimos, separate huts are built for the use of menstruating women and special dietary regulations are prescribed for them. Further, the women use cups and utensils that are kept exclusively for their use. Similar isolation was also observed among the Tlingit, an indigenous group of people present in the Pacific Northwest Coast of North America. Tlingit women were not even allowed to lie down or chew their own foods. They had to sleep propped up with logs.

They consumed already masticated food. Among the Dene, there was similar dread towards menstruation. Speaking of the more southerly plains tribes, Major Marston says: The women of these nations are very particular to remove from their lodge to one erected for the particular purpose when their menstrual time approaches; no article of furniture which is used in the hut is ever used in any other, not even the steel and flint with which to strike fire. No Indian ever approaches the lodge when a woman occupies it.[3]

Central and South America

Briffault notes that similar menstrual practices are prevalent among the tribes of Central and South America, as well. Among the Bribri Indians of Costa Rica, menstruating women use banana leaves (instead of normal household utensils) and these are carefully buried afterwards, for they believe that if such used leaves happen to be eaten by cows, it would kill them. Among the Mosquito Indians and the Caribbean tribes, women retire into forest huts during their menses and they are not allowed to cook even their own food, since it is considered dangerous. Instead, food is brought to them. The Macusi of Guiana believe that menstruating girls are in a state of impurity, and hence they must rest. They believe that menstruating women are more prone to be bitten by snakes, and hence, must avoid going into the forest. During menarche, the girl is expected to remain in her hammock all day, and she may cook and eat a little food only at night. The vessels used for the purpose are thereafter broken and the shreds buried in the ground. The girls belonging to the Guayquiry of the Orinoco fast for forty days before their marriage to become free from the dangerous effects of menstruation. Women belonging to many Brazilian tribes retire to hammocks suspended from the roofs of their huts during menstruation and they are subjected to fumigation and fasting. Many tribes have special isolation huts for the use of menstruating women. Among the Ticunas, menstruating girls are also subjected to plucking of their hairs and flagellation. Similar practices were observed among the Araucanians of Chile, the Kamchatka, the Yukaghir, the Koryak, the Samoyeds and the Ostyak. The women of the Araucanians were 'debarred from attending places of public amusement, and was [sic] not on any account to visit a sick person, lest her presence might give the *coup de grace* to the invalid'.[4] Menstruating Women of the Samoyeds and the Ostyak are 'segregated in an inner chamber of the "yurta", and must be purified with fumigation from burnt reindeer hair before resuming their duties...'.[5]

Australian and African Tribes

NN Bhattacharyya notes that such seclusions were practised by Australian and African tribes, as well. Bhattacharyya writes: 'The Australian tribes strictly seclude their women at their monthly courses. The reason for this is the dread with which they regard the menstrual period of women. This also holds good in the case of many African tribes. Among the Bagandas, a menstruating woman cannot drink milk, come into contact with any milk-vessel, touch anything that belongs to her husband and even she cannot cook for him. They believe that if a menstruating woman handles anything of her husband, he will surely fall ill; if she touches his weapons, he will certainly be killed in the next battle; if she touches a well, it will surely go dry.'[6] Writing about notions of menstruation among African tribes, Briffault observes:

> Among the Bushmen a menstruating woman is an object of terror, and the community is protected by her complete segregation. Among the Kaffir of South Africa, women are entirely secluded for six days at their periods and by a curious regulation have to be particularly careful at that time not to

> touch cow dung. They are not permitted to speak above a whisper. Among the Baila of Rhodesia a menstruating woman must not sit down in other people's company; on no account may she touch her husband's bed but must sleep on the floor; nor can she cook any food for him. Among the Akikuyu, if a woman menstruates in a hut, even if it has just been built, it is at once pulled down and destroyed as unfit for human habitation.[7]

Similar practices were observed among people from Bakongo, Loango, Angola, Ashanti etc. of the African continent.

South and South-East Asia

In South Asia, we have already examined the menstruation notions regarding impurity prevalent among the Indic traditions of Hinduism, Buddhism, and Jainism in the earlier chapters. Noting the wide prevalence of such notions of menstrual impurity across India, Bhattacharya writes:

> This fear for menstrual blood also prevails in India. Among the Bhuiyas of South Mirzapur the menstrual blood is dreaded much. Among the Kharwars of the same region a menstruous woman is kept in outer varanda; she is not allowed to enter the kitchen or cowshed, nor can she touch the cooking vessels. The South Indian women generally seclude themselves at their monthly periods and observe a number of rules such as not to drink milk, not to milk cows, not to touch fire, not to lie on a high bed, not to walk on common paths, not to walk by the side of flowering plants and not to observe heavenly bodies.[8]

Notions of impurity are also prevalent among people of South-East Asia. People of the Malay Peninsula, for example, associate danger with menstruation and childbirth. Among the Orang Belenda and the Orang Laut, it is the young girls who shoulders the duty of carrying lit sticks to kindle a new fire, but menstruating girls were prohibited from this due to impurity. They were also 'confined to a hut, no man would dare to come near, nor must they cook for a man or touch anything belonging to him, and the vessels which they use must be kept carefully separate'.[9] Among the Menankabau of Sumatra, menstruating women avoided going near the rice crop for it was believed that her going there will cause the crop to fail. In the island of Wetar, menstruating women practised seclusion during their periods. Bhattacharyya notes that 'In Cambodia a girl at her first menstruation has to stay under a mosquito curtain for a hundred days, though at present four, five, ten or twenty days are thought enough. She has to observe a number of rules such as not to be seen by a stranger, not to eat flesh or fish, not to go to the Pagoda, and so on'.[10] In Sri Lanka, 'when the girl has her first monthly course, she has to undergo a confinement of two weeks. During this period of seclusion, she must remain unseen by the males. When the period of seclusion is over, she comes back with her face covered by hands. A ceremonial bath of purification is then followed under a jak tree, Sometimes the hut, in which she was confined, is burnt'.[11]

Europe

The association of menstruation with impurity was widely prevalent in Europe, as well. Bhattacharyya writes: Among the peasants of Italy, Spain Germany and Holland, it is believed that flowers and fruit trees are withered by contact with a menstruating woman. In the wine districts of Bordeaux and of the Rhine, women, when menstruating, are strictly forbidden to approach the vats and cellers, lest the wine should turn to vinegar, and in Northern France, they are excluded from sugar refineries when sugar is boiling or cooking, for the presence of a menstruating woman would turn it black.[12]

Association with Sacredness

While the association with impurity is widely prevalent across the world as seen above, an association with sacredness is also quite prominent. We already saw this in the case of various Indian communities, which celebrate menstruation and menarche through rituals and festivals, even after associating impurity with it. The same is the case with many indigenous communities across the world.

Briffault, in fact, notes that a thing or a condition is designated as a 'tabu' i.e. prohibited from being approached by others, not only because it is associated with notions of impurity, but may be also because it is considered too sacred, too pure to be violated, with any such violation being considered 'sacrilege'. In fact, the Polynesian word 'tabu' or 'tapu' not only signifies menstruation, a variant of the word 'atua' also signifies 'God'. Similarly, the Dakotan word for taboo is 'Wakan', which is often described as referring to something mysterious, spiritual and wonderful.

The indigenous communities often marked what they considered sacred with blood or red paint. Briffault writes:

> The condition of women in a tabu state is commonly indicated by them painting themselves red. Thus, among the Dieri and other Australian tribes, menstruating women were marked with red paint round the mouth. Among the tribes of Victoria, a menstruating woman is painted red from the waist upwards. Among the Tapuya tribes of Brazil, a menstruating woman is also painted red. In some parts of the Gold Coast women painted themselves red when menstruating. In India, the condition of a menstruating woman is indicated by her wearing round her neck a handkerchief stained with menstrual blood.[13]

Illustrating the association of menstruation with sacredness among indigenous communities, Briffault provides these examples:

> Among the Ainu, menstrual blood is chiefly regarded as a talisman. When a man sees some on the floor of a hut he wipes it up with a piece of paper and rubs it over his breast.

> He believes he will thereby secure success in all his enterprises. Among the Aborigines themselves, whose 'horror' of a woman's blood is so pronounced, if a man is seriously ill, he is sometimes treated with blood from a woman's vulva; her labora minora is scarified so as to make them bleed, and she rubs the blood all over his body, after which a coating of grease is applied. Again, among the Warundi of East Africa, the menstruating girl, who is almost everywhere segregated as if she were a leper, is led all over the house, and obliged to touch everything as if her touch imparted a benediction instead of a curse. Among the Déné, who, it will be remembered, regard menstruating women with extravagant dread, if a child is not thriving, or several of his brothers and sisters have died, his mother will fasten round his neck a small piece of cloth soiled with menstrual blood. In these instances, the menstrual blood is regarded as scaring away evil spirits, and thus, like a powerful poison, acts as a disinfectant.[14]

Stressing on the sacredness associated with menstruation among Native American tribes, Shannon F notes in her article titled 'Menstrual Rites of the Native Americans' that menstruation involved 'a strong oral tradition, rituals, ceremonies and more' with women being treated with great reverence.[15] She adds: 'Some tribes actually believed that women were the embodiment of a holy person during their periods. Others believed that women's bodies were purifying themselves during this time. Perhaps most fascinating of all is that many tribes believed women were more powerful, spiritually, during their periods – and that they even had special intuitive powers. Some Native American tribe members would call upon menstruating women for their advice, insight, guidance, or to connect them to higher powers.'[16] Not only was menstruation associated with sacredness, menarche was elaborately celebrated among the Navajo, Apache and many other Native American tribes. Writing about the menarche celebration of the Navajo tribe, Nicole G says: 'The Navajo tribes celebrate a girl's first menstrual period with an elaborate four-day celebration called the "Kinaalda." Symbolic dances, cleansing rituals, physical activities such as racing, and a special cake called "alkaan" are among some of the blessed rituals experienced during a girl's Kinaalda celebration. The festivities are supposed to symbolise a physical and spiritual closeness to Mother Nature, and a young girl's transformation into the very image of Mother Nature.'[17] Similarly, the Apache tribe practise a 'Sunrise Ceremony' wherein 'The young girls are showered with attention while other members of the tribe sing, pray and dance almost non-stop during the four-day celebration'.[18] Nicole G adds that these rituals 'not only given a renewed confidence and heightened sense of self, but also the significant recognition that they have just passed into a new role in their lives – that of wives and mothers to be'.[19]

Conclusion

From the above discussion, we can see that the association of menstruation with impurity and sacredness, and the unique cultural practices, including the seclusion that followed it, is prevalent across the globe among a wide range of indigenous communities with little or no contact with each other. Though these practices are distinct to each community owing to the different cultural conditions, they share a common knowledge in the form of impurity and sacredness, which seems to have informed all these communities to evolve their own practices around menstruation.

With regard to the implementation of these practices on the ground, Briffault makes a very important observation. He says: The women, it appears from most accounts, segregate themselves of their own accord; they isolate themselves without consulting the men and warn them not to approach them.[20]

He further adds that 'Compulsion of any kind is foreign to the character of primitive societies; the women in carrying out their arduous duties, never do so under compulsion, even where the men are most tyrannical. Indeed, the most rigorous observance take place in societies such as Micronesia and North America, where far from being tyrannised, the women exercise an almost despotic power over the men'.[21]

Menstruation Attitude Hinduism vs Modernity

THE MODERN narrative on menstruation, which is predominated by western cultural views rooted in a modern, scientific worldview, has de-rooted it from its sacred dimensions. Its non-physical aspects have been termed 'taboo', thereby reducing it to negative notions such as pain, cramps, an unavoidable physiological process, and an annoyance to be overcome (through drugs etc.).

Contrasting the Hindu views on menstruation that correlate it to sacredness and regeneration with the modern narrative, which connects it to mere reproduction and biology, Frederique Apffel-Marglin observes in her essay 'The Sacred Groves' thus: In my world menstruation is related to reproduction, rather than to generation or regeneration. It is a process understood scientifically and categorised as biology. Scientific knowledge concerning menstruation has profoundly affected the manner in which menstruation is lived, understood, and spoken about by many women. Although many women consciously or unconsciously resist or reject the scientific understanding of menstruation, that understanding is dominant in my lived world. It is the one taught to all girls and young women in high schools, and in biology classes in colleges. The scientific understanding of menstruation is the one that determines what is 'normal' and what is pathological. That understanding of menstruation, of reproduction, and of bodily processes in general as 'biological' is also the prism through which anthropology understands and relates to the menstrual practices and the acts that generate and regenerate the lived world of people such as the villagers living in Orissan.[1]

She then provides a detailed analysis of the consequences this purely biological approach to menstruation has resulted in. The very first thing that this approach has led to is to make menstruation a very private, intimate affair, to the extent of making it a taboo in the public sphere. Contrary to public celebration of menstruation among Hindus, especially in rural areas, Apffel-Marglin notes that 'In the west the idea of a large public event to celebrate menses is simply unthinkable'.[2] She gives the example of the advertisements of menstrual pads that makes it 'abundantly obvious' that they all 'promise to eliminate or disguise any outward signs'.[3] We can see that this is true for modern, urban India as well, where owing to the import of western modernity and its menstrual notions, the advertisements on television and the educational videos aim to portray menstruation as an annoyance, which can now be eliminated and hidden from public view, using pads and tampons etc. As Apffel-Marglin rightly observes, 'They are all designed to reassure one that the product (pads or tampons) will enable one to act as if one were not menstruating',[4] in effect, denying the very existence of menstruation in public.

Second, the obsession with imparting knowledge about menstruation to youngsters in a purely biological manner to the exclusion of the cultural experience, means that young girls are denied the opportunity to find a positive meaning and relevance to menstruation in their lives. Apffel-Marglin writes: Menstruation is, in my world, biology; it is taught in schools under the rubric of female anatomy and physiology. Menses happen on their own. They can be modified and controlled by drugs and many women use the pill to regulate, predict and control their menses…As biological phenomena, menses just happen, automatically, just because we are alive. This way of seeing these processes deprives them of meaning and creativity.[5] And since this modernity posits that 'To be truly human, creative, rational, is not to be "enslaved" by our biology',[6] women are expected to free themselves of the enslavement of menstruation using drugs, tampons, sanitary pads etc.

The desire to become free from the enslavement of menstruation is so strong that the very names chosen for some of the sanitary products make this obvious. As Apffel-Marglin notes, 'A quick perusal of napkins and tampons on the shelf yielded such names as Stayfree and Freedom, pithily capturing the desire to erase as much as possible the experience of menstruation, an event experienced as a curtailment of freedom of action'.[7]

Third, Apffel-Marglin notes that this obsession with biology has resulted in alienating people from their own bodies. Contrary to cultural experiences as in a Hindu society, wherein women retain the agency to feel, understand, and interpret their body and mind as part of their self-discovery and inner journey, modern scientific approach has reduced women to become passive describers of their bodily sensations, without an agency to interpret them or find meaning. Apffel-Marglin writes that the 'Privileged access to knowledge of the body belongs to those who systematically probe the body to yield its secrets. Those are anatomists, physiologists, molecular biologists, and other scientists'.[8] Modernity has, thus, alienated women from their own bodies, who can no longer interpret their bodily changes as part of their self-discovery but must instead rely only on 'science' to gain 'authentic' information about menstruation!

In other words, while cultural experiences have been relegated to the status of falsehood and superstition, biological information alone has been upheld as 'truth'. Apffel-Marglin gives a typical example regarding this, often found in the writings on menstruation. She writes:

> I want to focus on the word 'really' in the following: 'What comes out of your vagina is usually called blood because the blood in it makes it red, but it's really a mixture of tissue, mucus, and blood.' The vernacular understanding is relegated to the status of untrue knowledge. Truth is single and cognitive authority lodged only with the scientists.... Lived experience and vernacular knowledge do not deliver to us the 'real', that is, the monopoly of the certified knowledge makers.... The road to 'true' knowledge is single and it specifically eliminates lived experience as a source. Eighth graders reading this account of menstruation are placed outside their own bodies and must experience their bodies as a strange, alien entity.[9]

Apffel-Marglin notes that modernity has not only attempted to delegitimise the feelings and livid experiences of women regarding menstruation but that using the same 'scientific lens' through anthropology, it has tried to delegitimise the cultural experiences and the knowledge about menstruation that is prevalent in other non-western cultures and traditions. It has done so by trying to portray them as primitive knowledge as against western scientific understanding, which is considered progressive. She notes that this is accomplished through portraying the notions and practices around menstruation prevalent in non-western cultures as taboos rooted 'not on fact, but on fear'.

She sums up modernity's approach to menstruation thus:

> The lesson is relentless: the embodied self has no privileged access to knowledge about its body; feelings have nothing to do with knowledge of the body; only one kind of knowledge can deliver the Truth; other cultures with different systems of knowledge than the western scientific one are dismissed as ignorant and primitive. Primitives and atavistic modems only have menstrual taboos. In sum, there is no other avenue to truth but the scientific one.[10]

While modernity itself projects this scientific view as progressive and has been imported into non-western cultures like those of India, Apffel-Marglin cautions that:

> The supposedly disembodied, unsituated, uncontextualised rationality, radically outside not only of the body but of any particular lived world, is in fact very much embodied in a middle class, white, male body, situated in late industrial capitalism. It has also shown how this knowledge has penetrated deeply into vernacular lived experience and produced a modern consciousness in which 'women's lives are especially degraded, fragmented, and impoverished'.[11]

One example, which clearly illustrates this degrading of the menstrual experience in popular culture, especially in the West, is how the monthly periods are referred to as 'on the rag'. The Urban Dictionary gives some examples of the usage of the term 'on the rag':[12]

> *Her pants got stained because she was on the rag and had no tampons.*
>
> *'Damn, b**ch! Are you always on the rag?!?*
>
> *'Gee guys... i have cramps, im on the rag. It's been a couple days. no sex for me.'*

She's really in a mood, she's on the rag and complaining about everything.

*When i am on the rag, i get cranky and bitchy and scream at assh**es.*

In contrast to this, Hindu tradition promotes a positive notion, and asks women to perceive menstruation as a period of rest, austerity and self-purification, and as a privilege available only to them. It considers pain and depression as symptoms of abnormal menstruation, and has designed a mode of life to be adopted by menstruating women, which will help ease their discomfort.

Though it does associate menstruation with Ashaucha, it recognises it as a part of honoring this feminine process as a tapas, like the austerity of the yogis, a sacred cleansing, uniquely available to women. The cultural practices are designed to free women from the obligation of routine work and chores, and they offer seclusion as a form of spiritual retreat. More importantly, Hinduism celebrates menstruation as a sacred festival, and promotes a holistic view by aligning it with various ecological and cosmic principles.

Modernity either mocks the process or pretends it doesn't exist by expecting women to 'show up with a work face' regardless of their physical or emotional state. When that manifests as emotional disturbance, women are patronised as being 'on the rag'.

The Hindu tradition, one of the last surviving planetary traditions that honour the sacred feminine, can help women recover the sacred aspect of the menstrual process. Menstrual practices based on Yoga and Ayurveda, and an understanding of physical, mental and spiritual health will allow women to best manage this process for bodily comfort, emotional support and spiritual growth.

Conclusion

In our examination of various cultures, traditions, and religions of the world, we noticed how most cultures and communities attached some notion of impurity and sacredness to menstruation. While polytheistic cultures have understood menstruation in terms of lack of vitality and incompetence, monotheistic religions have associated menstruation with the notion of Original Sin. Within polytheistic cultures, while Hinduism and other Indic traditions have defined impurity through the category of Ashaucha, others like Greco-Romans and Egyptians have used the category of Miasma and Bwt, respectively. Mesopotamians used a number of terms like *urruštu* and *(m)usukkatu* to refer to the impurity aspect of menstruation. Similarly, different indigenous communities across the globe have used their own categories and definitions to understand the 'ritual impurity' aspect of menstruation.

Be it through the framework of Ashaucha or of Miasma, Bwt or as Original Sin, women in most cultures and religions across the world have adopted a special lifestyle during their monthly menses. While each culture and religion has evolved menstrual practices unique to its own cultural and social realities, there are some common elements. These include seclusion, dietary control and abstaining from sacred activities, to name a few. Polytheistic cultures have also associated a strong notion of sacredness with menstruation, going as far as designating specific deities such as Parvati, Durga, Artemis, Diana, Isis, Hathor, Innana, to name a few. These cultures perceive the sacred aspect as complementary rather than contradictory to the impurity aspect. Among the Abrahamic monotheists though, except for Judaism, none associates any sacredness to menstruation. In any case, in communities that associated both sacredness and impurity with menstruation, both aspects inform their menstrual beliefs and practices, and this makes menstruation a wholesome experience for women. A good example is Hinduism, wherein women celebrate menarche, practise monthly periods as austerity and purification, take rest, worship Goddesses and celebrate festivals that glorify menstruation.

Contrary to this, we saw how modernity, on the one hand, relies heavily on a positivistic and materialistic worldview, promoted by a modern, scientific narrative, and on the other hand, it has inherited certain misogynist[1] views from Abrahamic religions like Christianity. It also desacralises menstruation, and delegitimises the cultural experiences and the knowledge about menstruation prevalent in traditional societies, especially among non-western polytheistic cultures, by branding them as primitive knowledge as against western scientific understanding.

India is currently going through turbulent times where more and more women are becoming deracinated from their cultural roots owing to modernity and modernity-inspired misportrayal of menstrual notions prevalent in traditional societies. Those with commercial or other vested interests controlling various media of information are further adding to this confusion.

It is high time these assumptions were examined and challenged, and questions raised about the bias against traditional knowledge, and the aim to caricaturise it.

An unbiased examination of the Hindu view on menstruation will not only help us arrive at a better understanding of menstruation in Indian culture and civilisation, it will also provide a window and a framework for better understanding the menstrual notions prevalent among ancient polytheistic civilisations and other indigenous communities. After all, Hinduism is the last surviving and still flourishing ancient civilisation. One such attempt is made in this book and it is the hope of the author that this will pave way for further research in this direction.

Last Words

Even though in my own life I never practiced any menstrual taboos, yet I find this well compiled account by Nithin Sridhar an invaluable guide to how different civilisations have viewed one of the most quintessential qualities of being a woman-namely the power to being new life (a new jivaatma) into this world which is intrinsically connected to the monthly menstrual cycle that the feminine body undergoes from teenage to her 50s.

However, the book, *Menstrualion across Cultures – A Historical Perspective,* is not so much about India as we know it today, it is about Hindu civilisation's deep engagement with trying to understand and come to grips with the distinctive nature and role of the feminine principle in the divine scheme of things.

As with much else, the cultural values and knowledge traditions of Hindu civilisation have been wilfully demonised and caricatured by zealots of Abrahamic faiths because they consider it their God-given mission to either annihilate or convert Hindus. It is no surprise, therefore, that the menstrual taboos among diverse Hindu communities have been caricatured beyond recognition by modernists of all hues – feminists, communists and western 'liberals' who instinctively turn into authoritarian Stalinists when it comes to dealing with cherished values of Hindu culture and civilisation, as has been demonstrated yet again through the ongoing battle over Sabarimala shrine to Lord Ayappa. It is ironical that the malicious Evangelical critiques of Hindu civilisation have been adopted lock stock and barrel by westernised modernists, leftists of all hues and even feminists.

Even though the idea of this book was triggered off by the Sabarimala controversy, Sridhar's book is not about the pros and cons of women's entry into Sabarimala. Instead it introduces us to the writings reflecting deep intellectual, emotional and spiritual engagement of the most revered Hindu sages, authors of leading Shastras and Smritis in trying to understand the distinct bodily processes of women not just in relation to human society but also cosmic forces that govern this universe. Far from treating women as inferior beings on account of this biological rhythm linked as it is to the lunar cycle, the Hindu view of menstrual cycle is integrally linked to the deep-rooted culture of revering and worshipping the feminine as the Divine Power that moves the entire Universe.

That is why, it is not just mortal women who bleed every month but also the most powerful icons of Shakti – various goddesses enshrined in the most sacred shrines of India – with similar rituals and taboos that are assigned for women in order for them to use the menstrual period to rejuvenate themselves and experience the full power of this divine gift.

Sridhar's book documents the many celebratory rituals attached to the start of menstruation in the life of a young girl among different communities of India so that the entry into womanhood becomes a joyful experience and not a traumatic and shameful one, as it is in cultures which treat menstruation as God's own curse on women and link it to the role played by Eve in bringing about the fall of entire mankind from Grace.

Whether or not one agrees with the validity of the taboos mandated for menstruating women in the Indic tradition, it is noteworthy that each community was free to decide which of the taboos it considered worth observing and how to celebrate the beginning of menarche for young girls. No centralised authority decided the dos and don'ts on this issue. Nor is there any record of lethal punishments decreed for communities or individuals which defied the laid down norms. In any case, even the shastras differed with each other considerably though all of them share the same underlying concern – the health of the woman and the children she would be giving birth to. That is why all the taboos, rituals and practices make it mandatory for women to take complete rest during this period, including avoidance of routine household chores and sexual contact.

By contrast, western culture has in characteristic fashion, moved from one extreme to another following its secularisation. From treating the menstrual cycle as a manifestation of Evil and intrinsic flaws in the feminine being, they have found a magic wand for the 'disabilities' imposed due to monthly bleeding. Just wear a good sanitary pad which soaks all the blood or a tampon – and you are a free woman – liberated from the 'curse' God imposed on women. You can then play football, swim, climb mountains, go for wrestling matches and not have to take a day's leave from school or your job. In short, don't use this period as a period of physical and mental rest and reflection in order to get in tune with your cosmic rhythms. As someone who didn't observe any taboos but from experience I can say with conviction, treating the sanitary pad or a tampon as the be-all, end all solution is dangerous. It takes women in the direction of forgetting their feminine self as distinct from male physiology in their mindless quest for mere equality with men. From being treated as manifestation of Shakti, the feminist aspiration gets reduced to being 'as good as men'.

I might have dismissed the Hindu worldview as anachronistic but for the fact that classic texts of Yoga and Ayurveda lay great emphasis treating this period as a sacred phase in a woman's life, a period of rest, solitude and reflection. Yogic literature perceives menstruation as a physiological process that is deeply connected to the Apana Vayu – one of the five main vayus or forms of vital air – prana apana, vyana, samana and udana. 'One of the primary aims of a successful yogic process is to force the apana to move upwards inside the body, synchronise it with the prana and awaken a state of heightened awareness and concentration, refered to as *the kundalini awakening*.... Yogic literature perceives menstruation as a physiological process that is deeply connected with the Apana Vayu. Any hindrance caused to the functioning of Apana Vayu will result in unpleasant physiological conditions'.

However, the book does not dwell sufficiently on how some of the empowering rituals and taboos have in some regions turned misogynist and become instruments of oppression and cruelty. In any case, every single thing written in every shastra can't be and should not be taken as divine truth firstly because they differ abundantly among themselves and secondly, one must not become a total slave of textual authorities. I confess that some of the menstrual prohibitions do appear excessive and even irrational and harmful to me. To quote Mahatma Gandhi, 'It is good to swim in the waters of tradition, but to sink in them is suicide'.

However, this book forced me to reflect on my own life. I started off as a very healthy child who rarely fell ill. My menses started as healthy as could be for any teenager. But within a year certain allopathic medicines prescribed on some other account proved very harmful and messed up my periods for ever. This along with total disregard of all dos and don'ts during my menstrual periods may well have contributed to onset of health problems which have plagued my life ever since, including serious thyroid deficiency and its many attendant problems.

While the first half of the book deals with the Indic civilisation's norms, values and taboos dealing with menstruation, the second half provides an interesting glimpse into the myths, taboos and prejudices prevalent among followers of Abrahamic religions. It shows that ritual taboos during this period are prevalent in almost all religions and cultures of the world. They are not unique to Hinduism as is being made out in the course of the battle over Sabarimala. This comparative picture shows how in Hinduism the ritual impurity associated with the monthly cycle is not to mark women as an inferior species, as happened with Christianity and Islam, but to bestow special honour and powers on to women for their reproductive function. Sridhar's narrative describes how in medieval Europe the misogynist ideas linked to menstruation took the form of mass murders of women in the name of witch killings. Thus, while in Hindu culture, monthly bleeding links women to the cosmic and the Divine, the Christian theology saw in it manifestation of Evil and hence worthy of annihilation.

However, the book would have gained enormously if Sridhar had also documented what women sages, scholars, Smritikars and Shastrakars had to say on this subject through the ages. It is very unlikely that the large array of female sages and Smritikars India produced over millennia would have remained altogether silent on this subject. The absence of their voices makes it appear as though men laid down all rules while women merely imbibed and followed them. In a culture with deep matriarchal roots and a living tradition of worshipping women as Shakti incarnate, women are not likely to have remained passive recipients of male wisdom on an issue that impacts them so profoundly.

Nithin Sridhar doesn't hide the fact that he believes in the sanctity of the Hindu world view in this regard. But the book is a valuable addition to cultural studies even for those who may consider all the worldview reflected in menstrual practices and taboos as being superstitious mumbo-jumbo.

Madhu Purnima Kishwar, Founder Manushi
ICSSR Maulana Azad National Professor

Recommendations

Some practices that modern women can observe during their monthly periods

Food: Eating light meals made of ghee, rice and milk; or meal made of barley. Avoiding non-vegetarian food. Avoiding junk food and eating home-cooked food. Eating food using fingers, instead of metal spoons and forks. Using clay utensils, plates made out of leaves etc. and avoiding the use of metal utensils. Consuming food in less quantity.

Sex: Observing celibacy during the first three days of menstruation.

Sleep: Sleeping on a Mat or charpoi. Avoiding sleeping during day time.

Self-adorning: Avoiding bathing, brushing, make-up and anointment, use of collyrium, body massage, hair combing and nail pairing.

Physical work: Taking complete physical rest. Avoiding physical and mental exertion including running, travelling, cooking, household activities and any other tiring work. Taking a day or two off from office work whenever possible or at least opting to work from home during periods.

Mental stress: Keeping the mind calm and focussed on auspicious and joyful things. Avoiding laughing, indulging in long conversations and listening to loud music. Avoiding mental stress, crying and weeping as much as possible.

Religious activity: Avoiding performing any spiritual or religious activities like yoga, meditation, puja or visiting temples.

In today's fast moving society, while it may be difficult to practice all of these dos and don'ts all the time, women may choose to practice as many of them as they can for a better physical and mental health.

Hindu Texts Cited or Consulted for the Book

Ananga Ranga
Angirasa Smriti
Baudhayana Dharmasutra
Bhagavad Gita
Bhagavata Purana
Brihadaranyaka Upanishad
Charaka Samhita
Daksha Smriti
Dharma-Shastra Sangraha
Dharmasindhu of Kashinatha Upadhyaya
Garbha Upanishad
Kashyapa Samhita
Kaulajnananirnaya of Matsyendranath
Kaulavalinirnayah of Jnanananda Paramahamsa
Krityakalpataru of Bhatta Lakshmidhara
Mahabharata
Manu Smriti
Matrikabheda Tantra
Narada Bhakti Sutras
Panchadashi of Swami Vidyaranya

Parashara Smriti

Ratishastra

Shuddhikaumudhi of Govindananda

Shuddhiviveka of Rudradhara

Smritichandrika of Devana Bhatta

Stridharmapaddhati of Tryambakayajvan

Sushruta Samhita

Taittiriya Upanishad

Vadhula Smriti

Vamana Purana

Vashishta Dharmasutra

Vivekachoodamani

Vishnu Smriti

Yajnavalkya Smriti

Yajur Veda Taittiriya Samhita

Yoga-Shikha Upanishad

Yoga-Sutras of Patanjali

Yogasutra Bhashya by Vyasa

Yoni Tantra

Glossary

Preface

Dharma: Literally 'that which upholds' the universe. Cosmic order. Universal law. Refers to Righteous actions, duties, and responsibilities in the human context. All such actions that lead to the overall well-being of the individual, harmony in society, and maintains order in the cosmos.

Adharma: Opposite of Dharma. All actions that lead to sorrow, disharmony, and chaos.

Dharmic: related to Dharma. Related to Hindu Dharma.

Sanatana Dharma: Literally 'Eternal Dharma'. Or the eternal and perpetual principles that sustain the universe and which when practiced by humans lead to overall well-being. In the contemporary context, what is called Hinduism or Hindu religion is actually called as 'Sanatana Dharma' or Hindu Dharma by the practitioners.

Agama: Literally means 'That which has come down'. They refer to a large body of knowledge which has come down through tradition and deal with subjects like cosmology, epistemology, philosophical doctrines, meditation and practices related to worship, different types of kinds of yoga, mantras, temple construction, temple rituals, etc. The three main branches of Agama texts are those belonging to the traditions of Shaivism (Shiva), Vaishnavism (Vishnu), and Shaktism (Devi).

Ishta: Refers to the notion of 'Ishta Devata' or 'cherished divinity' denoting a worshipper's favourite deity among the Hindu pantheon.

Menarche: The the first occurrence of menstruation

Menopause: The ceasing of menstruation

Hindu View of Menstruation

Yuga: Yuga in Hinduism is an epoch or era within a four-age cycle. A complete Yuga starts with the Satya Yuga, via Treta Yuga and Dvapara Yuga ends into a Kali Yuga. Together, these four yugas constitute one Mahayuga and equal 4.32 million human years.

Samskara: In Hindu philosophy, it refers to mental impressions, recollections, or psychological imprints. They are the basis for the development of the karma doctrine.

Moksha: The final liberation from the Karmic cycle of birth and death.

Soma: A mystical ritual drink considered the elixir of immortality.

Prana Shakti: In yoga philosophy, prana shakti is the primordial cosmic energy that governs all physical functions. Prana is life force and Shakti is energy or power. It refers to the vital life-sustaining energy of both the individual body and the Universe.

Apana Vayu: The apana vayu is one of the five energy subdivisions of prana that involves the downward and outward flow of energy from the body. It influences digestion, elimination, and reproduction, and is active in the pelvic and lower abdominal areas.

Niyama: Literally means 'positive duties or observances'. In Yoga philosophy, Niyamas and its complement, Yamas, are recommended activities and habits for healthy living, spiritual enlightenment and liberated state of existence.

Yoga: Literally means 'Uniion' or 'To join'. It is one among the six major schools of Hindu philosophy. It refers to a group of physical, mental, and spiritual practices or disciplines which frees the practitioner from worldly bondages and leads him to the state of freedom.

Samanya Dharma: In Hindu philosophy, universal tenets of dharma like non-injury, truth, non-stealing, purity, and sense-control, which are applicable to every person irrespective of his class, gender or station in life is termed as 'sAmAnya dharma'.

Vedanta: Literally 'End of Vedas'. Considered the crown of Vedas, it refers to the latter philosophical portions of the Vedas enunciated in the Upanishads that deal with Knowledge of Brahman and how one can attain final Liberation from the cycle of birth and death. It is one of the six major schools of Hindu philosophy.

Karma: means action, work or deed; it also refers to the spiritual principle of cause and effect where intent and actions of an individual (cause) influence the future of that individual (effect).

Sandhyopasana: The ritual worship and meditation dedicated to the solar deity Surya to be performed every day at sunrise, noon and sunset.

Brahmana: A person belonging to Brahmana Varna. A Brahmana is one who has the following qualities: peacefulness, control of mind and senses; austerity, cleanliness, satisfaction, tolerance, simple straightforwardness, devotion to God, mercy, and truthfulness; and who engage in religious, educational, and spiritual duties like study and teaching of Vedas, performance of ritual yajnas for self and for others, etc.

Varna: Literally 'to choose'. Varna can be understood either as a reference to the svadharma (personal duty/purpose of life) chosen by each individual in his/her life according to his/her svabhava (inherent nature) or more appropriately as a descriptor tag referring to the svabhava that drives people to spontaneously choose particular paths of life as their svadharma. According to Hindu worldview, based on the innate temperaments and duties being performed in life, people can be divided into four such Varna groups: Brahmana, Kshatriya, Vaishya, and Shudra.

Mantra Japa: A mantra is a sacred utterance, a numinous sound, a syllable, word or phonemes, or group of words in Sanskrit. Japa is the meditative repetition of a mantra or a divine name to attain one-pointed concentration, purification of the mind, and spiritual wellbeing.

Nadi: Nadi literally means tube, channel or flow. It refers to the network of channels through which energy travels through the body. There are three principal nadis that weave through the spinal cord and the intense energy centers known as chakras.

Sampradaya: Refers to a 'tradition', 'spiritual lineage' or a 'religious system'. It relates to a succession of masters and disciples, which serves as a spiritual channel and ensures a continous and unbroken transmission of knowledge and practices unique to that tradition.

Panchatattwa: Five elements: Akash (Ether), Vayu (Air), Apa (Water), Agni (Fire) and Prithvi (Earth)

Mata: Also called Mathas or Mutts, they literally mean 'cloister, institute or college' and refer to Hindu religious, spiritual and education centers, as well as monasteries of Hindu Sannyasins.

Menstruation Notions in Other Indic Traditions

Daoism: A Chinese philosophy based on the writings of Lao-tzu, advocating humility and religious piety.

Tantric: Refers to the esoteric Hindu and Buddhist traditions of Tantra.

Ojas: In Sanskrit, ojas means 'vigor'. It is the essential energy of the body and mind. In Ayurveda, Ojas is understood to be responsible for vitality, strength, health, long life, immunity and mental/emotional wellness.

Menstruation Notions in Abrahamic Religions

Kabbahlah: It is an esoteric method, discipline, and school of thought of Judaism.

Chassid: A Jewish religious and mysticism group. It arose as a spiritual revival movement in contemporary Western Ukraine during the 18th century,

Kohen: He is a Jewish priest, a direct male descendant of the Biblical Aaron, brother of Moses.

Shekhinah: It literally means 'dwelling' and represents the divine presence of God. She is considered a female aspect of God.

Gentile: Refers to Non-Jewish people.

Halakhic: Related to Halakha. Halakha is the collective body of Jewish religious laws derived from the Written and Oral Torah.

Midrashic: Related to Midrash. Midrash is the biblical exegesis by ancient Judaic authorities, using a mode of interpretation prominent in the Talmud. The term is also used of a rabbinic work that interprets Scripture in that manner.

Challah: It is a special bread in Jewish cuisine, usually braided and typically eaten on ceremonial occasions such as Sabbath and major Jewish holidays.

Notes & References

Preface

1. Nithin Sridhar, 'Why Sabarimala controversy is religious issue, not women's rights issue', *NewsGram* [https://www.newsgram.com/why-sabarimala-controversy-is-religious-issue-not-womens-rights-issue]
2. The 6-part articles on menstruation published in *IndiaFacts* can be accessed here: [http://indiafacts.org/?s=Hindu+view+of+Menstruation]

Introduction

1. Vishakha Goyal (2016), 'Scope and Opportunities for Menstrual Health and Hygiene Products in India', *International Research Journal of Social Sciences*, Vol 5, Page 2319-3565.
2. '70% can't afford sanitary napkins, reveals study', *Times of India* (Jan 23, 2011). [https://timesofindia.indiatimes.com/india/70-cant-afford-sanitary-napkins-reveals-study/articleshow/7344998.cms]
3. 'Menstrual Hygiene Key to Keeping Girls in School', UNICEF India. (http://www.unicef.in/Story/122/Menstrual-Hygiene-Key-to-Keeping-Girls-in-School)

4. 'Sex Ki Adalat- Menstruation', *Main Kuch Bhi Kar Sakti Hoon*, Youtube [https://youtu.be/0juzmJx_Vb8]
5. The study by AC Nielsen and Plan India only interviewed 1033 women i.e. < 0.00029% of India's menstruating women! There are other issues with the study as well. See: Sinu Joseph, 'Why India Doesn't Need The Sanitary Napkin Revolution', *Swarajya*. [https://swarajyamag.com/culture/why-india-doesnt-need-the-sanitary-napkin-revolution]
6. AM van Eijk, M Sivakami, MB Thakkar, et al, 'Menstrual hygiene management among adolescent girls in India: a systematic review and meta-analysis', BMJ Open 2016;6:e010290. doi:10.1136/bmjopen-2015-010290. Cited from Sinu Joseph, 'Menstruation: Rhetoric, Research, Reality', Mythri Speaks. [https://mythrispeaks.wordpress.com/2016/06/13/menstruation-rhetoric-research-reality/]
7. Sinu Joseph, 'Menstrual Hygiene is not about Sanitary Napkins', Mythri Speaks. [https://mythrispeaks.wordpress.com/2013/04/08/menstrual-hygiene-is-not-about-sanitary-napkins-2/]
8. ibid.
9. Sinu Joseph, 'Menstruation: Rhetoric, Research, Reality', Mythri Speaks. [https://mythrispeaks.wordpress.com/2016/06/13/menstruation-rhetoric-research-reality/]
10. ibid.
11. ibid
12. Monica J Grant, Cynthia B Lloyd, and Barbara S Mensch, 'Menstruation and School Absenteeism: Evidence from Rural Malawi.' *Comparative Education Review* 57.2 (2013): 260–284. PMC. [https://www.ncbi.nlm.nih.gov/pmc/articles/PMC4286891/]
13. Oster, Emily and Rebecca Thornton. 2011. 'Menstruation, Sanitary Products, and School Attendance: Evidence from a Randomized Evaluation.' *American Economic Journal: Applied Economics*, 3(1): 91-100.

14. Frederique Apffel-Marglin, 'The Sacred Groves', *Manushi* (No. 82) [http://manushi.in/docs/106.%20The%20Sacred%20 Groves.pdf].
15. Sinu Joseph, 'Why India Doesn't Need The Sanitary Napkin Revolution', *Swarajya.* [https://swarajyamag.com/culture/why-india-doesnt-need-the-sanitary-napkin-revolution]

Hindu View of Menstruation

Introduction

1. 'Indus era 8,000 years old, not 5,500; ended because of weaker monsoon,' *Times of India* (2016). [https://timesofindia.indiatimes.com/india/Indus-era-8000-years-old-not-5500-ended-because-of-weaker-monsoon/articleshow/52485332.cms]
2. Surajit Dasgupta, 'We Were Always There', *Swarajya* magazine. [https://swarajyamag.com/magazine/we-were-always-there]
3. Nithin Sridhar, 'How Hindus Recreate Creation', *SirfNews.* [http://www.sirfnews.com/hindus-recreate-creation/]

Moon and Menstruation

1. Dr Arnold Leiber, 'The Lunar Effect: Biological Tides and Human Emotions', Cited from Arlini Singh, 'An Ayurvedic Perspective on The Lunar Effect', [http://www.ayurvedacollege.com/sites/ayurvedacollege.com/files/articles/The%20Lunar%20 Effect%20Arlini%20Singh.pdf]
2. Sandhiya Ramaswamy, 'Ayurveda – An ancient healing system's gifts to the Modern Woman', Research Paper submission as part of Ayurvedic Health Practitioner Certification California College of Ayurveda, Grass Valley, CA. [http://www.ayurvedacollege.com/sites/ayurvedacollege.com/files/articles/Ayurveda-SandhiyaRamaswamy.pdf]
3. ibid.
4. James G Bailey, 'By the Light of the Moon: Ayurveda, Yoga and Menstruation'. [http://ayurmater.blogspot.in/2012/07/by-light-of-moon-ayurveda-yoga-and.html]

5. ibid.
6. Cited from BM Hegde, 'Woman, Moon and Menstruation', *Journal, Indian Academy of Clinical Medicine*, Volume 5, No. 1 [http://medind.nic.in/jac/t04/i1/jact04i1p22.pdf]
7. Sir Richard Burton (Tr), 'The Ananga Ranga' of Kalyana Malla. [http://sacred-texts.com/sex/ar/index.htm]
8. ibid.
9. ibid.
10. Prof HS Gambers (Tr.), 'Ratishastra or The Hindu Science of Sex as expounded by God Siva, Page 114. [https://archive.org/details/in.ernet.dli.2015.142218]
11. ibid, Page 114-121.
12. ibid, Page 119-121.

The Story of Indra

1. Arthur Berriedale Keith (Tr.), 'The Yajur Veda (Taittiriya Sanhita),' [http://www.sacred-texts.com/hin/yv/index.htm]

Menstruation as Ashaucha

1. Also Vishnu Smriti 22.72: 'A woman in her courses becomes pure after four days by bathing.'
2. Also Vashishta Dharmasutra 28.4.
3. Also Angirasa Smriti Verse 36.
4. Tryam̃bakayajvan, Julia Leslie (tr.),'The Perfect Wife [stridharmapaddhati:Sanskrit]', Page 284
5. ibid. Page 286.
6. ibid.
7. One can find extensive descriptions about Pancha-Koshas in the Upanishads like Taittiriya Upanishad and in the writings of Hindu Acharyas like Adi Shankaracharya (Vivekachoodamani) and Swami Vidyaranya (Panchadashi).
8. Nithin Sridhar, 'Is Swacchata part of our culture?' *Swarajya magazine*. [Retrieved from https://nithinsridhar.wordpress.com/2014/12/29/the-concept-of-swacchata-in-hindu-dharma/]

9. Manu Smriti 10.63, Yajnavalkya Smriti (1.122), Vamana Purana (11.23-24).
10. Yoga-Sutras of Patanjali 2.32.
11. Narada Bhakti Sutra (Verse 78) says that a practitioner of bhakti is ever indulged in the practices of tenets like ahimsa (non-violence), satya (truth), shaucha (cleanliness), daya (compassion) and aastikya (conviction in God and vedas).
12. Vivekachoodamani (Verse 18-30) elaborates on competencies required for the practice of Vedanta i.e. Jnana Yoga or Atma-Vichara.
13. Daksha Smriti 5.2.
14. Vyasa Commentary on verse 2.32 of Patanjali Yoga-Sutra, also refer Vadhula Smriti Verse 19, Daksha Smriti 5.3 'Purification is of two types – external and internal. External purification is achieved through water and clay. Internal purification results from cleansing of one's inner thoughts (and emotions)'.
15. Five vital airs are: Prana vayu, Apana vayu, Samana vayu, Udana vayu and Vyana vayu. They handle various functions of the body and provides life support to the physical body.
16. Cited from KV Rangaswamy Aiyangar (Ed.), Introduction to 'Krityakalpataru of Bhatta Lakshmidhara,' Volume 10 Shuddhikhanda. Gaekwad's Oriental Series. Volume CXII. Baroda Oriental Institute.
17. ibid.
18. ibid.
19. 'Can I get pregnant just after my period has finished?' NHS.UK [https://www.nhs.uk/chq/Pages/981.aspx]

Menstruation as Austerity, Self-purification & a period of Rest

1. Yoga Sutras of Patanjanli 2.43.
2. Yoga-Sutras of Patanjali 2.32.
3. Vivekachoodamani (Verse 22-23) speaks about control of the mind and the senses.

4. The verse actually asks the husband to not have intercourse with a menstruating woman, and lists various unsavory results that befall one when such an intercourse is carried out with a menstruating woman who combs her hairs and anoints her eyes, etc. In other words, a practice of austerity by staying away from such activities is indirectly suggested.
5. Here the 'sin' is being used to refer to the Hindu concept of 'Paapa' that one incurs by performing Adharma. 'Punya' and 'Paapa' are pleasant and unpleasant Karmic results one receives by performing Dharma (righteous) and Adharma (unrighteous) activities. This should not be confused with the Abrahamic concept of original sin.
6. A Brahmana is one who has the following qualities: peacefulness, control of mind and senses; austerity, cleanliness, satisfaction, tolerance, simple straightforwardness, devotion to God, mercy, and truthfulness (Bhagavata Purana 11.17.16). Manu Smriti says a Brahmana is one who is a friend to everyone. In other words, a Brahmana is one who will harm no one, and hence, slaying such a Brahmana is considered a great Adharma.
7. Brihadaranyaka Upanishad (1.5. 16-17) says that it is the duty of the householders to strive to attain all the three worlds – the world of men, of forefathers, and of gods. It further says that one can attain the world of men only by having offsprings.
8. Garbha Upanishad Verse 3.
9. Chandasekhar in his book *Abortion in a Crowded World* writes: 'As for induced abortion, the Hindu scriptures from the Vedic age down to the Smritis (100 B.C. to 100 A.D.) called it bhrunahatya ('foetus murder') or Garbhahatya ('pregnancy destruction'), and condemned it as a serious sin. According to Vishnu Smriti (c. 100 B.C. to 100 A.D.), 'The destruction of an embryo is tantamount to killing a holy or learned person'. Chandrasekhar S (Ed), 'Abortion in a Crowded World: The Problem of Abortion with Special Reference to India', Cited from Vaidyanathan Gowri, 'Abortion and Ensoulment,' [https://www.ncbi.nlm.nih.gov/pmc/articles/PMC3616773/]

10. Yajurveda Taittiriya Samhita 6.5.10.
11. Vashishta Dharmasutra (28.5-6).
12. The association of menstruation cycle with the moon have been recognised by different cultures across the world. Even recent scientific studies have found that they both share a relation. [http://www.ncbi.nlm.nih.gov/pubmed/3716780]
13. Though a Buddhist text, it may well serve to point towards the Hindu view as well, since Buddhist and Hindu Tantras are intimately connected. Cited from *Three Days of Impurity: Menstruation and (In)Auspiciousness* [https://swordandflute.wordpress.com/2013/07/19/three-days-of-impurity-menstruation-and-inauspiciousness/]
14. 'Period pain: Overview', *PubMed Health* [https://www.ncbi.nlm.nih.gov/pubmedhealth/PMH0072508/]
15. 'Period pain cripples women's careers'. *Daily Mail.*[http://www.dailymail.co.uk/health/article-358454/Period-pain-cripples-womens-careers.html]
16. Frederique Apffel-Marglin, 'Rhythms of Life: Enacting the World with the Goddesses of Orissa,' Cited from *Three Days of Impurity: Menstruation and (In)Auspiciousness* [https://swordandflute.wordpress.com/2013/07/19/three-days-of-impurity-menstruation-and-inauspiciousness/]
17. Mitoo Das, 'Menstruation as Pollution: Taboos in Simlitola, Assam.' *Indian Anthropologist*, Vol. 38, No. 2, 2008, pp. 29–42. [www.jstor.org/stable/41920072]
18. Kumkum Bhatia, 'Menstrual Taboos in Hinduism', [http://www.sanskritimagazine.com/indian-religions/hinduism/menstrual-taboo-in-hinduism/]

Menstruation as a Sacred Celebration

1. LK Anantha Krishna Iyer, *The Cochin Tribes and Castes* (Vol 1), Page 200-201.
2. Frederique Apffel-Marglin, 'The Sacred Groves', *Manushi* (No. 82) [http://manushi.in/docs/106.%20The%20Sacred%20Groves.pdf]

3. A detailed account of the Tamil celebration of Menarche: Richard Clarke, 'Tamil Coming of Age – Manjal Neerattu Vizha', Living in the Embrace of Arunachala. [https://richardarunachala.wordpress.com/].
4. Dr NN Bhattacharyya, *Indian Puberty Rites*, Page 16.
5. ibid, Page 16-18.
6. Prof Nagaraja Gundappa, in a private communication shared with the author the Yogic insights into menarche practices and the dress-codes practiced by Hindu women as taught by Sriranga Mahaguru, an early 20th century Yogi.
7. Dr NN Bhattacharyya, *Indian Puberty Rites*, Page 25.
8. ibid. Page 33.
9. ibid.
10. ibid. Page 27-29.
11. Sankrant Sanu, 'Killing the feminine: Misogyny in Christianity', *India Facts.* [http://indiafacts.org/killing-the-feminine-misogyny-in-christianity/]
12. Michael Magee (Tr.), 'The Yoni Tantra', Third Patala. [https://archive.org/details/YoniTantraTr.MikeMagee]
13. Cited from Michael Magee (Tr.), 'The Yoni Tantra', Introduction. [https://archive.org/details/YoniTantraTr.MikeMagee]
14. ibid.
15. ibid.
16. ibid.
17. Sir John Woodroffe (Ed.), 'Kaulavalinirnayah of Jnanananda Paramahamsa', Introduction. [http://www.shivashakti.com/kaulav.htm]
18. Michael Magee (Tr.), 'The Yoni Tantra', Fifth Patala [https://archive.org/details/YoniTantraTr.MikeMagee]
19. June McDaniel, 'The Embodiment of God among the Bauls of Bengal', *Journal of Feminist Studies in Religion*, Vol. 8, No. 2, pp. 27-39. [www.jstor.org/stable/25002179]
20. Cited from 'The Yoga Upanishads', Translated into English by TR Srinivasa Ayyangar, The Adyar Library, 1938.

21. Sinu Joseph, 'Unearthing menstrual wisdom – Why we don't go to the temple, and other practices', Mythri Speaks [https://mythrispeaks.wordpress.com/2015/05/28/unearthing-menstrual-wisdom-why-we-dont-go-to-the-temple/]
22. Kashinatha Upadhyaya, 'Dharmasindhu', Translated into Kannada by Shambhu Sharma Najagara.
23. Kartikeya C Patel, 'Women, Earth, and the Goddess: A Shākta-Hindu Interpretation of Embodied Religion.' *Hypatia*, vol. 9, no. 4, pp. 69–87. [www.jstor.org/stable/3810423]
24. ibid.
25. Sinu Joeseph, 'In Search Of The Menstruating Goddess', Mythri Speaks [https://mythrispeaks.wordpress.com/2014/11/18/in-search-of-the-menstruating-goddess/]
26. 'Keddasa', Tulu Research [https://tulu-research.blogspot.in/2008/02/89-keasa.html]
27. Janet Chawla, 'Mythic Origins of Menstrual Taboo in Rig Veda.' *Economic and Political Weekly*, vol. 29, no. 43, pp. 2817–2827. [www.jstor.org/stable/4401940]
28. ibid.

Yogic & Ayurvedic perspectives on Menstruation

1. 'Yogasutras of Patanjali', Retrieved from [http://www.swamij.com/yoga-sutras-10104.htm]
2. Nithin Sridhar, 'Why Remove Yoga From Its Roots?' *Swarajya* [https://swarajyamag.com/culture/why-remove-yoga-from-its-roots]
3. ibid.
4. Kisari Mohan Ganguli (Tr.), 'Mahabharata,' Shanti Parva [http://www.sacred-texts.com/hin/m12/m12b011.htm]
5. Rajarshi Nandy, 'Sabarimala Discreet, Not Discriminatory', [http://www.sirfnews.com/sabarimala-discreet-not-discriminatory/]
6. Nithin Sridhar, 'Ayurveda Prakriti classification has genetic basis', *NewsGram* [http://www.newsgram.com/ayurveda-prakriti-classification-has-genetic-basis-study]

7. Shweta V Dabhade, AA Hawale, 'A conceptual study of rutuchakra', *Ayurlog: National Journal of Research in Ayurved Science*, Vol3, Special issue (16th Feb. 2015). [http://ayurlog.com/Archive/january_march/ssac/201502S060.pdf]. Also see: NishiJain, Anil Kumar Joshi, 'Analysis of Artava (Menstruation) in Context of Sharira Rachana', *Ayushdhara*, Vol 2, Issue 3 (May-June 2015).
8. Shweta V Dabhade, AA Hawale, 'A conceptual study of rutuchakra', *Ayurlog: National Journal of Research in Ayurved Science*, Vol 3, Special issue (16th Feb 2015). [http://ayurlog.com/Archive/january_march/ssac/201502S060.pdf]
9. 'An English Translation of Sushruta Samhita', Vol2, Edited by Kaviraj Kunjalal Bhishagratna. [https://archive.org/details/englishtranslati00susruoft]
10. Amrutha BL, 'Menstrual Health And Ayurveda', *International Ayurvedic medical Journal* {online} 2016 {cited 2016 April} [http://www.iamj.in/posts/images/upload/602_605.pdf]
11. 'Charaka Samhita: Handbook on Ayurveda', Vol1, Edited by Gabriel Van Loon. [http://yousigma.com/biographies/Charaka%20Samhita%20%28Acharya%20Charaka%29.pdf]
12. 'An English Translation of Sushruta Samhita', Vol2, Edited by Kaviraj Kunjalal Bhishagratna. [https://archive.org/details/englishtranslati00susruoft]
13. 'Can I get pregnant just after my period has finished?' NHS. [https://www.nhs.uk/chq/Pages/981.aspx]
14. Sushruta Samhita (Sharirasthana 2.31), Kashyapa Samhita (Sharirasthana 5.5)
15. The Table 1 has been compiled using information present in various Ayurvedic texts, especially Sushruta Samhita. The table has been reproduced with minor changes from: Dr Jasmine Gujarathi, Dr Dilip Jani and Dr ARV Murthy, 'Prevalence of Menstrual Related Taboos in Special Context with Ayurvedic Rajaswala Paricharya in Young Girls', Rasamruta, 6:4, February 2014. [https://www.researchgate.net/publication/260267973_Prevalence_of_Menstrual_Related_Taboos_in_Special_Context_with_Ayurvedic_Rajaswala_Paricharya_in_Young_Girls]

16. The comparison between Rajaswala Paricharya and dos and don'ts during Shodhana, Agnimandya and injury conditions have been taken from: Dr Pallavi Pai, Dr Sarita Bhutada, Dr Prasad Pandkar, 'Rajaswala Paricharya: Effect on Menstrual Cycle and Its Associated Symptoms', *IOSR Journal of Dental and Medical Sciences,* Volume 14, Issue 2 Ver. II (Feb. 2015). [http://www.iosrjournals.org/iosr-jdms/papers/Vol14-issue2/Version-2/R014228287.pdf]
17. Dr Pallavi Pai, Dr Sarita Bhutada, Dr Prasad Pandkar, 'Rajaswala Paricharya: Effect on Menstrual Cycle and Its Associated Symptoms', *IOSR Journal of Dental and Medical Sciences,* Volume 14, Issue 2 Ver. II (Feb. 2015). [http://www.iosrjournals.org/iosr-jdms/papers/Vol14-issue2/Version-2/R014228287.pdf]
18. ibid.
19. ibid.
20. Sonu, Hetal H Dave, and Vipin Kumar, 'Efficiency of Rajaswala Paricharya in Asrigdara (Dysfunctional Uterine Bleeding): A Case Study,' *Journal of Biological & Scientific Opinion,* Volume 4 (3). 2016. [http://www.jbsoweb.com/admin/php/uploads/273_pdf.pdf]

Menstruation Restrictions

1. LK Anantha Krishna Iyer, *The Cochin Tribes and Castes* (Vol 1), Page 202-2013.
2. Manu Smriti (4.40-41) states: 'Let him, though mad with desire, not approach his wife when her courses appear; nor let him sleep with her in the same bed. For the wisdom, the energy, the strength, the sight, and the vitality of a man who approaches a woman covered with menstrual excretions, utterly perish.' The reason for this injunction appears to be two-fold. One, if sexual intercourse with menstruating woman leads to conception and the subsequent death of the child, then the Karmic fruits equivalent to 'Brunahatya' – which is among the greatest Adharmic actions will come to the father, since it was he who initiated the sexual activity (as clear from verse 40); Two, since the menstruating

woman is in a heightened condition of Rajas, the interaction and energy exchange during sexual activity may have adverse effect on the male partner, thus weakening his energy, strength and vitality.

3. Sinu Joseph, 'Why India Doesn't Need the Sanitary Napkin Revolution', *Swarajya.* [https://swarajyamag.com/culture/why-india-doesnt-need-the-sanitary-napkin-revolution]
4. Rajarshi Nandy, 'Sabarimala Discreet, Not Discriminatory', *SirfNews.* [http://www.sirfnews.com/sabarimala-discreet-not-discriminatory/]
5. Dr Jasmine Gujarathi, Dr Dilip Jani and Dr ARV Murthy, 'Prevalence of Menstrual Related Taboos in Special Context with Ayurvedic Rajaswala Paricharya in Young Girls', Rasamruta, 6:4, February 2014. [https://www.researchgate.net/publication/260267973_Prevalence_of_Menstrual_Related_Taboos_in_Special_Context_with_Ayurvedic_Rajaswala_Paricharya_in_Young_Girls]
6. Dr Pallavi Pai, Dr Sarita Bhutada, Dr Prasad Pandkar, 'Rajaswala Paricharya: Effect on Menstrual Cycle and Its Associated Symptoms', *IOSR Journal of Dental and Medical Sciences,* Volume 14, Issue 2 Ver. II (Feb. 2015). [http://www.iosrjournals.org/iosr-jdms/papers/Vol14-issue2/Version-2/R014228287.pdf]

Menstruation Notions in Other Indic Traditions

Buddhism

1. Nastika, though translated as 'atheist' does not necessarily mean rejection of God in Indic Dharma-based traditions. Astika refers to acceptance of Veda as the valid Pramana, while Nastika refers to non-acceptance of Veda as a Pramana. Darshana means worldview. Indic tradition recognises six Astika Darshanas, which are collectively sometimes called as Sanatana Dharma and three Nastika Darshanas: Bauddha, Jaina and Charvaka, one of the Nastika Darshanas in Indian schools of philosophy which upholds a materialistic view of life.
2. Buddha Dharma Education Association in answer to the question: 'It is commonly believed that women are unclean.

How true is this belief?' [http://www.buddhanet.net/e-learning/history/wbq21.htm]

3. Cordia MingYeuk Chu, 'Menstrual Beliefs and Practices of Chinese Women', *Journal of the Folklore Institute*, Vol. 17, No. 1, pp. 38-55.
4. Yeshe Choekyi Lhamo, 'The fangs of reproduction: an analysis of taiwanese menstrual pollution in the context of buddhist philosophy and practice', *History & Anthropology*, Volume14(2), Page 157-178.
5. ibid.
6. ibid.
7. Alan Cole, 'Mothers and Sons in Chinese Buddhism', cited from ibid.
8. Yeshe Choekyi Lhamo, 'The fangs of reproduction: an analysis of Taiwanese menstrual pollution in the context of buddhist philosophy and practice', *History & Anthropology*, Volume 14(2), Page 157-178.
9. ibid.
10. ibid.
11. Sutra on Changing the Female Sex, cited from Diana Mary Paul, 'Women in Buddhism: Images of the Feminine in the Mahayana Tradition', Page 308.
12. Yeshe Choekyi Lhamo, 'The fangs of reproduction: an analysis of Taiwanese menstrual pollution in the context of buddhist philosophy and practice', *History & Anthropology*, Volume 14(2), Page 157-178.
13. ibid.
14. ibid.
15. Shiu-kuen Fan Tsung, 'Moms, nuns and hookers: Extrafamilial alternatives for village women in Taiwan', cited from ibid.
16. Aru Bhartiya, 'Menstruation, Religion and Society', *International Journal of Social Science and Humanity*, Volume 3 No. 6.
17. M Guterman, P Mehta, M Gibbs. 'Menstrual Taboos Among Major Religions'. *The Internet Journal of World Health and*

Societal Politics. 2007 Volume 5 Number 2. [http://ispub.com/IJWH/5/2/8213]

18. Yeshe Choekyi Lhamo, 'The fangs of reproduction: an analysis of Taiwanese menstrual pollution in the context of Buddhist philosophy and practice', *History & Anthropology*, Volume 14(2), Page 157-178.
19. ibid.
20. Renee Pinkston, 'Menstrual Taboos - Anthropology of Gender', [https://www.academia.edu/5316101/Menstrual_Taboos_-_Anthropology_of_Gender]
21. Yeshe Choekyi Lhamo, 'The fangs of reproduction: an analysis of Taiwanese menstrual pollution in the context of buddhist philosophy and practice', *History & Anthropology*, Volume 14(2), Page 157-178.
22. ibid.
23. ibid.
24. ibid.
25. ibid.
26. Cited from ibid.
27. Momoko Takemi, 'Menstruation Sutra Belief in Japan', *Japanese Journal of Religious Studies*, Vol. 10, No. 2/3, Women and Religion in Japan, Page 229-246.
28. ibid.
29. ibid.
30. ibid.
31. Kara Spafford, 'The Perception of Menstruation and Treatment of Menstrual Ailments among Tibetan Women in Mcleodganj, Himachal Pradesh,' India: Public Health, Policy Advocacy, and Community. Paper 1. [http://digitalcollections.sit.edu/inh/1]
32. ibid.
33. ibid.
34. Charlene Makley, The Meaning of Liberation: Representations of Tibetan Women, cited from ibid.

35. Kara Spafford, 'The Perception of Menstruation and Treatment of Menstrual Ailments among Tibetan Women in Mcleodganj, Himachal Pradesh,' India: Public Health, Policy Advocacy, and Community. Paper 1. [http://digitalcollections.sit.edu/inh/1]
36. ibid.
37. ibid.
38. ibid.
39. ibid.
40. ibid.
41. ibid.

Jainism

1. Champat RaiJain, 'Risabha Deva - The Founder of Jainism,' cited from Wikipedia [https://en.wikipedia.org/wiki/Sangha_(Jainism)]
2. Nalini Balbir, 'Women in the Jain tradition'. [http://www.jainpedia.org/themes/people/women-in-the-jain-tradition.html]
3. ibid.
4. ibid.
5. ibid.
6. ibid.
7. ibid.
8. Nalini Balbir, 'Women in Jainism'. In Arvind Sharma (Ed), *Religion and Women*, Page 122.
9. Alan Soble (Ed), *Sex from Plato to Paglia: A-L*, Page 512.
10. Nalini Balbir, 'Women in Jainism'. In Arvind Sharma (Ed), *Religion and Women*, Page 122.
11. Manisha Sethi, 'Asceticism Among Jaina Women: Power, Sexuality and Social Control in Selected Districts of North India', Page 75. [http://hdl.handle.net/10603/14456]
12. ibid. Page 76.
13. Cited from Nalini Balbir, 'Women in Jainism'. In Arvind Sharma (Ed), *Religion and Women*, Page 122.

14. Manisha Sethi, 'Asceticism Among Jaina Women: Power, Sexuality and Social Control in Selected Districts of North India', Page 85. [http://hdl.handle.net/10603/14456]
15. Nalini Balbir, 'Women in Jainism'. In Arvind Sharma (Ed), *Religion and Women*, Page 122-123.
16. Alan Soble (Ed), *Sex from Plato to Paglia: A-L*, Page 512.
17. Manisha Sethi, 'Asceticism Among Jaina Women: Power, Sexuality and Social Control in Selected Districts of North India', Page 100. [http://hdl.handle.net/10603/14456]
18. Nalini Balbir, 'Women in Jainism'. In Arvind Sharma (Ed), *Religion and Women*, Page 123.
19. Jeffery Long, *Jainism: An Introduction*, Chapter 1: What is Jainism.
20. ibid.
21. Digambara Acharya Prabhachandra's 'Nyqyakumudachandra' paraphrased in Manisha Sethi, 'Asceticism Among Jaina Women: Power, Sexuality and Social Control in Selected Districts of North India', Page 103-104. [http://hdl.handle.net/10603/14456]
22. Yapaniya Acharya Saktayana's view paraphrased in Manisha Sethi, 'Asceticism Among Jaina Women: Power, Sexuality and Social Control in Selected Districts of North India', Page 101. [http://hdl.handle.net/10603/14456]
23. Manisha Sethi, 'Asceticism Among Jaina Women: Power, Sexuality and Social Control in Selected Districts of North India', Page 102. [http://hdl.handle.net/10603/14456]
24. ibid, Page 98.
25. ibid.
26. ibid, Page 98-99.
27. ibid, Page 105.
28. ibid, Page 105.
29. ibid.
30. ibid.
31. ibid, Page 106.

32 ibid, Page 107.

33. ibid, Page 107.

34. ibid, Page 107.

35. ibid, Page 106.

Sikhism

1. 'Sikhism: What is the role and status of women in Sikh society?' [http://www.realsikhism.com/index.php?subaction=showfull&id=1248311765&ucat=7]
2. Guru Granth Sahib, Page 473. Cited from AH Kaur, 'Sikhism and the status of women'. [http://web.lemoyne.edu/arora/women.htm]
3. Aru Bhartiya, 'Menstruation, Religion and Society', *International Journal of Social Science and Humanity*, Volume 3 No. 6.
4. Nicky Guninder Kaur-Singh, *The Feminine Principle in the Sikh Vision of the Transcendent*. Page 4.
5. Guru Granth Sahib, Page 472.[http://www.sikhnet.com/oldsikhnet/sggs/translation/0472.html]
6. ibid.
7. AH Kaur, 'Sikhism and the status of women'. [http://web.lemoyne.edu/arora/women.htm]
8. Guru Granth Sahib, Page 472. [http://www.sikhnet.com/oldsikhnet/sggs/translation/0472.html]
9. Guru Granth Sahib, Page 1013. Cited from 'Role of Women in Sikhism', WaheguruNet. [http://www.wahegurunet.com/role-of-women-in-sikhism]

Comparison with Hindu Tradition

1. Details about the menarche rituals of Buddhists in Sri Lanka can be read here: Deborah Winslow, 'Rituals of First Menstruation in Sri Lanka,' Man, New Series, Vol. 15, No. 4. Page 603-625
2. Guru Granth Sahib, Page 472. [http://www.sikhnet.com/oldsikhnet/sggs/translation/0472.html]
3. ibid.

Menstruation Notions in Abrahamic Religions

Judaism

1. 'The Patriarchs and the Origins of Judaism', Judaism 101. [http://www.jewfaq.org/origins.htm]
2. ibid.
3. ibid.
4. Jacob Neusner, 'A Short History of Judaism', cited from 'Origins of Judaism', Wikipedia. [https://en.wikipedia.org/wiki/Origins_of_Judaism#]
5. 'God, Torah, and Israel', The Pluralism Project, Harvard University. [http://pluralism.org/religions/judaism/introduction-to-judaism/god-torah-and-israel/]
6. William E Phipps, 'The Menstrual Taboo in the Judeo-Christian Tradition', *Journal of Religion and Health*, Vol. 19, No. 4. (Winter, 1980), Page 298 [http://www.jstor.org/stable/27505592]
7. Glenda Lewin Hufnagel, *A History of Women's Menstruation From Ancient Greece to the Twenty-First Century*, Page 22.
8. ibid.
9. Sharon Faye Koren, 'The Menstruant as 'Other' in Medieval Judaism and Christianity', *Nashim: A Journal of Jewish Women's Studies & Gender Issues*, No. 17, Special Issue: Sexuality in Jewish Contexts (Spring 2009), Page 36. [http://www.jstor.org/stable/10.2979/nas.2009.-.17.33]
10. ibid.
11. Harold M. Kamsler, 'Hebrew Menstrual Taboos', *The Journal of American Folklore*, Vol. 51, No. 199. (Jan. - Mar., 1938) [http://www.jstor.org/stable/535946]
12. M Guterman, P Mehta, M Gibbs. Menstrual Taboos Among Major Religions. *The Internet Journal of World Health and Societal Politics*. 2007 Volume 5 Number 2. [http://ispub.com/IJWH/5/2/8213]
13. Sharon Faye Koren, 'The Menstruant as 'Other' in Medieval Judaism and Christianity', *Nashim: A Journal of Jewish Women's Studies & Gender Issues*, No. 17, Special Issue: Sexuality in

Jewish Contexts (Spring 2009), Page 34. [http://www.jstor.org/stable/10.2979/nas.2009 -.17.33]

14. Cited from Harold M Kamsler, 'Hebrew Menstrual Taboos', The Journal of American Folklore, Vol. 51, No. 199. (Jan. - Mar., 1938) [http://www.jstor.org/stable/535946]
15. Cited from ibid.
16. ibid.
17. Sharon Faye Koren, 'The Menstruant as 'Other' in Medieval Judaism and Christianity', *Nashim: A Journal of Jewish Women's Studies & Gender Issues*, No. 17, Special Issue: Sexuality in Jewish Contexts (Spring 2009), Page 39-40. [http://www.jstor.org/stable/10.2979/nas.2009.-.17.33]
18. Leviticus 15:16-33, Torah Reading for Tazria-Metzora. [http://www.chabad.org/parshah/torahreading.asp?aid=15578&p=7]
19. M Guterman, P Mehta, M Gibbs. Menstrual Taboos Among Major Religions. *The Internet Journal of World Health and Societal Politics*. 2007 Volume 5 Number 2. [http://ispub.com/IJWH/5/2/8213]
20. ibid.
21. Erubin 100b, cited from William E Phipps, 'The Menstrual Taboo in the Judeo-Christian Tradition', *Journal of Religion and Health*, Vol. 19, No. 4 (Winter, 1980), Page 300. [http://www.jstor.org/stable/27505592]
22. Cf Segal, JB, 'Popular Religion in Ancient Israel,' J Jewish Studies, 1976, 1, 5; Cited from William E Phipps, 'The Menstrual Taboo in the Judeo-Christian Tradition', *Journal of Religion and Health*, Vol. 19, No. 4 (Winter, 1980), Page 300. [http://www.jstor.org/stable/27505592]
23. Niddah 57b, cited from William E Phipps, 'The Menstrual Taboo in the Judeo-Christian Tradition', *Journal of Religion and Health*, Vol. 19, No. 4 (Winter, 1980), Page 300. [http://www.jstor.org/stable/27505592]
24. Sharon Faye Koren, 'The Menstruant as 'Other' in Medieval Judaism and Christianity', *Nashim: A Journal of Jewish Women's Studies & Gender Issues*, No. 17, Special Issue: Sexuality in

Jewish Contexts (Spring 2009), Page 34. [http://www.jstor.org/stable/10.2979/nas.2009.-.17.33]

25. ibid.
26. ibid.
27. Baraita deniddah, edited by Chaim Horowitz, cited from Sharon Faye Koren, 'The Menstruant as 'Other' in Medieval Judaism and Christianity', *Nashim: A Journal of Jewish Women's Studies & Gender Issues*, No. 17, Special Issue: Sexuality in Jewish Contexts (Spring 2009), Page 36. [http://www.jstor.org/stable/10.2979/nas.2009.-.17.33]
28. Sharon Faye Koren, 'The Menstruant as 'Other' in Medieval Judaism and Christianity', *Nashim: A Journal of Jewish Women's Studies & Gender Issues*, No. 17, Special Issue: Sexuality in Jewish Contexts (Spring 2009), Page 35. [http://www.jstor.org/stable/10.2979/nas.2009.-.17.33]
29. ibid.
30. ibid, Page 36.
31. ibid.
32. Zohar 2:60b (Ra'aya meheimna), cited from Sharon Faye Koren, 'The Menstruant as 'Other' in Medieval Judaism and Christianity', Nashim: *A Journal of Jewish Women's Studies & Gender Issues*, No. 17, Special Issue: Sexuality in Jewish Contexts (Spring 2009), Page 39. [http://www.jstor.org/stable/10.2979/nas.2009.-.17.33]
33. Moses de Leon, Mishkan 'edut, MS Cambridge Dd 4.2, f. 42b, cited from Sharon Faye Koren, 'The Menstruant as 'Other' in Medieval Judaism and Christianity', *Nashim: A Journal of Jewish Women's Studies & Gender Issues*, No. 17, Special Issue: Sexuality in Jewish Contexts (Spring 2009), Page 40. [http://www.jstor.org/stable/10.2979/nas.2009.-.17.33]
34. Sharon Faye Koren, 'The Menstruant as 'Other' in Medieval Judaism and Christianity', *Nashim: A Journal of Jewish Women's Studies & Gender Issues*, No. 17, Special Issue: Sexuality in Jewish Contexts (Spring 2009), Page 47-48. [http://www.jstor.org/stable/10.2979/nas.2009.-.17.33]

35. M Guterman, P Mehta, M Gibbs. Menstrual Taboos Among Major Religions. *The Internet Journal of World Health and Societal Politics*. 2007 Volume 5 Number 2. [http://ispub.com/IJWH/5/2/8213]

36. Charlotte Elisheva Fonrobert, 'Menstrual Purity: Rabbinic and Christian Reconstructions of Biblical Gender', Page 15.

37. Charlotte Elisheva Fonrobert, 'Menstrual Purity: Rabbinic and Christian Reconstructions of Biblical Gender.'

38. ibid. Page 17.

39. Jonah Steinberg, 'From a 'Pot of Filth' to a 'Hedge of Roses' (And Back): Changing Theorizations of Menstruation in Judaism', *Journal of Feminist Studies in Religion*, Vol. 13, No. 2 (Fall, 1997), Page 11.

40. Charlotte Elisheva Fonrobert, 'Menstrual Purity: Rabbinic and Christian Reconstructions of Biblical Gender', Page 17.

41. BA Levine's JPS Torah commentary volume on Leviticus (97), cited from Charlotte Elisheva Fonrobert, 'Menstrual Purity: Rabbinic and Christian Reconstructions of Biblical Gender', Page 17.

42. Jacob Milgrom's Anchor Bible volume on Leviticus 1-16 (744-45), cited from Charlotte Elisheva Fonrobert, 'Menstrual Purity: Rabbinic and Christian Reconstructions of Biblical Gender', Page 17.

43. BA Levine's JPS Torah commentary volume on Leviticus (97), cited from Charlotte Elisheva Fonrobert, 'Menstrual Purity: Rabbinic and Christian Reconstructions of Biblical Gender', Page 17.

44. BA Levine's JPS Torah commentary volume on Leviticus 1 - 16 (463-64), cited from Charlotte Elisheva Fonrobert, 'Menstrual Purity: Rabbinic and Christian Reconstructions of Biblical Gender', Page 17.

45. Jacob Milgrom's Anchor Bible volume on Leviticus 1-16 (745), cited from Charlotte Elisheva Fonrobert, 'Menstrual Purity: Rabbinic and Christian Reconstructions of Biblical Gender', Page 17.

46. Charlotte Elisheva Fonrobert, 'Menstrual Purity: Rabbinic and Christian Reconstructions of Biblical Gender', Page 17.
47. ibid, Page 18.
48. ibid, Page 18.
49. ibid, Page 17.
50. Moshe Greenberg, 'Etymology,' (76), cited from Charlotte Elisheva Fonrobert, 'Menstrual Purity: Rabbinic and Christian Reconstructions of Biblical Gender', Page 18.
51. Charlotte Elisheva Fonrobert, 'Menstrual Purity: Rabbinic and Christian Reconstructions of Biblical Gender', Page 19.
52. ibid, Page 20.
53. ibid, Page 21.
54. ibid, Page 27.
55. ibid, Page 27.
56. ibid, Page 25.
57. ibid, Page 26.
58. ibid, Page 29.
59. ibid, Page 21-22.
60. ibid, Page 29-30.
61. Cited from Harold M Kamsler, 'Hebrew Menstrual Taboos', *The Journal of American Folklore*, Vol. 51, No. 199 (Jan. - Mar., 1938). [http://www.jstor.org/stable/535946]
62. J Theodore and C. Albeck, eds. Midrash Bereshit Rabba, Page 160, cited from Charlotte Elisheva Fonrobert, 'Menstrual Purity: Rabbinic and Christian Reconstructions of Biblical Gender', Page 30.
63. Charlotte Elisheva Fonrobert, 'Menstrual Purity: Rabbinic and Christian Reconstructions of Biblical Gender', Page 30.
64. ibid.
65. pShab2:6, 5b, cited from Charlotte Elisheva Fonrobert, 'Menstrual Purity: Rabbinic and Christian Reconstructions of Biblical Gender', Page 31.
66. Charlotte Elisheva Fonrobert, 'Menstrual Purity: Rabbinic and Christian Reconstructions of Biblical Gender', Page 31.

67. Cited from ibid.
68. bShab 31b/32a, cited from Charlotte Elisheva Fonrobert, 'Menstrual Purity: Rabbinic and Christian Reconstructions of Biblical Gender,' Page 33.
69. Charlotte Elisheva Fonrobert, 'Menstrual Purity: Rabbinic and Christian Reconstructions of Biblical Gender,' Page 33.
70. I have borrowed the phrase 'rabbinic architecture of the woman's body' from Charlotte Elisheva Fonrobert, 'Menstrual Purity: Rabbinic and Christian Reconstructions of Biblical Gender', Page 49.
71. The biblical verses have been cited from Charlotte Elisheva Fonrobert, 'Menstrual Purity: Rabbinic and Christian Reconstructions of Biblical Gender', Page 58.
72. Charlotte Elisheva Fonrobert, 'Menstrual Purity: Rabbinic and Christian Reconstructions of Biblical Gender', Page 58.
73. ibid, Page 59.
74. bKet 10a, cited from ibid, Page 60.
75. bShab 118b, cited from Charlotte Elisheva Fonrobert, 'Menstrual Purity: Rabbinic and Christian Reconstructions of Biblical Gender', Page 63-64.
76. Charlotte Elisheva Fonrobert, 'Menstrual Purity: Rabbinic and Christian Reconstructions of Biblical Gender', Page 63.
77. ibid, Page 44.
78. The reading of Leviticus 15.2 and 15.19 adopted here follows the reading in Charlotte Elisheva Fonrobert, 'Menstrual Purity: Rabbinic and Christian Reconstructions of Biblical Gender', Page 44.
79. Cited from Charlotte Elisheva Fonrobert, 'Menstrual Purity: Rabbinic and Christian Reconstructions of Biblical Gender', Page 48.
80. Charlotte Elisheva Fonrobert, 'Menstrual Purity: Rabbinic and Christian Reconstructions of Biblical Gender', Page 44.
81. ibid, Page 48-49.
82. Cited from ibid, Page 50.

83. Cited from ibid.
84. Cited from ibid, Page 51.
85. Cited from ibid, Page 235.
86. Charlotte Elisheva Fonrobert, 'Menstrual Purity: Rabbinic and Christian Reconstructions of Biblical Gender', Page 52.
87. ibid.
88. ibid.
89. ibid, Page 50.
90. mNid 2:5, cited from Charlotte Elisheva Fonrobert, 'Menstrual Purity: Rabbinic and Christian Reconstructions of Biblical Gender,' Page 28
91. mNid 8:1, cited from ibid.
92. Charlotte Elisheva Fonrobert, 'Menstrual Purity: Rabbinic and Christian Reconstructions of Biblical Gender', Page 28.
93. Susan Handelman, 'On the Essence of Ritual Impurity'. [http://www.chabad.org/theJewishWoman/article_cdo/aid/1542/jewish/On-the-Essence-of-Ritual-Impurity.htm#footnoteRef2a1542]
94. 'Interview with Rivkah Slonim by Janice Lochansk' [http://www.chabad.org/theJewishWoman/article_cdo/aid/83805/jewish/A-Feminist-on-Mikvah.htm]
95. Tanya, part 1, chapter 6, cited from Susan Handelman, 'On the Essence of Ritual Impurity'. [http://www.chabad.org/theJewishWoman/article_cdo/aid/1542/jewish/On-the-Essence-of-Ritual-Impurity.htm#footnoteRef2a1542]
96. Susan Handelman, 'On the Essence of Ritual Impurity'. [http://www.chabad.org/theJewishWoman/article_cdo/aid/1542/jewish/On-the-Essence-of-Ritual-Impurity.htm#footnoteRef2a1542]
97. Nechoma Greisman, 'Chukas: The Value of Life'. [http://www.chabad.org/library/article_cdo/aid/97566/jewish/Chukas-The-Value-of-Life.htm]
98. ibid.

99. Susan Handelman, 'On the Essence of Ritual Impurity'. [http://www.chabad.org/theJewishWoman/article_cdo/aid/1542/jewish/On-the-Essence-of-Ritual-Impurity.htm#footnoteRef2a1542]
100. ibid.
101. ibid.
102. ibid.
103. ibid.
104. Jill Hammer, 'The Shekhinah'. [http://www.telshemesh.org/shekhinah/]
105. Dr Sharon Koren, 'The Shechinah: A Supernal Mother'. [http://www.myjewishlearning.com/article/the-shechinah-a-supernal-mother/]
106. ibid.
107. ibid.
108. ibid.
109. ibid.
110. Susan Handelman, 'On the Essence of Ritual Impurity'. [http://www.chabad.org/theJewishWoman/article_cdo/aid/1542/jewish/On-the-Essence-of-Ritual-Impurity.htm#footnoteRef2a1542]

Christianity

1. Stephen Benko,'Pagan Rome and the Early Christians', Page 22.
2. William E. Phipps, 'The Menstrual Taboo in the Judeo-Christian Tradition', *Journal of Religion and Health*, Vol. 19, No. 4 (Winter, 1980), Page 298. [http://www.jstor.org/stable/27505592]
3. ibid.
4. EM Whelan, Attitudes toward Menstruation.Studies in Family Planning, Vol. 6, No. 4. (Apr., 1975). [http://www.jstor.org/stable/1964817?]
5. William E. Phipps, 'The Menstrual Taboo in the Judeo-Christian Tradition', *Journal of Religion and Health*, Vol. 19, No. 4 (Winter, 1980), Page 298. [http://www.jstor.org/stable/27505592]

6. M Guterman, P Mehta, M Gibbs. Menstrual Taboos Among Major Religions. *The Internet Journal of World Health and Societal Politics.* 2007 Volume 5 Number 2. [http://ispub.com/IJWH/5/2/8213]
7. ibid.
8. ibid.
9. Sister Vassa Larin, 'Ritual Impurity'. [http://www.pravmir.com/article_660.html]
10. ibid.
11. David D Gilmore, 'Misogyny: The Male Malady', Page 49.
12. ibid.
13. ibid, Page 49-50.
14. Sister Vassa Larin, 'Ritual Impurity'. [http://www.pravmir.com/article_660.html]
15. Cited from ibid.
16. ibid.
17. Charlotte Elisheva Fonrobert, 'Menstrual Purity: Rabbinic and Christian Reconstructions of Biblical Gender', Page 170.
18. ibid, Page 167.
19. ibid, Page 168.
20. ibid, Page 172.
21. All citations from Didascalia has been extracted from Arthur Voobus, 'The Didascalia Apostolorum in Syriac I + II', cited from Charlotte Elisheva Fonrobert, 'Menstrual Purity: Rabbinic and Christian Reconstructions of Biblical Gender'.
22. Arthur Voobus, 'The Didascalia Apostolorum in Syriac I + II,' cited from Charlotte Elisheva Fonrobert, 'Menstrual Purity: Rabbinic and Christian Reconstructions of Biblical Gender', Page 175,
23. ibid.
24. ibid.
25. ibid, Page 176-177.
26. ibid, Page 176.

27. ibid, Page 287.
28. ibid, Page 176.
29. ibid, Page 177.
30. ibid. Page 179-180.
31. Charlotte Elisheva Fonrobert, 'Menstrual Purity: Rabbinic and Christian Reconstructions of Biblical Gender', Page 181-182.
32. ibid, Page 181.
33. William E. Phipps, 'The Menstrual Taboo in the Judeo-Christian Tradition', *Journal of Religion and Health*, Vol. 19, No. 4 (Winter, 1980), Page 301. [http://www.jstor.org/stable/27505592]
34. Arthur Voobus, 'The Didascalia Apostolorum in Syriac I + II', cited from Charlotte Elisheva Fonrobert, 'Menstrual Purity: Rabbinic and Christian Reconstructions of Biblical Gender', Page 187.
35. Charlotte Elisheva Fonrobert, 'Menstrual Purity: Rabbinic and Christian Reconstructions of Biblical Gender', Page 186.
36. Fonrobert quotes three slightly different accounts mentioned in the three Gospels. I have summarised by taking into account all the three versions of the story.
37. Selvidge, *Woman, Cult and MiracleRecital*, Page 30; Cited from Charlotte Elisheva Fonrobert, 'Menstrual Purity: Rabbinic and Christian Reconstructions of Biblical Gender', Page 189.
38. Charlotte Elisheva Fonrobert, 'Menstrual Purity: Rabbinic and Christian Reconstructions of Biblical Gender', Page 187.
39. ibid, Page 190-191.
40. ibid, Page 195.
41. ibid.
42. R Kraemer, *Maenads, Martyrs, Matrons, Monastics*, Page 43, cited from Charlotte Elisheva Fonrobert, 'Menstrual Purity: Rabbinic and Christian Reconstructions of Biblical Gender', Page 196.
43. Sister Vassa Larin, 'Ritual Impurity'. [http://www.pravmir.com/article_660.html]
44. William E Phipps, 'The Menstrual Taboo in the Judeo-Christian Tradition', Journal of Religion and Health, Vol. 19, No. 4 (Winter, 1980), Page 300. [http://www.jstor.org/stable/27505592]

45. ibid.
46. Glenda Lewin Hufnagel, *A History of Women's Menstruation From Ancient Greece to the Twenty-First Century*, Page 20.
47. ibid. Pahe 21.
48. St. Thomas Aquinas. 'Basic Writings of St. Thomas Aquinas'. Anton C Pegis (tr). Page 880. Cited from Glenda Lewin Hufnagel, *A History of Women's Menstruation From Ancient Greece to the Twenty-First Century*, 21.
49. Thomas Aquinas, Summa Theologica, Supplement, q. 64, 3. Cited from William E Phipps, 'The Menstrual Taboo in the Judeo-Christian Tradition', *Journal of Religion and Health*, Vol. 19, No. 4 (Winter, 1980), Page 300. [http://www.jstor.org/stable/27505592]
50. Sharon Faye Koren, 'The Menstruant as 'Other' in Medieval Judaism and Christianity', *Nashim: A Journal of Jewish Women's Studies & Gender Issues*, No. 17, Special Issue: Sexuality in Jewish Contexts (Spring 2009), Page 41. [http://www.jstor.org/stable/10.2979/nas.2009.-.17.33]
51. ibid.
52. Isidore of Seville, Etymologiae XI, 1.140–141; English transl. by William D Sharpe, 'Isidore of Seville: The Medical Writings: An English Translation with an Introduction and Commentary', Transactions of the American Philosophical Society, NS 54 (1964), p. 48. Cited from ibid. Page 41.
53. ibid.
54. ibid.
55. Sharon Faye Koren, 'The Menstruant as 'Other' in Medieval Judaism and Christianity', *Nashim: A Journal of Jewish Women's Studies & Gender Issues*, No. 17, Special Issue: Sexuality in Jewish Contexts (Spring 2009), Page 41. [http://www.jstor.org/stable/10.2979/nas.2009.-.17.33]
56. ibid.
57. Quoted from ibid. Page 42.
58. ibid.

59. M Guterman, P Mehta, M Gibbs. Menstrual Taboos Among Major Religions. *The Internet Journal of World Health and Societal Politics*. 2007 Volume 5 Number 2. [http://ispub.com/IJWH/5/2/8213

60. Sharon Faye Koren, 'The Menstruant as 'Other' in Medieval Judaism and Christianity', *Nashim: A Journal of Jewish Women's Studies & Gender Issues*, No. 17, Special Issue: Sexuality in Jewish Contexts (Spring 2009), Page 43. [http://www.jstor.org/stable/10.2979/nas.2009.-.17.33]

61. Glenda Lewin Hufnagel, *A History of Women's Menstruation From Ancient Greece to the Twenty-First Century*, Page 26-27.

62. Charles T Wood, 'The Doctors' Dilemma: Sin, Salvation and the Menstrual Cycle in Medieval thought.' *Speculam: A Journal of Medieval Studies*. 56 (4). Cited from Glenda Lewin Hufnagel, *A History of Women's Menstruation From Ancient Greece to the Twenty-First Century*, Page 26-27.

63. ibid.

64. This section heavily draws upon the work of Sharon Faye Koren: 'The Menstruant as 'Other' in Medieval Judaism and Christianity', *Nashim: A Journal of Jewish Women's Studies & Gender Issues*, No. 17, Special Issue: Sexuality in Jewish Contexts (Spring 2009). [http://www.jstor.org/stable/10.2979/nas.2009.-.17.33]

65. Rabanus Maurus, 'De Rerum Naturis', VI.243b–244b; PL 111, cols. 174–175, ed.William Schipper, transcribed from MS Augiensis 96 and 68, Karlsruhe, Badische, Landes bibliothek (http://www.mun.ca/rabanus/). Cited from Sharon Faye Koren, 'The Menstruant as 'Other' in Medieval Judaism and Christianity', *Nashim: A Journal of Jewish Women's Studies & Gender Issues*, No. 17, Special Issue: Sexuality in Jewish Contexts (Spring 2009), Page 43. [http://www.jstor.org/stable/10.2979/nas.2009.-.17.33]

66. Sharon Faye Koren, 'The Menstruant as 'Other' in Medieval Judaism and Christianity', *Nashim: A Journal of Jewish Women's Studies & Gender Issues*, No. 17, SpecialIssue: Sexuality in

Jewish Contexts (Spring 2009), Page 43. [http://www.jstor.org/stable/10.2979/nas.2009.-.17.33]

67. ibid.
68. Biblia Latina cum Glossa Ordinaria: Facsimile Reprint of the Editio PrincepsAdolph Rusch of Strassburg 1480/81 (Brepols: Turnhout, 1992).Cited from ibid.
69. ibid.
70. Sharon Faye Koren, 'The Menstruant as 'Other' in Medieval Judaism and Christianity', *Nashim: A Journal of Jewish Women's Studies & Gender Issues*, No. 17, Special Issue: Sexuality in Jewish Contexts (Spring 2009), Page 44. [http://www.jstor.org/stable/10.2979/nas.2009.-.17.33]
71. ibid.
72. ibid.
73. ibid, Page 44-45.
74. ibid, Page 45.
75. ibid.
76. ibid, Page 47.
77. Elizabeth Clark and Herbert Richardson, *Women and Religion: A Feminist Sourcebook of Christian Thought*, Page 119.
78. Glenda Lewin Hufnagel, *A History of Women's Menstruation From Ancient Greece to the Twenty-First Century*, Page 25.
79. Elizabeth Clark and Herbert Richardson, *Women and Religion: A Feminist Sourcebook of Christian Thought*, Page 119.
80. Glenda Lewin Hufnagel, *A History of Women's Menstruation From Ancient Greece to the Twenty-First Century*, Page 25.
81. ibid, Page 24.
82. Miriam Simos, 'The Spiral Dance: A Rebirth of the Ancient Religion of the Great Goddess,' Page 6, cited from ibid.
83. Francesca Matteoni, 'Blood beliefs in early modern Europe', Page 27. [https://core.ac.uk/download/pdf/1640372.pdf]
84. ibid.
85. ibid.

86. Glenda Lewin Hufnagel, *A History of Women's Menstruation From Ancient Greece to the Twenty-First Century*, Page 27.
87. Penelope Shuttle and Peter Redgrove, 'The wise wound: Eve's curse and every woman', cited in Glenda Lewin Hufnagel, *A History of Women's Menstruation From Ancient Greece to the Twenty-First Century*, Page 21.
88. ibid, Page 21-22.
89. Monica Sjoo and Mor Barbara, 'The Great Cosmic Mother: Rediscovering the Religion of the Earth', cited from ibid.
90. Francesca Matteoni, 'Blood beliefs in early modern Europe', Page 34. [https://core.ac.uk/download/pdf/1640372.pdf]
91. Demosthenes Savramis, 'The Satanizing of Woman: Religion versus Sexuality', Page 22, cited from Glenda Lewin Hufnagel, *A History of Women's Menstruation From Ancient Greece to the Twenty-First Century*, Page 22.
92. Purva Shoor, 'A study of knowledge, attitude, and practices of menstrual health among adolescent school girls in urban field practice area of medical college, Tumkur', *Indian Journal of Health Sciences Biomed Res* 2017;10:249-55. [http://www.ijournalhs.org/text.asp?2017/10/3/249/213999]
93. Surinder S Jodhka, 'Community and Identities: Contemporary Discourses on Culture and Politics in India'.
94. Soumya & Leena Sequira, 'A descriptive study on cultural practices about menarche and menstruation', Nitte University *Journal of Health Science* (2016). Volume 6. No 2. Page 10-13. [http://nitte.edu.in/journal/june2016/7o.pdf]
95. K Kamaljit, A Balwinder, KS Gurmeet, & NS Neki, 'Social beliefs and practices associated with menstrual hygiene among adolescent girls of Amritsar, Punjab, India', *JIMSA* (2012). Volume 25. No 2. Page 69-70. [http://medind.nic.in/jav/t12/i2/javt12i2p69.pdf]

    Also see: AJ Singh, 'Place of menstruation in the reproductive lives of women of rural North India', *Indian Journal of Community Medicine* 2006;31:10-4. [http://www.ijcm.org.in/text.asp?2006/31/1/10/54923]

And see: Kaliyamoorthi Tamilselvi, 'Socio-cultural Taboos concerning Menstruation: A Micro Level Study in the Cuddalore District of Tamil Nadu, India', *IJSRP* (2012). Volume 2, Issue 8. [http://www.ijsrp.org/research-paper-0812/ijsrp-p0861.pdf]

Islam

1. 'People of the Book'. Islam: Empire of Faith. PBS. [https://www.pbs.org/empires/islam/faithpeople.html]
2. ibid.
3. Catherine Cartwright Jones, *Menstruation and Henna: Pollution and Purification*, Page 2. [http://www.hennapage.com/henna/encyclopedia/HennaMenstruation.pdf]
4. Nitzan Ziv, 'Interpreting Their Blood: The Contradictions of Approaches to Menstruation Through Religious Education, Ritual andCulture in Rabat, Morocco' (2006). Independent Study Project (ISP) Collection. Paper 331. Page 7-8.
5. ibid. Page 8.
6. Quran 2.222. Translation by Abdullah Yusuf Ali. [http://www.islam101.com/quran/yusufAli/QURAN/2.htm]
7. Nitzan Ziv, 'Interpreting Their Blood: The Contradictions of Approaches to Menstruation Through Religious Education, Ritual andCulture in Rabat, Morocco' (2006). Independent Study Project (ISP) Collection. Paper 331. Page 10
8. ibid.
9. ibid.
10. M Guterman, P Mehta, M Gibbs. Menstrual Taboos Among Major Religions. *The Internet Journal of World Health and Societal Politics*. 2007 Volume 5 Number 2. [http://ispub.com/IJWH/5/2/8213]
11. Rashida Esakjee & Abdur-Rahman (Compilers), 'The Laws of Menstruation, Postnatal Bleeding, & Dysfunctional Uterine Bleeding: Based on the Hanafi School of Islamic Law'. Page 4-6. [http://www.zamzamacademy.com/files/docs/articles/01The%20Laws%20of%20Menstruation,%20

Postnatal%20Bleeding%20&%20Dysfunctional%20Uterine%20Bleeding.pdf]

12. ibid.
13. ibid.
14. Quran 2.222. Translation by Abdullah Yusuf Ali. [http://www.islam101.com/quran/yusufAli/QURAN/2.htm]
15. Mohammed Rahimuddin. 'Muwatta Imam Malik'. Ch. 34 #125. Cited from Nitzan Ziv, 'Interpreting Their Blood: The Contradictions of Approaches to Menstruation Through Religious Education, Ritual and Culture in Rabat, Morocco' (2006). Independent Study Project (ISP) Collection. Paper 331. Page 21.
16. Mohammed Rahimuddin. 'Muwatta Imam Malik'. Ch. 33 #122. Cited from ibid.
17. Nitzan Ziv, 'Interpreting Their Blood: The Contradictions of Approaches to Menstruation Through Religious Education, Ritual andCulture in Rabat, Morocco' (2006). Independent Study Project (ISP) Collection. Paper 331. Page 13.
18. ibid.
19. DA Spellberg, 'Writing the Unwritten Life of the Islamic Eve: Menstruation and the Demonization ofMotherhood', *International Journal of Middle East Studies*, Vol. 28, No. 3 (Aug., 1996), Page 305-324. [http://www.jstor.org/stable/176389]
20. ibid.
21. ibid.
22. ibid.
23. ibid.
24. ibid.
25. ibid.
26. ibid.
27. Al-Tabari, 'Ta'rikh al-Rusul wa'l-Muluk', 1:109. Ibid.
28. Catherine Cartwright Jones, 'Menstruation and Henna: Pollution and Purification', Page 4. [http://www.hennapage.com/henna/encyclopedia/HennaMenstruation.pdf]

29. ibid, Page 5.
30. ibid, Page 6.
31. ibid, Page 29.
32. ibid, Page 11.
33. ibid, Page 12.
34. ibid, Page 18-19.
35. ibid, Page 4.
36. ibid, Page 21.
37. ibid, Page 22.
38. Edward Westermarck, 'Ritual and Belief in Morocco Vols 1 & 2', cited from ibid, Page 22-23.
39. Catherine Cartwright Jones, 'Menstruation and Henna: Pollution and Purification', Page 8. [http://www.hennapage.com/henna/encyclopedia/HennaMenstruation.pdf]
40. Aru Bhartiya, 'Menstruation, Religion and Society', *International Journal of Social Science and Humanity*, Volume 3 No. 6.
41. Sarika Manhas and Rabia Salem, 'A Study Of Menstrual Taboos Prevalent Among Muslim Females Of Banihal, J&K', *International Journal of Recent Scientific Research* (2015), Vol. 6, Issue 7, pp.4930-4934. [http://www.recentscientific.com/sites/default/files/2792.pdf]
42. Suneela Garg, Nandini Sharma & Ragini Sahay, 'Socio-cultural aspects of menstruation in an urban slum in Delhi, India', *Reproductive Health Matters* (2001), Volume 9:17, Page 16-25. [https://www.tandfonline.com/doi/pdf/10.1016/S0968-8080(01)90004-7]
43. ibid.

Menstruation Notions in Ancient Western Civilisations

Greek Civilisation

1. Lesley Dean-Jones, 'Women's bodies in Classical Greek Science', cited in Glenda Lewin Hufnagel, *A History of Women's Menstruation From Ancient Greece to the Twenty-First Century*, Page 16.

2. ibid.
3. ibid. Page 20.
4. Phillip Slater, 'The glory of Hera: Greek mythology and the Greek family', cited in Glenda Lewin Hufnagel, *A History of Women's Menstruation From Ancient Greece to the Twenty-First Century*, Page 17.
5. Penelope Shuttle and Peter Redgrove, 'The wise wound: Eve's curse and everywoman', cited in Glenda Lewin Hufnagel, *A History of Women's Menstruation From Ancient Greece to the Twenty-First Century*, Page 17.
6. Lesley Dean-Jones, 'Women's bodies in Classical Greek Science', cited in Glenda Lewin Hufnagel, *A History of Women's Menstruation From Ancient Greece to the Twenty-First Century*, Page 20.
7. Rufus of Ephesus, 'Oribasius, Liber Incertus, XVIII', cited in Glenda Lewin Hufnagel, *A History of Women's Menstruation From Ancient Greece to the Twenty-First Century*, Page 16.
8. Helen King, *Hippocrates' Women: Reading the female body in Ancient Greece*, Page 76.
9. Helen King, *Hippocrates' Women: Reading the female body in Ancient Greece*, Page 76.
10. Susan Guettel Cole, in 'Domesticating Artemis', included in *The Sacred and the Feminine in Ancient Greece*, Edited by Sue Blundell andMargaret Williamson, Page 29.
11. Susan Guettel Cole, in 'Domesticating Artemis', included in *The Sacred and the Feminine in Ancient Greece*, Edited by Sue Blundell and Margaret Williamson, Page 29.
12. Helen King, 'Hippocrates' Women: Reading the female body in Ancient Greece', Page 77.
13. Hilary Alton (Editor), Robert Briffault (Author), 'The Moon and Menstruation: A Taboo Subject'. [http://radicalanthropologygroup.org/sites/default/files/pdf/pub_the%20mothers.pdf]
14. Jenny Kien, 'The Battle between the Moon and Sun', Page 39-42.

15. Glenda Lewin Hufnagel, *A History of Women's Menstruation From Ancient Greece to the Twenty-First Century*, Page 17.
16. Bharat Gupt, 'Indo-European Beliefs in Classical Greek and Indian Drama'. [http://ifihhome.tripod.com/articles/bg001.html]
17. Linda-Marie Günther, 'Concepts of Purity in Ancient Greece, with Particular Emphasis on Sacred Sites', included in *Purity and the Forming of Religious Traditions in the Ancient Mediterranean World and Ancient Judaism'* dited by Christian Frevel and Christophe Nihan, Page 250.
18. Linda-Marie Günther, 'Concepts of Purity in Ancient Greece, with Particular Emphasis on Sacred Sites', included in *Purity and the Forming of Religious Traditions in the Ancient Mediterranean World and Ancient Judaism*, Edited by Christian Frevel and Christophe Nihan, Page 247.
19. Andreas Bendlin, 'Purity and Pollution', *A Companion to Greek Religion*, Edited by Daniel Ogden, Page 178.
20. Robin Osborne, 'Women and Sacrifice in Classical Greece', *The Classical Quarterly*, Volume-43, No. 2 (1993), Page 398.
21. The story cited from Susan Guettel Cole, in 'Domesticating Artemis', included in *The Sacred and the Feminine in Ancient Greece*, Edited by Sue Blundell and Margaret Williamson, Page 29.
22. ibid. Page 25.
23. ibid. Page 27.
24. Helen King, 'Hippocrates' Women: Reading the female body inAncient Greece', Page 83.
25. Susan Guettel Cole, in 'Domesticating Artemis', included in *The Sacred and the Feminine in Ancient Greece*, Edited by Sue Blundell and Margaret Williamson, Page 27. Also cited from Helen King, 'Hippocrates' Women: Reading the female body inAncient Greece', Page 83.
26. Susan Guettel Cole, in 'Domesticating Artemis', included in *The Sacred and the Feminine in Ancient Greece*, Edited by Sue Blundell and Margaret Williamson, Page 28.

27. Helen King, *Hippocrates' Women: Reading the female body inAncient Greece*, Page 84.
28. ibid.
29. ibid. page 98.
30. Susan Guettel Cole, in 'Domesticating Artemis', included in *The Sacred and the Feminine in Ancient Greece*', Edited by Sue Blundell andMargaret Williamson, Page 28,29.
31. Helen King, *Hippocrates' Women: Reading the female body inAncient Greece*, Page 84-85.
32. Apollo and Artemis: Culture and Instinct, *astrosynthesis.com* [http://www.astrosynthesis.com.au/wp-content/uploads/2015/02/apollo_and_artemis.pdf]
33. De octimestri partu 1, (CMG. 1.2,1, 78); cited from Lesley Dean-Jones, Menstrual Bleeding according to the Hippocratics and Aristotle, Page 186, Transactions of the American Philological Association (1974-), Vol. 119 (1989). [http://www.jstor.org/stable/284268]
34. Lesley Dean-Jones, Menstrual Bleeding according to the Hippocratics and Aristotle, Page 187, Transactions of the American Philological Association (1974-), Vol. 119 (1989). [http://www.jstor.org/stable/284268]
35. Gynecology 1.2, cited from Lesley Dean-Jones, Menstrual Bleeding according to the Hippocratics and Aristotle, Page 187, Transactions of the American Philological Association (1974), Vol. 119 (1989). [http://www.jstor.org/stable/284268]
36. Generatione Animalium767a 2-6, cited from Lesley Dean-Jones, Menstrual Bleeding according to the Hippocratics and Aristotle, Page 188, Transactions of the American Philological Association (1974-), Vol. 119 (1989). [http://www.jstor.org/stable/284268]
37. Lesley Dean-Jones, Menstrual Bleeding according to the Hippocratics and Aristotle, Page 189, Transactions of the American Philological Association (1974-), Vol. 119 (1989). [http://www.jstor.org/stable/284268]
38. Historia Animalium 582a 34, cited from Lesley Dean-Jones, Menstrual Bleeding according to the Hippocratics and Aristotle,

Page 190, Transactions of the American Philological Association (1974-), Vol. 119 (1989). [http://www.jstor.org/stable/284268]

39. Shweta V Dabhade, AA Hawale, A conceptual study of rutuchakra, *Ayurlog: National Journal of Research in Ayurved Science*, Vol3, Special issue (16th Feb. 2015). [http://ayurlog.com/Archive/january_march/ssac/201502S060.pdf].
40. Helen King, *Hippocrates' Women: Reading the female body inAncient Greece.*
41. As cited in Robin Osborne, 'Women and Sacrifice in Classical Greece', *The Classical Quarterly*, Vol. 43, No. 2 (1993), Page 394-397.
42. Robin Osborne, 'Women and Sacrifice in Classical Greece', *The Classical Quarterly*, Volume-43, No. 2 (1993), Page 397.
43. ibid. Page 400-401.
44. ibid. Page 298.
45. W Burkert, 'Greek religion Archaic and Classical', cited in Robin Osborne, 'Women and Sacrifice in Classical Greece', *The Classical Quarterly*, Volume-43, No. 2 (1993), Page 394.
46. Robin Osborne, 'Women and Sacrifice in Classical Greece', *The Classical Quarterly*, Volume-43, No. 2 (1993), Page 403.
47. Helen King, *Hippocrates' Women: Reading the female body in Ancient Greece*, Page 94.
48. Helen King, *Hippocrates' Women: Reading the female body inAncient Greece*, Page 96
49. 'Ritual and Sacrifice.' *Ancient Greece and Rome: An Encyclopedia for Students.* Edited by Carroll Moulton. Vol. 3. New York: Charles Scribner's Sons, 1998. 178-180. World History in Context. Web. 11 Oct. 2016. [http://ic.galegroup.com/ic/whic/ReferenceDetailsPage/ReferenceDetailsWindow?zid=0769e7eef519dffc52f95d3e0369f225&action=2&catId=&documentId=GALE%7CCX2897200404&userGroupName=tlc199095657&source=Bookmark&u=tlc199095657&jsid=450e7b46d893a733e47a925f984365f3]
50. Rigveda 10.90.6-11.

51. Helen King, *Hippocrates' Women: Reading the female body in Ancient Greece*, Page 98.
52. Elsimar M Coutinho and Sheldon J Segal, 'Is Menstruation Obsolete?' Page 18.
53. Hippocrates: 'Diseases of Women 1', Translated by Ann Ellis Hanson, Signs, Vol. 1, No. 2 (Winter, 1975), pp. 567. [http://www.jstor.org/stable/3173068]
54. Various names for menstruation used in Greek medical texts have been cited from: Helen King, *Hippocrates' Women: Reading the female body in Ancient Greece*, Page 60.
55. ibid, Page 76.
56. All quotes from 'Diseases of women-1' are cited from: Hippocrates: 'Diseases of Women 1', Translated by Ann Ellis Hanson, Signs, Vol. 1, No. 2 (Winter, 1975), pp. 567-584. [http://www.jstor.org/stable/3173068]
57. Cited from Lesley Dean-Jones, Menstrual Bleeding according to the Hippocratics and Aristotle, Page 181, Transactions of the American Philological Association (1974-), Vol. 119 (1989). [http://www.jstor.org/stable/284268]
58. Views of Aristotle from De Generatione Animalium has been cited from: Lesley Dean-Jones, Menstrual Bleeding according to the Hippocratics and Aristotle, Page 177-191, Transactions of the American Philological Association (1974-), Vol. 119 (1989). [http://www.jstor.org/stable/284268]
59. Lesley Dean-Jones, Menstrual Bleeding according to the Hippocratics and Aristotle, Page 177, Transactions of the American Philological Association (1974-), Vol. 119 (1989). [http://www.jstor.org/stable/284268]
60. ibid, Page 177-178.

Roman Civilisation

1. Elsimar M Coutinho and Sheldon J Segal, 'Is Menstruation Obsolete?' Page 19.
2. ibid.
3. ibid.

4. Christian Frevel and Christophe Nihan, Introduction in *Purity and the Forming of Religious Traditions in the Ancient Mediterranean World and Ancient Judaism*, Page 28.
5. Bernhard Linke, 'Sacral Purity and Social Order in Ancient Rome' included in *Purity and the Forming of Religious Traditions in the Ancient Mediterranean World and Ancient Judaism*, Edited by Christian Frevel and Christophe Nihan, Page 293.
6. ibid, Page 294.
7. R Beck, 'Sin, Pollution and Purity: Rome', cited in Jack Lennon, 'Menstrual Blood in Rome: An Unspeakable Impurity?' included in *Classica Et Mediaevalia*, Edited by Tonnes Bekker Nielsen and Marianne Pade, Vol 61, Page 72. [http://www.mtp.hum.ku.dk/cgibin/PDFmedopenaccess/Classica_et_Mediaev_61_0_9788763538114.pdf]
8. Cited in Jack Lennon, 'Menstrual Blood in Rome: An Unspeakable Impurity?' included in *Classica Et Mediaevalia*, Edited by Tonnes Bekker Nielsen and Marianne Pade, Vol 61, Page 74. [http://www.mtp.hum.ku.dk/cgibin/PDFmedopenaccess/Classica_et_Mediaev_61_0_9788763538114.pdf]
9. Jack Lennon, 'Menstrual Blood in Rome: An Unspeakable Impurity?' included in *Classica Et Mediaevalia*, Edited by Tonnes Bekker Nielsen and Marianne Pade, Vol 61, Page 83. [http://www.mtp.hum.ku.dk/cgibin/PDFmedopenaccess/Classica_et_Mediaev_61_0_9788763538114.pdf]
10. Pliny the Elder, *The Natural History*, Translated by John Bostock. [http://www.perseus.tufts.edu/hopper/text?doc=Perseus:text:1999.02.0137]
11. All quotes from Columella have been cited from Victoria Louise Newton,'Everyday Discourses of Menstruation: Cultural and Social Perspectives', Ch.2 'Periods: Historical and Cultural Interpretations of Menstruation', Page 24-25.
12. Jack Lennon, 'Menstrual Blood in Rome: An Unspeakable Impurity?' included in *Classica Et Mediaevalia*, Edited by Tonnes Bekker Nielsen and Marianne Pade, Vol 61, Page 73. [http://

www.mtp.hum.ku.dk/cgibin/PDFmedopenaccess/Classica_et_Mediaev_61_0_9788763538114.pdf]

13. ibid. Page 83.
14. ibid. Page 73.
15. Glenda Lewin Hufnagel, *A History of Women's Menstruation From Ancient Greece to the Twenty-First Century*, Page 21.
16. Mary Beard, John North, Simon Price, *Religions of Rome: Volume 2: A Sourcebook*, Page 15.
17. EM Berens, *The Myths & Legendsof Ancient Greece and Rome.*
18. Mary Beard, John North, Simon Price, *Religions of Rome: Volume 2: A Sourcebook*, Page 29.
19. ibid.
20. CMC Green, *Roman Religion and the Cult of Diana at Aricia*, Page 136.
21. ibid. Page 80-81.
22. Lilian Portefaix, 'Sisters Rejoice', cited in Joseph A Marchal, *Hierarchy, Unity, and Imitation: A Feminist Rhetorical Analysis of Power Dynamics in Paul's Letter to the Philippians*, Page 74.
23. ibid. Page 75.
24. CMC Green, *Roman Religion and the Cult of Diana at Aricia*, Page 118.
25. Elsimar M Coutinho and Sheldon J Segal, 'Is Menstruation Obsolete?' Page 19.
26. ibid.
27. Cited from Janice Delaney, Mary Jane Lupton, Emily Toth, *The Curse: A Cultural History of Menstruation*, Page 47.
28. ibid.
29. Jack J Lennon, *Pollution and Religion in Ancient Rome*, Page 82.
30. Elsimar M Coutinho and Sheldon J Segal, *Is Menstruation Obsolete?* Page 22.
31. ibid. Page 19.
32. ibid.
33. Soranus, Gynaecology, Translat in by O Temkin. [http://www.stoa.org/diotima/anthology/wlgr/wlgr-medicine355.shtml]

Mesopotamian Civilisation

1. M Stol, 'Women in Mesopotamia', *Journal of the Economic and Social History of the Orient.*

   Vol. 38, No. 2, Women's History (1995), Page 123. [https://www.jstor.org/stable/3632512]
2. Erica Reiner, 'Babylonian Birth Prognoses', Page 129, Cited in A R George, IL Finkel, 'Wisdom, Gods and Literature: Studies in Assyriology in Honour of WG Lambert', Page 3.
3. AR George, IL Finkel, 'Wisdom, Gods and Literature: Studies in Assyriology in Honour of WG Lambert', Page 3.
4. M Stol, 'Women in Mesopotamia', *Journal of the Economic and Social History of the Orient* Vol. 38, No. 2, Women's History (1995), Page 124. [https://www.jstor.org/stable/3632512]
5. ibid.
6. ibid.
7. ibid.
8. ibid. Page 125.
9. Karen Nemet-Nejat, 'Women's Roles in Ancient Mesopotamia' included in *Women's Role in Ancient Civilizations: A Reference Guide*, Edited by Bella Vivante, Page 87-88 .
10. M Stol, 'Women in Mesopotamia', *Journal of the Economic and Social History of the Orient* Vol. 38, No. 2, Women's History (1995), Page 125. [https://www.jstor.org/stable/3632512]
11. Jerrold S Cooper, 'Virginity in Ancient Mesopotamia', Page 100-102, in Parpola and Whiting, *Sex and Gender in the Ancient Near East.*
12. ibid. Page 100-101.
13. ibid. Page 102.
14. Karen Nemet-Nejat, 'Women's Roles in Ancient Mesopotamia' included in *Women's Role in Ancient Civilizations: A Reference Guide*', Edited by Bella Vivante, Page 88.
15. ibid.
16. ibid.

17. Elsimar M Coutinho and Sheldon J Segal, '*Is Menstruation Obsolete?*' Page 15-16.
18. I thank Dr Ulrike Steinert for sharing the abstract of her current yet-to-be-published research paper titled 'Created to bleed: Blood, women's bodies and gender in ancient Mesopotamian medicine' and the PPT presentation of the same title presented at 'Near East and Egyptology Seminar' at Oriental Institute, Oxford on February 23, 2016, containing many of the Mesopotamian source texts in translation, both of which I have extensively used in my presentation of this section.
19. Ulrike Steinert, Abstract of a current yet-to-be-published research paper titled 'Created to bleed: Blood, women's bodies and gender in ancient Mesopotamian medicine', shared in personal communication.
20. ibid.
21. This cuneiform tablet is Neo-Babylonian, from Nineveh, first half 1st mill. BCE. Cited from Ulrike Steinert, 'K. 263+10934, A Tablet with Recipes Against the Abnormal Flow of a Woman's Blood'. [https://www.ncbi.nlm.nih.gov/pmc/articles/PMC3636454/]
22. This cuneiform tablet is Late Babylonian, from Babylon. Cited from Ulrike Steinert, 'Fluids, rivers, and vessels: metaphors and body concepts in Mesopotamian gynaecological texts'. [https://www.ncbi.nlm.nih.gov/pmc/articles/PMC3791376/#FN1]
23. This cuneiform tablet is Late Babylonian, from Sippar. ibid.
24. This cuneiform tablet Late Babylonian, from Uruk, 4th/3rd century BCE. Ibid.
25. This cuneiform tablet is Neo-Assyrian, from Assur. ibid.
26. This cuneiform tablet is Neo-Assyrian, from Assur. ibid.
27. This cuneiform tablet is Neo-Assyrian, from Assur, 8th/7th century BCE. ibid.
28. This cuneiform tablet is Neo-Babylonian, from Babylon. Cited from Ulrike Steinert, PPT presentation on 'Created to bleed: Blood, women's bodies and gender in ancient Mesopotamian medicine'.

29. This cuneiform tablet is Late Babylonian, probably from Sippar. ibid.
30. Ulrike Steinert, 'Fluids, rivers, and vessels: metaphors and body concepts in Mesopotamian gynaecological texts'. [https://www.ncbi.nlm.nih.gov/pmc/articles/PMC3791376/#FN1]
31. The medical texts use another term 'ulpu lupputu' meaning 'soiled rag', which was used to absorb blood. Though, it most appears in the context of postpartum women, it may have been used during menstruation as well.
32. Ulrike Steinert, 'Fluids, rivers, and vessels: metaphors and body concepts in Mesopotamian gynaecological texts'. [https://www.ncbi.nlm.nih.gov/pmc/articles/PMC3791376/#FN1]
33. Ulrike Steinert, 'K. 263+10934, A Tablet with Recipes Against the Abnormal Flow of a Woman's Blood'. [https://www.ncbi.nlm.nih.gov/pmc/articles/PMC3636454/]
34. The discussion on K. 263+10934 is summarized from Ulrike Steinert, 'K. 263+10934, A Tablet with Recipes Against the Abnormal Flow of a Woman's Blood', with my comments appended to it wherever necessary. [https://www.ncbi.nlm.nih.gov/pmc/articles/PMC3636454/]
35. This cuneiform tablet is Neo-Babylonian, from Babylon. Cited from Ulrike Steinert, 'Fluids, rivers, and vessels: metaphors and body concepts in Mesopotamian gynaecological texts'. [https://www.ncbi.nlm.nih.gov/pmc/articles/PMC3791376/#FN1]
36. This cuneiform tablet is Neo-Assyrian from Aššur. Ibid.
37. The discussion on the 'fumigation from below' treatment is summarized from Ulrike Steinert, 'I smell a rat! Fumigation in Mesopotamian and Hippocratic recipes for women's ailments' – Part 1. [https://recipes.hypotheses.org/3278] and Part 2 [https://recipes.hypotheses.org/3284]
38. Cited from ibid.
39. ibid.
40. ibid.
41. ibid.

42. Ulrike Steinert, 'Fluids, rivers, and vessels: metaphors and body concepts in Mesopotamian gynaecological texts' [https://www.ncbi.nlm.nih.gov/pmc/articles/PMC3791376/#FN1]
43. Ulrike Steinert, Abstract of a current yet-to-be-published research paper titled 'Created to bleed: Blood, women's bodies and gender in ancient Mesopotamian medicine', shared in personal communication.
44. Cited from Ulrike Steinert, PPT presentation on 'Created to bleed: Blood, women's bodies and gender in ancient Mesopotamian medicine'.
45. ibid.
46. ibid.
47. ibid.
48. ibid.
49. Yitzhaq Feder, 'The Semantics of Purity in the Ancient Near East: Lexical Meaning as a Projection of Embodied Experience', *Journal of Ancient Near Eastern Religions* 14(1):87-113 · May 2014. Also, Yitzhaq Feder, 'Deflement, Disgust, and Disease: The Experiential Basis of Hittite and Akkadian Terms for Impurity,' *Journal of the American Oriental Society*, Vol. 136, No. 1 (January–March 2016), pp. 99-116.
50. Erica Couto-Ferreira and Agnes Garcia-Ventura, 'Engendering Purity and Impurity in Assyriological Studies: A Historiographical Overview' included in Joanna de Groot (Editor) and Sue Morgan (Editor), *Sex, Gender and the Sacred: Reconfiguring Religion in Gender History*.
51. Yitzhaq Feder, 'The Semantics of Purity in the Ancient Near East: Lexical Meaning as a Projection of Embodied Experience,' *Journal of Ancient Near Eastern Religions* 14(1):87-113 · May 2014.
52. ibid.
53. ibid.
54. ibid.
55. ibid.

56. ibid
57. ibid
58. Yitzhaq Feder, 'Deflement, Disgust, and Disease: The Experiential Basis of Hittite and Akkadian Terms for Impurity,' *Journal of the American Oriental Society*, Vol. 136, No. 1 (January–March 2016), pp. 99-116.
59. ibid.
60. ibid.
61. ibid.
62. ibid.
63. ibid.
64. ibid.
65. ibid.
66. ibid.
67. ibid.
68. Erica Couto-Ferreira and Agnes Garcia-Ventura, 'Engendering Purity and Impurity in Assyriological Studies: A Historiographical Overview' included in Joanna de Groot (Editor) and Sue Morgan (Editor), *Sex, Gender and the Sacred: Reconfiguring Religion in Gender History*.
69. Yitzhaq Feder, 'Deflement, Disgust, and Disease: The Experiential Basis of Hittite and Akkadian Terms for Impurity,' *Journal of the American Oriental Society*, Vol. 136, No. 1 (January–March 2016), pp. 99-116.
70. ibid.
71. Cited from Ulrike Steinert, PPT presentation on 'Created to bleed: Blood, women's bodies and gender in ancient Mesopotamian medicine'.
72. CT 23, 2f.: 1-14 // AMT 31/2: 2ff. (W Farber, JNES 49 (1990), 311f.), cited from ibid.
73. W Farber, Lamaštu (2014) II 34-60, cited from ibid.
74. KAR 300 rev. 6 (omens drawn from the behaviour of animals and humans, NP Heeßel, KAL 1 (2007), 113ff. No. 39), cited from ibid.

75. Tablet 85, Köcher / Oppenheim 1957-58, 76 Text B Funck 3, obv. 26, cited from ibid.
76. Marten Stol, 'Women in the Ancient Near East'.
77. Marten Stol, 'Women in the Ancient Near East'.
78. W Farber, Beschwörungsrituale an Ištar und Dumuzi, 226ff. ll. 1-8, cited from Ulrike Steinert, PPT presentation on 'Created to bleed: Blood, women's bodies and gender in ancient Mesopotamian medicine'.
79. T Abusch and D Schwemer, Corpus of Mesopotamian Anti-Witchcraft Literature, 104 Text 2.5 sub 3: 1-7, cited from ibid.
80. Cited from Ulrike Steinert, PPT presentation on 'Created to bleed: Blood, women's bodies and gender in ancient Mesopotamian medicine'.
81. ibid.
82. ibid.
83. ibid.
84. ibid.
85. Gwendolyn Leick, 'Sex and Eroticism in Mesopotamian Literature', Page 65.
86. Gwendolyn Leick, 'Sex and Eroticism in Mesopotamian Literature', Page 65.
87. Karen Rhea Nemet-Nejat, 'Women's Roles in Ancient Mesopotamia', included in 'Women's Role in Ancient Civilizations, A Reference Guide', Edited by Bella Vivante, Page 103.
88. ibid.
89. Yamur Heffron, 'Inana/Ištar (goddess)', Ancient Mesopotamian Gods and Goddesses, Oracc and the UK Higher Education Academy. [http://oracc.museum.upenn.edu/amgg/listofdeities/inanaitar/]
90. Judy Grahn, 'Ecology of the Erotic in a Myth of Inanna', *International Journal of Transpersonal Studies*, Volume 29, Issue 2, Page 62.
91. Sandra Bart Heimann, 'The Biography of Goddess Inanna; Indomitable Queen of Heaven, Earth and Almost Everything'.

92. ibid.
93. ibid.

Egyptian Civilisation

1. Cited from 'The Status of Women in Egyptian Society'. [http://collectiondevelopment.library.cornell.edu/mideast/womneg.htm]
2. Carolyn Graves-Brown, 'Dancing For Hathor: Women in Ancient Egypt', Page 55.
3. ibid.
4. Cited from Rudolf Cronau, 'Woman Triumphant', Page 47. [https://en.wikisource.org/wiki/Woman_Triumphant/Women_During_the_Ages_of_Antiquity]
5. Barbara Watterson, 'The Egyptians (Peoples of Africa)', cited from Mark, Joshua J 'Women in Ancient Egypt.' *Ancient History Encyclopedia*. [http://www.ancient.eu/article/623/]
6. Bob Brier and Hoyt Hobbs, 'Ancient Egypt: Everyday Life in the Land of the Nile', cited from Mark, Joshua J 'Women in Ancient Egypt.' *Ancient History Encyclopedia*. [http://www.ancient.eu/article/623/]
7. Mark, Joshua J 'Women in Ancient Egypt.' *Ancient History Encyclopedia*. [http://www.ancient.eu/article/623/]
8. James C Thompson, 'Women in Ancient Egypt'. [http://www.womenintheancientworld.com/women_in_ancient_egypt.htm]
9. Mark, Joshua J 'Women in Ancient Egypt.' *Ancient History Encyclopedia*. [http://www.ancient.eu/article/623/]
10. Carolyn Graves-Brown, 'Dancing For Hathor: Women in Ancient Egypt', Page 53.
11. ibid. Page 54.
12. ibid.
13. ibid.
14. ibid.
15. ibid. Page 55.

16. Cited from 'The Status of Women in Egyptian Society'. [http://collectiondevelopment.library.cornell.edu/mideast/womneg.htm]

17. Mark, Joshua J 'Women in Ancient Egypt.' *Ancient History Encyclopedia*. [http://www.ancient.eu/article/623/]

18. Cited from Rudolf Cronau, 'Woman Triumphant', Page 47. [https://en.wikisource.org/wiki/Woman_Triumphant/Women_During_the_Ages_of_Antiquity]

19. Malcolm Potts and Martha Campbell, 'History of Contraception', Vol. 6, Chp. 8, Gynecology and Obstetrics, 2002. [https://web.archive.org/web/20030701162741/http://big.berkeley.edu/ifplp.history.pdf]

    Alternatively, can be accessed at: [http://www.glowm.com/section_view/item/375]

20. Joachim Friedrich Quack, 'Conceptions of Purity in Egyptian Religion,' included in *Purity and the Forming of Religious Traditions in the Ancient Mediterranean World and Ancient Judaism*, Edited by Christian Frevel and Christophe Nihan

21. ibid, Page 115.

22. ibid.

23. ibid.

24. ibid, Page 117.

25. ibid.

26. ibid, Page 118.

27. ibid, Page 120.

28. For a detailed treatment of the competency requirements for a Hindu temple archaka, see Nithin Sridhar, 'Caste Considerations have no locus standi in appointment of temple priests', *IndiaFacts*, December, 2016. [http://indiafacts.org/caste-no-locus-standi-temple-priests/]

29. Joachim Friedrich Quack, 'Conceptions of Purity in Egyptian Religion,' included in *Purity and the Forming of Religious Traditions in the Ancient Mediterranean World and Ancient Judaism*, Edited by Christian Frevel and Christophe Nihan, Page 122.

30. ibid, Page 127.
31. ibid.
32. Kom Ombo, text 878 with parallel in Edfu III, 360,12-362, 4, cited from Joachim Friedrich Quack, 'Conceptions of Purity in Egyptian Religion,' included in *Purity and the Forming of Religious Traditions in the Ancient Mediterranean World and Ancient Judaism*, Edited by Christian Frevel and Christophe Nihan, Page 124-125.
33. Joachim Friedrich Quack, 'Conceptions of Purity in Egyptian Religion,' included in *Purity and the Forming of Religious Traditions in the Ancient Mediterranean World and Ancient Judaism*, Edited by Christian Frevel and Christophe Nihan, Page 128.
34. ibid. Page 136.
35. ibid. Page 135.
36. ibid.
37. ibid. Page 129-133.
38. ibid. Page 137.
39. ibid. Page 136.
40. ibid. Page 140.
41. The birth of the three Pharaohs, 'Westcar Papyrus', Adapted from translations by Marc Jan Nederhof and AM Blackman, Ancient Egypt Online. [http://www.ancientegyptonline.co.uk/westcar-pharaohs-birth.html]
42. Joachim Friedrich Quack, 'Conceptions of Purity in Egyptian Religion,' included in *Purity and the Forming of Religious Traditions in the Ancient Mediterranean World and Ancient Judaism*, Edited by Christian Frevel and Christophe Nihan, Page 143.
43. ibid Page 144.
44. ibid.
45. ibid.
46. ibid.
47. Paul John Frandsen, 'The Menstrual 'Taboo' in Ancient Egypt,' *Journal of Near Eastern Studies*, Vol. 66, No. 2 (April 2007), Page 82 [http://www.jstor.org/stable/10.1086/519030]

48. JJ Janssen, 'Absence from Work by the Necropolis Workmen of Thebes', Studien zur altägyptischen Kultur (SAK) 8 (1980): Page 141–43, cited from Paul John Frandsen, 'The Menstrual 'Taboo' in Ancient Egypt', *Journal of Near Eastern Studies*, Vol. 66, No. 2 (April 2007), Page 82. [http://www.jstor.org/stable/10.1086/519030]
49. KA Kitchen, Ramesside Inscriptions Translated and Annotated: Translations, vol. 3 (Oxford, 2000), Page 361–68, cited from Paul John Frandsen, 'The Menstrual 'Taboo' in Ancient Egypt', *Journal of Near Eastern Studies*, Vol. 66, No. 2 (April 2007), Page 82. [http://www.jstor.org/stable/10.1086/519030]
50. Cited from Carolyn Graves-Brown, 'Dancing For Hathor: Women in Ancient Egypt', Page 55.
51. Paul John Frandsen, 'The Menstrual 'Taboo' in Ancient Egypt', *Journal of Near Eastern Studies*, Vol. 66, No. 2 (April 2007), Page 84 [http://www.jstor.org/stable/10.1086/519030]
52. ibid.
53. ibid.
54. Terry G Wilfong, 'Menstrual Synchrony and the 'Place of Women' in Ancient Egypt (OIM 13512),' included in 'Gold of Praise: Studies on Ancient Egypt in Honor of Edward F Wente', edited by Emily Teeter and John A. Larson, Page 422.
55. Cited from Carolyn Graves-Brown, 'Dancing For Hathor: Women in Ancient Egypt', Page 55.
56. ibid. Page 56.
57. Paul John Frandsen, 'The Menstrual 'Taboo' in Ancient Egypt', *Journal of Near Eastern Studies*, Vol. 66, No. 2 (April 2007), Page 87. [http://www.jstor.org/stable/10.1086/519030]
58. ibid.
59. ibid.
60. ibid. Page 88.
61. ibid.
62. ibid.
63. ibid Page 87.

64. ibid.
65. ibid Page 89.
66. Siegfried Morenz, 'Egyptian Religion', trans. Ann E Keep, Page 113, cited from Ferguson, R James, 'The ancient Egyptian concept of Maat: Reflections on social justice and natural order,' CEWCES, Research Papers. Paper 13. [http://epublications.bond.edu.au/cewces_papers/13]
67. Sarah Iles Johnston, 'Religions of the Ancient World: A Guide,' Page 497.
68. ibid.
69. For a detailed discussion on what *Dharma* is, See: Nithin Sridhar, 'Samanya Dharma and Spirituality', *Prabuddha Bharata*, September, 2015.
70. Paul John Frandsen, 'Tabu', in: Lexicon der Ägyptologie, VI,cited from Terry G Wilfong, 'Menstrual Synchrony and the 'Place of Women' in Ancient Egypt (OIM 13512),' included in 'Gold of Praise: Studies on Ancient Egypt in Honor of Edward F Wente', edited by Emily Teeter and John A Larson, Page 422.
71. Terry G Wilfong, 'Menstrual Synchrony and the 'Place of Women' in Ancient Egypt (OIM 13512),' included in 'Gold of Praise: Studies on Ancient Egypt in Honor of Edward F Wente', edited by Emily Teeter and John A Larson, Page 422.
72. Cited from ibid, Page 420.
73. ibid. Page 426.
74. ibid. Page 429.
75. Carolyn Graves-Brown, 'Dancing For Hathor: Women in Ancient Egypt', Page 56.
76. Terry G Wilfong, 'Menstrual Synchrony and the 'Place of Women' in Ancient Egypt (OIM 13512)', included in 'Gold of Praise: Studies on Ancient Egypt in Honor of Edward F Wente', edited by Emily Teeter and John A Larson, Page 424.
77. ibid.
78. Paul John Frandsen, 'The Menstrual 'Taboo' in Ancient Egypt', *Journal of Near Eastern Studies*, Vol. 66, No. 2 (April 2007), Page 97. [http://www.jstor.org/stable/10.1086/519030]

79. Carolyn Graves-Brown, 'Dancing For Hathor: Women in Ancient Egypt', Page 56.
80. Paul John Frandsen, 'The Menstrual 'Taboo' in Ancient Egypt', *Journal of Near Eastern Studies*, Vol. 66, No. 2. (April 2007), Page 99. [http://www.jstor.org/stable/10.1086/519030]
81. ibid. Page 100.
82. ibid.
83. ibid. Page 103.
84. Papyrus Ebers 808 = 95, 1–3, cited from ibid.
85. Paul John Frandsen, 'The Menstrual 'Taboo' in Ancient Egypt', *Journal of Near Eastern Studies*, Vol. 66, No. 2. (April 2007), Page 103. [http://www.jstor.org/stable/10.1086/519030]
86. ibid. Page 103-104.
87. Carolyn Graves-Brown, 'Dancing For Hathor: Women in Ancient Egypt', Page 164.
88. RE Witt, 'Isis in the Ancient World', Page 23.
89. M Isidora Forrest, 'What does the Knot of Isis mean?' [https://isiopolis.com/2012/06/16/what-does-the-knot-of-isis-mean/]
90. ibid.
91. Spell 156, *Book of Coming Forth by Day*, Cited from ibid.
92. M Isidora Forrest, 'What does the Knot of Isis mean?' [https://isiopolis.com/2012/06/16/what-does-the-knot-of-isis-mean/]
93. Carolyn Graves-Brown, 'Dancing For Hathor: Women in Ancient Egypt', Page 166.
94. ibid.
95. ibid, Page 167.
96. David Leeming and Jake Page, 'Goddess: Myths of the Female Divine', Page 43.
97. ibid.
98. Normandi Ellis, 'Sekhmet, Bast, and Hathor: Power, Passion, and Transformation through the Egyptian Goddess Trinity', included in *Goddesses in World Culture*, Volume 1, Edited by Patricia Monaghan.

99. ibid. Page 205.
100. ibid. Page 206.
101. ibid.

Comparison with Hindu Tradition

1. Bharat Gupt, 'Indo-European Beliefsi n Classical Greek and Indian Drama'. [http://ifihhome.tripod.com/articles/bg001.html]

Menstruation Notions Among Indigenous Communities

1. Hilary Alton (Ed.), 'The Moon and Menstruation: A Taboo Subject, Selected extracts from Robert Briffault's The Mothers', A Radical Anthropology Group Publication. [http://radicalanthropologygroup.org/sites/default/files/pdf/pub_the%20mothers.pdf]
2. Carver, J 'Travels through the Interior Parts of North America'. Cited ibid.
3. Letter of Major Marston to Rev Dr Morse. In Blair, Emma Helen, The Indian Tribes of the Upper Mississippi Valley and the Great Lakes. 2 vols. Cited from Hilary Alton (Ed.), 'The Moon and Menstruation: A Taboo Subject, Selected extracts from Robert Briffault's The Mothers', A Radical Anthropology Group Publication. [http://radicalanthropologygroup.org/sites/default/files/pdf/pub_the%20mothers.pdf]
4. Hilary Alton (Ed.), 'The Moon and Menstruation: A Taboo Subject, Selected extracts from Robert Briffault's The Mothers', A Radical Anthropology Group Publication. [http://radicalanthropologygroup.org/sites/default/files/pdf/pub_the%20mothers.pdf]
5. ibid.
6. Dr NN Bhattacharyya, *Indian Puberty Rites*, Page 8.
7. Hilary Alton (Ed.), 'The Moon and Menstruation: A Taboo Subject, Selected extracts from Robert Briffault's The Mothers', A Radical Anthropology Group Publication. [http://radicalanthropologygroup.org/sites/default/files/pdf/pub_the%20mothers.pdf]

8. Dr NN Bhattacharyya, *Indian Puberty Rites*, Page 9.
9. Hilary Alton (Ed.), 'The Moon and Menstruation: A Taboo Subject, Selected extracts from Robert Briffault's The Mothers', A Radical Anthropology Group Publication. [http://radicalanthropologygroup.org/sites/default/files/pdf/pub_the%20mothers.pdf]
10. Dr NN Bhattacharyya, 'Indian Puberty Rites', Page 15.
11. ibid.
12. ibid, Page 9.
13. Hilary Alton (Ed.), 'The Moon and Menstruation: A Taboo Subject, Selected extracts from Robert Briffault's The Mothers', A Radical Anthropology Group Publication. [http://radicalanthropologygroup.org/sites/default/files/pdf/pub_the%20mothers.pdf]
14. ibid.
15. Shannon F, 'Menstrual Rites of the Native Americans', Cycle Harmony. [http://www.cycleharmony.com/stories/menstrual-myths-a-rituals/menstrual-rites-of-the-native-americans]
16. ibid.
17. Nicole G, 'Rites of Passage into Womanhood in Native American Cultures', Cycle Harmony. [http://www.cycleharmony.com/stories/menstrual-myths-a-rituals/rites-of-passage-into-womanhood-in-native-american-cultures]
18. ibid.
19. ibid.
20. Hilary Alton (Ed.), 'The Moon and Menstruation: A Taboo Subject, Selected extracts from Robert Briffault's The Mothers', A Radical Anthropology Group Publication. [http://radicalanthropologygroup.org/sites/default/files/pdf/pub_the%20mothers.pdf]
21. ibid.

Menstruation Attitude Hinduism vs Modernity

1. Frederique Apffel-Marglin, 'The Sacred Groves', *Manushi* (No. 82). [http://manushi.in/docs/106.%20The%20Sacred%20Groves.pdf]

2. ibid.
3. ibid.
4. ibid.
5. ibid.
6. ibid.
7. ibid.
8. ibid.
9. ibid.
10. ibid.
11. ibid.
12. 'On the rag', Urban Dictionary. [https://www.urbandictionary.com/define.php?term=on%20the%20rag]

Conclusion

1. Sankrant Sanu, 'Killing the feminine: Misogyny in Christianity', *IndiaFacts* [http://indiafacts.org/killing-the-feminine-misogyny-in-christianity/]

* The author and publishers acknowledge Open Source material from the Creative Commons, Wikipedia and other online sources.

The Adda Seal depicting Ishtar and others

Greenstone cylinder seal from Akkadian period dated to 2300 BC. A hunting god (full-face) has a bow and an arrow over his shoulder; a quiver with tassel attached hangs on his back. On the left hand mountain stands a small tree and Ishtar (full-face) who is winged and armed with weapons including an axe and a mace rising from her shoulders. She is holding a bush-like object, probably a bunch of dates, above the sun-god Shamash's head. The water god Ea stands to the right with one foot placed on the right-hand mountain. Behind him stands Usimu, his two-faced vizier (chief minister).

Source: The British Museum Collections, Image retrieved from Open Source.

Cylindrical seal showing Ishtar and a worshipper below a canopy

From the Neo-Assyrian period dated to the eighth-seventh century BC. A statue of the goddess Ishtar stands on a platform within a canopied enclosure. Ishtar is identified by crossed quivers, a starred crown, and stars encircling her body. Two winged genies protect the enclosure, while a kneeling figure worships.

Source: The Metropolitan Museum of Art, US.

Statuette of Isis and Horus

From the Ptolemaic Period dated to 332–30 BC. For the Ancient Egyptians the image of the goddess Isis suckling her son Horus was a powerful symbol of rebirth that was carried into the Ptolemaic period and later transferred to Rome. On the goddess's head is the throne hieroglyph that represents her name. She also wears a vulture head-covering reserved for queens and goddesses. Following ancient conventions for indicating childhood, Horus is naked and wears a single lock of hair on the right side of his head.

Source: The Metropolitan Museum of Art, US.

Figure of Isis-Aphrodite

From the Roman Period dated to the second century A.D. Terracotta. Isis-Aphrodite is a form of the great goddess Isis that emphasises the fertility aspects associated with Aphrodite. She was concerned with marriage and childbirth and, following very ancient pharaonic prototypes, also with rebirth.

Source: The Metropolitan Museum of Art, US.

Tit Amulet orlsis Knot

Dated to 1550–1275 BC. The tit symbol illustrates a knotted piece of cloth which was associated with the goddess Isis, the great magician and wife of Osiris. The tit was also associated with the blood of Isis. It was considered a potent symbol of protection in the afterlife, and the Book of the Dead specifies that the tit be made of blood-red stone, and placec at the deceased's neck.

Source: The Metropolitan Museum of Art, US.

Hathor Amulet

Dated to 1086–332 BC. The goddess Hathor was generally associated with love, music, and fertility. The particular form of this amulet though alludes to her dangerous and protective role in the myth of the destruction of mankind. The amulet was probably meant to put its wearer under the protection of the goddess and her appearance as a cobra was probably thought to be particularly effective to ward of dangers.

Source: The Metropolitan Museum of Art, US.

Column with Hathor-emblem capital

Limestone Column dated to 380–362 BC. Hathor columns were particularly favored at temples connected with goddesses or with mammisi-temples ('birth houses'), which were devoted to the birth of the divine son of a goddess. However, smaller versions like this one may have served as cult emblems as well.

Source: The Metropolitan Museum of Art, US.

Statue of Sekhmet

Granite Statue from the temple of Mut belonging to the period of the New Kingdom dated to1403-1365 BC.

Source: Image retrieved from Open Source.